THE RABBIT
FACTORY

BY MARSHALL KARP

For details and sample chapters please visit www.karpkills.com

THE RABBIT FACTORY

FACTORY

A Lomax and Biggs Mystery

Marshall Karp

ISBN-978-1-7363792-2-6

Jacket design by Dennis Woloch
Book design by Kathleen Otis
Author photo by Fran Gormley

For information, email contact@karpkills.com.

for Emily,

the best thing that ever happened to me,

and

for Adam and Sarah,

the best thing that ever happened to me and Emily

PART ONE

KILLING RAMBO

CHAPTER 1

EDDIE ELKINS AMBLED down Fantasy Avenue. A light breeze penetrated his costume, and he felt relatively cool inside the furry white rabbit suit.

Of course, these were the balmy days of April. July and August would be unbearable, but for Eddie, it would be a small price to pay.

Six weeks ago he had lied, cheated, and bribed his way into the best job in the world. And now, he was Rambo. Rambunctious Rabbit, the most famous character Dean Lamaar ever created. The acknowledged superstar at Lamaar's Familyland.

Eddie waved at the kids as he wandered through the sprawling theme park. Occasionally some wiseass teenager would give him the finger, but for the most part kids loved him.

And Eddie loved kids. In fact, he loved them so much that he was mandated by Megan's Law to register with the Los Angeles police, so they could notify people in his community that he had moved into their neighborhood.

But he hadn't registered. Not this time. He had complied with the law when he lived in Boston. But the Irish bastard across the street keyed Eddie's car, slashed his tires, and put dog shit in his mailbox. Eddie tried to explain that there's a big difference between high-risk offenders who are violent and regular guys like Eddie, who would never hurt anyone, but the guy wouldn't listen.

3

Then one day Eddie made the mistake of saying hello to the man's ten-year-old son. That night two bullets came flying through his bedroom window.

Eddie moved to Rhode Island and registered with the Woonsocket police. Life was better there. Nobody wanted to kill him, but nobody wanted to hire him either. Not for the kind of jobs Eddie wanted. He finally got work as a clerk in a paintball supply store, where he had plenty of time to think about his life.

He was born Edward Warren Ellison in Trenton, New Jersey, majored in English Lit at Rutgers, was never any good at sports and was never really comfortable with women, although he had had sex with four of them. People said he looked like Buddy Holly, or at least what Buddy would have looked like at age thirty-six, if not for that plane crash. Eddie even wore the black horn-rimmed glasses to heighten the effect.

He tried real hard to break his pattern with the kids, especially after the first conviction. He had a smart therapist, but stopping wasn't as easy as the shrinks make it sound. He didn't want to hurt the children, but fondling wasn't hurting. After three months in Rhode Island, he decided it would be easier to find a better job in a big city. Especially if he didn't register.

He moved to Los Angeles. Getting a new name and new identity cards were easier than he thought. Other men like him had done it and there was the New Beginnings Network on the Web. His closest confidant, whom he e-mailed almost every day, was Vandy333.

Vandy was divorced with two kids of his own and had been a school principal in Tennessee for twelve years. "Changing my identity made all the difference," Vandy had told him.

So Eddie Ellison became Eddie Elkins. He found a nice clean place to live and set up his new persona just the way New Beginnings instructed him. Finally came his big break. They told him about Caleo.

Anthony Caleo was a scumbag, but he was a great guy to know.

4

He worked in Human Resources at Familyland. His job was to verify the résumés of people applying for jobs. Caleo didn't care about New Beginnings. He only cared about what was in it for Caleo. He charged Eddie six thousand bucks.

For that he cleared Eddie's bogus résumé and prepped him on how to handle the one-on-one interview with Marjorie Mac-Bride. And that's how Eddie landed the job of his dreams.

His first day at work he reported to the Wardrobe Department. One of the Dressers, a chatty little Mexican woman whose name tag said Provi, helped him into the furry white Rambunctious Rabbit costume, with its distinctive red, white, and blue denim overalls. Provi was prattling on, but Elkins's mind and heart were racing too loud and fast for him to hear.

He couldn't believe it. He was Rambunctious Fucking Rabbit. More recognizable than The President of the United States. Maybe even The Pope. Children would literally flock to him. How many guys did he know who would trade their left nut for this gig?

"Elkins?"

He looked up, as Provi's thick-toothed black comb raked over his hairy white rabbit arms. The speaker, standing ten feet away, was Danny DeVito tall with an Arnold Schwarzenegger chest. His face and close-cropped gray hair had the wear and tear of a fifty-year-old. But the body, in black nylon warm-up pants and a tight black tank top, had the muscle tone of a college wrestler.

"I'm Dante, your Character Coach," he said. "Let's see what kind of a rabbit you are. Don't put the head on yet. Just let me see you walk over here."

Provi gave the suit one final fluff and stood back. Elkins inhaled, took one bold step forward and immediately hooked the front edge of one giant rabbit's foot to the back of the other. Gravity took over and down he went, floppy ears over cottontail, onto the rubber-matted floor. Provi let out a loud *aye-aye-aye*.

"That's why you don't put the head on yet," Dante said, help-

5

ing him up. "Don't want you to break it."

"But it's okay if I break my own head? Why didn't you warn me?"

"You learn faster this way," Dante said. "What size shoes do you wear?"

"Ten and a half."

"Well now you're wearing size twenty-four rabbit's feet and eighteen pounds of fur. Why don't you try it again?" Dante said, stepping to the other side of the room.

Elkins hobbled his way toward Dante and made it to the other side without falling. "How's that?" he asked.

"Fantastic," Dante said, "if you were one of Jerry's Kids. You gotta be animated. Bouncy, springy," Dante said, bouncing and springing across the room. "Don't worry. By the time I'm finished you'll be dancing around the park like Adolf Nureyev."

It took ten hours. "Tomorrow I'll show you how to find your way around every inch of this park," Dante said. "Then we'll go over the rules for handling kids. There's a right way and a wrong way, and you gotta be real careful. Don't scare 'em, don't drop 'em and don't touch 'em in any wrong places."

They worked with dolls. Eddie had no problem not touching them in any wrong places. On the last day of training, Dante introduced him to a squat, moon-faced woman with a thick mane of bottled blonde hair, a dozen tiny gold earrings on each side of her head, and eyes that convinced Eddie there was nothing going on between the earrings. "This is Noreen Stubiak," he said. "She'll be your Keeper."

Caleo had prepared him for this, but Eddie played dumb. "My what?"

"Every character gets a Keeper. They follow you around the park. Somebody messes with you, bam, she's right there to help."

Eddie smiled at her. "So you're going to protect me," he said. "You got a gun?" Noreen made a snorting sound that Eddie took for a laugh.

"Don't give her no ideas," Dante said. "She's got a walk-ie-talkie. Anybody starts up with you, she calls Security to bail you out."

Eddie knew the truth. Noreen was a spy. He hated the idea of having a watchdog follow him around, but it didn't take long to figure out that Noreen was the best possible Keeper he could have. She was a highly unmotivated, twice-divorced piece of flotsam from the Total Loser's Section of Trailer Park City, and Stubiak, Eddie decided, was Polish for 'dumb as shit.' But she had one redeeming quality. It didn't take much to get her to look the other way.

Every few days Eddie would give her a little gift. A Faith Hill CD. A bag of scrunchies for her mop of revolting yellow hair. Or a bottle of her favorite perfume, Eau de Wal-Mart. Maybe she knew what he was up to; maybe she didn't. Either way, she never said a word.

The weeks that followed were the happiest of his life. Four times a day Eddie, dressed as Rambunctious Rabbit, would hop on the Easy Street Trolley and head for Tyke Town. That's where the younger kids were. Just this afternoon, he had spotted the boy. Asian. Stunning. Six years old, maybe seven. The perfect age. A little shy, but not afraid.

Eddie had waved at him. The kid waved back. Eddie followed up with a little hippety-hoppety dance, and the kid smiled. Then he walked over, purposely almost tripping over his two giant rabbit's feet. The kid laughed.

Eddie stretched out his white-gloved paws and Mom helped her son jump into the eager arms of Rambunctious Rabbit. Eddie slid one hand between the boy's legs and the other behind his head. He touched his rabbit nose to the kid's nose and got another laugh from the boy and a happy shriek from the mother.

The father scrambled for his camera. "Can we get the statue in the background?" he said, in surprisingly perfect English.

Eddie snuggled the tiny genitals in his palm and walked toward the thirty-foot bronze likeness of the late Dean Lamaar. Dad took a picture. Then another. Take your time, Eddie thought, re-cupping his hand so that his thumb rested in the crack of the sweet little butt.

This, he thought, as cold, clammy sweat trickled from every pore, is even better than the school bus driving days. Good pay, good benefits, and parents who lift up their kids and hand them to me crotch first.

At that moment, Eddie had less than an hour to live.

He spent another twenty minutes in Tyke Town, then he and Noreen headed for the tunnel that led to The Rabbit Hole, the vast underground world hidden beneath Familyland's 866 acres. Above ground was fantasy. Below ground was the hard reality of hundreds of miles of electric cable, sewage lines, refrigeration pipes, and of course, scores of locker rooms, cafeterias, toilet facilities, and rest areas for the 6,200 employees who made the fantasy happen.

There was still another half hour till quitting time, and Eddie needed a smoke. As soon as they got through the tunnel, Eddie pulled off the rabbit head. "I got something to do before I change," he said. "See you tomorrow."

"Goodnight Eddie," Noreen said. "Thanks again for the video."

Eddie had picked up an old Brad Pitt movie at a flea market for two bucks. "My pleasure," he said. "I know how much you like him."

The entire Rabbit Hole was a No Smoking Zone, but Eddie knew a spot where he could light up out of view of the security cameras. He wound his way through a maze of ductwork, plopped down on the cool tile floor, and set the giant Rambo head down next to him. He lit a Marlboro Light, inhaled deeply, leaned back against a water pipe, and exhaled the smoke from his lungs with a long, slow breath.

It was his last.

The rope came from nowhere, cutting deep into his neck. He tried to scream, but nothing came out. He tried to inhale, but nothing came in.

Thirty-seven seconds later, Eddie Elkins, a.k.a. Edward Ellison, sex offender, child molester, and convicted pedophile, had his last conscious thought.

God, I was so happy. Why now?

He knew better than to ask, *why me?*

CHAPTER 2

I WISH I still smoked. Some occasions just seem to go better when I inhale deadly toxins. Occasions such as opening Joanie's monthly letter. But I gave up tobacco seven years ago, so I had to resort to other self-inflicted pain. Exercise.

I did forty-five minutes on the bike, managed 114 sit-ups, then hit the shower, slowly edging the hot water from invigorating to excruciating. I switched to cold just before my back started to blister.

I was out of coffee, but there was half a pot of Juan Valdez's finest still on the counter from yesterday. I poured a cup and nuked it. It tasted like Juan's donkey's finest, but at seven in the morning, I'll take my caffeine any way I can get it.

I poured myself a bowl of Cheerios. Andre heard me chewing and showed up before I swallowed my first mouthful. "We're giving out numbers this morning," I told him. "I'm One. You're Two. Wait your turn."

Andre does not grasp the finer points of math, but he got my gist and sprawled out on the floor, waiting patiently for his number to be called.

I propped the envelope against the cereal box. On the front was my name in Joanie's girly-girl handwriting. Plus the number six. Only she didn't write the number. There were just hash marks. Like an inmate counting days.

I sat there staring at the envelope and spooning up my Cheerios. Andre remained a polite two feet away, both eyes riveted on the spoon. "Explain something to me," I said to him. "How come the Cheerios commercials always show happy Moms with perky breasts, Dads who seem to be on the right career path, and teenage kids with no substance abuse problems? What about real families like us? A middle-aged widower and his Cheerios-loving dog?"

Andre shifted positions and started licking his dick. "You keep doing that at the breakfast table," I told him, "and we'll never wind up on television."

I always put in too much milk, so I grabbed another fistful of cereal, to establish a better oats-to-milk ratio in the bowl. I still wasn't ready to open the letter, so I read the box and was delighted to find that Cheerios may reduce my cholesterol if I make them part of my heart-healthy diet. I decided not to order a Cheerios T-shirt for only $4.99 and wondered why they had to print "Limit 4 T-shirts per household." Are there actually households that need more than four? And if so, why would General Mills deprive them?

I left an inch of milk and about two dozen floaters in the bowl and set it down on the floor next to Andre. He stopped gratifying himself sexually and immediately dove into the heart-healthier choice.

I waited for him to finish so I could pick up the bowl, otherwise Rosa, my cleaning lady, would find it on the floor and have to go to church to ask God to forgive me for feeding the dog out of my dead wife's good dishes.

Andre finished his Cheerios and went back to his dick. I put the bowl in the sink, went back to the bedroom, and plopped down on the big stuffed chair. I used Joanie's best cake knife to open the envelope. *Dios mio*; pray for me, Rosa.

Dearest Mike,

Are these letters driving you crazy? Tough shit. I've never been dying before, and I'm trying to figure this out as I go along. It serves you right for marrying a firstborn, perfectionist, Gemini control freak.

Assuming you're following my orders and reading these on schedule (if you don't I'll come back and haunt you) it's been six months. Hopefully Rosa is still coming, or by now there are 180 pairs of dirty socks and underwear piled up on the bedroom floor.

I wrote the first five letters when I was between chemo sessions. Today I'm vomiting between paragraphs, so bear with me.

I'm sad for you. The hardest part of this whole ordeal is not that I'm dying (although believe me that sucks big time). It's trying to imagine you without me.

How can I not be there every morning when you roll over all shaggy, scruffy, and if I'm lucky, horny. How can I not be there on Sunday nights at Gino's to split a sausage and pineapple pizza and a bottle of dago red? How can I not be with you? How can you be—how can you exist—without me?

I don't know how many more letters I've got left in me, but I'll write #7 tomorrow. Just to whet your appetite, I promise to reveal the biggest secret I ever kept from you. No cheating. You can't open it for another month.

Michael, my sweet lover, I know these messages from your dear departed wife must be like getting greeting cards from the Surreal Section of the Hallmark store. But I can't stop writing. I've accepted the fact that I can't hold onto my own life. I just can't let go of being part of yours.

I will love you for eternity. Give Big Jim and Andre big wet kisses for me.

Joanie

I closed my eyes and let it soak in. Then I read the letter again. I was about to read it for the third time when the annoying little voice that lives rent-free inside my head told me to put the letter away now.

I try not to argue with the voice. I extricated myself from the sagging green chair as gracefully as one can extricate 180 pounds from anything.

I walked over to Joanie's dressing table, and picked up the double-sided silver picture frame she gave me for our first anniversary. On the left side of the frame was our wedding picture with her handwritten inscription below. *"To my darling Mike, We've only just begun. Love, Joanie"*

On the opposite side was the identical picture, but through the miracle of Photoshop, Joanie had digitally aged us fifty years. My hair was silver and thinning, but at least she gave me hair. I was thirty pounds heavier, and my face was lined with crags and crevices.

Joanie was even harder on herself, thickening out her middle, bluing her beautiful strawberry blonde hair, and adding liberal amounts of wrinkles and liver spots to her glowing skin. But she didn't change her eyes. There were crow's feet on the outside, but inside they were still the color I told her was Cavu Blue. My father flies a Piper Warrior on the weekends, and CAVU is pilot talk for a sky that has 'Ceiling And Visibility Unlimited.' To me nothing is bluer.

"I resent the fact that you think I can't function without Rosa cleaning up after me," I said to the left side of the frame. "For your information, I was recently honored by *Good Housekeeping* as one of the only men on the planet who has actually mastered the art of picking up his own dirty socks and underwear. And you thought I couldn't live without you."

Andre paddled in. Andre, just for the record, is a six-year-old black Standard French Poodle. Not the kind of dog you'd expect to be living with a cop. But this dog has instincts like Sherlock

Holmes and better communication skills than a kennel full of movie Lassies.

He cocked his big curly head and gave me his most serious man-to-man look, which I clearly understood to say, "Hey, Lomax, I heard you talking, and now I see that it's just you and the picture of your dead wife. I'm starting to worry about you, pal."

I half-put the frame back down on the dressing table, then pulled it back to my lips, pressed my face to the glass, and set it back down. Andre, realizing that this was a private moment and that there was nothing edible in it for him, toddled off back to the living room.

The phone rang. It was my partner, Terry Biggs.

"Hey, Mike, we got a live one." A 'live one' was Terry's standard lame joke for a homicide victim.

"Ask me if the vic was a man or a woman," he said. Terry is a wannabe stand-up comic, but he's never sure he's going to get the straight line, so he helps you serve it up to him. I was in no mood to resist.

"Okay, Terry, who bought it? A man or a woman?"

"A rabbit," he answered, hoping to get a bigger reaction from me than I was capable of giving. "Actually a guy in a Rambo Rabbit suit. It happened out at Lamaar's Familyland."

"Familyland?" I said. "Is no place sacred?"

"I guess the scumbags are branching out. More work for you and me," Terry said. "I'll pick you up in fifteen."

I hung up. The letter was still in my other hand. There was a wooden box on top of Joanie's dressing table. I had found it gift wrapped at the bottom of my shirt drawer a few days after the funeral.

A brass plaque on top was engraved *Mike and Joan...till death us do part*. That's where I found the letters. I put Number Six back in the box. There were still three more to be opened.

I picked up my gun and my shield and had one more go at the picture. "This is not easy reading, Joanie," I said. "Don't be surprised if I come home tonight and flush all these love letters from the grave down the toilet."

"Don't be an asshole," said the annoying little voice inside my head who hasn't paid a day's rent in forty-two years.

CHAPTER 3

A HORN HONKED and my partner pulled up in his 2002 silver Lexus ES 250. "Hey, kids," he yelled out the window. "We're going to Familyland! Yayyyy!"

That's Terry, the Fun Homicide Cop.

I got into the Lexus ES 250, which I love to remind Terry is actually a Toyota Camry with a wood-paneled dash and a few other non-essentials to jack up the price. "Good morning, Detective," I said. "Are you looking for the guy who slapped a Lexus logo on the front of your Camry?"

"Nice way to talk to the man who brought you breakfast." There was a container of Starbucks in the cup holder plus a bag of Krispy Kremes on the floor. "Today's the 18th," he said, pulling away from the curb.

"Yeah, I saw that," I said, sipping the coffee and trying hard to ignore the aroma of fried dough and sugar wafting up from the waxy bag of carbs at my feet. "It made Page One of today's paper."

Terry was one of three people who knew about Joanie's letters. "It's that time of the month," he said. "You get mail?"

"Yeah," I said. "She's having a great time. I don't get the sense she's coming back."

Terry was there for me when Joanie was dying. Not intruding. Not giving advice. Just there. A lifeline. He knows when to keep quiet, and this was one of those times. Carbs, be damned, I decided, and unbagged a glazed donut as we headed for the 405 South.

Terry Biggs is the best partner I ever worked with. For starters, he's not very L.A. He's one hundred percent Da Bronx. From the time he was a kid, he knew he was going to become a cop. But in the late seventies when he was ready to apply, the city of New York was in financial hell, and the NYPD had a hiring freeze. Los Angeles, on the other hand, had money, criminals, and jobs. Terry switched coasts and joined LAPD.

Terry is tall, dark, and ugly. Don't get me wrong. I love him. We've been friends and partners for seven years. But he'd be the first to back up my description. Six-foot-three, a mop of greasy black hair and a face that's kind of muley, but more pock marked than a real mule. The man is butt ugly.

Until he speaks. And his voice, soft and sweet as honey, warms you. He's funny, charming, loving, and before you know it, you're thinking what a beautiful guy. Women are particularly vulnerable to his special brand of ugliness. Terry Biggs had never had a problem getting girls.

Keeping them was a different story. He'd had three marriages go south. But number four was the charm. Marilyn. She's with LAPD Rescue. They met on the job.

About ten years ago, Terry stops at the Ralph's on Robertson. He's just parked his car when two guys with guns come tear-assing out of the market carrying a sack, which later turns out to contain $18,000 in cash and food stamps.

Terry pulls his service revolver and yells the standard, "Police, drop your guns, etcetera, etcetera." Now Terry is off duty, so he's wearing plaid shorts and a New York Yankees T-shirt. Apparently, this is not an intimidating outfit, and the robbers keep running. They jump into a moving car, and in two seconds flat, the car is barreling down on Terry.

He dives out of the way, but a fender catches his foot in midair and breaks his ankle. He still manages to get off three shots and blows out two of their tires. The car plows into one of those metal dividers where they collect the shopping carts. The driver gets a face full of air bag. One of the gunmen pulls his own trigger on impact and shoots himself in the leg. And before the last guy can figure out where the door handle is on their stolen car, Terry limps over and is singing "You Have the Right to Remain Silent."

The headline in the paper the next day says, *One of L.A.'s Finest Bags Three of L.A.'s Dumbest.* But there was a second part to the story that got even more coverage. Lots more.

A few minutes after Terry nails the bad guys, about a dozen black and whites converge on the scene, followed by LAPD Rescue. The cops are screaming, "Officer down! Officer down!" which lets the Rescue Squad know to bypass the dirtbag who is bleeding to death and take care of that cop over there with the Camel dangling from his mouth.

The ambulance screeches to a stop, the driver's side door flies open and out jumps Marilyn Cavanaugh. Marilyn has green eyes, curly red hair, and a big Irish smile. Sounds pretty good on paper, but she's what they politely refer to in the Personal Ads as full-figured. She's a hefty lass, Marilyn is, weighing in at about fourteen stone. But she's also a top-notch paramedic, and no one ever complains that their Angel of Mercy is too chunky. Certainly not Terry.

Big as she is, Marilyn is lightning on her feet. Wham, bam, she takes Terry's vitals and quickie-splints his ankle. Then together with her co-pilot, Marty Delaney, she hoists Terry onto a gurney and wheels him into the back of the bus. Marty hops in with the patient. Marilyn slams the rear doors, jumps in the cab, and flips on the siren. Terry, who has been operating on pure adrenaline, knows he's finally headed for a fistful of Advil, a six-pack of beer, and at least a week's paid leave. He closes his eyes and thanks God for another mission accomplished. Marilyn, feeling all the pressure of being responsible for an Officer Down, peels out, hell bent for Cedars-Sinai.

And that's when the A-M-B-U and the L-A-N-C-E part company. The back doors fly open, and the gurney catapults out onto the macadam, where it rolls about thirty feet until it runs head on into a Soccer Mom parking a minivan. The cops, who are still on the scene, scramble to help Terry, who now has a concussion to go along with his broken ankle. When they realize this is not particularly life threatening, they all have a huge laugh. But the camera crew from News Channel 4 has the biggest laugh of all. They had been shooting the departing ambulance for the evening news when the doors burst open. The video ran incessantly for three nights.

About sixty seconds later, a totally humiliated Marilyn returns for her Officer Down Twice. And that's how they met.

After that, she visited him every day, first in the hospital, then at home, offering to do whatever she could to make him happy. One night, it seemed that the thing that would make Terry the most happy was a roll in the sack. No problem for Marilyn. Rarely does a nice Irish girl get the opportunity to have sex with a man and actually diminish her Catholic guilt.

One thing, as they say, led to another, and despite the fact that Marilyn had seven-year-old twin daughters, and a third, age five, Terry signed on for the whole package. And that's how a guy from The Bronx winds up living in Sherman Oaks with a wife and three teenage Valley girls.

We plugged along the 405. "No sense using lights and sirens," Terry said. "With all this traffic, we'd wind up causing an accident. Besides, the guy we're going to see is already dead, so what's the hurry? You been to Familyland?"

"A bunch of times. You know Joanie," I said. "She was a kid at heart." What I didn't say was how much she wanted kids. We both wanted them. We spent three years and thousands of dollars trying to make one. It was our fertility doc who actually discovered the ovarian cancer. Congratulations, Mrs. Lomax. You're not going to have a baby, and you're going to die.

"I always thought of Lamaar as a rip-off of Disney," Terry said. "But that's sort of like saying Pepsi is a rip-off of Coke. There may be truth in it, but it's still an eight hundred-pound gorilla on its own."

He was right. Lamaar, like Disney, had started out as a small animation house. Rambunctious Rabbit, Slaphappy Puppy, Mc-Greedy the Moose, and a shitload of terminally jolly characters had captured the public's heart and transformed the little cartoon studio into a global entertainment company.

Today Lamaar made movies and TV shows, owned music and toy companies, operated hotels and a cruise line, licensed cartoon characters, and was traded on the New York Stock Exchange. Familyland was just one small piece of the corporate pie.

Terry recapped the highlights of his last two trips to Familyland with Marilyn and the girls. He made sure to give me some tips on how to get 'back-doored,' which is theme park jargon for entering a ride or attraction without waiting on line. Apparently, his ability to buck the long lines and get the VIP treatment at Familyland had made him even more lovable in the eyes of the four women who already adored him.

We don't like to talk about a case before we get to the scene, so Terry segued into the upcoming college hunt for the twins, who were juniors in high school. He never once mentioned how expensive it would be, which if you know Terry is just like him. He was just a button-popping proud Dad, who wanted the best for his girls. We were discussing the merits of applying for early admission when he pulled onto the off ramp. The arrow on the sign for the main entrance to Familyland pointed right. Terry turned left.

"They said don't go to the front gate," he told me. "We're going to the admin building on Happy Landings Boulevard. They want to keep this investigation low profile, so try not to look like a cop."

That's the nice thing about Terry. Sometimes he lobs out a straight line for me to take. "Okay," I said. "I'll leave the donuts in the car."

Terry gave a little chuckle, which from him is a rave. I, in turn, bowed to thank him for the set-up line. Sometimes homicide can be a lot of fun.

CHAPTER 4

UNTIL DEAN LAMAAR showed up with his world-famous rabbit and a bottomless checkbook in 1970, the little town of Costa Luna, California was exactly that. A little town. But after he gobbled up most of the town in one gulp, Lamaar wanted to make sure his investment would be protected by a real police force and not some Podunk constabulary.

Everybody agreed that the local cops could handle the small stuff, like Drunk and Disorderlies. But the supremely paranoid Mr. Lamaar was particularly jittery about a race riot breaking out on the carousel. The big stuff, he insisted, required big guns. And that meant LAPD.

Meetings were held. Palms were greased, backs were scratched, and eventually codes were rewritten. I've heard that the legalese goes on for 150 pages. The short version is that Lamaar's Familyland is technically outside of LAPD's jurisdiction. Unless the shit hits the fan. Defining 'the shit' takes up most of the 150 pages.

Over the years we had handled a few rape cases and the occasional "I-was-ahead-of-you-in-line-Mother-Fucker" stabbing. This was our first homicide in the Happy Little Kingdom.

We pulled up to the Dexter Duck Administration Building. Catchy name. So radically different from Donald or Daffy Duck. I hoped the murderer was as unoriginal as the guy who created Dexter.

There were a bunch of black and whites discreetly parked at odd angles, plus an EMS bus and the Medical Examiner's wagon. Most of the vehicles still had their lights flashing. That ought to keep it low profile.

A ruddy-faced local cop with a beer belly that any man could be proud of, sized up the Lexus/Camry from twenty feet away.

"Budweiser blimp at eleven o'clock," Biggs informed me.

The blimp was about fifty, wearing a Smokey hat and tan summer-weights that fit well despite his enormous girth. He lifted a finger to indicate he'd seen us, but had something more important to do first. He pulled a wrinkled red bandana out of his back pocket and honked into it hard. Then he moseyed on over. "Morning, Detectives," he said, downright friendlier than I'd expected.

I was prepared for an Archie Bunker voice to go with the Bunker-like physique. But he talked in a high-pitched squeak, and 'detectives' came out 'detectifth.' It wasn't the hissy, sibilant S that helps you spot a gay guy across a crowded room. It was more of a good old-fashioned childhood speech impediment that never went away. No wonder he became a cop. In a small redneck town like Costa Luna, a fat guy with a bad lisp needs to carry a gun.

I scanned the gold-and-black nameplate on the flap of his left breast pocket. "Good morning, Sheriff Davis," I said.

"It's not Davis; it's Daves," It came out 'Davthe.' "Marlon Daves. Like more than one Dave." He winked. "Welcome to Familyland, the unluckiest place in the world."

"How so, Sheriff?" Terry asked.

"Fella was wearing two rabbit's feet, and he still got iced." We all had a Big Hearty Cop Laugh over that.

"Lucky that Dean Lamaar is dead," Daves said. "He'd be all tore up if he knew someone kilt his star attraction."

I'm so used to cynical, wiseass L.A. cops that it took me a beat to realize that the statement was heartfelt. Terry and I agreed with Daves that it was excellent fortune for Mr. Lamaar to be dead at this point in his career. Daves went on. "I met with him a couple of times y'know," he said with obvious pride. "We have monthly meetings with their security people. Sometimes the old man would stop by and say hello. He'd ask me how the missus was. Give me free passes for the kids. Things like that." He paused, waiting for our reaction.

Police work is all about respect. It's the key to our psyche. Did you ever get pulled over for speeding and try to talk your way out of a ticket? If you whine, make lame excuses, or tell the cop how important you are, it only pisses him off. If you apologize, show remorse, and promise it won't happen again sir, you have half a chance of getting off with a warning.

Terry and I both gave the Sheriff an appreciative nod to let him know how impressed we were that he had spent quality time with Dean Lamaar.

"Anything going on around here we should know about?" Terry asked. "Problems in the company that might get one of their characters murdered?"

"What makes you think it's about the company?" Daves said, his tinny voice piercing the air. "Could be that the guy in the bunny suit had an enemy. Maybe he owed somebody money or he had his dick in the wrong place."

"Possible," Terry said, "but I figured you'd know more about the company than the rabbit's dick."

"Sure I know about the company. Bought their stock. It was headed south for a while, till Nakamachi bought them out and brought in Ike Rose to run the place. Sharp guy. Stock's been going up. Dean Lamaar died about three years ago, so the place isn't as homey as it used to be. But hell, it's a business, not a home. My opinion—there's no problems in the company that would cause a murder. If it was my investigation, I'd find out who that bunny rabbit was humping. Of course, I'm just a country boy. You're the ones who do this every day."

"Marlon," Terry said, crossing over to first-name familiarity, "any more country boys as smart as you, and us city boys would be out of a job."

The fat man smiled and his chest puffed out a little. You could practically hear Aretha Franklin singing R-E-S-P-E-C-T. Terry asked where the DOA was.

"They got these tunnels under the park. They call it The Rabbit Hole. Employees only. Your vic is down there."

"We appreciate your help, Sheriff," Terry said.

"One more thing," Daves said. "There's a woman waiting for you in the Duck Building. Amy, the gal with the big boobs. She just showed up from Lamaar headquarters in Burbank. Told me to stand out here and keep everybody away. This company don't like publicity, and she's in charge of Corporate Miscommunications. She's gonna do her best to get you fellas to keep this investigation under wraps. Just thought you should know up front."

Marlon was no country bumpkin. His theory about the rabbit's dick was iffy at best, but he was a smart enough cop who apparently paid attention. We thanked him for the heads-up and turned toward the Dexter Duck Building and the gal with the big boobth.

CHAPTER 5

DEXTER DUCK WAS your basic low-rise, earthquake-resistant Southern California office building. No real architectural point of view, which surprised me. Shouldn't it have been covered with feathers, or at least shaped like a duck?

We walked through two sets of glass doors. A receptionist sat dead center about twenty feet in. The first hint that this office building was different from your average insurance company was the fact that the walls were covered with oversized color glossies of cartoon characters.

Before we could even cross to the receptionist's desk, I heard the rapid click-clack of heels on the marble floor, and a woman hurried over to us. She was thirty-fiveish, brunette, white-bread pretty, no wedding ring. The photo ID card on a chain around her neck had come to rest on her left breast, which I sized up to be a 38C or D, which is a popular size among men. The tag simply said 'Amy,' but I stared at it long enough to read the Gettysburg Address.

Biggs and I flashed Amy our Big City Cop credentials, and she introduced herself. "I'm Amy Cheever, Corporate Communications."

Terry pulled out his pad. "How do you spell that, ma'am?" he asked.

"Cheever," she said. "Like John Cheever, the writer."

"Thank you, ma'am," Terry said. "And how does he spell it?"

Her brown eyes crackled, but she kept her cool and proceeded to spell Cheever. She took a beat, then added, "And Amy is spelled A-M-Y." This girl didn't take no sass. Not even from the Big City Cops.

We had been forewarned by Daves. Amy was the enemy. Our job was to gather as much information as possible. Her job was to keep it from us. Terry had opted to play Nasty Cop. "How long you work here at Familyland?" he said. He already knew the answer.

"I don't work here," she said. "I told you I'm with Corporate. I work out of Lamaar Studios in Burbank. Press relations for Familyland is one of my responsibilities. I got here as soon as I heard the news."

"Thanks for coming, but we're not press," Terry said.

Amy handed me an official-looking folder. "This is Eddie Elkins's personnel file. He's the man who was killed. He's a new employee, been with us a few months. There's a sister in Baltimore to notify in case of emergency."

"I think this qualifies," Nasty Cop said. "Did you call her?"

"Several times. No answer. No machine."

"Just as well," Terry said. "We'll call her."

She took a deep breath and let it out slowly. I know a little about body language, and her breathing told me that she was about to say something she knew we wouldn't like.

"It's important that we keep this crime from being blown out of proportion in the press," she said. "It would be good if we could keep it out of the press entirely."

Thank you, Sheriff Daves. Underneath those 38s, Amy Cheever's corporate heart was definitely in the right place. Let's all sweep it under the rug.

"We can't control the press," I said with a Friendly Cop smile.

"I understand," she said. "That's my job. I went to business school. They taught me how to handle the harsh realities of a bad situation."

"Did they teach you how to handle the harsh reality of a homicide?" It was Biggs. He seemed to really enjoy sparring with her.

"Listen," she said, without a hint of Cop Respect in her tone. "Half of our business is aimed at children under twelve. If Mr. Elkins had been a third-grade teacher, and he were murdered in a gay bar, I'm sure the police would cooperate in trying to protect the children from the details. All I'm asking is that you treat this case with the same discretion. We really do care about the children."

Terry and I both nodded to communicate that we understood, but that was all the commitment we would give her.

"Thank you very much," she said. I wondered how she'd spin this conversation to her boss. Something like, 'I spoke to LAPD, sir. They promised to take a vow of silence.'

Terry spoke. "If it's not too much trouble, ma'am, we'd like to see the dead body now."

"Your forensic people are on the scene. I'll take you there."

Our forensic people? On the scene? Everybody loves cop-speak.

Amy did an about-face and headed for the elevator. Terry threw me one of those quick Man Looks to let me know that Amy Cheever also had a fabulous ass.

I threw him back the Man Look that says, "What am I, Mr. Magoo?" We fell in behind her. I had the distinct sense that she was enjoying the fact that we were enjoying her ass.

All in all, I thought we were off to a pretty good start.

CHAPTER 6

TERRY AND I stepped to the back of the elevator. Amy stood in front. I inhaled deeply to get a better take on her perfume. This was not official police work. In fact it wasn't work at all. She smelled fantastic. Not your typical office fragrance. More bedroom than boardroom.

There were no buttons to push. Just a panel with a series of locks, each one marked with the corresponding floor. I gawked at Amy as she inserted a chrome key into the fourth lock from the top. The light next to it went from red to green. Then before the doors could close, one more passenger jumped aboard. Surprise, surprise, it was the little voice that lives inside my head.

"And what do we have here?" it said. "Is this Detective Lomax fantasizing about a principal in a homicide case? How quickly one forgets the letter from one's wife, who is lying in the ground these six short months."

I've accepted the fact that I can't hold onto my own life. I just can't let go of being part of yours.

I thanked the voice for stopping by and looked away from Amy's seductive butt and down at my loafers. I also began to breathe through my mouth, but the scent of Amy still hung in the air. I took one last gawk to see if I could make out a panty line. Nothing visible. Civilians have no idea what goes on inside a cop's head when he's working the job.

The elevator took us four floors down. D Level. The doors opened, and we got our first look at The Rabbit Hole. It was hardly a hole. It was wide and spacious and well lit. It reminded me of the American Airlines terminal at LAX.

We hopped on a golf cart and headed down a corridor that was not quite as wide as the Ventura Freeway. Amy was our driver and tour guide.

"On your right is the employee cafeteria. We serve over twelve thousand meals a day. Up ahead is our laundry facility. How many pounds of laundry would you guess we handle on a daily basis?"

"We're cops, ma'am," Terry said. "We can't guess without clues."

"Fifty-two tons," she said, with a hint of self-congratulation that one doesn't usually associate with getting laundry dirty. "And believe it or not, that generates over one hundred pounds of dryer lint every day."

I had to hand it to her. She acted like this was just another day at the office. Let's see, what's on the agenda today? Staff meeting, write a press release, dash over to Familyland, drive cops to dead body, then lunch. The gal in charge of Corporate Miscommunications. Calm and composed on the outside, but I'd bet that deep down she was scared shitless.

The cart stopped to let a zebra cross in front of us. Not a man in a zebra suit. A real zebra, like you see on the savannah. The handler, or whatever you call those guys who pull exotic animals around underground tunnels, waved at us. Amy said, "Hi, Harold," and for a second I was impressed that she knew him by name. Then I saw the name tag on his shirt. Can't fool this detective.

The cart took off again. Like I told Terry, I had been to Familyland. This was better. It was like being backstage at the circus. Actually it was more like being in the circus. Everyone was in costume. We passed a group of three young women who must have been on a coffee break. One of them looked like Dolley Madison and had to stand about five feet back from the others to make clearance for her hoop skirt. The second was in a tiger suit, with the head resting on the ground nearby. The third was some sort of a Martian drinking a Fresca.

"You think maybe our killer was wearing a costume to help him blend in?" Terry asked, practically reading my mind.

"I was just wondering the same thing," I said.

"But it would have to be something simple," Terry said. "I can't imagine being able to kill somebody if you're dressed up like a six-foot duck."

The golf cart hummed along, and I sat back and enjoyed the show. It was difficult to think of this place as a business. Or a murder scene. This was the underbelly of one of the greatest entertainment institutions in the world. The part the public never gets to see; hardly even knows about. I couldn't help but think how much Joanie would have loved this special secret world down here.

We drove past hundreds of people, most of whom seemed to be in a hurry to get to God-knows-where. Just like an airport. Except in the airport, you don't see that many people dressed in sequins, sparkles, and spangles. Well, maybe San Francisco Airport.

We turned off the Ventura Freeway onto a narrow passageway, a cul-de-sac about fifty feet deep. At the far end was a cluster of people inside a perimeter of yellow plastic tape. Amy stopped the cart, and Terry jumped off. "What the hell is this?" he said, grabbing the tape.

It should have said, *Crime Scene. Do Not Cross*. Instead it said *This Area Closed For Renovations. Sorry For The Inconvenience*. Terry was furious. "Are we investigating a homicide, or an inconvenience?"

"We need to keep a low profile," Amy said. "We can't have employees gawking at a big yellow police banner that says *Mur-*

der Committed Here."

"You *need* to keep it low profile?" Terry barked. "Are you aware that it's against the law to remove the Crime Scene tape?"

"We didn't remove it. We just added our own tape and extended the perimeter. The whole world doesn't have to know there was a murder here."

"Well, LAPD just might want the whole world to know," Terry said, loud enough for a good chunk of the world to hear him, "just in case one of them happened to be a witness. Did you ever think of that?"

"Gentlemen, can I help?" a voice called out.

The people behind the tape stopped working to see what the yelling was about. One by one they lost interest and went back to what they were doing. Except for the guy who offered to help. He headed toward us.

He was a light-skinned African-American, big and well-built, his head shaved smooth and buffed to a soft glow. His eyes locked on me and Terry, slicing and dicing us as he approached. He stopped a foot away and stood eyeball to eyeball with me, which made him six-foot-one. But he had at least twenty pounds on me, about nineteen and a half of which were muscle.

His face, his bearing, his look, everything about him, said Cop. Everything but his clothes, which said Handsomely Paid Executive. I was right on both counts.

"Gentlemen," he said, "I'm Brian Curry, Head of Security at Familyland."

CHAPTER 7

COP-TO-COP introductions at the scene of a homicide don't usually call for hearty handshakes, but Curry extended his hand, so I shook it. Terry hung about six feet back, folded his arms across his chest and nodded at him.

"I'm glad you're here," Curry said. That surprised me. Private cops are never glad to see city cops show up on their turf. "This is a terrible day for us. Whatever I can do to help you solve this crime quickly..." he cleared his throat, "and quietly, just say the word."

He walked over to Terry and extended his hand again, this time with a business card in it. "If it's really critical, I'll take down the little barrier we put up to discourage people from rubbernecking. However..."

Terry took the card. "Let's just leave it for now."

"Hey, guys... Lomax... Biggs... over here."

Another voice from the business side of the Crime Scene tape. This time it was the unmistakable twang of Jessica Keating. Nobody in all of LAPD sounds quite like Jessica. She's from Chicago where they apparently teach their young to run every word through their nasal passages before actually speaking it. She could really mutilate the name Lomax, but I was thrilled to hear her. There are a couple of hard-ass, self-absorbed, this-is-my-job-not-yours LAPD Crime Scene Investigators. Jessica

Keating is not one of them.

Jess is an amalgam of visual counterpoints. She's Janet Reno tall, with curly blonde Shirley Temple hair. Her face has wonderful hints of Audrey Hepburn. Creamy white skin, unblemished by a single ray of California sunshine, tapering off into an elegant slender neck. At the other end are two oversized Bozo the Clown feet.

She's Midwestern friendly with a glorious smile and a big goofy laugh. Homicide cases are inherently depressing, but if anyone can brighten up a murder scene, it's Jessica. I always tell her she's the Ghoul of my Dreams. The only time I ever saw her cry was in a high school gymnasium in Van Nuys. Every cop has a breaking point. For Jessica it was four dead kids and a gym teacher sprawled across a painted hardwood floor.

Terry and I gave her a big "Hey, Jess" and walked over with Curry and Amy close behind. Jess was on one knee, fiddling with the DOA, who was still inside his bunny suit. His size 42 rabbit head, an open pack of Marlboro Lights, and a red translucent plastic Bic lighter were on the floor nearby.

Terry and I hadn't crossed paths with Jessica for about a week, so she had a little catching up to do. "Nice going on the Marlar case," she said.

"Couldn't have done it without you, Keating," I said. It was true. She had determined that the murder weapon was a rock-hard rawhide bone that had been the chew toy of the victim's dog, a massive golden retriever named Rudy. The dog hadn't done it, but apparently the victim's husband had. Jessica had put us on the path to success when she picked up a single drool-covered Rudy hair from the victim's skull.

"What do we have?" I asked, getting down to the business at hand.

She smiled real perky and put on her instructor face, as if she were now going to teach us a simple, basic life skill, like how to stuff a turkey. "Cause of death, strangulation. This is a No

Smoking facility. Looks like the vic snuck back here to cop a cigarette. Someone came up from behind him, wrapped a rope around his neck, and strangled him."

"You sure the killer came from behind?" Biggs said.

"Not a hundred percent, but if he attacked from the front, there'd be signs of a struggle. I'm thinking the killer snuck through these pipes and got behind Elkins while he was lighting up. Elkins never knew what hit him. Once the rope was around his neck, he was probably unconscious in thirty seconds, dead in sixty. A maintenance guy found him this morning, but I'd put the time of death between 3 and 5 p.m. yesterday."

"There's a million people down here," Terry said. "It took that long for someone to discover the body?"

"This is a blind alley, a dead-end junction for ducts and pipes. No security cameras. No reason for people to be here."

Amy was hovering at our side listening to every word. "So there wouldn't be any witnesses," she said, with a smug look at Terry.

Terry ignored her and turned to Curry. "Come to think of it, Brian, there is something you can do. Explain the concept of obstruction of justice to your people." He turned back to Jessica. "You sure the murder weapon was a rope?"

"You tell me. Let's call this Exhibit One." She used a tongue depressor to hold up a kid's jump rope. It was flecked with dried blood, and when I leaned closer I could see little shriveled bits and shreds of Eddie Elkins's neck hanging off it. The handles at each end of the rope were plastic cartoon characters. Gerbils, maybe. Or hamsters. Definitely some kind of fun vermin for little kids.

"It's the Wacky Pack Rat jump rope," Brian said. "We sell it here in the park."

"We'll need surveillance tapes from the gift shops," I said, "and the names of anyone who put that jump rope on their credit card in the past thirty days." I turned back to Jessica. "Anything else?"

"The killer cut an ear off the rabbit head; took it as a souvenir. Then there's this. We found it in the victim's right paw... hand... whatever."

With two gloved fingers, she held up a little book, two inches long, an inch and a half wide. It was forty or fifty pages thick. "It's an old-fashioned flipbook," she said. "Y'know, the picture is slightly different on each page. When you flip the pages, the picture looks like it's moving. Take a look."

There was a drawing of a closed hand on the cover page. She placed her thumb on the front edge and began flipping. As the pages flew by, the picture animated, and the middle digit of the hand popped up, giving us the finger.

"Definitely not available at a Lamaar gift shop," Curry said.

Biggs began writing in his notebook. Homicide cops are supposed to write in pads. You see it on all the TV shows. So nobody paid attention. But I knew he wasn't taking notes. He was quietly communicating with me. I leaned left so I could see the pad. He wrote *TTT???* I responded with a shrug. Terry closed the pad. He wasn't about to pursue his theory in public.

"Brian," I said, "we'll need to talk to the people Elkins worked with."

"Can do," he said. "Each character is assigned a Keeper. Someone to tag along, so they never walk through the park solo. I've checked the roster, and Elkins's Keeper is Noreen Stubiak. We can track her down for you. Also, a lot of the characters work in teams for the Character Breakfast Events, so I'm sure there are a number of people who knew him. Plus there's the men's dressing room. I'll get you a list of all the guys who had lockers near his."

"I have a problem with that." It was Amy.

"You got a problem with what?" I was real close to becoming Bad Cop.

"I know this will sound heartless," she said, "but we were fortunate that Mr. Elkins was murdered in this out-of-the-way area. The maintenance man who found him has agreed not to discuss it publicly. Then there were another fourteen employees who were attracted to the commotion before we were able to close off the area. They too have agreed not to discuss the incident publicly."

"You seem to have an abundance of agreeable employees," I said.

"It's not against the law to encourage our people to protect the company's privacy. Why broadcast the murder by talking to every employee who knows him? I thought we were trying to keep this out of the press."

"You're the one trying to keep this out of the press." I said. "We're the ones trying to solve it. That means talking to everybody Elkins worked with."

Brian shook his head slowly. "This is premeditated, isn't it? Somebody had it in for this guy and hunted him down. Maybe another employee."

"Looks planned out to me," Terry said. "Nobody stumbled on this guy, rolled him for his wallet, and took the time to draw a flipbook. This is a crime of passion. Someone was really pissed off at this guy."

"A crime of passion," Amy said. "That sounds like you should be interviewing people Elkins knew personally. Maybe a girlfriend, a jealous husband, something like that."

"What are you talking about, Amy?" Curry said. "Since when do jealous husbands leave flipbooks? I'm afraid whoever did this was pissed off, but not at Elkins. I think the killer is pissed at Lamaar, so he murders Rambunctious Rabbit. That flipbook really bothers me. I think it's a message to the company."

"And what message is that?" Amy said, pursing her lips and squinching up her pretty little White Anglo Saxon-Protestant face.

"'Fuck you.' What else do you think this means?" He gave her the finger and her face turned to Red Anglo-Saxon Protestant. "I think there could be some maniac roaming around the park right now, planning to kill off our characters."

Amy glared at him. She wanted us looking for jealous husbands, not scouring the park for homicidal maniacs.

"Suppose Brian is right," I said. "Can you think of anyone who is angry enough at the company that they would randomly kill one of your employees?"

"Rambo is not a random employee. He's the living, breathing symbol of the company. And while I would never say this on the record, as long as Brian opened this can of worms, with six thousand people working for us, yes, it is possible that one of them is angry or crazy enough to kill another employee."

"I'd say a lot of our employees are that crazy," Brian said. "Sometimes I get the feeling this place is the Post Office with costumes."

"Jesus, Brian!" Amy threw her hands up at him, then turned back to me. "That comment was off the record too."

Brian Curry was clearly unhinged by the thought that it might be Open Season on Dexter Duck. "I'm sorry, Amy. But this is unnerving. What if somebody deliberately killed this man because he was wearing the Rambo suit? What if this is a series of... of..."

"Character assassinations?" Terry chimed in.

Amy's face went red again, but Terry kept going before she could say anything. "How many people have access to this tunnel system?"

"About six thousand," Brian answered. "All our people are costumed. Not just the characters, but everyone. We don't even call them employees. They're cast members. Ride operators, restaurant staff, everyone dresses up in theme wardrobe that's appropriate to where they work. They come down here to change in and out of costume. Plus there are facilities for them down here. Food services, training classrooms, and of course, bathrooms. Cast members are not allowed to use the same restrooms as the public."

"Why not?" I asked.

"It sort of spoils the magic to see McGreedy the Moose taking a piss in the men's room."

"You have a security system to keep non-employees out of these tunnels?" Terry asked.

It was not a complicated question. Yes or no? But Curry clasped his hands and took five seconds to formulate an answer. Terry and I call it the Fudge Pause or the Waffle Beat. We were about to get a version of the truth.

"Think of the park as a giant ship," Curry began. Metaphors are handy when you're telling half-truths. They're nice and muddy. "Now on a ship, the engine room, the radio room, and the other critical areas are all under tight security." He paused, either to make sure we understood or to invent some more bullshit. "But they don't monitor every passageway or every stateroom. It's the same thing here. There are so many corridors and doors that connect us to the buildings up top, that we can't possibly watch them all."

"So anyone who buys a ticket can just stroll down here?" Terry asked.

"It's not that easy," Curry said, defending the Mother Ship. "We've got visual security at all the main entrances that connect with public thoroughfares. My guards are well trained. They can tell the difference between a cast member and a curious tourist."

"But the killer could have been another cast member," Terry said. "Or he could've been anybody who got past the guards dressed as Donald Duck."

"Dexter Duck," Amy said, correcting him. Terry acknowledged her with his best "don't-mistake-me-for-someone-who-gives-a-shit" smile.

Curry nodded his head. "The security system was originally designed to keep out nosy parkers, not homicidal maniacs. But after 9/11 we issued every employee an ID card. They have to swipe it to get into this area."

"And how hard would it be for somebody who doesn't work here to steal somebody's ID card?" Terry asked.

"This is a theme park, not Fort Knox. Somebody who was really determined could sneak down here. But believe me, it's going to change."

My cell phone rang, which totally surprised me. "You guys get cell reception down here?"

"We get better reception down here than they get at Spago," Curry said. "A lot of our cast members are aspiring actors. They'd bitch if we didn't have air conditioning, but they'd quit if we didn't have cell service."

I answered my phone. It was Big Jim, my father.

"Hey, Mike," came the booming voice. "How's my boy?" I could picture his fifty-six-inch barrel chest swelling up and his cobalt blue eyes twinkling the way they always did whenever he called me his boy.

"I'm fine, Jim," I said. I never call him Dad when I'm trying to impress others during a homicide investigation. "But I'm busy here."

"I'll make it quick. Angel wants to know if you want chicken or fish tonight."

"What is this?" I said, walking out of the group's earshot. "A family dinner or a wedding reception? Tell Angel I'll have whatever she serves."

"Fine," he said. "Then I'll definitely see you tonight at 7:30."

"Oh, I get it. This isn't about menu options. This is your way of making sure I haven't forgotten and that I'll actually show up tonight."

"You're way off base," he said, which confirmed that I was totally on base. "You'd make a lousy detective. See you tonight." He hung up, just in case I thought about changing my mind about dinner.

He didn't have to worry. I definitely wanted to see my father as soon as possible. He used to be a driver for Lamaar Studios.

CHAPTER 8

I FLIPPED MY cell shut and flagged Terry to come over. I wanted to pursue his TTT theory.

TTT stands for Tony the Tiger, who is on every box of Frosted Flakes, which is Terry's favorite cereal, which sounds like serial, which is a word we don't like to blurt out when we're investigating a homicide, so Terry came up with the code.

"We've only got one dead body, plus an MO we've never seen before," I said. "You think this could be a serial killer?"

"I wouldn't rule it out. Start with the flipbook. If you're pissed at Elkins, just kill him and be done with it. Why go to the trouble of creating a fifty-page going-away gift? It's a signature, so we recognize him the next time."

He held up Elkins's personnel folder. "The vic lived in West Hollywood. Not exactly a gated community. Why not kill him there? Why go to the trouble of getting past Lamaar security? Even if it's Mickey Mouse security, they still have guards and cameras. Killing Elkins down here, while he's dressed in a Lamaar costume, feels like maybe the killer is out to hurt the company."

"You think Elkins is dead because he just happened to be the guy in the rabbit suit?"

"I like it better than Amy's jealous husband theory." He laughed. "Shit man, if I was crazy enough to strangle someone who was banging my wife, I might cut something off the bastard. But it wouldn't be his bunny ears. Curry's got the right idea. This is way too slick to be a one-shot deal just to kill Elkins. Maybe somebody has a hard-on for the company."

"I think you could be right, but as long as we're here, let's find out if anybody had a hard-on for Elkins."

Easier said than done. We spent three hours talking to people who supposedly knew Elkins. Apparently nobody knew him that well. In deference to Amy's Corporate Paranoia, we just told the rank and file that he had been killed. We left out the fact that he died on the job, in uniform.

Our best shot was Elkins's Keeper, Noreen Stubiak. Curry explained that the Keepers were hired to follow the characters around. "Just in case," he said, without actually explaining in case of what. "They're not authorized to do anything but call Security if a character needs help. I had to fire one of them a few weeks ago because he used pepper spray on a bunch of teenage punks who were harassing Officer Jelly Belly."

"If I were you," Terry said to Curry, "I'd issue Officer Jelly Belly a .357 Magnum. Teach those little bastards not to dick around with cartoon cops."

"Don't tempt me," Curry said, laughing. "At the risk of prejudicing your investigation, I have to warn you that the Character Keepers are not trained security people. They're just whistle blowers who are paid burger-flipper wages. Don't expect much from Noreen."

Understatement. Noreen had the IQ of a pipe wrench and none of the personality. Her first question was, "What do you mean, he's dead?" Terry explained the concept to her and proceeded to ask a series of questions using one- and two-syllable words. After five minutes, he got as much as he could from her, which was practically nothing.

"He was a good person. He always treated me like a lady. I'm gonna miss him," Noreen said, as she left teary-eyed.

Terry hadn't written a single word in his note pad during the entire interview with Noreen. He tore out the blank page and handed it to me. "Here, file this under Clueless."

Nobody else seemed particularly broken up over Elkins's death. "He seemed like a nice guy but he kept to himself" was the prevailing response.

At noon Curry invited us to break bread in the executive dining room. We took a Pasadena. Terry and I wanted to thrash out our first impressions over a more private, less executive lunch, without having to resort to code. Amy and Curry gave us their home phone numbers, cell phones, beepers, pagers, and mothers' maiden names, and made us promise to keep in touch. We left the park with Elkins's personnel file and very little insight into whodunit.

CHAPTER 9

WHEN WE GOT back to the parking lot, Sheriff Daves was still standing guard. "Sheriff," I said, "don't you have deputies who can take over for you?"

"The way I figure," Daves said, "Lamaar is the biggest taxpayer in the county. They got a homicide. Even if I can't do much, it's smarter for me to hang out here than chase skateboarders off of Mrs. DeFrancis's driveway."

"Well, we're glad you're still here, Sheriff," I said. "You've had a lot of contact with Lamaar Security. What's your take on Brian Curry?"

"Smart," he said. "Corporate type, but not a candy ass. Man of his word. Got some real integrity, far as I can tell. But he's totally out of his league to solve a homicide. They'd have been much better off with the last guy."

"What last guy?" I said.

"This Texas cop. From Dallas or Houston, I forget which. He had one of them double names like Billy Bob. Only his was real weird. Ben Don. Ben Don Marvin. He was Head of Security till six months ago. Then he got canned. Brian Curry filled his boots."

"Why did he get sacked?" Terry asked.

"Marvin ran a little operation where he was stealing stuff and selling it. Not valuable stuff, but shit that collectors will pay a bundle for."

"Like what?"

"Like costumes."

Sometimes I play Dumb Cop to pump more information out of people. In this case, I felt like Dumb Cop. "I don't get it," I said. "The Head of Security is probably pulling down 125 big ones plus stock options and other goodies, and he's stealing what— rabbit suits?"

Daves shook his head. "People pay good money for those sweatshirts and hats and shit with the characters' pictures on it. Imagine what they'd pay if they could get their hands on an actual costume that Rambo Rabbit wore. Thousands. I'm not kidding, thousands of American dollars."

"Un-freaking-believable," Terry said.

"And not just costumes. It was all sorts of gewgaws and what-nots. Like if the characters marched in a parade waving flags, them flags would just vanish into thin air. Sometimes, even piec-es of floats would disappear. Shit like that."

"How did this Ben Don guy get caught?" I asked.

"He didn't really get caught. Somebody high up in the orga-nization was on eBay one day and saw that a woman in Kansas was selling a pair of shoes that she claims was worn by an actual Lamaar character. So the executive, he bids on it, and he buys it. Sure enough, it's the real deal. That's when the shit hit the fan. They audited the books and realized they were replacing a ton of items that had gone missing. They couldn't pin it on Marvin, but they knew it was too big an operation to be going down without him. So they canned him."

"Do you think he did it?" I asked.

"Oh, yeah," Daves said, without missing a beat. "Ben Don was smart. As scams go, I'd say it was pretty clever. Plus it didn't really hurt nobody."

"Thanks, you've been a big help, Marlon," I said.

"One more thing before we go," Terry said. "You're thinking

that Elkins was killed by someone who knew him. But is it possible Ben Don was so angry at getting fired that he decided to come back and get even with the company?"

Daves didn't ponder this one either. "Nope," he said. "Black-marketing the costumes was your basic victimless crime. Marvin made a bundle, got caught, and was shipped out, hush-hush. Never prosecuted. Why would he come back and commit Murder One? It doesn't add up."

"You think anyone else would want to hurt the company?"

"Nobody I know. Most folks love Lamaar. If somebody has a beef with the company, they ain't gonna come around and kill Rambo. I'm sticking with my original theory. Find out who this Elkins guy was fucking and follow the rabbit droppings."

CHAPTER 10

FIVE MINUTES LATER we were back on the 405, doing eighty. "We did real good, partner," Terry said. "The Sheriff told us to keep our eye on the rabbit shit, and Amy Cheever wants us to keep the murder out of the press for the sake of the children. For the sake of her corporate ass is what she means. Which by the way I couldn't help notice that you were noticing. You interested?"

"First, I'm not about to date a principal in a homicide investigation, and second, I thought we had an agreement. No meddling in my social life."

"I wasn't meddling in your social life. I was trying to help you get one."

"I'm having dinner with my father tonight. You can help me with a good Teamster joke."

"Okay, how do you know if a Teamster is dead?"

"The Danish falls out of his hand. I need a *new* joke."

"I got a new fat joke."

"He doesn't think of himself as fat," I said. "He's big. His name is Big Jim, not Fat Jim. And he's a Teamster. I need Teamster jokes."

"It's too bad he's not a proctologist. I got a great proctology joke."

"Gosh, when I was a kid, I always wished my Dad were an

astronaut or a quarterback. I never thought about wishing for a proctologist."

He thought for a few seconds. "Alright, here's my best shot. How come Teamsters don't have anal sex?"

"I give up."

"They're too lazy to get off their fat asses and bend over."

I actually laughed. "Not bad," I said, "but it's got the word fat in it. Plus with that anal reference, it's got overtones of proctology. Don't quit your day job, Detective Biggs. Speaking of your day job…"

"You want my take on all this?" he said. "It's not about Elkins. Don't be surprised if another lovable cartoon character gets whacked. Curry thinks so too. I guarantee you he's going to beef up security and keep a tight watch on those critters. He won't be letting them prance around the park with idiots like Noreen Stubiak."

I know my partner. He sees innocent people get zipped into body bags every day, and his way of coping with the injustice of it all is to deflect his emotions with humor. But sooner or later it gets to him. I watched his jaw tighten and his eyes burn holes in the windshield. He smacked his hand down hard on the steering wheel.

"Damn," he said. "What a shitty reason to die. Just because you dressed up like Donald Fucking Duck."

He meant Dexter Fucking Duck, but I let it go.

CHAPTER 11

WE HAD ONE more stop to make before we could head for the office. We still hadn't solved last week's murder mystery, so we took the 405 to LAX to interview a JAL flight attendant.

Kiro Hakai was built like a Japanese jockey. I've never been totally comfortable around tiny men, and the fact that he had shaved his head and his eyebrows made him extra creepy. He was also screamingly effeminate.

We had proof that Hakai had been at Bottoms Up, a gay bar on Sunset, the previous Thursday night. We also had reason to believe that he had been in a stall in the men's room at the very moment that Alan C. Trachtenberg, a dentist from Sherman Oaks, wound up with a six-inch ice pick between his third and fourth ribs.

Unfortunately, Hakai didn't remember being at said club on said night and swore he had spent that evening at the Galleria 12-Plex with a friend. We had no doubt that the friend would back him up. They always do.

When we held up the grainy black-and-white photo of him, dated and time-stamped by the surveillance camera at the front door of the bar, Mr. Hakai remarked that there was a slight resemblance, but then don't all Japanese men look alike. Only the ones who shave their eyebrows, I thought.

I know when to throw in the towel with a hostile interviewee, but Terry wouldn't quit. "What movie did you and your buddy see that night?"

"Pearl Harbor," he said, with a smirk. An hour later the hairless little bastard was on a 777 bound for Tokyo.

We had already asked Trachtenberg's widow what her husband was doing in a gay bar. She swore up and down that the man was straighter than Warren Beatty. There aren't too many reasons why heterosexual men find themselves surrounded by the other team, so I asked her the next obvious question. Did the good doctor use recreational drugs? This time she did not swear up, down, left, or right. She started crying.

Our pint-sized flight attendant friend probably thought he screwed us by not cooperating. But his reluctance to talk said a lot. Truly innocent bystanders are quite vocal when it's a crime of passion. They clam up when drugs are involved. Usually, on the grounds that it might tend to incriminate them.

A drug-deal-gone-sour seemed like a worthwhile avenue to pursue, so I called my old buddy Irv Ziffer in Narcotics. Ziff the Sniff they call him, because he's probably caught more drug pushers than the entire K-9 Corps at Schiphol Airport in Amsterdam. Ziff knew the bar in question and asked me if the stabbing had occurred last Thursday night. Bingo. I asked how he knew.

Apparently he keeps flow charts of when stuff hits the streets and when the supply dries up. That Thursday was a buyer's market after a ten-day product shortage. But the sellers are particularly paranoid after a long drought, plus there was a full moon that night. "In a volatile business environment," Ziff said, "shit happens." He's quite the philosopher.

He also knew who was dealing at the clubs in that area, and it was clear to me that our Homicide team could use a little help from Narcotics. In the spirit of interdepartmental cooperation, we asked, and Ziff said sure. I felt that much closer to finding the guy who left three kids fatherless and hundreds of Valley residents without adequate dental care.

CHAPTER 12

IT WAS 4:45 by the time we got to the precinct. I plopped down on my pea green vinyl chair and rolled it up to the cigarette-scorched, coffee-ringed slab of laminated pine that the City refers to as Detective Lomax's office.

My messages were stacked in a neat little pile. Four of the nine were from my boss, Lieutenant Brendan Kilcullen, a ruddy-faced Irishman who believes in The Good Lord and Bill W. The latter had shown him the twelve steps to getting sober twenty-three years ago, which is how Lt. Kilcullen came to believe in the former.

He was on the phone when I knocked, but he waved me in. His office is a photo gallery, so there's always plenty to look at while you wait. The desk top is reserved for family pictures, and there are lots of them. Brendan Kilcullen is a good Catholic who procreates the way the Pope told him.

The walls are divided into sections. On the left side are the Kilcullen Career Highlight photos. Promotions, awards ceremonies, and other dress uniform occasions. The period from Academy graduation to getting his Lieutenant's bar spanned eighteen years and about forty pounds.

The center section features a dozen or more pictures of Kilcullen With People of Consequence. The coolest by far is Kilcullen with his arm around Jack Nicholson. It was taken at a Lakers game, and they appear to be the best of friends, which I know for a fact they're not. I doubt if Kilcullen had met the actor before or after that single click of the shutter. The picture I had long ago voted Most Pathetic is an eight-by-ten glossy of Kilcullen and Walter Mondale.

The right side is dedicated to bowling. Kilcullen is a league bowler who averages 180. There are a number of shots of a victorious Kilcullen holding up a trophy with his pinmates, none of whom is Jack Nicholson.

About ninety seconds later I heard Kilcullen say, "I love you too, Sweet Pea." He hung up the phone and smiled at me. "That was the Mayor."

"I'm glad you and Mayor Sweet Pea are on such good terms." I dropped his four messages on the desk. "What can I do for you, Loo?"

"Catch this rabbit killer, and catch him fast. A lot of people in important places are rooting for us."

"Did the real Mayor call you?" I asked.

"No. The real Governor did."

He wasn't smiling. He wasn't kidding.

"Did he call out the National Guard to protect the rest of the animals?"

"No, but I suspect he called a couple of publishers. Don't look for this rabbit shit to be on Page One of tomorrow's *Times*. Or Page Forty-One for that matter."

No press. It sounded like Amy Cheever had been busy.

"I'm doling out your case load to the other boys and girls in the squad."

I told him we'd already recruited Ziff the Sniff to help us out on the Trachtenberg stabbing. "Good," he said. Then Terry knocked.

"Gentlemen, I got a riddle for you. What's white and fluffy and likes to bugger little boys? Give up? It's Rambunctious Rabbit, also known as Eddie Elkins, also known as Edward Ellison, convicted sex offender."

He threw a computer printout on Kilcullen's desk. "We ran his prints. He's been a busy little pervert."

Kilcullen stood up. "Jesus, Lord, how in Christ's name does a goddamn pedophile get a job hugging and fondling kids all day?"

"He must've interviewed really, really good," Terry said.

Kilcullen, the father of six, ignored the crack. "What do you got so far?"

"We got dick," I said. "Murder weapon and a sicko calling card. Terry was thinking it could be a serial killer stepping up to the plate."

"Jesus, Mary, and Joseph, that is exactly what they're shitting bricks about. They're afraid some bozo is going to start picking off their cartoon characters one at a time. Biggs, I was just telling your partner, this one is on you boys. In fact, if you have anything else to do, like eat, sleep, or wipe your ass, cancel it."

Brick shitting and ass wiping. Kilcullen was usually good for at least three scatological references.

"Yes, sir," Biggs said, answering for both of us.

"Good, because I got the goddamn Governor of California crawling up my butt," he said, completing the trinity of rectal references.

"Now that we've made Elkins for a sex offender," I said, "I'm leaning back to our original instinct. It's just as likely this is a vendetta against Elkins as a crime against the company. It could be some father whose kid got manhandled by Elkins, and now he's getting revenge."

"I agree," Kilcullen said. "If some bastard violated one of my kids, I'd cut his dick off and shove it up his..." The phone rang and interrupted yet another trip down Hershey Highway. Kilcullen grabbed the phone. "Hold on," he said, putting his hand over the mouthpiece.

He turned to us and stared hard. His Irish eyes were definitely not smiling. "Solve it," he said. "Fast."

We didn't stick around to hear if the person on the other end of the phone was the Governor, Sweet Pea, or the King of Siam.

We walked to the coffee room. It was 6 p.m. and the stuff in the pot was like mud, so we each only had half a cup. Terry added half a cup of sugar to his. "I still think we got the makings of a serial killer," he said, "but let's run a check on all his victims and see if any were in the vicinity of Familyland yesterday."

"Maybe we should track down some of the victims themselves," I said. "Remember that case in Jersey? Thirty-year-old guy murders a priest who molested him back when he was an altar boy?"

"When do we tell Amy and Brian that the dead guy inside the rabbit suit was a wolf in sheep's clothing?"

"Let's wait till tomorrow. First let's toss Elkins's apartment," I said. "Is Muller around? We'll need him." Muller was our resident computer guru. When you visit a pedophile's apartment, you head straight for the PC.

"Gone for the day. I saw him split about five," Terry said.

"Good. If he were still around I'd feel obligated to search Elkins's place tonight. Now I can get out of here and not be late for dinner with Big Jim."

"That reminds me," Terry said. "How can you spot a Teamster's kid in the schoolyard?"

I took a sip of mud and shrugged.

"He's the one sitting on the side of the sandbox watching all the other kids play."

I dumped the rest of my coffee in the sink. "Like I said, Detective Biggs, don't quit your day job."

CHAPTER 13

TERRY DROVE ME home and we beat out a game plan for the next day. Pick up Muller, search Elkins's apartment, meet with Brian and Amy, get a list of people who had a grudge against the Lamaar Company.

He said good night, pulled out, and headed toward the Valley. He was probably thinking about Marilyn and the kids before his car was out of my sight.

I live in a sweet little house on Selma just on the edge of Laurel Canyon. It's a rental. A white saltbox with blue shutters. More New England than L.A. Joanie found it. We were going to live there a few years, have a baby, then buy a real house. *We had it all planned, didn't we, Joanie?*

It took me fifteen minutes to shower, change clothes, skim the mail and check my messages. For fourteen of those minutes Andre got to take care of Official Poodle Business in the back yard. Then he joined me in the kitchen, where we popped the tops on a couple of cans. Bud Light for me, Alpo for him. We male-bonded for five minutes, while the cold beer and the chunky beef with gravy washed away some of the cares of the day.

There was a message on the machine from Big Jim. A pilot friend of his might join us for dinner and could I pick up a bottle of wine. Jim flies his Piper on weekends, and he has a habit of striking up instant friendships with the other part-time pilots.

There was a bottle of Murphy-Goode Sauvignon Blanc in the fridge that Joanie never got around to opening. I figured with a name like Murphy-Goode, what could be bad? I grabbed the bottle, turned on the Animal Planet channel for Andre, and told him not to wait up for me.

Big Jim lives in Riverside, less than an hour from my place if the 10 is moving. It's close enough so he can commute to the studio every day, but far enough from 90210 that he can afford to own a four-acre spread.

He needs the space. He owns over fifty cars and trucks which he rents to film crews. Jim is a card-carrying member of the Teamsters Union who spent his entire career working for the TV and movie studios as a Transportation Captain. He's driven everything from eighteen-wheelers hauling film equipment to super-stretch limos hauling the world's biggest assholes. If it has wheels and an engine, Big Jim can get it for you, and he can deliver it wherever you want. Assuming, of course, he can fit into it. The man wears shirts marked XXXXX-L.

He's built like an offensive lineman. Six-foot-four, three hundred pounds, some of which are a direct consequence of too many idle hours around the catering trucks, but a lot of Big Jim is solid muscle. Let me put it this way: If he walked into a biker bar wearing silver slippers and a ball gown, nobody would fuck with him.

On the outside he looks like the poster boy for the World Wrestling Federation. Inside, he's three hundred pounds of marshmallow. He's an avowed Oprah-holic. Loves her. Tapes every show. When Oprah flew to AIDS-infested Africa to bring Christmas to fifty thousand kids, Jim asked me to watch the tape with him. He cried openly while he watched. That's who he is. All my grown life I've heard guys complain about fathers who weren't there, didn't hug them, kiss them, or say 'I love you.' Not me. I'm blessed. Jim Lomax is the most loving, adoring Dad a kid could grow up with. If I'm screwed up, it definitely was not his fault.

My mother was equally fantastic and even more colorful. When Big Jim first met Tess Delehanty, she had just fallen off a horse. She had to fall off three more times before the director felt he had it on film. She was one of the top stuntwomen of her day and worked in over two hundred movies, five of them with John Wayne. Every now and then, Joanie and I would be watching an old video, and some woman would fall down a flight of stairs, jump off a bridge, or get hit by a truck, and I'd smile and proudly say, "That's my Mom."

Jim and Tess got engaged two months after they met. A week later they broke up, and for the next three years they were on-again-off-again. They were so well matched that I never could figure out why their courtship was so stormy. But family legend has it that Mom had trouble letting go of an old boyfriend. I could understand how that would piss Big Jim off. They finally got married on a ranch in the Napa Valley. Mom was three months pregnant at the time with me.

After I was born my mother stopped taking the high-paying, high-risk Hollywood stunt jobs. Instead, she opted to help Jim with the driving and do the occasional job as a film extra. But she never lost her stunt skills, and at an age when most kids are learning their ABCs, Tess was teaching me how to fall down the porch steps, crash my bike, take a fake punch, and do a roll and tuck without getting hurt. I thought she was the coolest Mom in the neighborhood. My kid brother Frankie, on the other hand, was totally embarrassed having a truck-driver father and a daredevil mother. He wanted Ozzie and Harriet. Mom and Dad didn't even come close.

During her heyday my mother broke seventeen bones, got three concussions, lost four teeth, and punctured a lung. She took it all in stride. No fear. Always relying on her God-given talent, a vigilant stunt coordinator, and the occasional air bag. When she died of congestive heart failure five years ago, she went just the way she always said she would. Peacefully, in her sleep.

Big Jim, of course, was a mess. Some people drink to deal with death. Some eat. Jim shut down. One of the most outgoing guys on the planet just went into hibernation. He asked Chico, one of his drivers, to take charge of renting out the vehicles, and then notified the studios that he personally was not available. After four months he started driving long hauls, which got him out of the house, but kept him isolated for weeks on end.

Thank God for Oprah. One of her shows was about widowhood. A grief counselor suggested that the surviving spouse return to a place where they had the happiest times of their marriage. Then she gave a list of spiritual exercises to help them accept the death of their husbands or wives.

If I had suggested it, my father would have blown me off. But I didn't suggest it. Oprah did. So he went to the spot where he and my Mom had spent some of the happiest moments of their lives.

The Hillview Country Inn is a hundred-year-old estate in the Napa Valley, just off Highway 29 between Napa and Yountville. Mom and Dad went there on their honeymoon and about twenty more times after that. Except for the color TVs in every room, central air conditioning, and the annual price increases, time has pretty much stood still at The Hillview. The Old English Rose Garden looks just like it did when they saw it together for the first time. Entering the parlor, where you start your morning with a two-thousand-calorie country breakfast, is like stepping into the nineteenth century.

Dad has told me every detail of his journey back to The Hillview, and every year on the anniversary of my mother's death he tells me the story again. When he first drove up to the property his chest clenched so hard he was sure he'd have to be taken to the ICU instead of his room. The owners, Victor and Gerri Gomperts, greeted him the same way they had greeted him every time since his honeymoon—with a pot of tea, a basket of scones, and a gargantuan side of clotted cream and jam. They gave him their best suite and their deepest sympathies. For a while he just sat there on the big white iron bed, staring out the window, wondering if this was such a good idea. Finally he undressed and got into this big, Spanish-tiled shower built for two.

And every time he tells the story, he says these exact words: "Son, there's nothing sadder than a two-person shower, a two-person bed, and a two-person room, when one person is gone forever."

I wasn't there, but I've heard him tell it enough times to be able to picture what happened next. The big man slowly sank to the shower floor and let the water beat on him for twenty minutes while he wept for the piece of him that was missing. Oprah, he thought, you were wrong.

That night, he was sitting in the parlor when Angel came over and extended her condolences. Angel Cruz is at least twenty years younger than Jim, with wide dark eyes, creamy caramel skin and that lustrous black hair that so many Mexican women are blessed with. She had been a fixture at The Hillview for years. By day she waited on tables; at night she served espresso and after-dinner drinks to the few guests who actually hung around after dinner. She had always taken excellent care of my parents, and my Mom adored her.

"Face it, Jim, she's your fantasy girl," my mother used to say. "Beautiful, exotic, and she waits on you hand and foot. Next time we go up to The Hillview we should bring her back home with us."

"I don't need a fantasy girl," Jim would answer. "I need a feisty old woman who can jump off a burning building but is totally dependent on me to light the barbecue."

"Feisty old women die," my Mom would tell him. "When I do, take my advice and go back for this one."

They used to joke about it, but somehow that night it seemed to make perfect sense. Jim offered Angel a job as his housekeeper. Much to his surprise she said, Gracias, but no.

He called me the next morning, totally wounded. "Can you

believe it? I offered her more money than she makes at the hotel, plus free room and board, and she said no."

"So hire somebody else," I said. "L.A. is knee-deep in house-keepers. There's got to be at least one out there who could tolerate working for you."

"No dice," he said. "This is the one your mother thought would make a good housekeeper. I'm going back next weekend and offer her the job again."

Angel said no again. Now Jim was pissed. He drove back to L.A. and bitched and moaned to Joanie and me over fried chicken and beer. "I offered her an extra hundred a week, her own car, a TV in her room, a VCR, whatever she needs, and she still turns me down. I give up."

"Give it one more shot," Joanie said. "Try offering her dinner."

Jim and Angel started dating. Six months later, he asked her if she'd like to leave The Hillview and move in with him.

Permanently. This time she said, I do.

CHAPTER 14

IT WAS 8 P.M. when I pulled into El Rancho Lomax. Only thirty minutes late. Not bad for a cop. Angel's spring flowers were starting to bloom and the Mexican-style decorative lights along the pathways heralded their arrival.

The house itself started out in the 1930s as a rambling, single-story California Hacienda. It was, I am told, semi-tasteful for its day. But over the years, it expanded without any architectural rhyme or reason. The original white stucco exterior has been joined by an eclectic combination of red brick, bluestone, clapboards, and oak beams. In the ultimate insult, my parents, who were far more pragmatic than artistic, covered several of the add-on sections with vulgar vinyl siding from Sears. There are also four undistinguished, industrial-strength outbuildings on the property, whose sole function is to house vehicles, not people. Buckingham Palace it's not, but every time I pull into the driveway, that big old eyesore feels like home to me.

There was a car in the driveway that I didn't recognize. A black Jeep Cherokee. I figured it must belong to the pilot, and right now he's waiting for his wine to arrive. I've met more than my share of Jim's fly-boy friends, usually colorful war veterans who can regale you for hours with the gory details of every bombing mission they ever flew. Boy, was I not in the mood for that.

Angel opened the front door. "Mike," she said, singing my

name, her eyes radiating joy like she was genuinely happy just to hear me ring the bell. "You're looking well."

"And you look like a Latin movie star ready for her close-up. Perfect hair, perfect makeup." She gave me a big, stepmotherly hug and kiss. "And you smell fantastic," I said. "I hope my father knows what a lucky man he is."

"I tell him ten times a day, but it couldn't hurt if you remind him."

Skunkie was right behind Angel, patiently waiting for me to notice him. The Skunk is a photogenic mutt with shaggy hair that's black and white and about forty shades of gray. In a world full of yapping, high-strung, Type-A dogs, Skunkie is the low-maintenance exception. He's loving, mellow, and zero trouble, which is why he's the only dog allowed to live in the house. The other three have to be content with the kennel out back.

Skunkie sat at my feet, his tail sweeping the floor as I bent down to say hello. He tilted his head quizzically, which I decided was his way of asking about Joanie. He hadn't seen her since she got sick over a year ago, so I'm pretty sure he was concerned. He's that kind of dog. No pedigree, but extremely sensitive.

I handed Angel the bottle of wine and followed her into the living room. Big Jim was already out of his oversized brown La-Z-Boy and bounding over so he could crush me to death in his loving arms.

"Detective Lomax, I'm so pleased you could make it," he bellowed after I came out of the bear hug. "I want you to meet one of my fellow pilots. This is Diana Trantanella. Diana's one of those misguided pilots who still flies a high wing. A Cessna 172. I'm trying to get her to switch to a real airplane."

I had hardly noticed her sitting in the corner of the sofa when I entered the room. She stood up, and I could immediately see there was a lot to notice. This was definitely not some ancient bombardier here to share war stories. Diana had the clean, wholesome look of a high school cheerleader who had made a graceful transition into her early forties. Her hair was that curious shade of California dirty blonde which I'm never sure is real or store-bought, but which works for me, no matter what its origins. She was wearing a casual summery dress, that salmony, pinkish color that blondes always look great in. She had what my mother used to call a 'lovely figure,' which meant that she'd never make the centerfold of *Playboy*, but any man who spent the night with her would surely thank the Almighty for His generosity.

She extended her right hand, which had, of all things, a Rambunctious Rabbit watch on the wrist. Small weird world. I'd have to tell Biggs. There appeared to be no jewelry on her left hand, emphasis on the ring finger. "Big Jim has told me so much about you. It's a pleasure to finally meet you," she said, shaking my hand. I quickly made a few more mental notes. Five-foot-six. Pretty blue eyes. Sexy voice. Drop dead smile. I was really pissed.

Pilot, schmilot, this was a goddamn fix-up. Granted, at first sight, she looked to be a nine and a half on a scale of one to ten, but that didn't change the fact that my well-meaning father had ambushed me with an unwanted dinner date. There are worse fates, I know, but I was not prepared to make an evening of it with this woman. Not this evening.

I shook her hand grudgingly, giving only about five percent of the enthusiasm that she gave when she shook mine. I then muttered that I had brought wine and excused myself to go to the little boys' room.

In addition to all her other attributes, Diana apparently also has excellent antennae. She caught my I'm-not-interested vibe and turned on a dime. By the time I got back from the bathroom, she had gone from happy-to-meet-me to politely chatting with Angel in the kitchen. Jim and I had our drinks in the living room and quietly watched the Dodgers get their asses kicked by the Mets.

Dinner was a little more sociable. Four people sitting around a table tend to make small talk. We tried. Jim asked what I was working on these days. In deference to Amy Cheever and the Governor of California, I decided it wouldn't be wise to bring up the Lamaar murder with Diana in the room. So I mentioned the dentist who got stabbed at the Bottoms Up.

Diana literally dropped her fork. "Oh, my God. Alan Trachtenberg?"

"You knew him?" I asked.

"Not well, but I work with his wife, Jan. We're nurses at Valley General. She's in Maternity; I'm in Pediatrics. Have you caught whoever killed him?"

"Not yet." I said. "But a lot of things say it could be drug-related."

"That doesn't shock me. Alan had a real problem. Jan and I have talked about it many times. I'm sure she told you."

"Not right away," I said. "But we're aware of it now."

"This chicken is delicious, Angel," Diana said. "And I can't get over how fluffy this rice is." My connection to the Trachtenberg case had briefly opened the door to a real dialogue. Diana was now shutting the door.

"Thank you, Diana," Angel said. "It's just regular rice from the box."

"My rice usually cooks up into one big sticky lump," Diana said.

I caught the look on my father's face. *The women are now talking about rice. I hope you're happy.*

I decided to make an effort. "So, Diana, how long have you been flying?"

"A year and a half. I took it up after my husband died. It helped a lot with the grieving process." She smiled, "Plus it gets me four thousand feet closer to God." She let the smile dissolve into a look of concern and compassion. "I understand your wife died recently. I'm sorry for your loss."

"Thanks, and I'm sorry for yours." *Now I understood Jim's*

logic. Recent widower meets recent widow. A match made in Teamster Heaven.

"Have you ever considered taking up flying?" she asked.

"About ten years ago my brother Frankie and I took a few lessons," I said. "It just didn't do it for us."

"Speaking of Frankie," our father said, "what do you hear from him?"

"Not much. It's been over a week," I said. "But you know Frankie, the telephone is not his favorite way to communicate."

"Unless he's putting his money down on a basketball team," Jim said. I could tell he regretted it as soon as it left his mouth. He tried lamely to recover. "He's a good kid," he told Diana. "Runs a health club in Beverly Hills." Jim turned back to me. "If you hear from him, tell him to call his aging father."

The main course was over, and we all heaped mucho praise on Angel. I helped clear the table. "I made flan for dessert," she announced.

"I'll have to take a rain check," Diana said. "I'm on an early morning shift this week."

We all expressed our regrets as Diana threw a white cardigan sweater over her shoulders and picked up her purse. "Thank you for a lovely evening," she said. "Mike, the Sauvignon Blanc was particularly excellent."

I smiled. Mr. Big Shot Wine Connoisseur.

"Mike, do me a favor," Big Jim said. "Let me know if those automatic floodlights over the truck garage went on. They've been giving me trouble lately. And as long as you're going out, you may as well walk Diana to her car."

"Oooh, a police escort," Diana said, and once again I caught a glimpse of the bouncy cheerleader from days gone by. "How exciting."

She kissed Jim and Angel goodnight. I clucked to Skunkie, and the three of us walked to her car. The sky was peppered with stars. The moon was a few nights away from being full, and Diana Trantanella looked extremely desirable in the heavenly blue-white glow of night. Under different circumstances, it could have been a hell of a moment. I took her hand.

"I'm sorry," I said. "I'm usually better company. I really do apologize."

"I'm sorry too. I didn't mean to sandbag you," she said, squeezing my hand ever so slightly. "I didn't even know you were coming. Big Jim told me ten minutes before you got here."

I shook my head. "There's nothing worse than a well-meaning parent."

"What do you expect from a jerk who flies a Piper?" She smiled. Her mouth looked very kissable in the moonlight. But I had been a total asshole this evening. I know the rules. I was in no way entitled to a good-night kiss.

And then she kissed me. She leaned forward and gently pressed her lips to my cheek. It was just a kindhearted little peck to let me know that she accepted my apology, but her lips were soft and full and warm, and I felt a tingle run from my brain to the pit of my stomach.

"'Night, Mike," she said, and she got into the Jeep and drove off.

Skunkie was parked at my feet, and I crouched down to scratch him behind the ears. "What do you think, boy?" I asked him. "Interesting woman."

He didn't answer. He just rolled over on his back so I could scratch his belly. Hey, we've all got an agenda.

CHAPTER 15

WHEN I GOT back into the house Big Jim had finished eating his flan and was already working on Diana's.

I sat back down at the table, picked up a spoon and toyed with my dessert. "The outdoor floodlights seem to have come on just fine," I said, drilling a hole in him with my best pissed-off stare.

"I'm not surprised. They've been working well for years," he said, inhaling the rest of his second bowl of custard. "I didn't send you out there to check on the lights. Did you apologize to her for behaving like an asshole?"

"Me? What I should have done is apologize for *you* behaving like an asshole. What the hell were you thinking? Since when do I need you to mastermind my playdates?"

"It's six months today, isn't it? I loved Joanie like a daughter, but it's time to move on with your goddamn life," he said.

"Look who's talking. When Mom died you spent the first six months holed up in this house."

"That was different. Your mother and I were married almost forty years. I needed more time." He eyeballed my dessert. "You gonna eat that?"

I shoved the bowl his way.

"So," he said, digging into the caramelized gooey brown sugar topping, "now that the ice is broken, are you gonna call Diana?"

"No," I answered loudly. "I am not calling her."

"Don't be an idiot," he said. "I have all her phone numbers. Work, home, cell. She's not doing anything Saturday night. I checked."

"You asked her if she... Jesus F. Christ!" I tried to count to ten. I got to three and exploded. I started furiously tapping my fingers on the tabletop as if it were a computer keyboard. *"Dear Abby,"* I said, typing. *"I am a forty-two-year-old widower. It's only been six months since my wife died, and in my heart I don't feel ready to start dating. My problem is that my meddlesome father won't mind his own business. He invited a recently widowed woman over to dinner in a pitiful attempt to jumpstart a relationship for me. I love my father, and I really don't want to hurt his feelings, but how do I tell the fat, nosy bastard to back the hell off? Signed, Pissed-Off Police Officer in L.A."*

Jim swept aside the dessert bowls in front of him so he could create his own imaginary computer. He began to type. In real life, he can barely hunt and peck using two fingers. But now he raised both hands and let all ten fingers fly across the phantom keyboard with all the passion of Billy Joel in concert. *"Dear Pissed-Off Police Officer,"* he said, spitting out each word. *"First of all, I'll bet your father has more brains in his left butt cheek than you do in your entire head. Do you think he wants you to be miserable? No, he's looking after your happiness. Don't be a schmuck. Do what he says. He's never been wrong. And he never will be. Love and kisses, Abby."*

I stomped into the kitchen. Angel was making coffee. "I hear much yelling," she said, setting a creamer and a sugar bowl on a gleaming silver tray.

"I'm sorry, Angel, but your husband is driving me crazy."

"In my family, yelling is another way to say *te amo.* I am making Irish coffee. That will make you both feel better."

"I'm driving," I said. "I'll have the coffee. Hold the Irish."

I helped her carry the tray into the dining room. Big Jim had finished my flan, his third. "Do you believe this guy, Angel?" he said, angling for spousal support. "He won't ask Diana out on a date."

She set a cup of aromatic, steaming black coffee in front of him and added a hefty shot of Bushmills. "Maybe he should invite Diana to move in with him and become his housekeeper. It worked for you."

Jim's face flushed. I burst out laughing. It's always a joy for me when someone nails the big guy, and Angel was getting to be almost as good at it as my mother. Finally, Big Jim let loose. "Fuck you both," he erupted, and then all three hundred pounds of him shook and whooped with laughter. "Just what we need around here. A drop-dead gorgeous Mexican wiseass."

Angel poured me some coffee, but it didn't smell half as comforting as Big Jim's. So I put my two fingers very close together and said, "*un poquito, por favor*." She added a tiny splash of the whiskey, and I inhaled deeply. The heady blend of rich, dark French Roast and smoky Irish spirits wafted up my nostrils and into my brain. Without even taking a sip, I felt that warm calming buzz. I inhaled a second noseful.

Angel sat down with us and shared her flan with Big Jim. He had long ago converted her to his Oprah religion, and she recounted some of the highlights of that afternoon's show. It was all about aging gracefully and accepting where you are in your life right now. "So many women, they resent growing old," she said. "They can only think about the wrinkles, the sagging breasts, the menopause. But what they forget is that now we have so much more wisdom, we have life experience, we are in touch with our inner spirit. Getting older can be a joy." She stopped abruptly. "I'm sorry, Mike. This is not good talk for you."

She had suddenly thought of Joanie, who would never see menopause or wrinkles or experience the joy of growing old with grace. "No, please, it's fine." I said.

Angel's eyes welled up, and a tear trickled slowly down her cheek, leaving a visible streak across her perfect makeup. "It's my bedtime," she said, quickly blotting her face with a dinner napkin and standing up. "You two macho men can stay up and yell at each other all night. It won't keep me awake."

I stood up, and she hugged me. Not a perfunctory goodnight squeeze, but the compassionate, consoling embrace reserved for loved ones in pain. "I miss her too," she whispered.

Then she put her arms around Jim's neck and kissed him gently, and I could see him melt. I wondered what my mother would think about Jim and Angel. Was she joking when she used to say "next time we go up to The Hillview we should bring her back home with us," or did she have a vision?

Angel left the room. Skunkie curled up at the foot of Jim's chair. I tuned in to the rhythm of his breathing as he drifted into Happy Doggie Slumberland.

"Can we drop the Diana thing?" I said. "I'm working on a homicide, and I need your help."

He bowed his head. "I live to serve."

I took him through the Elkins murder. The jump rope, the flipbook, the missing ear, every detail. He didn't utter a single word until I got to the part about Rambunctious Rabbit being a convicted pedophile. "When you find the killer," he said, "somebody should pin a medal on him."

When I finished, he simply said, "How can I help?"

"All my cop training tells me to follow the pedophile path. Somewhere in Elkins's past is a person whom he hurt so bad that they had to kill him."

"That's what your cop training tells you. What do your instincts say?"

"Something is rotten at Lamaar. Terry was there ahead of me," I said, giving credit where credit was due. "He says if you want to kill the guy who molested your child, why not go to his house? But whoever killed Elkins took the trouble to get through Lamaar's security and killed him on Lamaar property while Elkins was dressed up as Lamaar's signature character."

"Sounds like Terry's right. The killer's got a grudge against Lamaar."

"It feels like a real possibility, and if that's the case, then the bodies will start piling up. Victim Number Two, Number Three, Number Four," I said, counting them off on my fingers. "I've seen it before. Then it won't stop."

"Did you see what you just did?" Jim asked.

"No, what'd I do?"

"You counted the victims off on your fingers," he said.

"So?"

"Show me Victim Number Four again."

I held up four fingers.

"Now show me Victim Number One."

I held up my index finger.

"Now show me Victim Number One, but use a different finger."

It took a few seconds for me to process what he was getting at. Then I slowly closed my index finger and held up a different finger. The middle one. "Damn," I said. "The finger in the flipbook. It doesn't mean 'fuck you.'"

"Sure it does," he said. "But I think it also means 'Victim Number One.'"

"Big Jim Lomax, you're one goddamn smart Teamster," I said.

"I guess the three years I spent working on the set of *Murder She Wrote* finally paid off."

"So Terry nailed it from the get-go," I said. "Somebody is out to kill off the Lamaar characters, one at a time."

"That would be my take on it."

"Terry and I are going to have to learn a lot more about this company if we're ever going to figure this out."

"There's a couple of real good books on Lamaar," Jim said. "You could just turn to the last chapter and find out who the killer is." He sipped his coffee. "Or you could just ask your dear old Dad to help."

"I already asked for your help," I said. "What do want me to do, beg?"

"Hell, no." He grinned, and I knew what was coming next. "I just want you to go out with Diana."

"You realize you're blackmailing an officer of the law," I said.

"Arrest me," he said.

If there's one thing I learned growing up, it's that Teamsters know all the studio dirt. They're the first ones on the job in the morning and the last ones to punch out at night. It's a long day, but there's a big chunk in the middle where they don't have much to do except sit on their asses near the catering truck and soak up the gossip. They're like flies on the wall. He had me and he knew it.

"Give me her phone number," I said. "I'll ask her out." He passed me a folded piece of paper, which he already had palmed in his hand.

I took a sip of my Irish coffee. It felt good. I took two more sips, then I put it down. I like alcohol, but I drink more like a schoolmarm than a homicide detective. I know a lot of cops who can't sip. They pound. Their shift ends and they deadhead for some cop-friendly bar so they can drink the demons away. A few of the more desperate ones can't always wait till the end of their shift.

Lt. Kilcullen, who sponsors six recovering alcoholics in the department, is always on the lookout for number seven. Any cop who doesn't show up on time for duty on a Monday morning is immediately on the suspect list. Be a no-show two Mondays in a month, and he'll interrogate you till you're ready to confess to kidnapping the Lindbergh baby.

I'm lucky. I don't get shit-faced. Some guys get that little glow on, then kick it into high gear. I stop at the little glow. It drives my two-fisted friends crazy. I've only been drunk twice since I got out of college. The night my mother died, and exactly six months ago today.

I tell people I'm a beer man, but the truth is I'm an alcohol slut. I'll drink almost anything. Joanie taught me the pleasures of red wine; I love a good Cognac, especially when somebody else is buying; and while I would never walk into a pub and order an Irish coffee, when your family tree branches all the way to County Cork, there's no better beverage for a father and son to bond over.

And now we were ready to bond over a homicide. But first I had to lay out the ground rules. "You're a veritable Font of Industry Insider Information," I said. "I have no doubt that you can help with my investigation."

"But?" he said. "I can hear a 'but' at the end of that sentence."

"But, it's late. I want to get home by midnight."

"And you think I'm just gonna sit here and talk your ear off?"

"I just want the straight 4-1-1. None of the usual colorful details."

"I see," he said. He played hurt. The wounded giant.

"Please, Dad. Just this once, give me the short version."

"Fine," he said. "I'll bet Danny Eeg killed Elkins."

I pulled out my pad and pen. "I didn't expect an actual name. Who is Danny Eeg?"

"That's the long version," he said with a little victory shrug. "Want to hear it?"

CHAPTER 16

THE SWATCH OF pink-and-white polyester that had been sliced from Rambunctious Rabbit's head sat in the center of the black lacquered writing desk.

It had been delivered by courier just hours ago. By now, the swarthy man who had sent it was back in the hills of Sicily counting his American dollars.

Never to be heard from again, the proud new owner of Rambo's left ear told himself as he picked it up and held it to the light.

Sitting in his faded leather desk chair, wearing a frayed terry bathrobe, he hardly looked like a murderer. His face was white and bloated. Over the years it had taken on the color and texture of the Sta-Puf Marshmallow Man.

He had never plotted a real murder before. But he had approached the execution of Eddie Elkins with the same systematic, careful planning that went into every script he ever conceived.

During his writing career he had created hundreds of stories for feature films and television shows. He was mediocre on dialogue and passable on character, but when it came to plot development, nobody could touch him. He was known in the business as the Story Guru.

He set the ear down, picked up a fresh yellow pencil, and began chewing on it. He had been writing on a computer for fifteen years now, but he still couldn't think without gnawing on a No. 2 Ticonderoga.

There had never been any question in his mind that the job required a professional killer. "We have to hire someone," he had told the others when the plan was first being hatched. "I mean really, who among us is capable of wet work?"

"I haven't been capable of wet work since I had my prostate removed," one of his partners in crime had said.

They had a good laugh over that one. That had been over two years ago. Slowly, methodically, the plan came together. Then they took a month-long trip to Europe to recruit the man who eventually killed Elkins. A working vacation they called it. Museums, fine restaurants, four-star hotels, and as they loved to say, "cloak and dagger meetings with potential hit men."

In truth, there was nothing cloak or dagger about the meetings. Finding candidates was easy enough if you asked the right questions in the right neighborhoods.

They found their assassin in Palermo. "A Sicilian hit man," one of them had said. "How stereotypical can we get?"

But they agreed he was the right man for the job. Now, two years later, Elkins was dead and the Story Guru was alone in his den, having a quiet victory drink. So how come I'm not feeling victorious, he thought.

Fear. He felt it bubbling up in his belly. Planning is one thing, he thought. Pulling it off is something else. At first it had been an adventure. Hatching a real murder plot was a thrill. Cruising the continent for professional killers was better than sex. But now it had gone from a dream to a reality and with that came the possibility of getting caught. His plot was airtight. He knew he was too smart to get caught, but he was a worrier by nature.

He took a deep breath and looked at the top right hand corner of his monitor. Monday, April 18, 11:09 p.m. He had been sitting at his computer for three hours searching for news about the murder.

Pencil still clenched between his teeth, he went back to the Google site and for about the fiftieth time that night he typed the words 'Murder at Familyland' into the Search bar. And like every time before, he got thousands of pages of Familyland references, but nothing about the man who had been strangled in the Rabbit Hole more than twenty-four hours ago.

"I know how Ike Rose and those people at Lamaar operate," he had said from the very start. "The guy inside the Rambunctious Rabbit suit at Familyland will get whacked, and there won't be a whisper about it on TV, radio or newspaper. They'll bury it."

He searched the *L.A. Times* site. Then cnn.com. Nada. Not a word. Just as he predicted. The Lamaar Company didn't want the public to know about the death of Eddie Elkins.

He removed the splintered pencil, spit a few yellow flakes onto the rug, and poured another two inches of Grand Marnier into his glass. "Here's looking at you, Rambo," he said, downing half the amber liquid in one swallow.

He sat back in his chair and stared up at the ceiling. There's no reason to be nervous, he told himself. Everything is going according to script.

CHAPTER 17

BIG JIM SETTLED into his chair. "The movie business is all about power," the smug professor explained to his captive audience. I put my pad down on the table and nodded my head in surrender.

"But the people in power change about every five minutes. A few bombs at the box office, and the hotshot who had the vision suddenly finds himself with a lot of time for golf and martinis. Then a new messiah shows up with *his* vision. Usually some retread who got fired from another studio. It didn't work that way at Lamaar. From the time he went into business until a few years before he died, Dean Lamaar didn't just run the company. He *was* the company. My way or the highway.

"There's no Mr. Paramount, no Mr. Columbia, but there was a Mr. Warner and a Mr. Disney and a Mr. Lamaar, and if it's your name on that front gate, you are God Almighty. You think I'm a control freak? Imagine if I had a power base."

"I shudder at the concept," I said.

"Dean Lamaar came from one of those Bible Belt states. His father was one of those old-time religion ministers, a real bitter son of a bitch because he got his leg blown off in World War I. Plus he was a drunk. He'd hobble up to the pulpit with his wooden leg and preach against the evils of booze, then go home, get wasted, and beat the shit out of his son."

"Stop! Stop!" I said so loud that Skunkie opened his eyes to see what the problem was. "I don't want the life story of some dead guy. I want to know why you think Danny Eeg killed Elkins and where do I find him."

"Y'know, Mike, you just don't appreciate what a source I am. I used to drive Dean Lamaar around in the early seventies. Most of the time, he'd just be polite, ask how I'm doing, stuff like that. But a few times he'd be a little plastered, and he'd open up. He even showed me the scars on his hands where his father burned them when he caught him drawing cartoons."

"Dad, you are confusing me with someone who gives a shit. I don't want to know about Dean Lamaar's unhappy childhood and his sadistic father."

"Okay, okay, just one last juicy little tidbit on the subject. One day the preacher climbs a ladder to fix some shingles on the roof. He's a drunk and a gimp, so he loses his balance, falls off the roof, and lands on a rake. Bleeds to death in a couple of minutes. Now, is that divine justice or what?"

"Apparently God punishes fathers who are cruel to their sons," I said. "Process that little tidbit."

"God doesn't punish fathers who introduce their ungrateful sons to beautiful, intelligent, eligible women."

"I'll make you a deal," I said. "If you hurry up and get to the part about Danny Eeg, I'll marry Diana and give you twelve grandchildren."

He took a sip of his Irish. "It started right after the Japs bombed Pearl Harbor. Lamaar enlisted in the army and since by now he's a working cartoonist, they assign him to a unit that makes military training films, and he becomes fast friends with four other soldier boys. They called themselves The Cartoon Corps. They worked together as a team, learned their craft at the Army's expense."

"One of them better be Danny Eeg."

"No, but one of them was Lars Eeg. Danny is his son. He was

born about a year after the war ended."

I put my hand over my eyes. Jim wasn't even up to the part where my suspect was born yet. I removed my hand to signal him to go on.

"Lars was a brilliant cartoonist. Way better than Lamaar. When the war ended the other three went their separate ways, but Lamaar and Eeg went off to Hollywood together and landed a job in some nickel-and-dime animation house. After a year Lamaar hates working for other people, so, without a pot to piss in he opens his own company. But by now Eeg's got a wife and kid, and he can't afford to live hand to mouth, so he turns down the partnership."

"Bad call," I volunteered.

"Lamaar struggles. Finally he gets the big call. RKO wants six cartoons starring this new character he created, Rambunctious Rabbit. He does one. It comes out good, but not great. Plus he's such a perfectionist that he spent more than RKO paid him, so he's losing his shirt. He needs help, so he uses part of the front money to hire his old buddy Lars Eeg, who Lamaar knows is much more talented than he is.

"A few months later it's all turned around. Eeg really develops the character. The drawings, the attitudes, the whole persona. He doesn't give Rambunctious a girlfriend like Mickey Mouse has. No, he gives him a wife. And kids. A shitload of kids, because what the hell, he's a rabbit. And they don't live in a hole like Bugs Bunny. They live in suburbia. The whole rabbit family becomes the symbol of middle-class, post-war America. It's brilliant. And it's perfect timing. Because now it's 1950, and along comes television. The demand for animation is bigger than the supply.

"Lamaar Studios explodes. Now Dean's got hundreds of employees working around the clock, and he knows he needs a management team, but he doesn't trust anybody. So he sends for his old Army buddies, The Cartoon Corps. In less than ten years they go from a mom-and-pop operation to an entertainment giant. Movies, TV, music, licensing, and of course, since Walt had Disneyland, Dean had to build Familyland.

"They go public and the money is pouring in. Dean Lamaar is one of the most powerful men in Hollywood, and his buddies do whatever he asks. They helped run the show, but they are all yes men. Yes, Deanie, yes, Deanie, yes Deanie. I'd hear it in the car. And then one day, Lars Eeg says No.

"Dean wanted to make an animated feature about the Civil War. The others kissed Lamaar's ass for his creative genius, but Eeg thought it was a bad idea. He had butted heads with the boss before, but by now Lamaar is a full-blown paranoid and he sees this as a threat to his power. He decides that Eeg has to go."

"My way or the highway," I said, just to let him know I was paying attention.

"Exactly. Lamaar offered Eeg $250,000 to cash in his chips. Eeg knew he was the odd man out, so he agreed to take the money. But he had to sign away all his creative rights to any of the work he did while he worked for Lamaar. Do you know how much Eeg would be worth today if he hadn't been squeezed out? Over a billion dollars. Lars died, but he's got a son, Danny, who's been fighting for that money for years. Years! And he still hasn't collected a penny."

"And you think Danny Eeg murdered the guy in the rabbit costume as a way of getting back at Lamaar Studios for screwing his father?"

"To make a long story short," he stopped, and we both laughed, "yes, I do. If it turns out I'm wrong, and someone killed Elkins because he molested their kid, you'll figure that out soon enough. But if I'm right about that flipbook, and those Lamaar characters start dropping like flies, you'll know it's a hate crime against the corporation. There's always hundreds of disgruntled employees at a company, but there's only one person in the world who hates Lamaar enough to do this. Lars Eeg's son, Danny."

"But if what you told me is common knowledge, Danny would

know he'd be the first suspect on a list of one."

"Right. And he'll have an ironclad alibi. Probably was in another part of the world when the murder happened."

"So he hired someone."

"Getting screwed out of a billion bucks can make a normal man do a lot of crazy things," he said. "By the way, Lamaar did make that Civil War movie. It was called *Divided We Fall*. It sank without a ripple. It was his only flop."

"Dad, thanks a lot. This is an amazing backgrounder. I owe you. I'm sorry if I called you an overblown windbag."

"You didn't call me a windbag."

"Then I must've just been thinking it."

He raised his huge hand and slowly lifted the middle finger in my direction. Just like the flipbook. "This does not mean 'one,'" he said.

Greater love hath no father and son.

CHAPTER 18

WE TALKED FOR another ten minutes. I was about to say good night, when Skunkie sat up and barked. Big Jim looked at me and said, "Company."

The doorbell rang. Skunkie raced to the front door. I was right behind him. I pressed the thumb latch and pulled the door open. It was my brother Frankie. He looked like a train wreck.

Frankie hadn't shaved or combed his hair for days. His clothes looked like he'd slept in them, but his pupils were so dilated, it was obvious that he hadn't slept anywhere for quite a while. He was carrying a small black duffel bag, which he dropped on the rug as he entered. His eyes were bloodshot, the rims red. I know my brother doesn't do drugs, but he looked like a candidate for a one-way ticket to Betty Ford.

"Mike?" he said, like he'd just encountered a total stranger. His voice resonated with fear. "I didn't know… I didn't know you'd be here."

"It's a good thing I am." He smelled even worse than he looked. A gamy mixture of body odor, booze, dried vomit, and the unmistakable stench of fear.

Jim came up behind me. Frankie threw his arms as far around his father as they could go. He's four inches shorter than I am, small, like my mother's side of the family. Big Jim gathered him up like a rag doll and held him tight.

Frankie buried his face into Jim's massive chest, pressing hard, digging deep to tap into that familiar well of comfort and closeness. A Pavlovian wave of relief rippled through his body as once again he let himself be wrapped in Daddy's loving arms. It's that primal physical contact between parent and child that says, As long as you are here with me, you are safe from harm. And when that touch finally came, Frankie's emotional fabric split at the seams, and he began to sob. "Pop," he said, "I am in such deep shit."

Without letting go of Frankie, Jim turned toward me, and he became the second person that day to communicate with me in code. He spoke softly, so he wouldn't disturb the boy inside the cocoon of safety. I could barely hear him over Frankie's wailing, but I could read Jim's lips. C.T.W. they said.

C.T.W. was something my mother had taught us before we even knew the other twenty-three letters of the alphabet. She had learned it from her father, and who knows how many generations had handed it down before him.

It is only used in times of family crisis. It is a rallying cry that says, No matter what your priorities, something else is now more important. Someone in the family needs your help. It's not like 9-1-1, which means call the cops or call an ambulance. C.T.W. is, in fact, the opposite of 9-1-1. It means, Call no one. This is a family problem, and only family can solve it. Outsiders are the enemy.

"Frankie," my father said into his ear. "Did you kill anybody?"

Frankie choked back a few last sobs and shook his head. "No."

"Well, that's good," Jim said. "Because anything else can be fixed. Plus now your brother won't have to be an accessory after the fact to murder. Next question, is this about gambling?"

"No," Frankie said. "Well, partly… it's a long story."

Some families have heart disease or diabetes or hemophilia running rampant through their genes. The Lomaxes are afflicted with diarrhea of the mouth. We hemorrhage long stories. There seems to be no cure.

"Did you steal anything?" Jim asked. Frankie was not a thief, but there were times when his gambling addiction had led him to make some very stupid, not to mention illegal, choices.

"No. Yes. I don't know."

If Frankie were a homicide suspect, this would be a perfect time for the cops to grill him. The exhaustion gives the good guys an edge. But this was my brother. "Dad," I said, "this kid needs sleep." Then I turned to the kid. "Frankie, honest truth—you got any drugs or alcohol inside you?"

"Yeah, some of each."

"Dad, let's clean him up and put him to bed."

"One last question. You're shaking with fear. What are you afraid of?"

Frankie's body rocked against Jim's. This wasn't fear. It was terror. He opened his mouth, but no human sounds came forth. Only puppy whimpers. Finally, he found his voice. "Someone has a contract out on me."

"No one will come for you here," Jim said. "If they do, Mike and I will kill them with our bare hands."

"And if you try to leave," I said to Frankie, "*we'll* kill you."

His body shook. Half a laugh, half a sob. But he knew he was safe. His family was there. To love him unconditionally. To support him without judgment, without recriminations. To protect him from any and all who might want to hurt him.

The Patriarch of the Lomax Clan has handed down the decree. Frankie's in trouble. C.T.W. Circle The Wagons.

CHAPTER 19

"WHO'S GOT A contract out on you?" Jim asked, as we peeled Frankie's clothes off and propped him up in the shower. No answer. We lathered him up with a bar of Angel's gardenia soap, which was perfect, because he wasn't really dirty; he just stank. I scrubbed him from head to waist, while Jim went to work on the lower half. At one point, Frankie said, "Dad, what are you — some kind of a homo?"

Jim answered "No, but your shower buddies in prison will be." I doubt if Frankie heard him. He was having enough trouble just standing upright.

We capped off the steaming hot shower with a fifteen-second blast of cold water, which shocked Frankie's system awake long enough to get two Balance bars and a glass of milk in his belly. Jim spiked the milk with a Halcyon. "Sleep insurance," Jim said.

"I'm not a doctor, " I said, " but I really doubt if he needs it."

"It's for me," Jim said. "I'll sleep better knowing he's comatose."

We tucked him into his old boyhood bed, which was conveniently located a short twelve feet away from the three-hundred-pound sentry who would guard him with his life. Jim owned an impressive collection of firearms, among them a Beretta, a Mauser, and a Glock. He also owned those two lethal bare hands. No mints on the pillow, but all in all, a pretty nice homecoming. The wagons were circled.

Jim dumped Frankie's duffel bag on the foyer floor and went through it while I hung back in the dining room. If there were drugs or guns or body parts in the bag, I didn't want to know about it. Just in case I ever had to testify.

After a few minutes, Jim yelled out, "Holy shit!" I braced myself. Then he yelled, "That crazy kid's got Jimmy Hoffa in this bag." Lomax humor. It never takes a holiday. Half a minute later, Jim called out again. "All clear. You can send in the cops now."

I entered to find the floor littered with a pitiful potpourri of underwear, socks, shirts, and khakis that smelled more of mold and mildew than of Frankie. Duffel bag rot. There was a grungy toiletry kit that resembled one I had seen being used a few months ago by a gray-skinned homeless man in the men's room at the bus terminal.

There were no telltale cocktail napkins or matchbooks from Vegas casinos, but there were several *Wall Street Journals*, the most recent of which was three days old. My brother had traded his gambling addiction for investing in the stock market, which I wasn't sure was all that different.

"Whoever's got a contract out on him, it's not for the contents of this bag," I said. "Unless you found something and you're hiding it from me."

"If I did, I wouldn't tell you anyway, because then I'd be jamming up both my sons," he said. "But I didn't."

Jim and I went back to the kitchen where he filled a large travel mug with black coffee. "Take it with you," he said. "I'm not a doctor either, but nine out of ten truck drivers recommend this for those late-night road trips."

"You're amazing," I said. "Your kids are forty-two and thirty-two, and you're still fathering."

"I slip one kid a Mickey and pump the other full of caffeine. You call that fathering?" He poured coffee for himself. "Weird, isn't it?" he said, blowing on the cup and taking a gulp while it was still too hot to drink. "I'm trying to help one son catch a murderer and the other one from getting himself murdered."

I let out a long, audible breath. A sigh, I guess, even though I don't like to think of myself as a guy who sighs. "When Joanie and I were trying to get pregnant, we made so many plans for the kid's future that we started to worry how old he'd be when he stopped needing us."

"It never stops. There are times when I still need my Dad, and he's been dead for twenty years."

"Did I ever tell you that Joanie wanted to call our first son Lincoln?" I said. "Link Lomax. She said it sounded like a movie star. I thought it sounded more like one of those dancers at Chippendales. When she couldn't get pregnant, she started calling him The Missing Link."

He too exhaled heavily. "You got another letter from her today, didn't you?" he said. "It's the 18th of the month."

"Yeah. Letter Number Six. Special delivery from heaven. She said she still loves me and that I should give you and Andre big wet kisses for her."

We had both gotten soaked when we showered Frankie. Jim squeezed a few drops of water from his shirt. "I'm already pretty goddamn wet as it is," he said. He took another Teamster-sized gulp of his coffee.

"Oh, yeah," I said. "She also said, Make sure you tell your father not to drink so much coffee."

"I'm only having half a cup," he said. "I want to be able to sleep with one eye open tonight."

We said good night and parted with mutual reminders to keep pagers and cell phones charged and at the ready. Jim said he'd let me know when and if Frankie said anything coherent.

I climbed into my Acura with my travel mug filled to the top and was dialing my cell phone before I made the first turn out of the driveway.

I had a date with a hooker and I was already an hour late.

CHAPTER 20

CORAL C. JONES is a beautiful, big-assed, chocolate-brown woman in her mid-thirties. She is a product of the streets of Los Angeles, and the streets are where she learned to ply her trade. I have friends in Vice who have had official police business with Coral C. over the years. Although she has numerous frequent flyer points with LAPD, they say she plays the game well and is usually cooperative with the cops. But she can be a tough negotiator when the stakes are high.

I never worked Vice. I met Coral C. two years ago in my capacity as a homicide detective. Her eighteen-year-old brother Tyrell had a starring role in a Seven-Eleven security tape. It opened with a run-of-the-mill, late-night stickup, and ended with a dead cashier—an unlucky Pakistani named Noor. He was a recent immigrant who obviously never studied Convenience Store 101, where the first rule they teach you is "Give Them The Fucking Money, Stupid!"

It seemed to be an open-and-shut case. Despite the fact that we were working with badly lit black-and-white security footage, we were able to read the name "Ty" sewn on the front of the perp's jacket. Within hours we had tracked down Tyrell Jones and booked him for murder.

Coral C. swore Ty was at home with her that night. It just happened to be a night she wasn't working, she said. Some people will swear to anything to protect someone they love, and since Coral C. had helped raise her younger brother, she was as much a mother to him as a sibling. What was different about Coral C. was that she swore on a Bible that she pulled out of her purse. But the Seven-Eleven tape showed Tyrell pulling the trigger.

Tyrell insisted it wasn't him. "Some dude stole my jacket to fuck me up," was his defense. "You think I'd be dumb enough to rob a store wearing a jacket with my name on it?" This got a big laugh around the squad room. We'd seen a lot dumber.

The D.A. assured us that the jury would convict Tyrell in fifteen minutes, start-to-finish, and still have plenty of time for a coffee break. They probably would have.

Except for Coral C. She knew that Tyrell was innocent, and she knew how to work the system. She called a lieutenant in Narcotics who owed her a favor for some insider information she had coughed up that had led to a Page One drug bust. The Narc Loo called Kilcullen, who in turn asked me to invest another twenty-four to see if Tyrell's bullshit impostor story held any water.

I gave it my best shot, something no cop would have done if Coral C. hadn't been able to cash in that chit from Narcotics. And guess what? It turns out it wasn't Tyrell in the video. It was a same-sized, same-color, same-age punk named Willie Washburn who not only wanted to fuck Tyrell up, but also wanted to fuck Tyrell's girlfriend.

Washburn *had* stolen Tyrell's jacket. He then pulled a cap down over his face, copied Tyrell's walk and his mannerisms, and held up the Seven-Eleven. When the robbery went sour and Tyrell was arrested for murder, Washburn felt like he'd hit a grand slam. He'd be banging Ty's girlfriend for the next fifteen to twenty. He would have gotten away with it, if he had worn different shoes.

The killer's feet were only on camera for a split second as he ran out of the store, but I freeze framed them and realized I'd never seen shoes like them before. There were four jagged lines attached to the Nike Swoosh. When we zoomed in, we could see that the lines were actually the letter W inked twice into the shoes. It didn't take long to find out that W.W. was the personal logo of Willie Washburn, who apparently had been dumb enough to rob a store wearing his signature shoes. Today he's doing a solid twenty in San Quentin. As for Tyrell, he's in his second year at a different state institution. UCLA.

On the day that Tyrell and Washburn traded places in the lockup, Coral C. came to thank me. "Without you," she said without a trace of tough street girl in her voice, "I'd be just another black hooker screaming for justice, and nobody would listen to me, and my baby brother would be rotting in prison."

Then she said those three little words. "I owe you."

There is a tradition of reciprocity between cops and hookers. Sometimes a girl gets in a jam and needs a favor. And sometimes a guy needs his pipes cleaned. It's a time-honored tradition that works out well for both parties.

I told Coral C., Thanks, but no thanks. I was happily married.

She put her hand on one hip and went into her Black Ho act. "Shit, White Boy, I don't wanna marry you. I jes' wanna thank you. I was gonna be sending you a Hallmark card, but I thought, Hell no, he'll trash that and forget all about it in two minutes. But if I suck his cock, he'll 'member that fo-ever."

"Ms. Jones," I said. "I'll remember *this* forever. It's not every day a grateful citizen stops by to express such deep appreciation. As for keeping your brother out of prison, I was as wrong as everyone else when I first saw that security tape. You're the one who saved his life. I'm just glad I could help."

Coral C.'s face softened. Her "you-can-do-me-anytime" body language morphed into the filled-with-gratitude loving sister. Her eyes welled up. She dropped the Ebonics. "Tell your wife I said she's a lucky woman. God bless you, Mike." She took my hand, leaned in, and kissed me gently on the cheek. And then she left the squad room. A lady.

And that was the last time I saw her. Until the night Joanie died. I was drunk. I dug out Coral C.'s number and called her. I told her I was ready to accept her offer. I wanted to spend the night with her. But first she had to agree to the ground rules.

I had never cheated on my wife, even in the last year of her illness, when our sex life was nothing more than a bittersweet memory. And now that she was dead I wanted to physically lose myself inside a woman. I wanted sex, but I didn't want charity. I didn't want payback for doing my job two years ago. I wanted a business arrangement. I wanted Coral C. to bang my brains out and charge me for the privilege. Full retail price. No policeman's discount.

She argued briefly, but she could tell I meant it. "I'm a cop, and I'm laying down the law," I said, drunk, belligerent, and hopelessly despondent. "Take it or leave it."

She took it. A month later, when I read Joanie's first letter from the grave, I gave Coral C. another call. Same deal. Since then we've spent the night together on the 18th of every month. Nobody knows about the arrangement. Not Terry, not even my father. It's not that they're judgmental. It's just that I've got enough guilt about paying a hooker every month on the anniversary of my wife's death. I don't want to think about what anyone else would be thinking.

I had planned to meet Coral C. at midnight, but my long-winded father and my bubble-headed brother had screwed up my plans. I dialed her cell phone to tell her I'd be late.

She answered on the first ring. "Hello."

"Hello," I said. We never used names on the cell phone.

"You're late. Should I start without you?" she said, laughing sexily.

"I have to cancel." It was the voice inside my head talking, but the words came out of my mouth, and, through the magic of wireless technology, went straight to her ear.

"You breaking our date?" She sounded surprised. Not nearly as surprised as I was. "You working a night shift?"

"No," I said, then added lamely, "family problems."

"You got yourself a girlfriend, don't you?" I could tell she was smiling.

"No way."

"But you're working on it." She was enjoying this.

I didn't answer. I wasn't even sure I knew the answer.

"Hey, baby, I'm cool with it," she said.

"How's our college student doing?" I asked, changing the subject.

"Two As, two Bs, and he's writing a sports column for the school paper. I might apply to college myself. Could you write me a reference?"

"Honey, I could write you a reference that would fog their glasses and get you a four-year scholarship."

"You sure you wanna break this date? Sounds to me like you still got pussy on the brain."

"I'll get over it," I said. We hung up, and for the rest of the ride home I tried to block the whole long day from my thoughts.

But every now and then the voice inside my head would say, "Don't forget, you promised Big Jim you'd call Diana."

CHAPTER 21

I MADE THE trip back from Big Jim's about three minutes shy of my personal-best door-to-door time. Speeding without fear of catching hell is one of the perks of being a cop. I turned into my driveway and automatically looked down at the clock on the dash.

Joanie had this little game she invented called Dashboard Poker. Whenever you get to your destination, you look at your car's digital clock and make a poker hand out of the numbers. There's no winning or losing, but a good hand means the stars are lining up in your favor. You're not allowed to plot your arrival time. It has to be completely random.

I arrived home at thirty-four minutes after midnight. The eerie green digits that the Acura designers had foolishly thought only served to tell time glowed happily with the good news that I had just been dealt a four-card straight: 1, 2, 3, 4, all lined up in a row. According to Joanie's rules, the better your poker hand, the greater your reward, so I knew excellent things were in store for me. Maybe Elkins's killer would be sitting in my kitchen, cuffed to the table, writing out his confession.

Joanie wasn't a mystic or a kook or any of those other labels we give people who don't rigorously follow the Accepted Path of Logic and Reason. Like millions of other perfectly sane people, she believed there are powers beyond the observable physical world. She would read our horoscopes daily, knock on wood whenever the occasion called for it, and was always on the lookout for Signs From God. So Dashboard Poker became much more than a game. To Joanie, it was one of God's many ways of communicating with us. G-mail.

Joanie had more than a passing need to hear from God. She desperately wanted a baby. Each month as her unfertilized eggs would drop, and the blood and the tears would flow from her body, she would pray for God's blessings and ask for His help. Some nights I would see her kneeling at her bedside, the angelic little Catholic girl, hands clasped, her lips moving in silent prayer. Other times she would storm out of the bathroom, the EPT strip in her hand unmistakably negative, and she'd thrust it up to the heavens and yell, "Thank you, God, but this is not the sign I was asking for."

Eventually, we turned to one of God's helpers on earth, Kristian Kraus, fertility doctor to the stars. His patients adored him, and from the moment you met him, you knew why. Kraus was about sixty, with silver hair, a golden tan, and blue eyes that radiated compassion, understanding, and most of all, hope.

But being a trained detective, I could see beyond the Marcus Welby façade. The man reeked of money. His suit cost more than my car. His Ferrari in the parking lot cost more than my house. And according to Joanie's estimate, he also had about $200,000 worth of limited-edition prints. And that was just in his waiting room. We were never invited to his home in Hancock Park or the beach house in Malibu.

The receptionist handed us a horse-choking bill after our "initial consultation," which is an expensive way of saying "first visit." On the drive home I gently asked Joanie if we really needed this pricey a doctor. "No," she said. "There's another guy who works out of the Kmart on La Cienega. Let's take the bus down there tomorrow and check him out." The subject was closed.

There was one wall in Kraus's office that had no expensive

art. Just pictures of expensive babies. Girl babies, boy babies, fat babies, wrinkled babies, twin babies, triplet babies, black babies, Asian babies, and of course, hundreds of silver-spoon-in-the-mouth, money-up-the-wazoo, rich white babies. Some of the kids posed with stuffed animals, some with real dogs, and some with easily identifiable *People Magazine* cover parents. In the middle of all those photos was a large plaque that read *Kristian's Miracles*.

The wall was sacred, and every seat in the waiting room faced it. You sat there for never less than an hour, and the wall spoke to you. "This is what you're here for, folks. See how easy it is? We do it every day." To me it said, Did you see Dr. Kraus's platinum Rolex and his ostrich-leather wing tips? Those are just some of the many things he spends your money on. This wall is dedicated to you. Thank you for your contribution.

After six visits that included poking, probing, sperm collecting, and various other procedures that were an amalgam of humiliation and comic relief, the good doctor announced his conclusions. "You appear to be in that very small category of couples where the tests are basically," he paused to clear his honeyed-voice throat, "inconclusive."

He couldn't find a thing wrong with either of us. He was, he consoled us, terribly, terribly disappointed to put us through all those tests and come up with no definitive diagnosis. But not so disappointed that he didn't cash our checks. His best advice was don't give up. Keep trying for another six months, and if you don't get pregnant, we should consider in vitro. By "we" he meant me, Joanie, and our checkbook.

One night, during our Just-Keep-Trying-For-Good-Old-Doctor-Kraus Phase, I got home around 9 p.m. I had just pulled my fourth sixteen-hour stakeout in a row, and I was cop-weary. I shucked my clothes in a heap on the floor and my body in a second heap on our bed. This is where my memory gets fuzzy, but I do remember bits and pieces of it. I had to rely on Joanie to fill me in on the finer points the next day.

Apparently two hours after I hit the pillow, she came home from a PTA meeting. Joanie taught third grade and loved it. She gently nudged me out of REM until she was convinced I had achieved a minimal state of auditory awareness. I, of course, couldn't hear shit.

"I had a rotten night," she said. "Suzie Dilallo's parents came directly from a cocktail party, and they were both half-sloshed. Doreen Riggins's father got so excited when I told him how well his daughter was doing in math that he threw his hands up and knocked over my diet Coke and spilled it on my next five reports." She waited for my usual husbandly concerned response. Getting none, she put her mouth to my ear. "Are you even listening to me?"

Technically I was listening, but I had not yet reached the stage where I could decipher. Her gentle nudging became aggressive prodding and quickly escalated into serious pummeling. Somewhere short of assault and battery, my brain opened up for business, and I managed to grumble, "Mmm, lis'ning."

"I'm sick and tired of going to PTA meetings as a 'T'," she said. "I want to go as a 'P.' All the way driving home, I was totally bummed, and then bam! I pulled into our driveway at exactly eleven minutes after eleven. Four aces, right there on the dashboard clock. It's the best hand you can get, so I know God has something spectacular planned for me."

"Hope you win the Lotto," I mumbled, still not opening my eyes.

"I'm ovulating, and I was thinking maybe a big handsome man would make mad passionate love to me and get me pregnant," she said.

"'Morrow," I said. "Inna morning."

"Dashboard Poker payoffs don't carry over to the next day," she explained as if I were coherent enough to comprehend the rules.

"Go way. Penis sleeping," I said.

"I have ways of arousing penises from their slumber," she said.

Indeed she did. The next day she told me that I had dozed off several times in the middle. I apologized. "No apologies required," she said. "It was very tender, very different. No heavy breathing. Just snoring."

I still think dashboard clocks contain messages from above, but that night four aces wasn't a winning hand.

I parked the Acura, turned off the ignition, and the 12:34 faded into oblivion. As I walked up to the front door I found myself singing "Ol' Man River." It's one of my all-time favorites and whenever my ass is dragging, I like to dig into the real soulful part about *Ah gets weary*. I always assumed it was an old Negro spiritual. Until my third date with Joanie. We were in her kitchen making pasta and small talk, when I heard "Ol' Man River" coming from her stereo. I would never have had the balls to do it with any other woman, but I grabbed the slotted spoon, turned it into a microphone, and sang along to the best of my limited Caucasian ability.

"And now I discover yet another facet of Detective Lomax," she said, applauding and kissing me on the cheek. "He does show tunes."

It was the first time she had kissed me so spontaneously, as if we were a couple who gave little cheek kisses all the time. I made a check mark on my mental scorecard and wondered if kitchen kissing could lead to bedroom kissing, which had been on my agenda since Day One, but which was as yet unchecked. It took me a few seconds to return to earth and realize that I couldn't process her post-kiss comment. "What do you mean 'show tunes'?" I said.

"That song is from *Showboat*. Oscar Hammerstein and Jerome Kern. If you eat all your pasta like a good boy, I'll buy you the album."

I stared at her in all my cultural ignorance. "It's a *show tune?*"

"Don't be upset," she said. "Just because you can sing show

tunes doesn't necessarily mean you're gay." Then she turned the burner off under the pasta, removed the spoon from my hand and kissed me for real. A few minutes later she gave me the chance to prove how absolutely heterosexual I could be.

I am now totally secure in my musical masculinity. I do, however, have difficulty reconciling the fact that my father, who bawls at Puppy Chow commercials, can dismiss a genius like Hammerstein, yet be totally enthralled by lyrics like *my wife ran away with my best friend, and I sure do miss him.*

I unlocked my front door. Andre was sacked out on the sofa. He stretched his legs, arched his back, and started to get up. "Stay," I said. "I have to make a phone call." He understood the 'stay' part and went back to sleep.

It was too late to call Terry at home, but I knew he'd check his office voicemail before he drank his first cup of coffee. I left a message with the highlights of my conversation with Big Jim, starting with his observations on the finger in the flipbook and ending with Danny Eeg and his billion-dollar motive.

I hung up the phone. "Oh, and one more thing," I said, once I was sure the connection was broken. "Someone has a contract out on my brother Frankie. But that's my problem."

I went to the fridge and took a few gulps of orange juice straight from the carton. The sugar hit would jolt me awake for about ten minutes and then I'd come down faster than an Austrian bobsled team. I just needed to stay awake long enough to re-read one of Joanie's letters.

I opened the back door, and before I let Andre out, I said, "Business!" which he knows means 'No sniffing for squirrels or other frivolous dog diversions. Just body functions.'

I stripped to my boxers, pressed the Oral B electric to my teeth for about one-tenth of the 120 seconds they recommend, and tended to my own business. Andre was waiting at the door when I got there. I locked up, turned off the TV, got Letter Number One from its wooden box, and crawled into bed.

CHAPTER 22

THE FIRST LETTER was seventeen pages. An epic. Longer by far than any of the ones that followed. I'd be lucky if I could stay awake long enough to read two pages. But I was jonesing for a connection with Joanie. I think it had something to do with the fact that I had met, and, okay I'll say it, mentally undressed not one but two women today. Amy Cheever and Diana...

Damn! I couldn't remember Diana's last name. Fried cop brain. It didn't matter. It's not like she was a murder suspect and I needed to get it right for my report to Kilcullen.

What's the suspect's name, Lomax? It's Diana, sir. Diana something or other. Darned if I can remember her last name, but she was wearing this cool Rambo Rabbit watch. You're fired, Lomax. Thank you, sir. Can I please read the letter from my dead wife now, sir?

I pulled a fistful of paper from the envelope and turned to page one.

Dearest Mike,

I love you. I love you. I love you.

Well, that's a good way to start. I've been trying to write this letter for weeks, but it keeps coming out maudlin or depressing or just plain dumb. Would you believe that the first ten drafts started out with, "By the time you read this, I'll be dead." I should have said, "By the time I write this, I'll be dead." I've torn up so many versions of this letter that I'm starting to feel guilty about how many trees I've killed.

Screw it. No more striving for perfection. This is the last draft.

The whole idea of writing to you came to me when I was lying in the hospital watching the chemo drip. For months they've been pumping my body full of this evil poison that has left me weak and hairless and no fun to be married to. They tell me it's the only way to kill the even more evil poison that is rotting out my insides. But that day on that table I realized it's not going to work. The cancer is going to win.

Don't try to argue with me, because if you're reading this, then I really am dead, which means I've won the argument.

Do you remember what you said that night I told you about the tumors? Your very first words were, "You'll beat it, Babe." Well, if I do beat it, I will shower you with kisses and burn this letter. But my Mom didn't beat it, my Aunt Lil didn't beat it, and after all these months of hospital stays, radiation treatments, and chemo sessions, I'm seeing the glass half empty.

Women don't have the same fears that men have. And I don't have the same fears most rational women have. Don't laugh, but what scares me the most right now (not counting the part where I get put in a box, which gets put in a hole, which gets covered with dirt) is that you won't remember me when I'm gone.

I know how stupid that sounds. I can hear your reaction. Are you crazy? How could I ever forget you?

I was 14 when my mother died, and even though I knew her for fourteen years, I can hardly remember her now. You've only known me for seven years. I know you'll have my pictures and those hideous family videotapes from Big Jim's Halloween parties, but I want you to have something else. My heart. My soul. My essence.

I figured if I just write what I feel and let it all pour out, you'll never be able to get me out of your mind. So I'm going to write as many letters as I can. This is the first in a series. You get to open one a month. You can't open them all at once. I don't want to be gone from your life so soon. I want you to still anticipate me, still wait to hear from me, still keep me in your head and in your heart.

Part of me thinks this is a very unhealthy, selfish, twisted thing to do to you. But the other part of me (the part that says it's not a sin for a girl to feel sorry for herself) says, Don't worry about Mike. He can handle it. He's one tough cop. He's a fantastic, resilient, extraordinary hell of a man. Just do what you've got to do for yourself and your own sanity.

I just stopped typing, hit the Print button and read back everything I've written so far. Yuck. It makes me want to throw up even more than the chemo. This is usually the point where I tear it to shreds. But if I keep going back to Page Zero, one day I won't be able to write, and all you'll have is zero. The other night I wanted to ask you if you would hate me for leaving you a letter like this. But I decided that you would rather I shared all my irradiated ruminations and emotions with you, than share nothing. I hope I made the right choice.

Where to start? First of all—most of all—I want to apologize for never bearing you a child. I know that's not what you want to hear, so I won't dwell on it. But I do have one semi-positive thought. Maybe it was God's will that we never had a baby. True, there will never be that tangible piece of me to leave behind who would love you unconditionally. But there will also be one less child in the world who has to suffer the early death of his mother. If little Link had been born, I would have become his Missing Link. Oh, God, that's awful. Feel free to tear up this drivel yourself.

Do you remember the day I met you? I went home that night and wrote pages and pages in my diary about my incredible adventure at the Dunkin' Donut Shop. I wrote a lot about poor Mr. Flores, because I knew no one else would write about just another junkie who got killed in just another stupid robbery. And then I wrote about the gorgeous homicide detective who took my statement and then offered to buy me a cup of coffee because mine spilled all over my skirt during the shooting.

I burned my diary a few weeks ago. It was filled with things I would have wanted you to read, but it was also filled with despair. My infertility haunted me, and there were so many times that the only way to get relief from the pain was to put all my anger and fears on paper. I don't want you to see that after I'm gone. But I saved the page with our first conversation. Here it is. Word for word.

Neatly taped to the letter was a page from her original diary. Blue ink on ivory paper. Her handwriting. Of everything she has written, this is the part that if I read out loud, I'll start to cry. I began to read. Out loud.

And then he said, Can I buy you another cup of coffee? And I said, Considering what just happened, I think they'll give me one for free. And he said, I meant some other time. Or if you've had it with coffee, I could buy you a drink.

I was so excited, but I had to be cool, so I said, You're asking me out? Isn't that frowned upon? And he said, Only if you frown upon it. I said, I've never gone out with a policeman. And he looked a little nervous, but he said, What kind of guys do you go out with? And I said, Usually jerks. Then he gives me this fantastic smile and he says, Heck, I can be a jerk if it'll help me get on the list. And my heart is racing, but not from the shooting, and I say, That won't be necessary. I've been thinking of branching out.

We're going out to dinner on Friday night. We'll sleep together on our third date, and then I'll marry him. Thank you God. It was 4:56 on the dashboard clock when I pulled into the donut shop. I knew something good would happen, but you had me worried when the bullets started flying.

My eyes were wet. That was as far as I could read tonight. I dropped the letter to the floor and turned off the light. I rolled over on my stomach and stretched one leg across the middle of the bed. The sheets on Joanie's side were crisp and cold. Her side was empty, but I could still feel her in the room. I found a cool part on the pillow and scrunched my face into it. "Good night," I said. "I love you."

Once again, our music drifted into my head.

Ah gets weary, and sick o' tryin.
Ah'm tired o' living and feared o' dyin',
Dat Ol' Man River,
He jes' keep rollin' along.

And then a voice inside my head whispered softly, "Trantanella. Diana's last name is Trantanella. Big Jim wrote it down for you."

I got that feeling you get when you finally remember something that's been driving you crazy all day, and I felt a little smile creep across my face. It's the same self-satisfied smile I get when I know the correct question to the Final Jeopardy answer.

I started to thank the voice inside my head for remembering Diana's name. But then I realized. It wasn't the usual nagging, heckling, judgmental voice. It was too polite, too helpful. This was a different voice. Sweeter. Gentler. Loving.

J-mail.

CHAPTER 23

THE NEXT MORNING I was sitting on the fender of my Acura waiting for Terry and Muller. I sipped coffee from the travel mug Big Jim had forced on me the night before. It had a Teamsters Union logo on one side and a big red Peterbilt decal stuck to the other, but in my gray Nordstrom's suit and my black Florsheims, I'm sure nobody mistook me for a long-haul trucker.

Even though he comes from the big city of Portland, Oregon, Muller looks like a farm boy. Clear blue eyes, straight-as-straw blond hair, and an all-American smile you're more likely to see in a milk commercial than in the halls of the LAPD. He's 6 feet tall, which is definitely man-sized, but his face is baby-butt hairless. He's thirty, but he can pass for seventeen, so even though he's assigned to Computer Crimes, he's been grabbed for more than a few undercover jobs at local high schools.

Muller is one part Bill Gates, one part Thelonius Monk, and one part Homer Simpson. The Gates part is obvious. He's the smartest Comp Tech I've worked with, maybe the best in the entire LAPD. He's also one of those rare individuals who uses both sides of his brain to the max. So on nights and weekends, he trades in his computer keyboard for the ebonies and ivories of a jazz piano. He's a great player, but lucky for the Department, he's not the same color as Thelonius. The geeky glasses, the white-as-rice face, and the Norman Rockwell aura work against him in the world of jazz. I may be wrong, but I'd bet that if Muller were African American instead of Velveeta American, he'd have been able to quit his day job long ago.

As for the Homer Simpson part—that's just pure Muller. He's a black belt in Simpson Trivia. His e-mails always close with some random Homerism, my favorite being, "Alcohol is the cause of all the world's problems. It's also the cure." Ask him why he relates to a loser like Homer Simpson, and he'll say, "It could be worse. I could idolize his brother O.J."

I drained the last of my coffee just as they pulled up in Muller's Dodge Caravan, a faded blue seven-seater, with the third row ripped out to make room for all kinds of bulky objects that fill up his life. I climbed into the center row.

Terry was wearing the black-and-brown hound's-tooth sport jacket that he'd worn at least fifty times since he bought it six months ago, plus the same burgundy tie with the Chinese lanterns on it that one of his daughters told him "looks great with that jacket, Dad." Muller's sartorial tastes are more eclectic. He rummages around the thrift shops looking for "previously owned clothing that gives off good vibes." Today he was wearing a blue herringbone jacket with suede patches on the elbows that must have belonged to an English professor for the first half-century of its existence. His shirt was off-white with white embroidery down the front. The vibe it gave me was Mexican barber. Black jeans and a pair of New Balance shoes rounded out the outfit.

"Hey, dude," Muller said. Like a lot of guys his age, Muller has a vocabulary that's rooted in the eighties. "Sorry, I'm late man, but Annetta really effed me up this morning. You're a smart cop. How many dogs can she bring home before I'm legally allowed to shoot her?"

Annetta is Muller's wife. As young as they are, they've been married nearly half their lives. They met at Portland High when she was an exchange student from Denmark. Annetta is blonde and pretty, which is the Official Look of all Scandinavian women, with an engaging personality that makes her instantly likeable. She also has a penchant for stray animals, which appeared to be the crux of this morning's marital stress.

"Good question," I said. "It was on the detective's exam. She can bring home as many dogs as she wants. It's different if she brings home another piano player. Him you could shoot. And how are you this morning, Mr. Biggs? Do you know when the coroner's report will be ready?"

"It's a rush," Terry said. "So I'd say end of April, middle of May at the latest. But after I got your voicemail, I figured to hell with the coroner. What we should do is deputize your father. The Big Jim Report was very encouraging. When we see Curry we'll pump him for some dope on this guy Eeg. But first let's get a little more dirt on our victim. Next stop, Pedophiles-R-Us."

Elkins's apartment was in a Spanish-style complex. Wrought iron gates up front. Big swimming pool in the courtyard. "Nice digs," Muller said. "Somehow I figured if the guy is a creep, he would live in a creepy place."

"I think they attract more kids if they live in a nice warm homey place. Remember Hansel and Gretel and the gingerbread house?" Terry said.

The manager was Helen Shotwell, a fifty-year-old redhead with a thirty-year-old boob job. When I told her that the tenant in Apartment 16 was a murder victim, she asked how soon she could rent it.

She claimed to know very little about Elkins and cared even less. "Been here eight months, paid on time, kept to himself," was her contribution to the investigation. When Terry flashed her the appropriate paperwork, she let us in the apartment and told us to lock up when we left. Then she disappeared. It's only in the movies that landladies and building managers are meddling busybodies who can fill the cops in on a tenant's darkest secrets.

Elkins's apartment was not exactly gingerbread, but with its red-tiled floor and brightly colored throw rugs, it had the festive, kid-friendly feel of a Tex-Mex restaurant. Close to the front door was a wrought iron and glass table. Nestled under it was a Cocker Spaniel puppy, with its head cocked to the side and its sad, penetrating black eyes looking up. I knew without bending down that it was a plaster Sandicast. Normal people collect them. Perverts buy them as kid bait.

"Welcome to Hacienda del Sicko," Terry said.

Dominating one living room wall was a sixty-inch plasma TV. Below that was a media center that contained a VCR, a DVD player, and enough video games and electronic gizmos to keep a kid fascinated for hours. Several rows of shelves were lined with game software plus hundreds of CDs and movies.

"Cool," Muller said. "How come I never get invited over by any pedophiles?"

We spot-checked the living room, kitchen, and dining alcove. If I hadn't read Elkins's rap sheet, I might have figured the tenant was a regular guy with an unlimited line of credit at Circuit City. But the normal-as-blueberry-pie appearance only went so far. The bedroom turned out to be the Perverts' Den from Hell. Three dresser drawers and one entire closet were filled with kiddy porn photos, magazines, and videos.

Terry flipped open a magazine. "Sick bastard," he said, dropping it like it was a biohazard.

Muller made a beeline toward the computer. I watched as his piano-player fingers flew across the keyboard. It reminded me of my *Dear Abby* exchange with Jim the night before, and I wondered how my brother was doing.

Terry and I sifted through the sordid souvenirs of Elkins's existence on the planet. Every few minutes he would spit out another "sick bastard."

Finally Muller stood up and stretched his lanky frame. "There's no doubt what the guy is. He's bookmarked every ped and anti-ped site on the Web. I want to hack into his e-mail and go to the chat rooms where he hangs out. It'll be easier if I take his PC back with us."

We spent another hour cataloguing the contents of the dresser and the closet. Then Muller packed up Elkins's computer plus three of the games for the PlayStation 2. I had watched him carefully check out every piece of software, so I asked why he had singled out those particular games.

"It's complicated," he said, "but all my years of training tell me that God of War, Soul Calibur III, and Grand Theft Auto: San Andreas will give us the best insight into Elkins's character."

"And let me guess," I said. "Those are the only ones you don't have at home."

"D'oh," said Homer Simpson, smacking his forehead with the heel of his hand.

CHAPTER 24

WE WERE BACK in Muller's van trying to decide whether to pull into Mel's Diner or go a few miles out of our way to The Farmer's Market. My cell phone beeped to let me know I had missed a call.

There was no message, but Caller ID said it came from Valley General Hospital. I called the main number and asked for Jan Trachtenberg. I got her voicemail.

"Mrs. Trachtenberg, this is Detective Lomax. Sorry I missed your call. If you're looking for an update on your husband's case, we've got some additional manpower working on it. I'll get back to you in a few days. Thanks."

"I just checked my voicemail," Terry said. "There's a message from Kilcullen."

"You say that calmly, but there's 'uh-oh' in your eyes. Is he homicidal or just psychotic?"

"Worse. All he said was, Let's get together at your earliest convenience."

"I guess Farmer's Market is out of the question," Muller said.

"Unless you want to see our balls hanging from the precinct flagpole, I think all forms of nourishment are out of the question," Terry said.

We made it back to the office by 10:45. Terry grabbed Elkins's folder, and we double-timed it to Kilcullen's door.

"Top o' the morning to ya, lads." Kilcullen was laying on the Irish brogue, which was a signal that he was going to be playful before he got down to business. 'Playful' is Police Academy code for Bust Our Balls.

"I was at the firing range this morning, don't ya know," he said, tapping his fingers on a Nike shoebox on his desk. He lifted the lid. It was filled with pieces of crushed black granite. Some of the chunks were lethal, big as a fist. Some were pebble-sized. The rest was powdery granules. He handed me the box. It weighed about fifteen pounds. I passed it to Terry.

"What is it, Loo?" Terry asked.

"That," he said, looking at the rock pile with contempt, "was my former bowling ball. It committed an egregious crime last night. A trial was held this morning in the shower, and the execution was completed at 8 a.m. You know that nice Sergeant Paris who runs the gun range? He's a bowler too, and I know you're supposed to shoot at paper targets, but he was very cooperative."

The fucker had shot his bowling ball.

He put his palms flat down on his desk and leaned forward. "So," he said, staring at us with the same crazy Jack Nicholson eyes I could see in the picture on the wall behind him. "I've successfully brought my criminal to justice this morning. What have you boys accomplished today?"

"We saw an old lady jaywalking," Terry said. "Gave her a warning. Not worth shooting her. Didn't seem as serious as a bowling ball gone bad."

"Shut the goddamn door," Kilcullen said, dropping the brogue, "and tell me where in Christ's name you are on the Lamaar case."

I filled him in on everything that happened since last night, including Big Jim's observation about the flipbook clue. But I didn't credit Jim.

When I finished, he said, "I agree. You gotta follow both tracks. First, let's nail down this whole pedophile revenge angle. Sutula and Langer can help you track down friends and relatives of vics who might be pissed off enough to kill him. You boys go back to Familyland and talk to the Head of Security. If we do have a serial killer looking to snuff cartoon characters, Lamaar could be headed for a real shit storm. LAPD needs to go on record with a warning. Plus it couldn't hurt for you to look around again."

"Good idea, boss," Terry said.

"Don't patronize me," Kilcullen said. "You guys already had that idea."

"It did cross our mind, sir," Terry said.

"You haven't said word one about the mob connection. Did that cross your mind? Because it crossed the Governor's mind and he's not even being paid to do police work."

He had us. We had missed something big and he was going to beat us over the head with it. "You don't know shit about a mob connection, do you?"

"No," Terry said. "I guess the Governor's more in touch with the mob than we are."

"I guess he reads the papers more than you do. Lamaar is building a big entertainment complex with the Camelot Hotel in Vegas. You know the Camelot. It was opened by Enrico Leone back in the day when the mob moved to Nevada. It's still run by the family. The granddaughter is in charge now."

"Arabella Leone," I said.

"Oh, so you did hear of them. Well, there's hope."

"Look, Loo," Terry said, "we've been on this case all of one day. The DOA is a convicted pedophile, so we're chasing that angle. There may be a vendetta against the company, so we're chasing that angle. Nobody we talked to even gave a hint of a mob connection, and there's nothing about this that makes it look like a mob hit. But if you think Sacramento can solve this faster than we can, here." He threw Elkins's file on the desk. "They can shove it up their..."

"Hey, hey, Bronx boy. Don't be so damn sensitive. The

politicians bust my ass; I bust yours. It's called the Hierarchy of Pain." He pushed the file back at Terry. "How long have you boys been under my command?"

"Three and a half wonderful years," Terry answered, taking the file.

"And have I ever leaned on you to solve a case?"

Terry gave him the raspberry.

"Hey, I may nudge you, but only because you're my Go-To Guys. Now, with this dead pervert in a rabbit suit, now I'm leaning on you. You understand what I'm saying? I've been easy on you in the past, but this time, I really have to push hard. The Governor is calling back at five for a progress report. A progress report!" His ruddy Irish face was a now deeper shade of rudd. "Do you know what he means when he says progress report?"

Rhetorical question. Don't answer it, Terry, I said, using mental telepathy. He didn't.

"He wants an arrest," Kilcullen said. "Those shit-for-brains in Sacramento think you can solve a homicide like on the TV shows. Murder at ten. Case closed at five to eleven. Stay tuned for scenes from next week's episode."

He reached into the shoebox and picked up a fistful of the late Mr. Brunswick. "This is a high-profile case, boys. Elkins is just another scumbag, but he got himself killed in a high-profile rabbit suit in a high-profile theme park in an election year. Don't fail me, boys. I don't do well with failure."

He slowly let the remains of the bowling ball sift through his fingers and back into its cardboard coffin. "Call me with anything I can use to keep the Governor from crawling any further up my rectum. Get to work."

We headed for the door. "One question," Terry said, before we made it out of the room. "This Hierarchy of Pain thing. The politicians take it out on you; you take it out on me. Who do I get to take it out on?"

"You got a dog?" Kilcullen said.

"No."

"Buy a bowling ball."

CHAPTER 25

I CALLED BRIAN Curry to tell him we wanted to talk to him and Amy.

"Amy's office is in Burbank," he said. "I can meet you there in an hour."

"Sorry, but Amy's going to have to meet us in Costa Luna," I said. "We want to take another look around the park. If she's too busy to..."

"Detective, Amy could be having a heart transplant and she'd hop off the operating table and drive down here. Ten bucks says she gets here before you."

"I've got lights and sirens."

"Twenty bucks."

"You realize that LAPD frowns on cops wagering on their arrival time."

"I'm just trying to make a point," Brian said. "She's a terrier. Nothing gets in her way."

"Well then it's too bad she's not the lead detective. I'll see you soon."

Then Terry and I briefed Detectives Sutula and Langer. They're known around the squad room as Penn and Teller. Sutula does all the talking. Langer is a man of few words. "Lots of people would have loved to murder this sicko," Terry said. "See if you can narrow it down for us."

Sutula asked questions, made comments, then let us know they were on the case. Langer just nodded.

Next we asked Muller to do some research on the Lamaar-Las Vegas possible mob connection.

"Why would the Camelot Casino want to get in bed with Lamaar?" Muller said. "The bottom fell out of that whole bring-the-family-to-Vegas crap. I was there a few months ago. They're ripping down the roller coasters and putting in more stripper poles. The real money is in nightclubs, high-end restaurants, and Texas Hold'em. Why would they do a deal with cartoon characters?"

"Hey, geek boy," Terry said. "You're not being paid to figure out if it's a smart business deal. Your job is to find out if the mob is in any way connected to this murder investigation. You got that?"

Muller laughed. "I guess you just got your ass chewed out by the boss, and now it's my turn in the barrel."

"Exactly," Terry said. "It's called the Hierarchy of Pain. If you want to pass it along, go home and kick your dogs."

"No problem. By the time I get there, I'm sure Annetta will have two or three new ones for me to kick."

Terry and I were twenty miles from Familyland when my cell rang. It was Big Jim. "This is a real bad connection," he said, clear as a bell. "Call me from a land line."

"Either you're super paranoid," I said, "or our boy did something so stupid that you can't even tell me on a cell phone."

"All of the above. You gonna call me back or what?"

"Can it wait? I'm on my way to a homicide investigation."

"What would you rather do," he said, "solve a murder or

prevent one?"

"Give me a few minutes to find a pay phone." I hung up.

"What's going on?" Terry said.

"Family shit," I said. "I need to call my father from a secure phone."

Terry gunned the Lexus, pulled into the left lane and smoked past traffic with the dashboard gumball strobing red. Three minutes later, we barreled up an off-ramp and came screeching to a stop at a sleepy little Mobil station like it was the final pit stop at the Indy 500.

"I love that I can get away with doing that," Terry said. "There's a phone, I'll go piss."

I dialed Big Jim. "Thank you for using Golden State Communications," the automated voice said, after I had punched in my AT&T Calling Card number.

Damn. It was one of those anonymous long-distance carriers that charge you whatever-the-hell-they-can-get-away-with per minute. I knew I could bypass it, but I didn't have the patience to dial thirty-two more digits, so I bit the bullet. Another reason to be pissed at my kid brother.

Jim picked up on the first ring. "Thanks for calling back."

"Talk fast, because I'm calling from 1-800-RIPOFF."

"As you know, your brother has been trying to get his gambling problem under control. He went to some of those twelve-step meetings, and he hasn't been to the track or bet on sports for six months."

"That's old news. Drop the other shoe."

"He's taken up investing in the stock market," Jim said.

"Yeah, I noticed he switched from the *Racing Form* to the *Wall Street Journal*. It's an expensive habit, but at least it's legal."

"It is, unless you're using OPM."

More initials. But this one everybody knows. Other People's Money. "Correct me if I'm wrong," I said. "But isn't one supposed to be licensed to use OPM when you buy and sell stocks?"

"Theoretically," Jim said.

There was knock on the phone booth door. It was Terry with two cans of Pepsi. He popped the top on one, passed it inside, and walked off. I took a swig. It was cold and sweet and felt good. "Let me get this straight," I said. "Frankie is investing other people's money without a license."

"I'm not at liberty to corroborate that," he said.

"Don't bother, I'm a detective. And I assume if he were making money hand over fist for his clients, he would look and smell prosperous, which is not how he looked or smelled last night."

"I'm not at liberty to corroborate that, either," he said.

"And knowing him, if he were losing OPM, he would want to make it all back in one night. So he fell down the entire flight of twelve steps, drove to Vegas, and came home in deeper shit than when he left. And please don't say corroborate again. Talk like a truck driver."

"Okay, I'd say he smelled like deep shit last night."

"That crazy ass dickhead," I said.

"That I can corroborate," Jim said.

"Listen, I hate doing this on a pay phone," I said, taking three long swallows of the Pepsi, "but as pissed off as I am personally, I need to ask a professional question. Did someone really put out a contract on him?"

"The boy has a tendency to be overly dramatic," Jim said. "But yeah, this time I think he's not kidding."

"Who?"

"He won't say."

"Why not? Because maybe you and I could help? How about if I come over and beat it out of him," I said, draining the last of the Pepsi.

"For now, I don't want you doing anything," Jim said. "If you replay this conversation in your mind, you'll note that I told you nothing of substance except that our friend plays the market and is indeed a crazy ass dickhead. Everything else is conjecture on your part."

"So that if I had to testify about what I know for sure, I could do it without perjuring myself."

"That's every father's dream for his son," he said.

"Dad, I gotta go. Terry and I are up to our nuts in dead rabbit. By the way, thanks again for last night. You were very helpful."

"You're welcome. Speaking of which, is there a reward for the kind of insight and detailed information I provided you with?"

"Not for blood relatives of a cop on the case. Why do you ask? Last night, the information was free."

"I suddenly find myself faced with some unexpected expenses."

"How much do you suddenly find yourself needing?" I asked.

"More than I got. More than I spent to save his ass a year ago, and ten times as much as I spent two years before that. Your brother's getting to be an expensive habit."

"I don't have time to talk about it now. I'll swing by the house tonight."

"Don't come," he said.

"Why the hell not?" I asked.

"Because I'm still basking in the glow of your presence from last night."

"Bullshit."

"I don't want you here. You're busy trying to solve a homicide."

"Dad, that is not a factor. I'm coming."

"James Michael Lomax, Jr.," he said, calling me by my real name, the one I never used. Most kids are proud to share their father's name. Growing up, a lot of my friends were Juniors. But when your Dad is called Big Jim, they don't call you Jim, Jr. They call you Little Jim. That I couldn't handle. So on my eighth birthday, I announced that I had given up my given name, and from that day forward I would only respond to my middle name.

Big Jim was furious. He didn't show up for my birthday party, and he didn't talk to me for what seemed like months. Finally, he blinked. One day at breakfast he simply said, "Morning, Mike." I've been Mike Lomax ever since. The only person who ever used my real name was my mother. She would save it for those rare occasions when she was really pissed at me. This was the first time Big Jim had used it on me. I answered him. "Yes, Mother," I said.

"I'm telling you, don't come. Because if you see what I do to your kid brother, you'll be forced to arrest me for child abuse."

"Fine, I won't come," I said, crushing the soda can in defeat.

"I knew you'd see it my way. Goodbye."

I hung up, flung the empty Pepsi can at a trash basket and missed. I walked over to Terry's car. He was sitting behind the wheel reading a book.

"Sorry," I said. "Ever since my Mom died, Dad's been having a rough time raising young Frankie."

He nodded his head with a father's wisdom. "Shoulda taken him to Familyland a couple of times when he was a kid."

CHAPTER 26

I WOULD HAVE lost the bet. Amy was there when we arrived. We met in Curry's office on the second floor of what Terry now referred to as The Dumbass Duck Building. The furniture was functional, without a hint of Hollywood chic, and the room itself was neat, sparse actually.

On his desk was a silver picture frame, hinged in the middle. On one side was an older couple, obviously his parents. Mom held a cane in her right hand, while her left hand interlaced fingers with her husband, who was the spitting image of Curry. Side two was a picture of Curry on a ski slope with an attractive woman and two young kids. "That was taken a few years ago," he said when he caught me looking at it. "The kids are ten and twelve now."

The one other personal item was an aging football with faded autographs. It sat on a bookshelf filled with three-ring binders, security videocassettes and other official Lamaar business. The room was a far cry from Kilcullen's Tribute-to-Myself Office. Curry was either a very private person or too modest to bombard strangers with a photomontage of his career.

"I hope this visit means you have good news," Curry said as he grabbed four bottles of Perrier from a small black refrigerator and passed them around.

"I'm afraid not," I said. "Eddie Elkins is a convicted pedophile.

He has a sex offender record as long as your arm. It goes back twenty years."

Amy almost spit out her designer water. "Oh God! We hired a pedophile?" She smashed her Perrier down on an end table. Sparkling water erupted, but the bottle itself remained intact, as if the French had designed it for a nation of hot-blooded bottle-bangers. "Who else knows about this?"

"The cops working on the case and you two," I said.

"Brian, how could this happen?" Amy barked at her Head of Security.

"I don't know, but it's a damn good question to be asking Steve." He turned to me and Terry. "Steve Darien is Head of HR. His department does a thorough background check on every single job applicant. I don't know how Elkins could have slipped through."

"Well, you better find out," Amy said. "Because that's the first question Ike Rose is going to ask you. The second question will be how many other perverts have we hired to wander around the park stalking children."

Curry took the high road. He ignored her. "If Elkins was a pedophile," he said to me and Terry, "maybe somebody from his past killed him."

"We're looking into that," Terry said. "But it's still possible that the real target is Lamaar. We have a theory that the finger in the flipbook may not mean 'up yours.' It could mean 'This is Number One. More killings to follow.' We think you should beef up security and warn your people to be on the lookout for..."

"We are not warning our people to be on the lookout for anything," Amy said springing up from the sofa. "If you want to see widespread panic, just tell those wannabe actors that someone wants to strangle them with a jump rope. They will exit Stage Right faster than you can say Rambunctious Rabbit."

"It's your call, Ms. Cheever," Terry said.

"It's my call, Detective," Brian said, turning back to Amy to see if she had a problem with that. "I'll beef up security, but I'll do it quietly. I'm not sending a memo to the troops about a killer running around loose. Anything else?"

"Yeah," Terry said. "We heard you're going into business with the Leone family in Las Vegas. How did a company that wants to *protect the children* from the details of Eddie Elkins's murder get mixed up with a bunch of scumbags who are four generations deep into organized crime?"

If Terry was hoping to throw Amy into another rant, he missed by a mile. She just waved her hand at him and sat back down on the sofa. "Oh, please, Detective, don't be so naïve. It's okay for Coca-Cola, McDonald's, American Airlines and the rest of the Fortune 500 to do business with the Vegas casinos, but Lamaar can't? And the people who run the casinos are organized criminals, but the people who run the oil companies, the pharmaceutical firms, or the tobacco industry are what? Saints? Lamaar is a publicly held company. Las Vegas is a major profit opportunity. We owe it to our stockholders to be there."

"Nicely put, Ms. Cheever. Although it sounds like you've delivered that little speech before," Terry said.

"I've been asked the same dumb question before."

"I may be dumb, but I know the difference between white-collar crooks at Enron and the Mafia. The Fortune 500 tends to resolve their business conflicts with lawsuits, not homicide."

She stood up again, ready to square off. "Detective, we don't have any business conflicts with the Camelot organization or any of its principals. And if we did, I can assure you they would not sneak down into a tunnel and strangle one of our employees to resolve it. You're fishing in a dry hole, so unless you have something of substance to ask, this area of questioning is closed."

"We'd like to take another look around the park," Terry said. "We'll need an all-access pass so we can roam around at will."

"What do you mean roam around?" Amy asked. "Where?"

I expected Terry to come back with, "Anywhere we damn

well please, bitch." But Brian stood up first. "Amy," he said, "they're investigating a murder. And whether we like it or not, we cooperate. Anything short of that is an obstruction of justice. Detectives, I'll be glad to give you access, but it will have to be with an escort from my department."

"No problem," Terry said.

"I'll escort them," Amy said.

Terry smiled at her. "That's very generous, Ms. Cheever, but you're a busy executive. We don't want to interrupt whatever you have planned."

"Detective, our CEO Ike Rose called me from Singapore last night. From now until the time we—you—find this killer, whatever I have planned doesn't matter. This is my first priority."

"Then we finally have something in common," Terry said.

"One more thing," Curry said. "Did you track down Elkins's sister?"

"We ran that Baltimore number you gave me," I said. "It's a pay phone at the airport."

"You're telling me the victim didn't have a family?" Curry said.

"No," I said. "The victim mostly had victims."

Curry picked up the phone and dialed a four-digit number. "Lily," he said, "tell Darien I need to see him right away. No, it can't wait. Interrupt the meeting and tell him Buddy Longo is on the phone."

Curry looked up at us. "Buddy Longo is company code for 'Serious Problem.' Sort of like yelling 'Hey Rube' in the…" He went back to the phone. "Steve, how fast can you clear out your office? Great, I'll be there in a minute."

He turned to us. "Gentlemen, Amy will now give you the VIP tour."

"Should we walk?" she asked. "It's a lot less conspicuous than riding around on a golf cart."

"Good idea," Terry said. "Two guys wearing jackets, ties and shoulder holsters…We'll blend right in."

We opted to lose the ties and walk.

If you have to investigate a homicide, there's no more pleasant place to do it than Familyland. The sun was shining, bouncy music was emanating from invisible speakers, and the air was filled with the sweet smell of cotton candy and other midway junk food.

I remember the first time Joanie and I went there together. "I like it better than Disneyland," she said. "I don't know why. They both have rides and cartoon characters running around, but there's something about Familyland I just love."

"Shorter lines," I said. "It's not as popular."

"Maybe it's the soft colors," she said. "Lamaar uses a lot of pastels."

She never did figure it out.

"There's a difference between Familyland and Disneyland," I said to Amy, as we retraced Elkins's final tour of the park, "but I'm not sure what it is."

"Thank you for noticing that there is one," she said. "Not everyone does. It's all about intent. Disney built a place for people to escape to. Dean Lamaar wanted to create a place for people to come home to. A family place. The differences are all over the park, but they're subtle."

"Like the pastel colors," I said.

"Very perceptive," she said. "I guess that's why you're a detective."

We started at the main gate and walked along Fantasy Avenue. Gift shops dominated the front of the park, but they were relatively empty.

"People don't buy much early in the day," Amy said. "But they can't get out of the park without going past these stores again. That's when the Mommy-Buy-Me madness begins."

When we got to Friendship Square a fat man stopped Amy and asked if she would take a picture. "Me and my wife by the statue," he said.

The man, who had a hot dog in one hand and a mammoth soft drink in the other, shoveled the entire frank into his moon-face so he could free up one hand and pull out his disposable Kodak.

Chomping noisily and dribbling brown juices down his chin, he edged Amy over to a bronze statue of Dean Lamaar and Rambunctious Rabbit. The plaque at the base said, *Dean Lamaar, October 15, 1924—May 21, 2002. He Lives On in the Hearts of Children Everywhere.*

Amy took the picture of the man and his even fatter wife and we moved on to The Rock Quarry. The RQ was a huge amphitheater that looked from the outside like a prehistoric cave dwelling. But inside were laser light shows, virtual reality rides, and loud, obnoxious hip-hop that could melt your fillings.

"The characters don't like this place," Amy said. "It's where a lot of teenagers gravitate. At that age they no longer think the characters are cute and cuddly. So they harass them."

We moved through the Quarry and hopped a ride on the Easy Street Trolley. Ten minutes later we arrived at the Tyke Town Arch.

"This is where the little kids are," Amy said.

The overriding sounds were the squeals and happy hollers of kids who were six, five, four, and younger. About fifty feet from where we stood was a character, some sort of frog or green lizard, holding a small child in his arms and posing for a picture that the Dad was taking.

"And I'll bet this is where Elkins liked to hang out," Terry said.

"Anyone who knew Elkins was a sex offender might have been stalking him here," I said. "How many surveillance cameras do you have in the park?"

"Close to a thousand, and our insurance carriers want us to add more," Amy said. "The good news is that almost everything that happens in Familyland is recorded and burned onto a DVD. The bad news is it would take one person about two years to screen one day's worth of DVDs."

"We'll put more than one person on it and they'll be watching it at high speed. Let's get everything that was shot on Elkins's last stroll through the park in this area on Sunday," I said. "Especially anything shot here in Tyke Town."

"I'll talk to Brian. We'll get them for you." She shook her head. "How did a man like Elkins..." She bit her lip. "Excuse me, I need a ladies room."

We walked to a rest area and Terry and I went into the men's room. Half a dozen guys were staring at the white wall, taking care of business.

Wherever you go in Familyland you're greeted by an automated voice. "Welcome to Fantasy World; Welcome to Global Village." Then it gives you the dos and don'ts of the attraction. It's supposed to be friendly, but it's pretty damn cold and annoying.

Terry and I stepped up to a pair of urinals. Then, in his best pre-recorded robotic voice, he said out loud, "Welcome to Urinal World. Please remove your dick from its holster. Please keep your hands inside your pants at all times. If you have any difficulty, an attendant will be glad to assist you. Thank you for urinating at Familyland. Don't forget to flush. Have a nice day."

I laughed, but not the big laugh Terry was hoping for. I managed to keep my shoes dry.

Unfortunately, that was pretty much the highlight of our second trip to Familyland.

We revisited The Rabbit Hole, this time entering through Ramp 17, which was the same way Elkins had entered. The ramp was a good fifty feet wide in order to accommodate the oversized horse-drawn parade floats.

A white-haired guard sat at the top, nodding to the few employees who said hello. When we approached, Amy flashed a badge and the guard waved us on in.

"If this is Brian's version of beefed up security," Terry said, "you need more beef."

We wound our way through the tunnel until we got to the maze of duct work where Eddie had lit up a cigarette and gotten himself killed out of range of the nearest security camera. That was it. The last stop in Rambo's last tour.

We regrouped in Curry's office and were told that HR did indeed do background checks on all job applicants, but they somehow missed the fact that Elkins had an extensive background in pedophilia.

"They're looking into it," Curry said. "And so am I. Just in case they had any conflict of interest, like covering their asses."

After four hours, Terry and I left Familyland the same way we had arrived. Empty-handed.

CHAPTER 27

IT WAS AFTER 6:00 when Terry and I got back to the office. Kilcullen had gone, but Muller was still there. "The boss left you both a message," he said.

A generous chunk of black bowling ball sat in the center of each of our desks. There was a hand-written note under my piece of the rock. "*Lomax, Don't let Biggs drag his ass. Keep after him. Kilcullen.*"

Terry was reading a note of his own. "Let me guess," I said. "It's from the boss and it says 'Don't let Lomax drag his ass. Keep after him.'"

Terry frowned. "The man's management skills never cease to amaze me. Now I'm really fired up to catch this killer."

"Sutula and Langer pulled this together from NCIC," Muller said, dropping a manila folder on my desk. "It's the collected perversions of Eddie Elkins. There are twenty-four victims on record. It's bad enough these families went through hell, but now they're suspects because somebody killed Elkins. It's gonna take a few days to track them all down."

"What about the Governor's theory that there's a connection between Lamaar and the mob?" Terry said.

"What mob? That's a myth perpetrated by the conspiracy to defame Italian-Americans," Muller said, dropping a second fat folder on my desk. "However, if you believe some of the things

129

you read, the mob is still alive and well and living large in Vegas. Did you ever hear of Meyer Lansky?"

"Old-time Jewish mob boss," Terry said.

"He was pals with Bugsy Siegel. The two of them saw the future of Vegas back in the forties. They were backed by the New York, New Jersey and Philadelphia crime syndicates, but they decided Bugsy was stealing, so they killed him."

"I know," Terry said. "I saw the movie with Warren Beatty."

"One of the syndicate guys was Enrico Leone. He moved to Vegas in 1955 and opened his own casino, the Camelot. It's been family-owned and family-run for the past fifty years. The granddaughter, Arabella, runs the operation. It's basically legit. I mean as legit as it gets in Vegas. She's the one who made the joint venture deal with Lamaar."

"Doesn't sound like a marriage made in heaven," I said.

"It's great for the casino. Lamaar's got the film, TV and rock stars who can do live appearances and draw the crowds. Plus they've got a squeaky clean image that's a nice counterpoint to the legacy of Rico Leone."

"But why would Lamaar want to get in bed with lowlifes who are one degree of separation from Bugsy Siegel and Meyer Lansky?"

"Duh, money. The company was hurting when the Japanese bought it. According to the *Wall Street Journal* this Vegas deal can take them from a nine-percent loss to an eleven-percent gain over the next five years. That's a twenty-percent swing. Big business will get into bed with lepers for a lot less.

"There's another reason. It's in the *Forbes* article. Lamaar started as an animation company. They've made their fair share of decent grown-up movies, especially since Ike Rose took over, but they're still saddled with that cartoon kiddy image. Vegas attracts a young, hip crowd. They got money to spend, and they don't want to spend it on Mickey Mouse. Lamaar wants a piece of that market. This is a smart deal for them and a smarter one for the Camelot."

"You think the mob had anything to do with the homicide?" Terry said.

"No. It's a win-win deal. It doesn't make sense for either player to screw it up. If anything, it would hurt them if it got out that Elkins was a pedophile."

"You did a great job, Muller," I said.

"Yeah. Thanks for executive summary," Terry said. "Now we don't even have to wade through all this crap."

"I didn't think you would, but I figured you'd be happy with a couple of pounds of paper to drop on Kilcullen's desk."

"It'll help keep the Junior Crime Stoppers in Sacramento off our backs for a few days, so we can solve this case," Terry said. "We owe you one."

"It was a lot more fun than researching pedophiles," Muller said. "Hey, one cool piece of Vegas trivia. You ever hear of Oscar Goodman?"

"No."

"He was a lawyer who defended a lot of mob bosses, including Meyer Lansky himself. Anyway, guess where Oscar Goodman is today."

"Leavenworth," I said.

"Nah, I don't think the Feds nailed him," Terry said. "I'm guessing he knew too much, the mob got nervous, and now he's at the bottom of some lake wearing size twelve cement shoes."

"You're both wrong," Muller said. "Oscar Goodman, defender of the much-maligned Italian-American businessman, is currently the mayor of Las Vegas. It's a great country we're defending, boys. See you tomorrow."

Muller went home, and Terry and I left the Vegas file on Kilcullen's desk, along with a note summarizing why we didn't think it was a critical path to follow at this time. We had decided to spend another hour wading through the Elkins files, when my phone rang. Caller ID told me it was coming from Valley General

Hospital. Not the case I wanted to deal with, but I answered.

"Hi, Detective Lomax. This is Jan Trachtenberg. I'm calling to thank you for returning my call, but I didn't call you this morning."

It had been a long day. The best I could come up with was, "What do you mean you didn't call me this morning?"

"I've been on Valium all week," she said, "but I'm functioning enough to know who I call. This morning I got my daughters off to school, and then I drove to Tarzana to pick up my Mom. She's moving in with us to help with the girls. I decided to work the night shift for a while. It's easier. I can't sleep nights anyway." She took a deep breath and let out a sigh. "I just got to the hospital a few minutes ago. This is my first day back since Alan was killed. I was really glad to hear that you've got more people trying to solve my husband's murder."

"I promise you, Jan, we will find the guy. Don't lose faith just because I can't figure out who called me from Valley General."

"I know who called you," she said. "It was Diana Trantanella. She left me a voicemail too. She said she met you socially last night."

"That's true," I said. "Small world."

"Yes. Two widows, working together, calling the same police officer. She's very sweet. I think you and Diana will make a real cute couple."

I was about to explain that Diana and I were a long way from being a couple, but for the first time since I met her, I could hear joy in Jan Trachtenberg's voice. I decided to let it go. "Thank you," I said.

"I've got to get to work," she said. "Keep me posted."

"Jan, what happens between me and Diana is personal."

"I mean about my husband's murder investigation."

"Oh, that. Sure."

She actually laughed. "I'm not that nosy, Detective. Besides, anything that happens between you and Diana will be the hot topic in the Nurses' Lounge."

"Well, then maybe you should keep me posted," I said.

She laughed again, which made me feel good, even if it was at my expense. We said good night, and I hung up. I looked over at Biggs, who was at his desk chuckling. "And you are laughing because…?" I said.

"Because all I needed was your half of the conversation to figure out what's going on. But I think that's the best detective work I'm going to do all night. How about we bag this Elkins shit and go for a beer or three?"

"Sure," I said. "What's the worst that could happen if we leave early?" I picked up my chunk of bowling ball, tossed it in the air, and caught it.

Thirty seconds later, we were out the door.

CHAPTER 28

THE NEXT MORNING at 5:15, the Twenty-Third Most Powerful Person in Hollywood pulled out of his driveway on Amalfi Drive in Pacific Palisades.

He could have had one of Lamaar Studios' drivers pick him up. Truth be told, he could have had one of Lamaar's Vice-Presidents pick him up. But Ronnie Lucas preferred to drive himself in his three-year-old Toyota Land Cruiser.

Today, as on every Wednesday, he was headed for the United Methodist Church's Homeless Shelter on Pico Boulevard and Fourth Street in Santa Monica.

Ronnie Lucas was an Industry Enigma. When the press asked him how it felt to jump from Number 87 to Number 23 in *Entertainment Weekly*'s "Top 100 Most Powerful People in Hollywood" issue, he said, "You gotta put it all in perspective. Last year Katie and I only had our one son, Jeremy, and I was the Third Most Powerful Person in our house. This year, we had the twins, and we got a Springer Spaniel puppy, and I've slipped to Number 6."

Ten years before Ronnie had been a nobody, a young actor from Munster, Indiana, surviving on his wife's small salary, waiting on tables and going to auditions. Then Joe Diggs died. Joe was the black comic who played the cantankerous old weatherman in *TV Daze*, a marginally successful sitcom.

The producers weren't about to replace one old black man with another. They had their reasons. *It's just not done. Tends to draw comparisons. We already had the funniest black guy; we're not settling for the second funniest.*

So they created a new character, Sonny Day, a twenty-something white guy who was totally inept at predicting the weather, but who was so sweet and lovable that the fictional TV station's ratings went through the roof.

Ronnie landed the part, and in a rare case of life imitating sitcoms, people were captivated by the blue-eyed, honey-haired, boyish hunk-next-door, and the series shot straight to the Top Ten.

Ronnie Lucas went from, "Good evening, I'll be your waiter tonight," to the cover of *TV Guide*. Fame is addictive and Ronnie was hooked. He loved the parties, the fans, even the paparazzi. But Katie, his high school sweetheart and wife of three years, would have no part of it. One night shortly after he became Flavor of the Month, Ronnie stumbled home reeking of booze, pot, and perfume, and found a note on his pillow. *"I've gone back to Indiana. I love you but I refuse to be married to a Hollywood asshole."*

The next day Ronnie was on the porch of Katie's parents' house in Munster. He rang the doorbell, and when she opened it, he got down on one knee and said, "I'm sorry. If you come back to L.A. with me, I promise to be the biggest anti-asshole in all of Hollywood."

Katie came back and Ronnie kept his word. He settled into the role of genuine nice guy who loves his wife, his kids, and his work—hardly the stuff the gossip columnists write about. And while he didn't agree that he was powerful, he couldn't deny that he was popular. He had won a People's Choice Award three years in a row.

Ronnie made the transition from TV to movies, and, while none of them were Oscar contenders, they each got respectable reviews and phenomenal box office grosses. Any studio would have sold their collective souls, assuming they could find one, just to bring Ronnie Lucas into their stable. But so far he'd been loyal to the one company that gave him his first big break in television. Lamaar.

He had gone from doing television for Lamaar to making movies and personal appearances for them, and they had just signed him to another five-year, five-picture deal. Lamaar loved Ronnie, and the feeling was mutual.

With Katie as his moral compass, Ronnie remained as unspoiled as the day he left Indiana a decade ago with two hundred and six bucks in his jeans.

This morning, he was feeding the homeless. By 6 a.m. Ronnie Lucas was piling food onto shiny plastic plates and joking with the regulars. He wasn't quite as big an attraction as the free breakfast, but they all knew who he was. And they respected the boundaries he had established early on. No autographs; no photographs. Ronnie wanted to be treated like any other church volunteer.

"*Buenos dias*, Manny," he said to a dark-skinned Mexican man, whose forty-eight-inch belly was spilling over his size 42 sweat pants. "*Como esta usted?*"

"*Yo tengo una hambre canino,*" Manny bellowed. It was the same repartee every time. "I am hungry as a wolf."

Ronnie dished up three heaping spoons full of eggs, covering most of the plate. "Just what you need, Manny," he said. "A little more cholesterol."

"I was reading the trades amigo, and I see you got like fifteen million dollars for your next picture."

"No kidding. I don't read the trades myself," Ronnie said.

"Truss me," Manny said. "*Es verdad*. So I am thinking, maybe you could spare four, five million, so I could buy a nice house in your neighborhood."

"Good idea. Have your people call my people, and we'll work

it out."

"Ah, my peoples," Manny said, shaking his head. "The problem is my peoples, they got no telephone." They both laughed. Two regular guys. One living in a ten-million-dollar house; the other in a GE refrigerator carton.

A black woman in faded Levi's and a yellow Old Navy sweatshirt was next. Beatrice Templeton was thirty-six years old and had spent twenty of those years on the streets of L.A. She held out her plate in her left hand. Her right hand covered her mouth. "You ready for this, honey?"

Ronnie put one hand on his heart. "Yes," he said. "I can't wait."

"Teeth!" Beatrice screamed and pulled her hand away, revealing a mouthful of brand new white teeth. A few heads looked up from their breakfasts, then quickly went back to plying their plastic forks. Screaming was part of the dynamics of the room. "I finally got me some teeth."

"Beatrice, you look absolutely beautiful," he said. His blue eyes gave her a loving look that millions of women would kill to get.

Tears streamed down her weathered face. "I feel beautiful. God bless you, Ronnie. You are my White Knight. I can't thank you enough."

"Cut it out," he said. "My friend Sandy is a dentist. He loves doing this kind of thing."

"Oh, yeah, he does Halle Berry, JLo, Janet Jackson, and now he can tell everybody he just added Beatrice Templeton to his list of famous patients."

"Hey, I bet he's bragging about you all over town," Ronnie said, scooping eggs onto her plate.

"You think?" she said, striking a Hollywood pose and flashing her teeth.

"Sure. Anyone can make those other women look gorgeous. You were a real challenge."

She let out a high-pitched whoop. "Oh, Lord, that's a good

one! I love you, Ronnie," she said, as she moved on.

He looked up at the next person in line. Way up. The man was tall. A white guy, fortyish, road-weary. He hadn't seen a razor or a bottle of shampoo in a week. He wore dirty chinos, a plaid shirt, and a raincoat that was grungy enough to embarrass Columbo. Ronnie had never seen him before. "Hi, I'm Ronnie. Welcome to the Shelter."

"Mark," the man said, looking down at his feet.

Like most actors, Ronnie studied people's speech patterns and body language. It had always intrigued him that his agent, Syd Resnick, was five-foot-two, yet whenever he entered a room, he strutted in with his chest puffed out and his head high. Syd was short, but he didn't think short or behave short.

Mark, on the other hand, was like a lot of the big guys in the room. His head drooped and his shoulders slouched as if he were trying to make himself less noticeable.

"First time here?" Ronnie asked.

The man grunted a "Yeah," but he still wouldn't look Ronnie in the eye. "Eggs, please," the man said, anxious to move along.

But Ronnie's brain was already on a Rescue Mission. This man needed help, and Ronnie never gave up on newcomers. "Where you from?" he asked.

"Munster."

"Munster, Indiana? You're kidding. I grew up in Munster. My Mom and Dad still have a house on Hohman."

"I know. I taught Phys Ed at Munster High. It was after you left, but they talk a lot about you. You were already on that TV show when I started."

"My wife and I are going back for the Munster High reunion in June."

"At least you can go back," Mark said. "I'm not welcome any more. They frown on faculty members getting arrested for cocaine possession."

"Sorry to hear that," Ronnie said, slowly dishing up the man's breakfast. "But whatever you did in the past, you're in the right place now. There's a lot of recovering addicts in this room. They have meetings here every day at noon. I'd be glad to introduce you around to some of the guys."

"I don't want to be no trouble."

"It's no trouble. Helping people get back on their feet is what we do. Let me know if there's anything special I can do for you."

"I could use a couple of extra sausages."

Ronnie added more food to the man's plate. "It's nice to meet a fellow Munsterite, although I gotta say, you don't have much of a Hoosier accent. Where you from originally?"

"Eastern Europe, but with my drug problem I don't stay in one place too long." He looked down at his tattered Nikes. "Nice to meetcha. Go Mustangs."

"Go Mustangs," Ronnie said, echoing Mark's rhythm and tone, which had turned his high school cheer into a chant of despair.

He watched the big man shuffle away. Good guy, Ronnie thought, and wondered if he'd ever see him again.

He would see him one more time. Forty minutes later Mark approached Ronnie in the parking lot and asked if they could spend a few minutes talking. "Maybe help me get my life straightened out," he said.

Ronnie felt like he had made a breakthrough, and the two of them walked over to a cluster of palm trees so they could talk in private.

When they were out of sight, away from the prying eyes, judgmental ears, and gossiping tongues of those homeless buttinskis, the man who called himself Mark and claimed to be from Munster, Indiana, produced a baseball bat from his greasy, threadbare raincoat and bashed in Ronnie Lucas's skull.

"Thanks for breakfast," the man said, as he set the brain-spattered bat alongside the bloody heap that had only moments ago been the Twenty-Third Most Powerful Person in Hollywood.

CHAPTER 29

ANDRE TOTALLY IGNORED me. I was trying to pick his poodle brain on whether I should call Diana today or not. I already had Terry's opinion. "Call her every five minutes," he had said last night over beers.

But Andre was too busy pushing my cereal bowl around the floor. He finally wedged it into a corner and with a few flicks of his tongue nailed the last of the rogue Cheerios that were clinging to the side of the dish.

"Not that you care, but I'm going to call her tonight," I said, as Andre headed for the toilet bowl to wash down his breakfast.

Thirty seconds later she called me. "Hi, this is Diana Trantanella," the perky voice on the other end of the phone said.

"This is so amazing. I was just talking about you."

"Really? To whom?"

"Andre. He's my dog. You may think that's a little weird."

"Not at all. I have a cat, Blanche. Your name hasn't come up yet, but I'll see if I can work it into the conversation. I called your cell yesterday to ask you a favor, but I didn't leave a message, because I decided it was more business than personal. Then I was going to call you at the police station, but I decided I didn't want to interrupt your homicide investigation. So now I'm calling you at home. Over-thinking is part of my charm."

"It's okay. I've been over-thinking about calling you. What's the favor?"

"I told you I'm a nurse at Valley General. What I didn't tell you was that I work in the Pediatric Oncology Unit. My patients are kids with terminal illnesses. Some of them are in remission, but a lot of them are not so lucky."

"That's gotta be a tough job," I said.

"It's the best job in the world. I love coming in to work every day. But some nights I go home and cry my eyes out." Her voice cracked. She took a deep breath and exhaled slowly. "The best thing we do is the 'I Have A Dream' Program. The kids tell us what they want to do or who they want to meet, and if it's humanly possible, we make their dream come true. A lot of kids want to meet basketball players or movie stars, or sit in the dugout at a Dodger game. One girl wanted to meet Senator Feinstein, and we were able to arrange it."

"And I'm guessing one of these kids wants to meet somebody I know."

"Oh, it's somebody you know, alright. It's you."

"Me? You're kidding. Are you sure he asked for Mike Lomax? Y'know a lot of kids confuse me with Shaquille O'Neal."

She laughed. "His name is Hugo Cordner. He's fourteen and he devours books. His favorite characters are smart people who solve murders. Everyone from the Hardy Boys to Sherlock Holmes to Alex Cross. But they're fictional. He wants to meet a real live detective who catches murderers."

"And you just happened to tell him that you know one?"

"No. I wouldn't do that to him or you. I don't want to put pressure on you to say yes, and I wouldn't want to disappoint him if you say no."

"Yes," I said without hesitating. "I don't think I've ever been anybody's dream before, but I'll do what I can to not disappoint him."

"Thank you," she said.

"I've been thinking that I owe you a more civil dinner than the one we had at Big Jim's house the other night."

"Well, you don't *owe* me one, but it sure would be nice."

"How's Friday night?"

"Perfect. Why don't you meet me at Valley General about six, spend some time with Hugo, and we can have dinner afterwards."

We hung up. Big Jim will be tickled, I thought. But I'd be damned if I'd tell him just yet.

The phone rang again. Busy morning. I grabbed it.

"What are you wearing?" It was Terry.

"The usual. Blue blazer, gray slacks, women's panties. Why do you ask?"

"Because there's a good chance your picture's gonna wind up on the front page of every newspaper in the country."

"I doubt it. Lots of cops wear ladies' underwear. It's no longer that newsworthy."

"We got another live one. A second homicide in the rabbit case. This is a biggie. Ronnie Lucas."

"Whoa! The kid from *TV Daze*? Ronnie Lucas, the actor?"

"He's currently playing dead in a church parking lot at Fourth and Pico."

"Pico isn't our turf," I said. "How did we get the call?"

"Jessica Keating is on the scene. She sent for us. There is no question in her curly blonde head that this is connected to the rabbit homicide."

"I'm on my way," I said. "What's the exact address?"

"Just go to Fourth and Pico. Look for the yellow tape and a couple of hundred photographers."

Terry is cynical, but he knows what to expect. A celebrity homicide in Tinseltown is a magnet for anyone with a camera. The paparazzi come out in such large numbers that rumor has it that whenever an A-List Hollywood personality is murdered, brokers tell their best clients to buy Kodak stock.

"I'll be there in ten minutes, at which point I will commence shooting photographers," Terry said. "What's your E.T.A.?"

"Ten and a half," I said. "Don't shoot them all. I look fantastic. I want one alive to shoot me."

CHAPTER 30

FOURTEEN MINUTES LATER I threaded the Acura through a maze of cop cars, news vans, and rubberneckers, and found a convenient parking spot on the sidewalk, a block from the action. I badge-flashed my way to the scene.

There weren't many cars in the parking lot, but the place was crawling with bums. I know the PC term is 'homeless,' but I have no idea whether these people had homes to go to or not. Most of them were dressed in clothes that Goodwill would reject. About a dozen were clutching plastic garbage bags, and one wispy-haired man of indeterminate age and race was hanging onto a shopping cart like it was the last lifeboat off the Titanic. Call me politically incorrect, but they looked like bums to me.

I could hear Terry before I spotted him. He was barking orders at three uniformed cops he had just recruited to be Bum Wranglers.

"Don't let any of them go," he yelled. "I want their names, some kind of address or how to get in touch with them. They're all material witnesses." Several shutters clicked in his direction and he exploded. "And get those effing reporters back behind the tape, or I'll cap their lenses and their knees!" That little piece of drama caused a chain reaction of rapid-fire shutter clicking.

Terry Biggs, Media Darling of the Moment, had ignored his own fashion advice and was wearing a shit-brown suit and one of his trademark stained ties. He gave me a quick wave and went back to the uniforms.

I did a 360° eyeball of the scene and counted nine photographers, all shoving cameras and microphones into the face of any bum, hobo, vagrant, or filthy person who would talk to them.

However, unlike most citizens of Los Angeles, these bums did not aspire to fifteen minutes of fame. They'd rather have cash. I watched several members of the press corps dig into their wallets, while the homeless deftly shoved green wads into their pockets. God bless the American economy.

While my partner worked the perimeter, I headed for the chalk outline. Jessica Keating was kneeling next to the body. She didn't have the same look of professional disassociation she'd had two days ago at Familyland. Her face was taut, bothered. I knelt down beside her. "This one got to you," I said.

She let out a long, slow sigh. "I know I'm not supposed to get emotional about dead people, but this one really sucks. A decent guy with a wife and kids starts out his day as a healthy, productive member of God's Green Earth and winds up with his brains beaten out before lunch."

"You sent for us. You think this is connected to the Familyland job?"

She held up a flipbook in her gloved hand. Same drawing of a closed fist on the cover page. Then she flipped the pages, and two animated fingers popped up, making the sign of the V. "It doesn't mean 'V for Victory,'" she said.

"Victim Number Two," I said.

A baseball bat covered with blood, hair, and chunks of gray matter was on the ground. "And that's the murder weapon." I said it, rather than asked it.

"Conveniently located," she said, "so even the dumbest cop could find it."

I took a closer look, but I didn't pick it up. "It doesn't look very Lamaar-like," I said. "It's just a baseball bat."

"Here's where we separate the dumb cops from the smart ones." She stood up. Gratefully, I stood too. I was too old to be kneeling next to dead people for extended periods of time. I arched my back into a stretch. This is the way cats stretch, I thought. From there, my brain made a sharp left turn and suddenly I was thinking about my new cat friend, Diana Trantanella.

Jess didn't stretch or let her mind wander. "Ronnie Lucas did a movie for Lamaar called *The Bat That Couldn't Miss*," she said. "It's about a Little Leaguer who's in a batting slump, and Ronnie, who's the coach, gives him this special bat that he says belonged to Mark McGwire, so it can't miss. The kid starts using it, and of course, now he's full of confidence, so he starts hitting again."

"What are you doing watching kid flicks?" I said. "You don't have kids."

"Gabe and Liana, my sister's kids. She lets me baby-sit if I promise not to say the 'F word.' Anyway, at the end of the movie, it's the Big Game, and the bat breaks. Now the kid can't hit. Bottom of the ninth, he's got two strikes against him. Ronnie calls time out, and he tells the kid, 'It's not really the bat that's got the talent. It's you.' Bam, the kid hits a grand slam home run and wins the game."

"Just like *Dumbo* the Elephant with the feather," I said. "Same premise. He didn't need the feather to fly. It was all inside him."

"How do you know that? You don't have kids either."

"Yeah, but I was one. Dumbo's a classic. It's like fifty years old."

"Anyway," she said, "they came out with a bat that had the movie logo on it and Ronnie Lucas's autograph. This is it."

"We've already got people checking gift shop receipts at Familyland," I said. "Maybe if our killer bought the bat and the jump rope at the same time…"

"He didn't. This is off the record," she said, dropping her voice. "Based on the angle of the rope marks, I'm positive that the guy who killed Elkins was five-foot-eight or nine. But the angle of the blows to Lucas's head indicates that the killer was six-four or six-five. I won't know for sure till I get back to the lab."

"But the flipbooks..." I started to say.

"I know. The flipbooks say one killer. But I think the geometry is saying short man, tall man—two different killers. The only other hypothesis is that the killer wore eight-inch platform shoes when he committed the second murder."

Terry was headed our way, talking into his cell phone. Just as he reached me he slammed it shut. "Damn telemarketers. Why do they always seem to call during a major homicide investigation? You and Keating look more bummed out than usual. What's the bad news?"

I told him about the second flipbook. It didn't surprise him. It fit our serial killer theory. Then Jessica hit him with her tall man, short man scenario.

"Two killers," he said. "We are totally screwed."

"Not as screwed as Ronnie Lucas," Jessica said.

"Who was that on the phone?" I asked.

"The usual suspects," he said. "First Amy Cheever. She and Curry are on their way over here. She asked what we could do to keep this out of the press. I suggested repealing the First Amendment. Then Kilcullen called. The Governor wants to know how long it's going to take us to find out who the hell is killing the valued employees of one of the state's most valued taxpayers. Unquote."

I shrugged. I didn't know what to say to the Governor. I didn't know what to say to Kilcullen. I didn't even know what I was going to say to Hugo Cordner, the fourteen-year-old boy who was hoping to meet a real live smart LAPD cop who catches murderers.

CHAPTER 31

IT TOOK US about three hours to interview eighty-three homeless people. Except for the few who offered up dubious addresses like "under the 101 by Sepulveda," or "behind the dumpsters at Vons on Robertson," I could now vouch for the fact they were indeed homeless. Most of them were also penniless, some were toothless and a few were mindless. But despite the fact that they had more than their fair share of Hep C, Hep B and HIV, very few were hopeless.

As a group they seemed to be much more upbeat than eighty-three random Los Angelinos you might find at the Century City Mall. One of them was so optimistic about life's possibilities that he had a cell phone. No roof over his head, but he made sure he had a mobile connection to his service in case they had any openings for film extras. There's no people like show people. If you live in L.A. long enough, you come to despise that phrase.

They may not have been bums, but Ronnie Lucas's murder had left most of them bummed. Most of them loved him, although a small minority thought he only worked at the shelter because it made for great publicity. "He was just like one of us," said a black man, who gave his name as Johnny B. Goode. "Except he was young and handsome and rich and successful." I couldn't quite figure out if Mr. Goode was one of the people who liked Lucas or not.

At least ten of them told us about a new guy who walked off with Ronnie in the general direction of where he had been killed. They described him as tall. Tall was good. I wanted to tell Jessica, but I knew she wouldn't want to be influenced by eyewitnesses. Her evidence was somewhere on Lucas's body or at the scene of the crime. She just had to find it.

Several people said the new guy's name was Mark. One woman swore it was Claudius Maximus. Since the murder weapon was a Mark McGwire bat, I figured Mark was the kind of phony name a sicko would use.

Within a few hours we had a police artist's sketch of our suspect, a raggedy-ass-middle-aged white guy with a scraggly beard and a head full of uncombed dirty brown hair.

"This ain't worth shit," Terry said, waving the sketch at me. "We may as well send out a picture of Dustin Hoffman as Ratso Rizzo. By now, our man Mark is showered, shaved, manicured, and dressed for the cover of GQ."

"But he's still tall," I said.

"So was Osama Bin Laden, and they had home movies of him," Terry said. "I can just hear Kilcullen calling the Governor. We've narrowed it down to a tall white guy, sir. Considering that California is chock full of short Hispanics, that's pretty good police work, don't you think?"

Dealing with eighty-three homeless people turned out to be cake compared to dealing with Amy Cheever. Elkins's murder had unhinged her, but this one had driven her off the charts. Ronnie Lucas's movies generated huge bucks for Lamaar, and his murder was front-page, worldwide news. The Queen of Miscommunications had a global damage control-job on her hands.

That was fine by me and Terry. She'd have less time to meddle in our investigation. Brian Curry was easier to manage. We deputized him. "We need a list of every person you can come up with who might have a big enough grudge against the company to do this," I told him.

"I wouldn't have thought anybody had this big a grudge," Curry said.

"How about Danny Eeg?" I asked. "How about Ben Don Marvin?"

Curry's head snapped back and his eyes widened. "You've been doing your homework. Okay, Eeg's got a big enough grudge, but it's about money. And Marvin is a white-collar crook. This guy has killed two people."

"Brian, your job is to give us suspects, not eliminate them," I said.

"You're right. What do you need?"

"Go back five years in your employee database. Look for wrongful termination lawsuits or any other aggressive reactions to being canned."

"We should also take a look at dissatisfied customers, rival studios, even people who lost money when Lamaar scooped up the real estate for Familyland dirt cheap, thirty-plus years ago," Curry said.

"Now you're talking. We need last-known addresses, phones, family members, whatever your computer can cough up. And put Daniel Eeg's name at the top of the list."

"I'm putting Ben Don Marvin at the top of the list," Curry said.

"I thought you said he's a crook, not a killer."

"Yeah, but I took his job," Curry said. "If I'm wrong, and it is him, it could be my ass that's next." He half-smiled, but he didn't look happy.

CHAPTER 32

MULLER WAS WAITING for us when we rolled into the office. "Good news. I hacked Elkins's passwords and went online pretending I was him. I've been in chat rooms with his buddies and I got a list of probable suspects. I also found out how he got the job at Familyland."

He was beaming like a kid who had just won the State Spelling Bee, but of course, he was still one murder behind. I knew that chasing down pedophile-haters wasn't going to crack the case. "We got some bad news," I said. "This case is not about Elkins." We filled him in on the Lucas homicide.

"Damn," Muller said. "That puts us right back at Square One."

"You still did a great job," I said.

"Yeah, thanks. Feel free to express your appreciation," he said, pointing to the large brandy snifter on his desk. He'd put it there a few months ago with a single dollar bill in it and a sign that said *Save The Geeks*. Since then, the rest of the squad had fed the kitty. Contributions included a box of condoms, a tube of Preparation H, a Tampax, a Tootsie Pop, and a glassine bag of white powder, most likely Sweet'N Low. Cops. A laugh a minute.

"You say you know how Elkins got the job at Familyland," Terry said.

"Yeah, is there a second prize for solving that?" Muller is not your basic tough street cop. He's a sensitive crime fighter who wails the blues when Truth, Justice, and the American Way do not immediately prevail.

"I love it when you sulk," Terry said. "Don't make me beg."

"Alright, alright," Muller said. "I was chatting online with a perv named Organ Grinder. Love the name. Who said pedophiles weren't subtle? There's a guy at Lamaar HR who's a fact checker on résumés. He's got a sideline business selling spotless background checks. Grinder was trying to buy one himself, only this guy suddenly disappeared."

"Who's on the take at Lamaar?" Terry asked.

"Grinder only had the guy's cell phone number, but once I got that, it was easy. His name is Anthony Caleo, a.k.a. Tony Cales, a.k.a. Anton Colello. Low-level bozo who runs nickel-and-dime scams. He worked at Wells Fargo and got caught selling good credit ratings to deadbeats. Eventually, they dropped all charges, so he never did time."

"That won't solve the case, but I'm sure Brian Curry will back-door you and Annetta to Familyland, when we tell him you tracked down the guy that helped Elkins get the job," Terry said. "Can you do us one other favor as long as you have some free time? They're sending some surveillance DVDs over from Familyland. Can you sift through them?"

"Sure."

"There's about a thousand DVDs. How long do you think it will it take?"

"A thousand?" Muller said. "Three months, two if I get lucky."

"How about if you skip lunches?" Terry said.

My phone rang. I was happy for the interruption. "Detective Lomax."

"Detective, this is Ike Rose, Chairman of Lamaar Studios." The man on the other end had a strong, clear voice, with no detectable accent.

"Sorry to meet you under such circumstances. What can I do for you?"

"The question is what can I do for you," he said. "I want the person responsible for these two murders brought to justice, and whatever resources I can bring to bear for you, just let me know."

Get the Governor off our asses, I thought, but instead I just said, "We appreciate that, sir."

"I'm flying back from Singapore," he said. "Can you meet me tonight at eight o'clock? My home in Bel Air. I'm sorry to inconvenience you, but I have to leave for New York tonight at eleven."

"It's not an inconvenience," I said. "My partner and I will be there, but since I don't recognize your voice, I'll have to ask you to call your Head of Security and have him call me, repeat the invitation, and give me the address."

"Done," he said. "See you tonight. Thank you."

Thirty seconds later Curry called and made the invitation official. "He suggested that I tag along," Curry said.

"No problem," I said. "I'm glad you'll be there."

"Amy too."

"Now I'm really glad you'll be there," I said. "One more thing. You've got a crooked fact checker working for you. His name is Anthony Caleo."

"Caleo? The fact checker who cleared Elkins was Antonio Calleno."

"I think they're one and the same. Whatever his name is, your fact checker has a history of overlooking the facts if you pay him enough money. If I were you, I'd prosecute."

"He left town," Curry said. "His father died in Italy and he took off for the funeral."

"Brian, I have a feeling he isn't coming back to clean out his desk. When did he take off?"

"Monday afternoon. The day Elkins turned up dead."

"Dumb question, but if you wanted to keep the Elkins murder a secret from the employees, how did Caleo find out so fast that he was killed?"

"He worked in HR. They're the ones who keep all the secrets."

I almost laughed, but I didn't think Brian would think it was funny. "Look," I said, "LAPD can't invest any manpower trying to find Caleo. He's a small-time grifter. We're looking for a serial killer."

"Agreed," Curry said. "And if Mr. Rose wants to track him down, we'll hire private. Right now our priorities are to check all the résumés Caleo-Calleno green-lighted, and, of course, to get you that list of grudge holders. I've been working with Darien and a few others, and we've done a first pass on people who'd really like to hurt Lamaar. We came up with fifty-seven so far."

"*Fifty-seven*? I know I told you not to eliminate anyone, and now I'm paying for it. Do me a favor. You've got good cop instincts," I said. I wasn't sure he did, but I was trying to motivate him. "Take a hard look at the fifty-seven names you got and put a check mark next to the five you like best."

"How about if I circle the names instead of checking them?" he said.

"Brian," I said, losing patience fast. "Circles, squares, checks, stars, I don't give a shit. Just help me prioritize the list."

"I already zeroed in on six. They're circled. Go to your fax machine. I'll see you tonight." He hung up.

Six. Maybe Brian Curry wasn't such a bad cop after all.

CHAPTER 33

THE MAN BEHIND the wheel of the Cadillac Escalade SUV had a Boston Irish face that was puffy from the good life. The veins on his nose said that alcohol had played a big part in it. He pushed the Scan button on the radio, and the dial jumped from station to station every five seconds.

"Are you listening to this?" he said to his passenger. Despite the fact that he lived in L.A. for half a century, he still had a lot of Hah-vahd Yahd in his voice. "The news is all-Lucas-all-the-time. As writ, my friend. As writ."

The round-shouldered lump in the front seat couldn't help smiling at the compliment. Short of a Golden Globe or an Academy Award, 'as writ' was the ultimate praise a writer could get.

It meant that everything you wrote was produced as you wrote it. In a business rife with directors, divas, and studio executives whose sole purpose in life seemed to be rewriting what the writers had conceived, as writ was a rarity.

He shifted his body so he could look at the driver. "Thanks, but it didn't take a genius to predict that if we murdered an international movie star, the press would be all over it." He leaned over and turned off the radio. Then he shoved two Rolaids into his mouth and crunched down on them.

The driver shook his head. "How many of those damn things you gonna pop?"

"The doctor says I need the calcium."

"And I say you're full of shit. You got a nervous stomach over all this?"

The writer could feel the acid eating away at what was left of his stomach lining. He shrugged. "Maybe a little. Who wouldn't be?"

"We're two for two," the driver said. "What's to be nervous about?"

"My wife was crying when she heard Ronnie Lucas was dead. She said she really liked him. What was I supposed to say to her? Everyone likes Ronnie? That's one of the reasons we decided to kill him?"

"*You* decided," the Irishman said. "Credit where credit is due."

"Don't make me the mastermind behind all this. I went along with it. But it wasn't my idea."

"Relax, for Christ's sake. It went smooth. This next one will go smooth too. Keep cool."

"That's easy for you to say. You've got nothing to lose if we…"

"Get caught?" The driver laughed. "Lucky me to have cancer."

"Sorry, I didn't mean…it's just that…"

"You sorry you signed on for this?"

Damn right I'm sorry I signed on. But he didn't dare say it. The two men had known each other for decades. The short Texas Baptist and the strapping Boston Mick. They got drunk together, rich together, old together. But this was not the time to tell his old friend the truth. He had already written the scenario in his head. If the others caught on to the fact that he was having second thoughts, they would decide he was a weak link who might go to the cops, and they would hire someone to kill *him*.

"I believe in what we're doing a hundred percent," he said. "I just have to remember that when you go into battle there are always casualties. Let's drop it for now." He shoved a stubby finger against the CD button on the dashboard, and the two men listened to Sinatra for the rest of the trip.

CHAPTER 34

EIGHTY MILES FROM downtown Los Angeles, The Ojai Valley sits on the edge of the majestic Los Padres National Forest, a few minutes from the Pacific Ocean. The little town of Ojai, surrounded by citrus groves and spectacular views, offers perfect weather, clean air, and safe, friendly neighborhoods.

For all its charm and desirability, many of the homes in Ojai are priced under a half million dollars, modest by Southern California standards.

The Escalade passed through the gates of one of the more substantial residences, a six-bedroom, multimillion-dollar stone-and-cedar architectural gem. The sun was dropping fast and a few purple-pink clouds hung overhead.

"It's almost the end of April and you can still ski up there," the driver said, pointing to the jagged white peaks in the distance.

The Rolaids and the Sinatra had calmed his passenger, who put on his upbeat game face. "When was the last time your fat Irish ass went down a ski slope?" he said, as he pressed the doorbell.

The houseman opened the front door.

"Freddy, tell me that's liver and onions I smell," the Irishman said.

"Yes, sir," Freddy said. "But I was wondering if I could twist your arm and offer you a cocktail first."

"Liver and onions *and* booze. For that you can twist any body part I got. I hate the drive up here, but you always make it worth while."

"Thank you, sir," Freddy said, as the guests headed toward the bar in the media room.

"Good evening, boys," the tall, gaunt man said, when his two cohorts entered the room. "How was your meeting with Fellini?"

The group had decided each of the hired assassins would have a code name. The Sicilian who killed Elkins had been Brutus. The tall Albanian who murdered Ronnie Lucas was Tom Thumb. The third operative was Fellini.

"Fellini checked into the Familyland Hotel yesterday and began scouting for our next victim," the Irishman said, as he poured vodka into a tall glass.

The writer set a letter opener on the table. "Behold, the weapon."

Their host picked it up and ran a finger over the long, thin steel blade. "It's not very sharp."

"That's the way they sell it in the gift shop," the Irishman said. "Believe me, the real one is sharp enough to slice a cunt hair down the middle lengthwise. I personally handed it to Fellini along with the flipbook and the letter."

"Excellent. And did you discuss the victim?"

"We gave Fellini strict instructions," the writer said, pouring himself some ginger ale to settle his stomach. "The victim will be a woman. And not *just* a woman. The script calls for a woman with children."

A woman with children. That had been one of his finer plot nuances. "Ike Rose and the people at Lamaar will be afraid we're planning on killing another one of their icons," he had told the others, once he had worked out the scenario. "The fact that the next victim is a visitor will set their heads spinning, and the fact that she's a mother will throw them into total corporate hysteria."

"And who is this lucky woman who gets to die for our cause?"

the host said.

"That's up to Fellini. A single mom would be ideal. If she has a husband, the people at Lamaar will have a hard time keeping him quiet, and it works to our advantage if they can manage to sweep this one under the rug. But a single woman with kids may not be easy to find and then kill at Familyland."

"And we're still on target for Sunday?"

"Yes. It will be exactly one week since Elkins, and then," Irish said, refilling the vodka glass that had already gone dry, "the shit will really hit the fan."

"Eloquent, as usual," the host said, "but I prefer to borrow a phrase from my days in the theatre." He picked up the letter opener and pointed it playfully at the others. "And then, Curtain, End of Act One."

"As writ," the Irishman said, winking at his co-conspirator.

CHAPTER 35

SOME PEOPLE SAY that the true measure of a man is the size of his penis. Others, who are more enlightened, say it's the size of his soul. But in Los Angeles, like in many places where the rich and shallow gather, it's the size of his house.

If you live in this town, the odds are you've heard about Ike and Carolyn Rose's house. And like large penises, it's one thing to hear about it, but quite another to see it up close and personal.

I myself have never been impressed by big, expensive houses. They're like big, expensive cars. You got one? Good for you. I get around just fine in my Acura, and it costs a lot less to operate. But I must admit that if I were the type to fall victim to habitat envy, the Rose house on Mapleton Drive could do it.

Where do I begin? The front gate, I guess. Two ornate, rose-colored, wrought-iron arches, towering almost thirty feet high, anchored to a pair of even taller stone columns that were the perfect matching shade of rosy pink, as if they came from an artist's brush, and not an Italian quarry.

Terry and I, still in separate cars, arrived a few minutes before eight. I did a quick calculation, realized we were now in the thirteenth hour of our shift and the night was still young. Serial killers would get their rocks off knowing that they also shorten the life spans of a lot of homicide cops.

We each identified ourselves over the intercom, and a

video camera zoomed in on our IDs. The gates swung open electronically, and we drove onto a cobblestone courtyard that was dotted with statuary. Some male, some female, all nude. There was also an oversized fountain that looked like it would be more at home in Florence than in Southern California.

There were no painted lines saying *Poor People Park Here* so I pulled up to the only two cars in the lot—a black Lincoln Navigator, which I figured must be Curry's, and a fire-engine red Mazda Miata with the top down, which seemed like a fitting set of wheels for Amy. Terry pulled in next to me.

We climbed a short flight of wide, low-rise marble stairs and stood in front of a set of double doors which were only a modest fifteen feet high. The doormat, which was bigger than my living room rug, said *Welcome to Rambling Rose*. Obviously this house did not want to be treated like just another number. It had a name.

Before we could ring the bell, an Asian man in a dark suit opened one of the doors. "Good evening, Detectives," he said. "I'm Herbert Lu. Mr. Rose is expecting you."

I took a quick look around. The entranceway or foyer or whatever they call the vast space just inside the front door was only slightly smaller than the Astrodome. Fifty or sixty feet above us was a stained glass skylight, but it was too dark for me to get the full effect. A museum-quality chandelier was suspended from the center and stopped about twenty feet over our heads.

In front of us were the stairs. Not one of those trite, predictable, marble spiral staircases that seem to define New Money in Hollywood, but a gleaming, polished mahogany stairway that rose up from the center of the hall, then fanned out left and right, like a million-dollar version of the letter Y.

"Two words," Terry whispered. "This is beyond awesome."

Terry had grown up in a tiny Bronx apartment, which left him with a debilitating case of House Arousal. His palms sweat, his heart races, and he loses all ability to count. "That was four words," I said. "Take deep breaths. You'll be fine."

Mr. Lu had no time for Cop Banter. "Mr. Rose and the others are waiting in the Master Library," he said.

As opposed to what? The other six Minor Libraries that were sprinkled throughout the house? When does such a busy guy find time to read?

We followed Mr. Lu. He was lean, and even with the dark suit, I could see he was well defined. Probably worked out right here in one of the Minor Gyms reserved for the staff. He was in his fifties, maybe even sixty, but the way he carried himself I decided that however old he was, he'd have no trouble defending this fortress from invaders. I looked for the telltale bulge, but if he was strapped, it didn't show. My guess was that his large sinewy hands were as lethal as any gun and a lot easier to get through airport security. He was definitely more bodyguard than butler.

We walked at a brisk pace, and I got a quick glimpse at some of the paintings, sculpture, crystal, and antique furniture I never see at IKEA or Target when I'm shopping for Casa de Lomax.

The Master Library was filled with hard-cover books and leathery, manly-man furniture and Nice Things on the Walls, but that's as much attention as I paid to the décor. At that point, I was tired of seeing the things money could buy for others and fell back into my familiar "nice-house-but-who-gives-a-shit" mode. Terry, on the other hand, was still drooling.

Our new best friends, Curry and Amy, were there, talking to a dark-haired, good-looking man of about forty-five. He looked a lot like the Ike Rose I had seen on the cover of *Fortune*, except this guy was only about five-foot-four.

"Detectives," he said, striding over and shaking Terry's hand, then mine. "I'm Ike Rose. Thanks for coming over to the house." His voice was strong and deep and commanding. The voice of a linebacker inside the body of a jockey.

I said hello without mentioning that he was shorter than his pictures, and silently marveled that *he* lived where *he* lived, *I* lived where *I* lived, and we both referred to where we lived as "*the house*." Either he should have said, "Thanks for coming over to the hundred-million-dollar mansion," or I should start saying, "Thank you for visiting my embarrassing little hovel."

"I hope you don't mind, but I asked my assistant Richard to sit in and take notes." Richard was sitting in an armchair with a pad on his lap. He was about Rose's age and was wearing a buttery yellow, V-neck cashmere sweater and a pair of casual cream-colored slacks that cost about ten times what I pay for pants at The Gap. He also had on a thousand dollars' worth of shoe leather and a Patek Philippe wristwatch that cost in the general vicinity of a year of my hard-earned salary. Assistant, my ass. More likely, Richard was Rose's wealthy attorney sitting in on the meeting off the record, so his name wouldn't show up in any official police reports. He did not get up to shake hands.

Rose offered us refreshments, and we said, No thank you. Then he invited us to sit down in one of the many seating areas that peppered the room. We did, and the foreplay was over.

CHAPTER 36

"GENTLEMEN," ROSE SAID, "Brian and Amy have filled me in on where we are. What I'd like to know from you is where we're going from here."

"Sir," I said, "I'm sure there are politicians who count on your company for tax dollars and on you personally for campaign contributions. And I'm sure they would like me to spend the next ten minutes giving you the politically correct speech on how we are doing everything we can to bring to justice the person or persons who are responsible for committing these heinous crimes, blah, blah, blah. But since you're a busy man, let me just assure you that this *is* a Priority One case, we *are* doing everything we can, and I'll save you nine minutes and fifty seconds of political rhetoric."

Rose smiled. "Thank you. If the politicians ask, I'll tell them you gave me the full ten-minute song and dance. Go on."

"The top line is that when Elkins turned out to be a convicted sex offender, we thought the killer might be someone whose life he contaminated. But after Ronnie Lucas and the second flipbook, we focused on suspects who might want to damage your company."

"Did you talk to Danny Eeg?" he said.

"Not yet, but he's high on a list we got from Brian just a few hours ago." I opted not to tell him that my own father had pointed

164

to Eeg while Ronnie Lucas was still at home, having dinner with his kids and making love to his wife.

"I find it hard to believe that any man would solve his problems with the corporation by murdering our people," he said, "but it looks like somebody is gunning for us, and I guess Eeg is as good a place to start as anyone. How soon do you plan to question him?"

"He lives in upstate New York," I said. "I spoke to the Ulster County Sheriff's Office this afternoon. They're going to send someone to talk to him."

His face stiffened and his voice kicked up a notch. "A county sheriff? Why... why the hell don't you fly out there yourself?"

Considering all the cop movies Rose made, he knew nothing about police procedure. "Sir," I said, "if he lived nearby, we would. But we can't spend the taxpayers' money on airfare till we at least talk to him and see if he has an alibi."

"Screw the taxpayers' money. Take one of our corporate jets," he said. "Two first-class seats. No charge."

Fat chance, I thought. The D.A.'s office would scream Conflict of Interest, and tell me to go coach on the Redeye. Better to clear it with Kilcullen, who won't care how I go as long as I come back with a collar. "We may take you up on that," I said. "For now, there are too many names on the grudge list for us to meet them all face to face. We're looking for evidence that will point us toward one of them."

"What if Eeg hired someone?" It was Amy. "Check his bank records. He may have left a paper trail."

I didn't want to elaborate on the futility of getting our hands on people's financial records. Not to mention that you don't pay your hit man by personal check. "We'll look into it," I said. "Mr. Rose, let me ask you a question. You're a busy executive. Surely you didn't invite us here to have us fill you in on where we stand twelve hours after we've concluded these are serial murders. Your staff can give you updates any time of the day or night.

So… why are we here?"

Amy jumped up. "Why are you *here*? Do you know who this man is? You're here because Mr. Rose wants you here!"

"Amy," Rose said. That was all. Just the one word. He communicated the rest by looking down at the rich leather sofa. She sat. I can't get Andre to sit that fast, and I know damn well that Amy is a lot harder to train.

"Good question, Detective Lomax," Rose said. "Three reasons. First I wanted to meet you gentlemen. I've read your bios, or whatever you cops call your résumés, but I wanted to meet you face to face. I'm sure you know that I have enough clout to pull you off the case if I don't like what I see."

"If we'd have known we were auditioning for the head of a studio, we'd have dressed better. Apart from my partner's brown suit, how are we doing?"

Rose laughed and the others followed. Except Richard. He was playing the assistant, and I guess assistants don't participate in Executive Laughter. "You got your work cut out for you," Rose said, "but so far, you're doing okay."

He was full of shit. That wasn't why he sent for us. I nodded a polite thank you for the empty compliment.

"Second," he said, "I wanted to reiterate what I said earlier on the phone. We'll do whatever we can to help. This company has resources no police department ever dreamed of. We have over sixty thousand employees around the world. My personal Rolodex has corporate CEOs, international celebrities, presidents, prime ministers, princes—I don't know how any of these people can possibly help you, but if they can, they will. We also have deep pockets, which means if you need a plane to get somewhere, we've got twelve of them. If you need a satellite to spy on someone, we've got one of those. We are ready to do whatever we can to help you stop these murders from going past this…" He held up two fingers in a V. Just like the second flipbook.

Now he was really full of shit. He had already told me over the phone that his universe was at our disposal. We didn't need a face-to-face to repeat it. I waited for him to get to the real reason he asked us over.

"Daddy."

All eyes turned to the opposite end of the room, where a pretty little girl, about eight or nine, was standing in the doorway. She had dark eyes, dark curly hair, and was dressed in a pink nightgown that was hand-painted from collar to hem with a giant Rambunctious Rabbit.

Rose dissolved from Corporate Mogul to Fawning Father in half a second. A big grin fanned out across his face, and he stretched out both arms and said, "Hannah Banana."

The little girl came running across the room and jumped into his arms. He fell backward on the sofa and cuddled her. "Are you staying?" she said, wrapping her arms around his neck.

"Not tonight, sweetie. I have to go to New York. I just came home to tuck you in."

"I don't think so," she said, wagging her finger like she'd seen more than a few Shirley Temple movies. "You're not tucking. You're having a meeting."

"You caught me," he said, standing up from the sofa. He lifted her in his arms and introduced her. "Folks, this is my daughter Hannah. Hannah, you remember Mr. Curry and Ms. Cheever from Daddy's office, and this is Mr. Lomax and Mr. Biggs. They're working with Daddy on a special project."

"Boring," she said, and squirmed out of his arms to the floor. Then she turned to me and Terry. "Please let him go soon, so he can tuck me in."

"Yes ma'am," Terry said. "You're the boss."

"No, I'm not," she said, giggling. "I'm the boss's daughter." She put both hands on her hips and did another Shirley Temple move. Then she waved at the assistant. "Hi, Uncle Richard."

I had to give Richard credit. He didn't blow his cover. He

just waved back and said, "Hi, Hannah," as if he were just one of those lucky assistants whose boss's daughter calls him Uncle. Hannah bounced out of the room yelling, "Good night, everybody. Hurry up, Daddy."

Rose beamed. "You were right, Detective Biggs. She *is* the boss. Where was I?"

"The third reason we're here," Terry said.

This time Rose sneaked a less overt look at Richard, but he might as well have waved a red flag. I'm a cop. I took Furtive Glances 101 in Police Academy.

Rose sat up straight on the sofa, making himself as tall as he could without standing. "I feel terrible that a man like Elkins wound up working for us. I can assure you it will never happen again. I feel a million times worse over Ronnie Lucas's murder. He was such a sweet kid and a major talent. My heart goes out to his family. But my biggest concern is how do I protect the company."

Amy, corporate kiss-ass that she is, was wagging her head in agreement. But at least she had the good sense not to open her mouth.

"We're all concerned about other people being targeted," I said.

"I agree that we have to protect our people, but I'm more concerned with protecting the company. This is a business of images, and we need to keep the Lamaar image from being tarnished. I thought about offering a reward for the apprehension of Ronnie's killer, but that would only link Lamaar closer to Ronnie, and we need to downplay our connection to these murders."

"Reward money brings out the crazies," Terry said. "So we're fine if you don't offer any. But now that we know that these murders are linked, you should warn your employees that..."

Rose cut him off. "Our employees are not the same as the general public. They *work* for us. No matter what they do, they ultimately get paid to enhance our image. They bring laughter and music and joy to the world. They do not get strangled in a tunnel under the park. It's bad for ticket sales, and it's *really* bad for our image. I want the Elkins's murder swept under the rug. You can investigate, but the world doesn't have to know there was a sexual deviant inside the Rambunctious Rabbit suit. Lucas, on the other hand, is major news. But he was not a Lamaar icon—not the way Rambo was—so I've asked Amy to see how much distance the company can keep from the victim."

"Sir, this seems like a business decision. What role do we play?" I asked. I knew the answer, but I wanted him to go on record with his lawyer in the room.

"Quite simply, if you know where we stand, you can help us reach our goals. Keep Elkins's murder under wraps. If it should come out, don't go public and announce the alleged connection between the two murders. Don't talk about Ronnie as a Lamaar employee. He's a Hollywood star, stalked and killed by a rabid fan. Just do what it takes to keep the company out of the limelight."

"Even though the company is the target?" Terry asked, his voice edgy.

"That has yet to be proven." Rose gave us an icy stare, and I wondered what happened to the person who was just snuggling with little Hannah.

Terry looked ready to blow a fuse. "Mike," he said. "Got a minute?" Without excusing himself he walked toward the far end of the room. I followed.

When we were out of earshot, he whispered, "Do you believe the balls on that little Napoleon? Sweep Elkins under the rug, and, if we don't play ball, he calls the Governor, and we're history."

"Actually, I don't think *he'd* call the Governor," I said.

"Right," Terry said. "His *assistant* would do it."

"I don't know his name," I said, "but I'm guessing Uncle

Richard goes for about six hundred bucks an hour."

"It's Richard Villante. He's with Villante, Coleman, and Somebody, and he's more like a thousand an hour. Major smart lawyer, except he apparently underestimates his opponents."

"Since when did we get to be the opponents?" I said.

"Since they want these homicides settled out of court and out of the press. They're making our job even harder. What should we do?"

I tapped my piece. "Shoot 'em."

"I thought about it. I needed a sane solution, which is why I called you over here."

"You still want this case?"

"Now more than ever."

"Fine. Bend over and grab your ankles. Tell Rose we're on his team. Otherwise, your cell will ring before you get back to the office, and it will be the Governor inviting you to Sacramento for a special assignment cleaning latrines."

"At least I'd have my integrity," he said with half a heart.

"Right. Two daughters in college and a shit bucket full of integrity."

"Grabbing ankles now," he said. We rejoined the group.

"Sir," I said, looking squarely at Rose. "We understand your need to keep this low profile. Lucas was killed outside a soup kitchen, so there's no reason for us to drag the Lamaar name into the investigation... for now." I knew I had said what he wanted to hear, except for the last two words. I kept going. "On the other hand, the Elkins homicide and Familyland are all wrapped up in one package. There's no getting around that, but we'll do our best to keep our investigation under wraps. That said, don't underestimate the press. I've seen them dig up much better kept secrets than this one."

"Under the circumstances," he said, "that's the best I can hope for. I appreciate your understanding, gentlemen."

"Can we ask *you* a favor, sir?" I said.

"Get our asshole Governor off your backs?" he said, smiling that cryptic smile that Men of Power do so well.

"I was going to put it more delicately," I said, "but yes. It gets our boss all gooned up, and since he doesn't have a dog to kick…"

"Done." Then to make sure we knew he still was holding all the cards, he added, "For now." He turned to his quasi-assistant. "Richard, remind me to call the Governor on the way to the airport."

"Yes, Mr. Rose," Richard said, and efficiently made a note on his pad.

Now that Uncle Richard had been drawn into the conversation, I decided it was time to go after him. "We don't want to make Mr. Rose late for his flight," I said, as if Ike Rose were flying on a plane that could possibly leave without him. "What time is it, Richard?"

He looked at his wristwatch. "Eight…" he said, then stopped abruptly. He was staring at the face of a $50,000 platinum-and-diamond Patek Philippe. He knew it. I knew it. And now, he knew I knew it.

In a lame attempt to cover up for his sudden inability to give me the correct time, he squinted at the watch as if it were hard to read. "Eight thirty-seven," he said, his blurred vision finally recovering. He looked away. Rose hadn't seen me nail him, and I was sure Richard wouldn't bring it up. I love dicking with lawyers who think they're smarter than cops.

"One last question," I said. "You're doing a joint venture with the Camelot Hotel. Is there any bad blood between the two companies? Some of these Vegas folks have been known to settle their business differences outside of the conference room."

Rose laughed. "C'mon, Detective. The gambling business is like any other business. The big players are all tough, smart, even ruthless, but do you think guys like Merv Griffin, Steve Wynn, or Donald Trump solve their problems by rubbing people out?"

"No sir, but the Leone family was rubbing people out before they got into the casino business."

"I don't buy your logic," he said. "If your grandfather was a horse thief that doesn't mean you're a horse thief. Arabella Leone is a total professional. Don't waste your energy thinking about the Vegas connection. Concentrate on people who might have a grudge with the company. Brian, give them the folders."

Curry handed me a large, fat, gray envelope with a Lamaar logo in the corner. "We pulled together backgrounder files on our top contenders."

Brian was a good cop, but four pounds of backgrounder material pulled together on short notice had the fingerprints of a CEO. "Thanks," I said.

"Anything we can do," Rose said. "I put together a Task Force to be at your disposal until these crimes are solved. Brian and Amy will act as liaisons. Whatever you need, call them. On behalf of the entire company and Ronnie's poor family, I do appreciate your coming over tonight. Thanks."

He was dripping with sincerity. It reminded me of Big Jim's favorite joke. How do they say "Fuck you" in Hollywood? "Trust me."

Rose shook my hand, then Terry's. With movie-perfect timing, the door opened, and Mr. Lu appeared, ready to escort us out. Some people have silent alarms to call for the cops. Rose apparently had one to get rid of us.

Amy and Brian were dismissed as well, and the four of us followed Mr. Lu. I slowed down so Terry and I could have some distance from the others. Then I stopped to gawk at an abstract on the wall. "Look at that," I said loudly to Terry. Then I whispered, "Divide and conquer."

"Fantastic," Terry said, for everyone to hear. Then he muttered. "You take the girl. Marilyn will be happier if I take Curry."

Once he realized he had two stragglers, Mr. Lu stopped and turned to keep a well-trained eye on us. We pretended to love the artwork for a few more seconds, then caught up with the group. "Great painting," I said to Mr. Lu.

"Thank you," he said, as if he had painted it.

Actually, it looked like it was painted by a chimpanzee. Total crap. It probably cost millions. There's no people like show people.

CHAPTER 37

I WAS WRONG about the cars.

"I wouldn't have pegged you for the sports car type," I said to Curry as he opened the little red door to the Miata.

"I love the feel of the wind blowing in my hair," he said, rubbing his hand across his shaved head. "Actually it was a good call, Detective. If you check the registration, you'll see that this belongs to Sharon Samaroo, who is five-foot-nothing in heels and weighs about ninety pounds. She's my assistant. I myself drive a Toyota Land Cruiser, which is a great car until you get your first flat, in which case you need a good half hour to read how to unchain the spare from under the belly of the car, and another twenty minutes to change the tire."

"And you didn't want to be late for the boss's little soiree, so Sharon is stuck fixing your flat."

"Do not feel bad for Sharon," he said. "She's got my AAA Card, my eternal gratitude, and my Land Cruiser, which, even with only three good tires, drives better than this matchbox."

Terry ambled over and caught the last part of the conversation. "I got a shoehorn if it'll help," he said, as Curry positioned his linebacker body to get into the Sharon-sized front seat.

"Don't need it," Curry said. "I used to be a circus clown." Then in one move, he slid snugly but smoothly into the front seat. I applauded.

"You still got room in there for a couple of beers?" Terry asked.

Curry looked surprised. "If you're buying, sure, but my limit is one."

"You guys are on your own," I said. "I'll catch you tomorrow." Then I hurried over to the Lincoln Navigator. Amy had turned it around and was ready to pull out. I waved at her to roll down the window.

"I owe you an apology," I said.

"A lot of guys do, but you're the first one to actually follow up on it." She laughed. It was genuine and sort of girlish. The first non-corporate display of emotion I had seen from her. "Just kidding. What are you apologizing for?"

"When I saw the two cars parked here, I figured the Miata was yours."

"Yuck. You do owe me an apology."

"Can I buy you a drink?"

"Business or pleasure?" she said.

"Business."

"I thought cops don't drink on duty."

"Another Hollywood myth shattered," I said.

"If it's business, I can't say no." Then she shrugged halfheartedly, and I wondered how she'd have responded if I had said pleasure.

"Do you know a place around here?" I asked.

"My apartment is in Westwood. Do you mind driving in that direction?"

"No problem."

"Follow me," she said. Her electronic window glided up, the transmission thunked into Drive, and the big black SUV pulled out without waiting for me to follow. I'm sure she enjoyed watching me in her rear view mirror as I hustled over to my car so I could catch up.

CHAPTER 38

"POUR ME ONE, will ya," Ike Rose said as Villante dropped some ice cubes into a fat, square-bottomed rocks glass.

Villante cocked his head. "What do I look like? Your assistant?"

Rose laughed. "Hannah blew your cover, didn't she, *Uncle Richard?*"

Villante reached for the cut glass decanter labeled Scotch and changed the subject. "When do you leave for New York?"

"I'm blowing off New York. I think I should fly to Vegas."

"And do what?" Villante said, handing him a drink. "Talk to Mamma Leone?"

"Don't let *her* hear you call her that. You're liable to wind up inside a sausage casing." Ike sipped slowly at his drink, leaned back in his chair, closed his eyes, and let the Scotch begin to work on his frazzled nerves.

He could picture Arabella Leone, and she was nobody's Italian Mamma. She had it all—beauty, brains, and balls.

Four years ago, she had called him. Just like that. No advance warning. She didn't even have a secretary place the call. She just dialed the main number at Lamaar until she got to Ike's wolf-at-the-gate, Magi Durham. Magi recognized Arabella's name and buzzed Ike, who couldn't resist taking the call.

"Mr. Rose, this is Arabella Leone," she said. "I'm a shareholder."

"How many shares are you holding?" Ike asked.

"One," she said. "I'd like to buy more, but not based on my analysis of Lamaar's current financial picture. I have an idea how we might do business together and get the price of that stock where it should be."

"That sounds intriguing, Ms. Leone," Ike said. "Why don't I have my new business development team give you a call..."

"Ike," she interrupted. "May I call you Ike?" She didn't wait for an answer. "I heard you were smart, so I'm only going to say this one time. I don't need your new business development team. I know the business and I already have it developed. I'm looking for a partner at the level of Disney, TimeWarner or Lamaar. I called you first. You. Not your flunkies. I know you're a busy man, and I'm sure with your less-than-rosy financial picture, you're getting phone calls every day offering you all sorts of ideas on how you can keep the Lamaar Company from going in the crapper. When you're ready to hear mine, give me a ring. I'm listed in the Yellow Pages under Incredibly Successful CEOs."

She hung up.

He called her back the next day. They met in Vegas a week later. A car took him from the airport to the Camelot, and a private elevator took him to the penthouse floor. Ike imagined her waiting for him in a white, gold, and leopard skin Mafia Princess Suite. But the guard escorted him to a large, windowless office, which had all the style and personality of a mid-priced room on one of the hotel floors below. Arabella Leone didn't need Vegas chic to make a statement. All she had to do was stand when he entered the room.

She had lustrous olive skin, menacing brown eyes, and a kickass body six inches taller than his own. She was powerful, dangerous, and intensely magnetic. "Thanks for coming," she said, shaking his hand. "Have a seat."

There were four nondescript armchairs grouped around a faux-marble coffee table. He sat down in one of them. She sat opposite him.

"Vegas has lost its collective mind," she said. "Somebody got the bright idea that we could attract more people by becoming a family vacation spot. The casinos are spending millions to build theme parks, animal habitats, and video arcades. I think the only people they're going to attract is the fucking Brady Bunch who will ride the roller coaster, spend fifty bucks on the slot machines, go to bed at ten o'clock, and scare away the people who would have lost thousands playing craps till three in the morning."

"Sounds like you have a business problem," Ike said.

"Not me. The other casinos. I'm going to put a hundred million into a thousand more rooms, new restaurants, theatres, a state-of-the-art spa, and a string of high-end nightclubs. I've got the land, the financial backing, and the cooperation of every politician in Nevada. What I need is a creative partner who can conceive the clubs, theme the restaurants, dream up the shows, and bring in the big-name stars. I want the new Camelot to make the MGM Grand look as insignificant as a three-inch dick. You interested?"

Ike laughed. "You want Lamaar to makeover a Vegas casino?"

"Not Lamaar the cartoon factory. I want the Lamaar you're building. In the past six months you signed rap stars, rock groups and hip-hop promoters; you've cut deals with heavy duty writers and directors who never did a PG-13 film in their life; and you bought a company that makes blood-and-gore video games. You're smart. You know your business can't survive only selling family entertainment. You're going after young, sexy people who set trends and spend money. I want them too. Let's do it together. That's my pitch. I don't need a committee; I don't need lawyers. Just a handshake. You want in or not?"

God, she was hot. He wanted in. Into the deal. And into her. He reached out and shook her hand.

They spent the next four years conceiving, designing, and fine-tuning their joint venture. In three weeks the new Camelot would have its grand opening. A new, young, hip, sexy vacation spot would rise from the Nevada desert, and Lamaar's stock, profits, and reputation on Wall Street would rise with it.

"One shot of Scotch and you zone out on me," Villante said.

Ike opened his eyes and sat up in his chair.

"What do you plan on saying to Arabella?" Villante said.

"I'm gonna tell her about the two murders," Rose said. "If this is part of a plot to blow this deal apart, she should know."

"Why?"

"Because I don't think those cops are on the right track. They're looking for someone who wants to hurt our company. I think we should be looking for the people who want to hurt hers."

CHAPTER 39

THE LITTLE VOICE inside my head was having a field day. Amy's apartment is in Westwood. She asked if you'd mind heading in that direction to have a drink. What do you think she's thinking?

Twenty minutes of head noise later, I followed Amy into the garage of The W Hotel on Hilgard. A young Hispanic with a head full of glossy black hair and a mouthful of white teeth peppered with gold welcomed us.

"You been here before?" Amy asked, as we headed upstairs to the lobby.

"Five years ago. The hotel was called The Westwood Marquis back then. Terry and I came looking for one of the bartenders. He was a suspect in a homicide. He never showed up, but I remember the bar, all oak and leather, dark and musty. Sort of like a private men's club. I loved it."

"In that case, I have bad news," Amy said, as we turned into the bar.

The new management had totally neutered the men's club. The oak was now stainless steel and glass, and the thick drapes and plush leather furniture had given way to wispy orange curtains and those little Asian seating areas that are the essence of L.A. chic.

Our waiter, Randy, a thirty-something gay man with thinning blond hair and nice pecs, brought us a bowl of mixed nuts and our drinks. "I'll leave you two alone," he said, with a discreet smile.

Amy got right to it. "So what's on your mind, Detective?"

"It looks like we'll be working together," I said. "Your boss assigned you to help the Department with the case. But in the next breath he asked you to do whatever you can to keep these murders from damaging the company."

"He didn't have to ask. To me that would be Job One."

"I appreciate that you plan to do whatever you have to do to make your boss happy, but I'm concerned about you crossing the line."

"What line is that?" she asked, taking a sip of her wine and leaving a bright red semicircle on the rim of the glass.

"I don't know a lot about corporate communications, but I do know that people in your job have to lie through their teeth to keep the company from looking bad. That may be an acceptable business practice, but it's frowned upon in a homicide investigation."

"It's my responsibility to look after the company's image," she said. "And I don't lie through my teeth. I massage the truth. But surely you can't believe that Ike Rose expects me to bullshit the cops who are investigating the murders."

"Amy," I said, "Ike Rose just tried to pass off a high-powered attorney as his assistant. Smelled like bullshit to me."

"Well, that was just plain stupid," she said frowning. "It was completely Richard's idea. I told him it would never fly. I mean you're not that dumb."

"I'm sure there's a compliment in there somewhere. But this is what I was talking about. You're not concerned that your people lied to us; just that they did it badly. You may call it massaging the truth, but some judge may call it obstruction of justice, which is a crime whether you do it intentionally or not."

I bit into a salted Brazil nut. It was hideously bitter. Not burnt. More like wormy. At home I would have spit it into the sink.

The best I could do here was swill down some beer and try not to gag. Amy didn't notice.

"Right now I'm between a rock and a hard place," she said.

"Want to talk about it?" I said.

"Like what? Like you're my shrink?"

"More like I'm the homicide cop who might be able to help you with damage control if you play it straight with me."

"Lamaar is only the third company I ever worked for. After college I got a job at Geiger and Dennis, a PR firm in New York. I spent the next five years in Houston, working for Shell. Oil people are very secretive, very political. When I took the job at Lamaar, I figured I wouldn't have to be so evasive any more. Turned out to be just the opposite. Ike Rose wants everything buried."

"Even people getting killed?"

"Especially people getting killed. Can I go off the record for a minute?"

"Cops don't go off the record," I said. "Are you familiar with the phrase, anything you say can and will be held against you?"

She downed her wine and hand-signaled Randy for another round. I polished off my beer, swishing the last few gulps like mouthwash to make sure the wormy taste was gone.

"I'll tell you anyway," she said. "About six months ago four college kids were hog-riding Cosmic Cat's Space Plunge."

"Hog-riding?"

"It's what the kids call it, when they go on the same ride over and over trying to see how many times they can do it in one day."

"Isn't that sort of dictated by the lines?" I asked. "I mean, you wait on line for an hour, you get on the ride, and about three, four minutes later it's over, then you gotta get back on line for another hour."

"Not if the crowd cooperates. The word gets out that hog-riders are trying to break the record, and the crowd lets them buck the line and move to the front. The record for the Space Plunge is forty-three times in one day."

Terry and I had visited the ride on our second trip to Familyland. It consisted of sleek, chrome, bullet-shaped cars that travel along a plunging roller coaster track inside an enclosed amphitheater. The huge room is pitch black except for brilliant intermittent light shows that flare up at key turns. Essentially, it's a roller coaster ride in the dark, with lots of pyrotechnics.

"Anyway," Amy said, "the Space Plunge cars are like four-man-bobsleds with a divider in the middle. Two people sit in front, two in back. These kids took turns sitting in the different seats, but by about the twentieth time around, they had a brilliant idea. Squirm out of the restraining bars and have the guys in front switch seats with the guys in back before the ride was over."

"Isn't the ride designed to make it impossible to do that?" I asked.

"Right," she said. "And the Titanic was designed not to sink. Family parks like Disney World, Universal, Six Flags and Lamaar go out of our way to protect our customers. But you can't protect them from their own insanity. For obvious reasons, we don't sell alcohol in the park, but these boys had smuggled in enough booze to get totally shit-faced. And on a sharp turn at forty-five miles an hour, Justin Erickson, a nineteen-year-old sophomore from USC, tried to switch seats, got thrown from the car, and fell sixty feet. He was killed on impact."

"When did this happen?" I asked.

"About a year ago."

"I never saw it in the paper. Never even heard about it, and cops hear a lot more than civilians."

"That's my job. Avoiding headlines like *Student Plunges to His Death on Lamaar's Space Plunge.*"

Randy showed up with the next round. "Everything alright?" he asked. Amy nodded and waited for him to leave before she went on with her story.

"Within minutes of this kid hitting the ground, Operation

Buddy Longo went into effect."

"Brian mentioned that. It's code, like yelling 'Hey Rube' in the circus."

"Brian has a way with words," she said, "but it's a little more sophisticated than that. More like being on Apollo 13 and saying, 'Houston, we have a problem.' An entire organization goes into Crisis Management Mode. Ike Rose set it up when he became CEO. Whenever a major incident takes place in the park—a heart attack, a serious injury, or something as disastrous as this was—a page goes out on beepers and the PA system. 'Buddy Longo, please report to Cosmic Cat's Space Plunge. Thank you.' There's no urgency attached to the page, but employees know that 'Buddy Longo' means fatality or life-threatening injury. 'Tyrone Short' is the code phrase for a lower-level accident."

She took a swallow of wine. "The Lamaar SWAT Team, which is trained for these disasters, swept in. Within minutes the ride was closed for quote, unquote, repairs, and the people who had been waiting on line were given a twenty-five-dollar gift certificate for the gift shop. It helps reduce the resentment factor.

"At the same time, the police, the coroner, and the State Amusement Park Safety Investigators were called in and taken to the scene of the accident via the underground tunnels. No press. Now, here's where it gets interesting. In less than twenty-four hours the accident was determined to be the fault of the victim. A team of attorneys visited with the dead kid's family and the three surviving friends. Each boy got $200,000 and the Erickson family got $1.5 million for their total silence. Their other option was to have the offer withdrawn and then try to prove wrongful death on the company's part. Pretty difficult considering their kid was drunk. Ike Rose is willing to go to great lengths to avoid negative publicity. And so am I. That said, I heard what you said. I'll do what I can to help the company, but I won't obstruct justice."

She tossed down her second drink. "Can we have one more?"

she said.

"I'm not much of a drinker. This second beer could last me all night."

"How about you finish it at my place?" she asked. "I could make you a mean bowl of chili to go with the beer."

The voice inside my head screamed like a sportscaster calling a hockey game. 'Yes! There you have it folks! The hat trick. Chili, beer, and sex with a real piece of ass. What a night it's been for Mike Lomax.' If only, I thought. Then I said, "That's a very attractive invitation. But I can't."

"Spoken for?" she asked, dropping all pretense that it was about the chili.

"Recently widowed," I said. "But that's not it. We're working together."

"Lomax, this is Hollywood. In my business, people who work together sleep together." She leaned over and rested her hand on top of mine. "It's no big deal. When you asked me for a drink, you said it was business, but my ego took over and I just assumed you were interested. Driving to this bar, I had these fantastic flashes of the both of us naked, well, almost naked—you were still wearing your gun. We had just smoked a joint, John Coltrane was on the stereo, and you were fucking my brains out on my new Calvin Klein sheets."

If she was waiting for a response, she got one. But she couldn't see it. I was rock hard and my pulse rate had doubled.

"I understand," she said. "I'm very sorry about your wife, and I'm sorry if I shocked you." She laughed. "You should see the look on your face."

"I've been off the market a while. I don't remember women being so aggressive."

"Not women. Me. I see what I want, and I go after it. It doesn't hurt if I've had a couple of drinks first."

"I'm flattered, but I gotta tell you, these days, I'm not that good a catch."

"That wouldn't have been a problem," she said. "Right now, I'm totally focused on my career. Anything I do catch, I throw back."

She stood up abruptly. "If you don't mind, why don't you finish your drink and give me a five-minute head start. I don't think either of us want to stand around the garage and make small talk while they bring up our cars."

I nodded, grateful not to have to stand up. She blew me a kiss, turned around, and walked toward the door.

I sat there sipping my beer and watched her walk away. The voice inside my head knew better than to say a word.

CHAPTER 40

I DREAMT ABOUT Amy. We were living together in a huge house. I'm not sure if we were married, but we seemed happy. We were having drinks in the library, when the doorbell rang. Joanie. She still loved me and wanted me back. Amy laughed and said, "You had him; you left him; he's mine now."

Joanie sat down on the cold marble floor. She was wearing a flimsy white nightgown. Her lips were blue, and she was shivering. She hugged her knees and began to rock back and forth, sobbing. I put my arms around her, and she whispered in my ear, "I won't leave you, I won't leave you." Then a loud series of beeps interrupted her. Amy had hit the burglar alarm and called for the police. I begged Joanie to leave before the cops showed up, but she refused.

The beeping got louder and louder and finally became part of my reality. It was the alarm clock. I fought not to wake up. I wanted to spend one more minute with Joanie. I wanted to hold her and tell her how much I loved her, but consciousness crept in, and the dream was over. I stared at the ceiling and tried to bring Joanie back as real as she had been in my sleep. But the best I could do was conjure up a two-dimensional image. It felt like I'd lost her all over again.

I got out of bed, peed, opened the back door for Andre and the front door for the *L.A. Times*. I hopped on the stationary bike and read while I pedaled. There was a picture of Ronnie Lucas on the front page. *America's Boy Next Door Slain in Churchyard.* The inside pages had more pictures and eight stories related to Lucas's death, including the standard recap of Sal Mineo, Rebecca Schaeffer, and other Hollywood celebrities who were murdered in their prime.

The reporting was sketchy at best. Easy for me to say, since I knew more of the facts than Los Angeles's paper of record. There was no mention of a link to the Elkins murder or to Lamaar as the ultimate target. The lead article had the bare bones story of the soup kitchen, the baseball bat, and the homeless man, but most of the articles were rehashes of Lucas's show business career. Even the TV reviewer whose column is usually in the back of The Living Section had a Page One story. Apparently, dying sells more papers than living.

I drove to work with the radio tuned to KFWB, the all-news station that alternated between traffic, weather, and the Ronnie Lucas murder. By the time I pulled into the parking lot, they were on their fifth update, and so far the crime had not been solved, which made me feel relevant, since I had specifically come in to work this morning to solve it.

Terry was at his desk drinking black coffee out of a bacteria-infested *I Love New York* mug he hasn't washed in six years. Every now and then he wipes it out with a paper towel and tells me not to worry. "Our coffee tastes like Lysol," he says, "so I figure it kills germs on contact."

"Morning," I said. "According to the radio, you haven't cracked the Lucas case yet, but they only report on it every three minutes. You might have solved it during my long walk from the parking lot."

"You're in luck," Terry said. "The killer is still at large. Make that killers. Jessica just made it official. Elkins was whacked by someone five-foot-eight. Lucas's killer was about six-foot-four. Two vics, two perps."

"How'd it go with Brian?" I asked.

"He's gay. We slept together. How'd it go with you and Amy?"

"She's gay too. So we didn't sleep together."

Terry's phone rang, and he picked it up. "Biggs." He looked up at me. "Pick up; it's Falco," he said.

Detective F.X. Falco was with the Sheriff's Office in Ulster County, New York. We sent him out to talk to Eeg. I picked up the other phone. "Good morning," I said. "You got both of us. How you doing?"

"I'm fine," he said, "but my girlfriend just called. She's in labor. So I'm in the car, heading home, and calling from my cell, which is not great police procedure, but I figured you'd rather get the big picture now. I tried to get Mr. E. to come in and have a sit-down at our facilities but he flat-out refused. He agreed to let me visit him at home. He lives in Woodstock."

"*The* Woodstock?" Terry asked. "Where they had the rock concert?"

"That's a myth. The concert was fifty miles away. Woodstock itself is your basic unexciting small town in upstate New York, and Mr. E. is a respected citizen and a pretty popular Town Councilman."

"Clinton was a pretty popular President," Terry said. "It's not necessarily a character endorsement. How did Eeg do on the five questions?"

When you do a long-distance interrogation, like we were doing with New York, the investigating officers come up with five questions for the interrogating officer to ask the suspect. They generally cover areas like alibis and motive, but they're always case-specific and usually structured in a way that the first few questions are soft enough to lull the suspect into a comfort zone. The last one or two are more loaded and hopefully will rattle the guilty.

"First I asked if he'd been out of town in the past week," Falco said, "and he said he hasn't been out of the area since Christmas.

Then he got all put out and he wanted to know what this was about, so I asked if he heard about the Ronnie Lucas murder, which, of course, he had. Then I asked if he had a grudge against Lamaar. The answer was an unqualified yes. He hates them with a passion and he didn't try to hide it. Then I told him that Lucas was shooting a movie for Lamaar and that there were indications that someone with a grudge might have hired a professional to kill him."

"Let me guess," Terry said. "He went batshit."

"Did he ever," Falco said. "He started yelling that the people from Lamaar were trying to frame him for murder. Before he could cool down I hit him with the bank account question."

We had told Falco to ask Eeg if his bank accounts would show any unusual withdrawals in the past six months. If Eeg had hired a hit man, even if he had buried the financial transaction, just having the cops zero in on that area might unnerve him. A good detective should be able to read that. We didn't know much about Falco, but he sounded like a sharp guy.

"How did he react?" I asked.

"I might as well have asked him where he hid the weapons of mass destruction. He freaked. He said if those cocksuckers at Lamaar want to check his bank account, tell them it's a billion dollars short, because they screwed his father out of what should now rightfully be his."

"So he makes no bones about being at odds with Lamaar," I said.

"Not at odds. At war. He'd like to bring the company to its knees."

"Sounds like a first-class motive to me," Terry said.

"Yeah, but nothing about the way he handled the questions made me think he was anything more than just pissed off. Until just at the very end. He was all worked up about the Lamaar people trying to look at his bank records, so I fanned the flames. I said they had a right, even though I'm not really sure they do. I made it sound like Lamaar was in the driver's seat and he better cooperate with them. He goes into a tear-ass rage and screams, 'If those bastards at Lamaar think they're nailing me for those murders, they're crazy.'"

"'Those murders,'" Terry said. "Plural. How did he know about the second murder? Lucas is all over the news, but the Elkins job has a tight lid on it."

"Bingo," Falco said. "I never said Word One about Elkins. Eeg's the one who called it a multiple homicide. Hey, I'm turning into my driveway. Gotta go."

"Thanks a lot," I said. "Now get your girlfriend to a hospital."

"Worst case, I'll deliver it myself," he said. "Done it before, but never my own. Good working with you guys. I'll call you after she pops."

"Good luck," Terry said, but the phone was already dead.

"Murders," I said. "How does a guy three thousand miles away from the action know about the second murder, when nobody in L.A. knows?"

"Maybe he contacted the dead. Had a heart-to-heart with Rambo."

"I think we better have a heart-to-heart with Mr. Eeg," I said. "Let's talk to the boss and see if we can accept Rose's offer of a free plane ride."

"You do the talking," Terry said, as we headed toward Kilcullen's office. "If I ask him, we'll wind up going by Greyhound."

"No problem," Kilcullen said. "Screw the asshole D.A.'s Office and their dumbass rules. Ike Rose can pay my goddamn proctology bill if it will help solve these murders and get the Governor out of my rectum."

Three anal references in five seconds. The man was in rare form. "Anything else?" he said.

"Yeah," Terry said. "We talked to Ike Rose. He agreed to ask the Governor to give us a little breathing room."

191

We smiled and waited for a hearty Irish "Thank you, lads." Instead he said, "Why in God's name did you do that?" Then he waved us out of his office.

"That went well," Terry said. "He thinks we're idiots, but he gave us his blessing to fly on the corporate jet. Let's have F.X. set up a look-see with Eeg."

"Better wait till the girlfriend pops first. The man sure has got a way with words, doesn't he?"

"One quick personal question," Terry said. "If you slept with Amy, would you have told me?"

"I would have called you at home before I took off the condom," I said.

We worked the phones all day eliminating people on Brian's grudge list, which he kept adding to as the day dragged on. We were eating hoagies for dinner when Jessica called to say that she had nothing new except some clothing fibers she found on Lucas's body. "But since he was bumping up against a hundred homeless people, the fibers are meaningless, unless you nail the killer and he's wearing the matching outfit."

"You sound fried," I told her. "Go home."

"I will," she said. "Give me some good news before I go."

"Let's see," I said. "Our best suspect is an upstanding town councilman who was three thousand miles away when the murders went down, but he has a rock-solid motive for shopping at Hertz Rent-a-Killer."

"Good luck. You guys get anything else?"

I picked up the souvenir chunk of Kilcullen's bullet-riddled Brunswick and found a semi-smooth place to rub my thumb on it.

"Yeah," I said. "Bowling trophies."

CHAPTER 41

THANK GOD FOR earthquakes. While I was asleep they had one in Japan that the *L.A. Times* decided was devastating enough to push the Ronnie Lucas story below the fold. I stood outside my front door in my bathrobe and breathed deeply. It had April showered during the night, and the air tasted almost sweet. Very un-Southern California.

According to the paper, today was a Friday, a detail that might otherwise have escaped me. Was it only Monday when Terry called and said, We got a live one? Hard to believe that I had only earned four days pay since that call.

I woke up thinking about the same two things that were haunting me when I went to bed the night before. Who was killing Lamaar employees, and what should I wear when I saw Diana tonight? Not necessarily in that order.

At times like this, I lean towards blue. My eyes aren't as blue as Big Jim's, and they're not in the same league as Joanie's, but they had been blue when I was younger and now had brown speckles that the Department of Motor Vehicles called HZL. Nothing sets off hazel eyes, but I have a slate blue sweater that Joanie gave me that makes my eyes as blue as they're ever going to get. Plus it's cashmere, so women enjoy touching it. I'd put a white Oxford shirt on underneath and the gray slacks that do the most for my ass. Black briefs, shined shoes, a condom in my wallet, and I'd be ready to go. Harry High School gets dressed for the Sock Hop.

From out of nowhere, I remembered what Amy had said last night. The two of us naked, except I was wearing my gun. I distinctly recall the phrase "fucking our brains out on my Calvin Klein sheets." I wondered if Diana would prefer me with or without a gun. The lower half of my bathrobe started to stir.

The phone rang. "Hold that thought," I said to my robe, and I went back into the house. Caller ID let me know it was Big Jim. No doubt he was calling to beg forgiveness for not letting me help him raise my thirty-two-year-old brother.

"You have reached the Lomax residence," I said in a monotone. "Mike can't come to the phone, but if you say 'uncle' and leave a message of apology and contrition, he will get back to you whenever the hell he pleases. Beep."

I waited for Big Jim's bombastic reply. "Uncle," he said softly.

"What?" I said. "I'm not sure I heard you correctly."

"I ain't saying it twice," he said.

"I can't believe you said it once. What's going on?"

"Frankie needs a bigger shovel than the one I got. I've dug him out of deep shit in the past, but this time, I need your help. Come over after work?"

"I don't have an after work. Didn't you hear about the Lucas murder?"

"Son of a bitch. Of course I heard. I just didn't make the connection. Lucas was Victim Number Two. He worked for Lamaar, right?"

"He had a big fan club at Lamaar. All their accountants loved him."

"Did you get another flipbook? Two fingers?"

"That is privileged police information, so I won't respond. But I will tell you that you laid out the pattern for me a day before it actually happened."

"Does that make me a suspect?" he asked.

"No, you're just a jerk for thinking you could handle Frankie's problems on your own."

"You sure you can't come over tonight?"

"Besides the workload, I've got a date with Diana tonight."

"Fantastic. Hey, Angel, guess what. Mike's got a date with Diana."

I could hear Angel in the background instructing Jim to invite us over for dinner. I declined the offer before he could get past "Angel wants to know if…"

"Can Frankie's tale of woe wait another twenty-four hours?" I asked.

"It can wait a year if he stays holed up here with me. He just can't go far, as long as there's a contract out on him."

"Dad, you and Frankie keep using that word. What do you mean *contract*?"

"What do you mean, what do I mean? You're a cop. You never heard of a contract?"

"Yeah, I heard of it. It's what they say in the movies. Do you mean someone is so pissed at Frankie they want to kill him?"

"No, someone is so pissed at Frankie they hired *someone else* to kill him. Or maybe just to beat him to a pulp. Frankie's not sure, but neither one of those options is sitting well with him. He had diarrhea all day yesterday. You know how your brother gets when he's afraid. Mom tried to work with him, but he has this ridiculous fear of pain. Can you believe that? A stunt-woman's kid?"

"Question. This *wrong person* that Frankie fucked over. Mob connected?"

"Worse. A woman scorned."

I actually laughed. "You're kidding me," I said. "This is about a woman? I thought you said this was about money."

"It is. First he screwed her…"

"And then he screwed her out of her life savings," I said.

"Hardly. She's rich, but she's extremely pissed. Wants to boil his bunny."

"Boil his *what*?"

"His bunny. Don't you remember *Fatal Attraction* when Glenn Close sneaks into Michael Douglas's house and takes the kid's pet rabbit and boils it in a pot of water?"

"Oh yeah. These days when I hear anything to do with bunny rabbits…"

"One more thing," Jim said, like it was an afterthought. "She's married; her husband doesn't know about the affair; he's a heavy hitter, and he *is* Italian, but Frankie swears the guy isn't mob-connected."

"That was at least five more things," I said. "What am I supposed to do with all this information? Unless we have proof, I can't start arresting everybody who wants to kill Frankie."

"You'd have to lock *me* up," Jim said. "Look, you don't have to arrest anybody. I just might need a little cop clout. At the very worst I need your best thinking on this one. I can't come up with any solutions that qualify as legal."

"Well, don't do anything illegal till I show up."

"Don't worry. I'll take care of Frankie. Just have fun tonight," he said. "And give Diana a big kiss for me."

"Yeah," I said. "And you give Michael Douglas a big kiss for me."

I hung up, ate breakfast and drove to work. I didn't turn on the car radio. I was tired of hearing how the LAPD hadn't made an arrest yet in the Ronnie Lucas murder.

CHAPTER 42

TERRY WAS LOOKING smug as I walked through the door.

"You'll never guess who called," he said.

"What do I win if I get it right?"

"What? You want a prize?"

"It's early in the morning. I have no clues. I need some incentive."

He opened his wallet and pulled out a five-dollar bill. "Five bucks if you get it right. I'll give you three guesses."

"Okay," I said. "My first guess is Ben, my second guess is Don, my third is Marvin. Ben Don Marvin."

"You dick," Terry said. "He called you too?"

"I checked my voicemail from the car. Apparently he saw you on the news throwing a shit fit at the paparazzi. He lives in Arizona, has his own plane, and is flying in to Burbank to talk with us. Somebody we called when we were trying to hunt him down must've tipped him off. We'll leave for the airport at 9:30." I yanked the fiver from his hand.

F.X. Falco called. He and Lisa had a boy. Despite the fact that he was calling from a secure line, he still wouldn't call Eeg by name. "I told Mr. E. that LAPD is coming to talk to him and he said 'Bring 'em on.' American Airlines flies into Stewart Airport in Newburgh. It's only a half hour from here. I can pick you up."

"Actually, we can hitch a ride on Air Lamaar. Corporate jet."

"Even the cops in L.A. travel like movie stars. Should I wear one of those little caps when I pick you up?" He didn't expect an answer, just a laugh. I obliged and he went on. "I've got one nagging thought. Mr. E. seems to be a smart guy. If he is guilty, why would he blurt out the word *murders*?"

"If he's innocent, how would he know there's more than one murder?" I thanked him and told him I'd let him know when to expect us.

Diana called just as Terry and I were ready to leave. "I don't want to rush you," I said, "but I gotta rush you."

"I called to confirm," she said, "and to tell you how much Hugo is looking forward to tonight. He's changed his clothes four times. He wants to look cool."

"Tell him cops don't worry about clothes," I lied. "And tell him I'm looking forward to tonight too."

"So am I," she said. I was about to start fantasizing what she meant by that, when she added, "I have one problem."

"What is it?"

"It's going to make you mad."

"Diana," I said. I liked the sound of her name. "What's the problem?"

"Your father called and invited us to dinner tonight."

"Jesus! That son of…" I exhaled hard into the phone.

"It's okay. I told him no."

"God bless you. Thank you."

"I feel terrible," she said. "I don't want to insult him."

"I do. He keeps forgetting I'm forty-two years old."

"Promise me you won't yell at him."

"How about if I just promise I won't kill him."

She laughed. I like a woman who laughs at my jokes. "Please, Mike, don't make me beg. Just promise me you won't even mention this to him."

"Fine. And you promise me you'll keep turning down his invitations."

"I'll do no such thing," she said. "I'll see you tonight."

"It's a date. See you later." I paused, then said, "Diana." I wanted to add her last name, because I liked the sound of Diana Trantanella even better than Diana by itself. But that would have been dumb. Besides, by the time I made up my mind not to say it, she had said goodbye and hung up.

"Well, well, well," Terry said. "And who is Diana?"

"My new cleaning lady."

"She can start by cleaning the drool off your face."

"Actually she's a nurse, so she's used to dealing with people who can't control their bodily functions."

"I'll drive," Terry said, taking me by the arm. "You save your strength for Diana."

He spent most of the ride to Burbank trying to pump me for details. But I wasn't talking.

CHAPTER 43

WE GOT TO the airport and made our way to the Dennis M. Ehrlich Pilots Lounge. Donated in memory of a Naval officer killed in Vietnam, it was intended for the pilots of small aircraft who landed in Burbank for a pit stop, fuel, or possibly, since they sold a variety of maps at the main desk, for directions.

The room was big and airy, but the furniture was worn and mismatched, a patchwork collection of hand-me-downs from airlines that had either upgraded their passenger lounges or gone belly up.

Half a dozen men and two women were drinking coffee, taking catnaps, or talking about tail winds, vectors, and all that other gobbledygook that Big Jim and his friends find so fascinating. I remembered that Diana was a pilot, but I sensed there was more to her life than which way the wind sock was blowing.

A barrel-chested man rose bear-like from a red, white, and blue striped sofa that was one of several pieces of furniture with a patriotic motif. He had orange-gold, shoulder-length curly hair and a matching goatee.

"Ben Don Marvin," he said, offering his hand. "Thanks for coming."

Terry took the lead. "Detective Biggs. This is my partner Detective Lomax. Thanks for inviting us."

Ben Don let out a loud laugh. Actually it sounded more like

a bark, but in context, it seemed that laughing was a more appropriate response than barking, so I gave him the benefit of the doubt.

He walked us over to a corner seating area, and I got the feeling that the other pilots went out of their way to ignore us. Considering how many drug dealers fly private planes, I guess that disassociating yourself from other pilots' conversations is the healthiest form of Pilots Lounge Etiquette.

"Who else was murdered besides Lucas?" Ben Don said.

"What makes you think..." He cut me off.

"I was Head of Security at Lamaar. After 9/11 I pulled together a bunch of screenwriters and spent a weekend having them pitch scenarios on how terrorists could hurt the organization. By the end of the weekend they came up with three hundred scenarios, one of which involved killing people who contributed heavily to the company's bottom line. And when you talk about moneymakers for Lamaar, Ronnie Lucas has to be very close to the top of the food chain. So let me repeat my question. Who else got killed?"

"What makes you even think there's anyone else?" Terry said. "Why can't we just be looking for the guy who killed Lucas?"

"Because Lucas was murdered Wednesday morning. LAPD started looking for me on Tuesday. Do you always start rounding up suspects ahead of the crime? I can understand if you don't want to share your investigation with me, especially since I left the company under a dark cloud. However, I'm not dumb; I'm not a murderer; and I'm here to let you know that I have an airtight alibi for the time of the Lucas killing. I was in Washington, D.C., at a conference with two hundred people, all of whom can vouch for me."

"All of them honest as you?" Terry said.

"Touché, Detective Biggs. A guy sucks one cock, and he's a cocksucker for life. So, I stole some worthless studio crap, I sold it on the Internet to a bunch of idiots, and I got canned."

"But not prosecuted," I said.

"Jesus, when did they change the rules? You both don't have to treat me like shit," Ben Don said. "Haven't you guys ever heard of Good Cop, Bad Cop?"

"He *is* the Good Cop, asshole," Terry said. "He's just not that good at it."

"Let me try again," I said. "Suppose you're right. Suppose there was another murder. What would you do if you still had the job?"

"Me? I'd beef up security. Then I'd make a list of everyone who has a hard-on for the company, which is obviously why you wanted to talk to me. I bet Danny Eeg is on your list too. This Lucas thing doesn't seem like his style, but I wouldn't rule him out."

"What about the mob?" Terry asked. "Lamaar is getting into the casino business with Arabella Leone in Vegas. What's your take on that?"

"What's *your* take?" he said. "Did it look like a mob hit?"

"Answer the question, asshole," Terry said.

"Lamaar isn't *getting into* the casino business," he said. "They're designing the clubs, providing entertainers, shit like that. If they're into the gambling part at all it's just licensing some of their TV and film characters for the video slots. But a lot of the studios are doing that. There's no reason why there should be a mob hit on Ronnie Lucas because of Lamaar's connection to the Camelot. But like I said, if it looked like a mob hit..."

"Anything else?" Terry asked.

"I'd rule me out." He laughed or barked again. "I'd have to be dumb as dirt to kill any Lamaar employees. This company could have put me in prison for an easy three to five. They didn't. That wasn't out of kindness to me. They wanted to avoid bad publicity. It doesn't matter. They spared my ass, so why would I want to get even with them? It doesn't add up."

"Nothing on this case adds up," Terry said, "including why a smart guy with a great job would throw it all away by stealing a bunch of trinkets and selling them on eBay."

"Would it help if I told you my mother needed a kidney transplant?"

"Oh, in that case, why don't you just rip out one of mine."

"I'm a cop that went sour. Big surprise. Maybe I'm just not that smart."

"You came up with an ingenious new way to steal from your employer," Terry said. "Even if you didn't get away with it, you get an A for ingenuity."

"It wasn't my idea," Ben Don said. "One of the girl writers came up with it that weekend we were developing terrorist scenarios. She pitched it to me at the break, but I told her it was lame."

"Turns out you were right," Terry said.

"Look, I've got a good job in Arizona," Ben Don said. "Nobody knows about my past, and I'd like to keep it that way. Once I found out you were looking for me, I flew in here to keep you away from my turf. I'm not here to make friends. I want to get my name off the suspect list, and I'm prepared to give you my whereabouts since the day I left Lamaar. I got a whole new life, and I don't want to drag my old one through it. That's all I've got to say."

"What's your new job?" Terry asked.

"I left the security business. I'm teaching at Arizona State."

"What do you teach?"

Ben Don gave a little bark. "Criminology. God knows I'm qualified."

"And you can prove you were at this conference in Washington last Tuesday?" Terry said.

"Yes."

"How about last Sunday?" Terry said. "Four p.m. L.A. time."

"I was just checking into the Sheraton in D.C. The conference started Monday morning. I flew commercial. Landed at 6:00, which is 3:00 p.m. L.A. time."

"Write down your address and phone numbers and the details on your D.C. trip. We still gotta check you out."

He got out a pad and a pen and started writing. Terry and I walked over to the coffee area. "He didn't kill anybody," I said.

"No. Just a couple of self-inflicted wounds. But we'll check out his alibi and let him fade gently into the wild blue yonder."

"Don't lose total touch with him," I said. "He can probably put in a good word for your daughters at Arizona State."

Terry grinned. "That would be a big help. Especially if they want to major in selling hot merch on the Internet."

CHAPTER 44

WE DROVE BACK to the office. By now, dozens of other cops had been pulled onto our growing little task force. Our best detectives interviewed the people on Curry's list. Terry and I waded through their reports. So far, we'd gone through twenty-six possibles, most of whom had alibis, none of whom seemed motivated or capable of orchestrating a plot against the company.

Muller and his people dug deeper into the Elkins murder, looking for connections to Ronnie Lucas. They also sifted through the gift shop receipts and the surveillance DVDs. "You heard of a needle in a haystack?" Muller said. "That would be easy. This is like trying to find a needle in a stack full of needles. I don't even know which one I'm looking for."

A team of other cops sifted through the witness reports and the physical evidence of the Lucas case, as if it were an isolated homicide, unrelated to Elkins.

Terry and I also researched the FBI database on serial killings in the past five years, looking for similar patterns. I personally began immersing myself in the facts and myths about Dean Lamaar and his global empire. Big Jim's anecdotes from Monday night were helpful, but I knew they were the tip of the iceberg. Somebody hated this company enough to actually murder innocent employees. I corrected myself. There was nothing innocent about Eddie Elkins.

I told Terry that I had a date with the friend of Jim's who wore the Rambo wristwatch and who was a nurse at the same hospital as Jan Trachtenberg. I left out the part about visiting the fourteen-year-old boy who had terminal cancer. Over the course of the day, I became more nervous about my meeting with Hugo than my date with Diana. The kid hadn't asked for *me*. What he really wanted was to meet Super Cop, and I knew I couldn't live up to his expectations.

At 4:45, Terry told me to leave early. "It's Friday night. The 101 is going to suck no matter what. If you go now, it will suck that much less."

Instead of arguing with him, which would be my normal response, I agreed. "Thanks," I said. "I appreciate it. I'm coming in tomorrow. If you need some Saturday time with Marilyn and the girls, I'll cover for you."

"We'll see," he said, which meant he'd be in before me. "Have fun with Diana tonight."

"Thanks," I said again. I pulled my keys out of my pocket, locked my desk, then looked around as if I were leaving on a two-week vacation and I had to make sure the oven and the water were turned off.

Terry watched me procrastinate. "You want some free advice?"

The look in his eyes told me this wasn't going to be a joke.

"Be you," he said. "Don't write the script for the evening. Just be you and see what happens."

"She works in a children's cancer ward," I blurted out. "One of the kids has his heart set on meeting a homicide cop. Diana picked me."

"Lucky kid," Terry said. "He couldn't ask for any better than you."

I stared at him, and as ugly as I know he is, all I could see was the crinkle-eyed smile emanating from his mug. No wonder women fell for him. "Thanks," I said for the third time.

The 101 was not as bad as it could have been, and I got to

Valley General by 6 p.m. As soon as I saw the sign that said Hospital, I realized I should have brought something for the kid.

The Pediatric Oncology Unit was on the sixth floor. I expected it to be bright and cheery, but it outdid itself. It was sunny and colorful, and the walls were covered with artwork, all of which had been created by the patients. Not every painting was a masterpiece, but collectively they had a raw honesty and a powerful optimism. Some hospitals smell of despair. This one radiated hope.

There was a circular nurses' station just inside the door, and one of the nurses behind the desk looked up as I entered. It was Diana. Her face lit up when she saw me. Nobody had looked at me like that in a long time, and I melted. She came around to my side of the desk and took my hand. Then she gave me a little peck on the cheek. "Thank you for coming. Hugo is so excited."

She introduced me to several other nurses, one male, three female, but I would be hard-pressed to identify them in a lineup. I did, however, take careful note of Diana's white uniform, pink cardigan sweater, blue eyes, and blonde hair. I had forgotten how pretty she was. How could I possibly have ignored her that night at Jim's? Oh, yeah, because Jim had wanted me to pay attention to her.

She escorted me down the hall. "Hugo's parents went home about twenty minutes ago. They usually stay later, but he asked them if he could meet you on his own. He's in the Day Room. We encourage the kids to use the public space instead of having guests sit at their bedside. I'm so glad he's up to it. I'll leave you guys alone for fifteen minutes, then come back and bail you out."

The Day Room was like the inside of a rainbow. Color everywhere. There were so many colors on the walls, the floor, and the furniture, that it didn't matter what went with what. It was like going to the circus. You didn't say, "I think the orange clashes with the purple." It just all seemed to work. I'm sure nobody who spends a lot of time in this ward forgets why it exists, but the joyful décor certainly helped to make you forget about cold hard reality for a while.

Three family groups were sitting in various parts of the room, each with one kid and several adults. In a corner by himself, sitting in a wheelchair, was a boy who looked eleven years old, but I knew he was fourteen. "Hugo," Diana said, "this is Detective Mike Lomax. Mike, this is Hugo Cordner."

His father must have taught him how to shake hands, because even in his condition, he gave me a man's handshake. "What a grip," I said, rubbing my hand as if he had really hurt it.

"I'm not as weak as I look," he said, and smiled at me with a mouthful of metal braces. My mind went through a machine-gun thought process of Hugo's parents making a decision to spend thousands of dollars on dental work for a kid who might be dead before his teeth were straight enough to remove the braces.

"Now that is one cool T-shirt," I said, and stole a peek at Diana. Her eyes thanked me for remembering what she had said this morning. The T-shirt was white with a large press-on color photo of Hugo and his family on a ski slope.

"It's from Christmas two years ago. We went to Sundance."

"Let's see," I said pointing at the picture. "That's you in the middle. This must be your Mom and Dad. This has to be your big sister, whose name is...."

"Sophia."

"Sophia. And this short one in the front is definitely your grandmother. Tiny woman, isn't she?"

He laughed. "That's Grace, my little sister."

"Really," I said, trying to look completely baffled. "I'm not sure I had enough clues to solve that one. Cool shirt and a *very* cool hat."

He had on a black baseball cap that had the words BAD HAIR DAY in white letters. "Sophia gave it to me."

"Well, I brought you a hat, but it's not nearly as special as the one Sophia gave you." I produced a navy blue LAPD baseball cap that had been in my trunk only a few minutes before. "I'm afraid it's used, but if you don't mind a few cop cooties, it's yours."

"Wow. Is this like a real regulation hat?"

"Totally," I said. "Very regulation. I'm sorry I didn't get you a new one. It's a little beat up, but at least it doesn't have any bullet holes in it."

"This is better than new," he said. "Wait till I tell my Dad... and my friends... and everybody." He took the BAD HAIR DAY hat off, and I saw lots of skin and a few wispy survivors of chemotherapy. Images of Joanie, equally ravaged by her own chemo, came flooding back. I shook them off.

Hugo put the LAPD cap on, and it slid down, practically covering his eyes.

"That's the way the undercover cops wear it," I said. "Keeps them out of sight." I took the cap off, adjusted the strap, and put it back on. "That's better."

"I'll see you guys later," Diana said, and headed toward the door.

"So you want to be a homicide detective," I said.

"I'm gonna be," Hugo said, as if there were no doubt. "If I don't die," he added, with the same matter-of-factness he would have used if he had said, "If it doesn't rain."

CHAPTER 45

THE FIFTEEN MINUTES flew by. I outlined the steps Hugo would have to take to get from eighth grade to homicide detective. I've seen perfectly healthy cadets in Police Academy drop out when they hear all the work they have to put in, but this kid was undaunted.

Then I told him some of my best war stories. Finally, as I knew he would, he asked if he could see my gun. Under ordinary circumstances I'd have told him he was too young. But this kid was not an ordinary circumstance. I took it out of the holster, emptied it, double-checked, triple-checked, then handed it to him. He was inspecting it when Diana walked in. She put up her hands.

Hugo knew enough not point it at her. He just put on a stern face and said, "You have the right to remain silent."

She lowered her hands. "Fat chance. I am not famous for my silence. You have a busy day ahead of you tomorrow," she said, and I tried not to imagine what that entailed. "And so does Detective Lomax."

"I'll come back," I said. "I promise."

"Just one more story. Please."

"A short one. And I'm staying to make sure it's short, but first..." she said, trying to sound as tough as she could, "Drop the gun, Cordner."

He handed me the gun, butt first, and watched as I carefully put it back in my holster. "Thanks," he said. "What's the first murder you ever solved?"

"My first homicide? I was a teenager."

"No way."

"Way," I said. "I was fifteen. I didn't even want to be a cop like you do. My Mom was a stuntwoman, and I thought I was going to follow in her footsteps. We had a next-door neighbor, a sweet old lady named Mrs. Hovsepian. She loved to garden, and she would spend hours every day digging in her flowerbeds. I'd come home from school and there she'd be, trimming with a pair of scissors small enough to clip a baby's fingernails and talking to the flowers. She'd look up at me and say, 'Do you think I'm crazy?' And since I had read that talking to plants makes them grow better, I'd always say no. 'Well, Donny thinks I'm crazy,' she'd say."

"Who's Donny?" Hugo asked.

"Her son. He was fifty years old, but he still lived with his mother. He was always friendly to me, but I thought it was a weird-friendly and kept away from him. One afternoon I came home, but Mrs. Hovsepian wasn't in the garden. She was being wheeled into an ambulance, wrapped in a black body bag. They said she fell down the basement steps. Donny had found her."

"He killed her."

"That's what I thought. And when we went to her funeral he was crying, 'Mama, Mama,' throughout the entire service. But I didn't buy it. He didn't seem real. A few days after the funeral, I came home from school and saw that a big patch had been cut out of one of Mrs. Hovsepian's flowerbeds. It was so cruel, so mean, after all her hard work. Donny did it, I thought. First he killed his mother, and now he was killing her flowers.

"I went to the police and told them that I thought that Donny killed his mother because she paid more attention to the flowers than to him. He was jealous, and now he was wiping out her precious garden. The detectives told me they suspected she might have been pushed, but they had no evidence. They thanked me for my detective work, but there was nothing they could do."

"But I bet there was something you could do," Hugo said.

Diana put her hand over her mouth to cover a smile, but I could still see her eyes. They were glistening as she watched Hugo hang on my every word.

"At first I was very upset," I said. "I thought Crazy Donny had gotten away with murder. But I wouldn't give up, and a few days later I came up with this wild idea. If I couldn't prove Donny did it, I would get him to confess."

"How could you do that?"

"Well, I knew he was crazy. So I did something just as crazy. I called my plan The Revenge of the Flowers. I went to the nursery and bought trays and trays of flowers. Then I went to the stationery store and bought flowered notepaper. And the next morning when Donny headed out to work, there was a clump of fresh daisies right in the middle of a section of the garden he had destroyed. Along with the daisies was a note."

"What did the note say?"

"Hey, no jumping ahead. This is my story. I had been looking out my window, and I could see the horror in Donny's eyes when he saw the daisies. He tore them out of the ground, shoved the note in his pocket, ran to his car, and drove off to work. The next morning when Donny came out of the house, there was another note and another bunch of fresh flowers. This time it was violets. Donny went ballistic and ripped them out too."

"Cool."

"Every night I planted new flowers and left another note. I knew he was watching the garden, but it was dark enough for me to belly crawl and not get caught. On the seventh morning, I left roses, which were Mrs. Hovsepian's favorite. Instead of ripping out the flowers and going to work, Donny just sat down on the ground and cried. Then he went back in the house.

212

"Ten minutes later I heard the sirens. The cops came and banged on the door. Donny came out with his hands up. He was crying, saying 'I'm sorry, I'm sorry.' He had called the cops, and he had confessed. Case closed. My first one."

Hugo was in awe. "He confessed because of you."

"That's what the detectives told me."

"What did the notes say?"

"Each one said the same thing. *'Donny, you bad boy. We know what you did. Confess or we will come for you.'* Each one was signed with a different woman's name. Daisy. Violet. Iris. Petunia. Lily. Heather. And the last one was Rose."

"All flowers. The Revenge of the Flowers. How cool."

"The Chief of Police didn't think so. He and I had a long talk about how far the cops can push a suspect. He said I had gone too far, but since I wasn't a cop, nothing I did was against the law. Then he invited my parents to a private ceremony in his office and gave me a Civilian Hero Award for excellent police work, plus a letter that accepted me to the L.A. Police Academy, if I ever decided to make it my career. From that day on, I forgot about being a stuntman."

"Would you like Detective Lomax to wheel you to your room?" Diana said.

"Sure." He turned to me. "Do you really promise you'll come back?"

"Are you kidding? Now that I finally found someone to listen to my boring stories, I'm definitely coming back."

"Yeah, sure," he said. "Thanks for coming, Detective Lomax."

"You can call me Mike."

"Is it okay if I call you Detective Lomax?"

"It's fine. Don't you like Mike?"

"Yeah, but I have an Uncle Mike. And there's this kid in my class, Mike Jackman. And one of the nurses, his name is Mike. So there's plenty of people I can call Mike, but it's really cool to have a friend named Detective Lomax."

"Well, I think it's cool to have a friend named Hugo Cordner." I stuck out my hand and he shook it hard. "Ow, ow, ow!" I yelled, rubbing my palm and contorting my face in mock pain. I turned to Diana and pointed at Hugo's LAPD cap. "I'm reporting this man to the Department. He practically broke my hand." I stepped behind his wheel chair and began to push. Diana was laughing.

"Police brutality!" I called out as we rolled down the hall.

Hugo let out a loud joyful hoot, then started clapping his hands. His laughter bounced off the walls.

As we wound our way down the corridor, all the nurses, doctors, patients, and parents within hearing distance stopped to smile and watch us go by. Joy of this magnitude does not go unnoticed in a place like the kids' cancer ward at Valley General.

Diana blew me a kiss. I hadn't felt this good in a long, long time.

CHAPTER 46

"**BE YOU, BE** you, be you," I chanted as I followed Diana's Jeep Cherokee along Ventura Boulevard. It sounded lame. "Be Tom Cruise! Be Tom Cruise! Be Tom Cruise!" I yelled. Better. I just wasn't sure how to pull it off.

We turned into a little strip mall on Ventura. "I couldn't decide between this or the hospital cafeteria," Diana said, as we walked up to a door that said *Giorgio's*. "But this place definitely has the better wine list."

She had changed from her uniform into a tan skirt and a pale blue sweater with a matching cardigan. She looked soft and warm and accessible. As I held the door I caught a light lemony fragrance as she brushed past me. I was fantasizing about wrapping my arms around her when another guy beat me to it. "*Buona sera, Signora,*" he said, as he and Diana exchanged double cheek kisses.

She introduced him as the owner, George Imbriale, who hugged me like I was a long-lost relative. He sat us and said he'd be right back with the vino and a special antipasto with all of Diana's favorites.

"All your favorites," I said, after he left. "I guess you're a regular here."

"I try to come as often as I can on a nurse's salary."

"Well, tonight you're here on a cop's salary."

215

"Absolutely not. I asked you out."

"No, you asked me to visit Hugo. I invited you to dinner. I'm paying. I'm very old-fashioned that way. And you may also recall that I am armed."

"Oh my God," she said. "Did I look horrified when I walked in and saw Hugo with that gun?"

"I thought you handled it very well. I don't normally let young children play with my weapon, but..."

"I know. Special circumstances. I can't thank you enough for spending time with him and for promising to come back."

"Actually, you *have* thanked me enough. Three times before we even left the hospital. If you keep on thanking me, I'll have to keep apologizing for being such a jerk the other night. It wasn't about you. I was pissed at Big Jim."

"You think my father is any easier?" she said.

"What does he do?"

"He's a rabbi."

"Rabbi *Trantanella*?"

"Rabbi Silver, which is my maiden name. My husband was Italian."

"Do you have children?"

"Just the cat."

"Blanche, right?"

"You have a good memory," she said.

"That's because I'm still waiting to hear what Blanche thinks about me."

"I haven't mentioned you to her yet, but I will tonight. Promise."

We talked about her job and my job and the relative plusses and minuses of each. We shared how difficult it was to lose a spouse. Joanie's death had been a slow agonizing process, but at least it gave us time for closure. Diana's husband Paul had blown her a kiss from a ski lift one sunny Saturday morning. Two hours later he was being carried off the mountain in a body bag.

Finally she asked me how long I waited to start dating after Joanie died.

"I waited till about seven o'clock this evening," I said.

"This is your first date?" she said, genuinely surprised.

"I'm amazed that Big Jim hasn't briefed you on that."

"I'm... I don't know, I'm honored. Thank you for asking me."

"Thank you for accepting. I don't think I could have handled rejection."

Dinner was fantastico, and the service was attentive, without being in our face. We ordered espresso and one tiramisu for two. The waiter offered us an after-dinner drink "*on-dee-owza*," which Diana explained meant "on the house." I passed, already intoxicated with half a bottle of Chianti and two hours of gazing across the table at Diana.

A few days ago, I would have sworn I wasn't ready to date, but now I had to rethink my decision. This was a woman I wanted to see again. There was something about her that seemed to fill an emotional void I didn't even know existed. Maybe it was her concern and compassion for others, which had been Joanie's most endearing quality. Then again, it just might be that I was one of the loneliest heterosexual men in Southern California, and I would have fallen for a fat lady with chin whiskers and a bad haircut.

She graciously let me pay the check, and I tipped too much, because I knew that even if I never came back, she would. The night was cool, so we walked briskly to our cars. Ten feet from the Jeep she pressed the electronic clicker and the door locks thunked up. "Thank you one last time for visiting Hugo, and thanks for a lovely evening," she said, and kissed me on the cheek. "I can't wait to get home and tell Blanche all about you." She opened the car door.

"What are you going to tell her?" I asked, all the while wondering if that little peck was the only good-night kiss I was going to get.

"I'm going to tell her you're the real deal."

"I don't speak cat. What exactly does that mean?"

She took her hand off the door handle and turned to face me. Then she snuggled her body close to mine, put one hand gently behind my neck, and lowered my face to hers. Her lips were soft and sweet and tender, and it was all I could do to keep from wrestling her to the ground. The kiss was long and slow, but it ended about thirty or forty years too soon.

"Stop asking so many questions," she whispered.

I watched her get into the car and drive off. I didn't move from my spot until her taillights blended into the ribbon of red on Ventura Boulevard.

The voice inside my head cleared his throat. "If you dream about Amy Cheever tonight," it said, "I will personally step outside your body and shoot you with your own gun."

Fair enough, I replied.

CHAPTER 47

I WAS BACK on the 101, thinking about Hugo and fantasizing about Diana. But someone else kept cluttering up my head.

Ike Rose.

Something bothered me about him. Something he said; something he did. Maybe it was something he didn't say, or didn't do. I called Terry at home.

"I didn't expect to hear from you tonight," he said. "What's up?"

"I was just wondering…is anything gnawing at you about Ike Rose?"

"The only thing gnawing at me is why you'd be calling me about Ike Rose in the middle of your date with Diana."

"The date's over."

"It's not even 10:30," he said. "When I heard your voice I figured you were calling me because you forgot how to unhook a bra. What went wrong?"

"Nothing. She's bright, attractive, charming. You'd like her."

"*I'd* like her? How about the kid in the hospital? Would I like him too?"

"Yeah, he was terrific."

"So then you had a good time."

"I had a fantastic time."

"Great. You can tell me all about it tomorrow. Good night."

"Whoa, whoa. You don't want to talk about the case?"

"Not tonight, Mike. And neither do you. You can play detective in the morning. At the risk of repeating myself, why don't you spend the rest of the night being you. Good night."

He hung up on me.

I was about to call him back, but the little voice inside my head stopped me. "Terry knows you better than you know yourself," it said. "It's only six months since Joanie died. You haven't even finished reading the letters she wrote. You feel guilty about your attraction to Diana, so you want to quickly crawl back to the comfortable misery of a double homicide."

But Terry wouldn't let me. Which meant I had to spend the rest of the night being Mike.

There was a message on my machine from my father. It was uncharacteristically brief. "Hi. Frankie's doing okay. I told him you're coming tomorrow." He paused. I know Big Jim. He was editing himself. "I'm glad you went out with Diana tonight. Hope you had a good time. Goodnight."

Something cold and wet touched my hand. Andre wanted some attention. "Did you hear that message?" I asked him, as I scratched his ears. "It was the shortest, least annoying Big Jim message in history."

I went to the bedroom and took the wooden box off the top of Joanie's dressing table. I had decided from the moment I watched Diana's Jeep drive out of sight that I had to open Joanie's next letter. I couldn't wait another three and a half weeks for her seven-month anniversary.

I opened the box and took out the envelope with the seven hash marks. "Forgive me," I said, as I opened it.

My darling Mike,
I lied. I said that I would write letter #7 tomorrow. That was three weeks and two relapses ago. I'm getting physically weaker and mentally less able to construct sentences that make any

sense. It's a combination of the pain and the drugs.

I just re-read my first six letters, so I'll spare you the "How can we not be together" guilt trip that I've been laying on you. It's not your fault I'm dying. My life won't go on, but yours should. I think I went through the grief process they tell you happens when people die. When I first learned about the cancer, I went into denial. Then bargaining, then anger, and now, finally, I've come out the other side. Acceptance. I'm dying; you're living; and that's how God has planned it. Who am I to argue? I have to accept the fact that He has more information than I do, so I'll accept whatever He has in store for me.

I do wonder what He has in store for you, and my fondest wish is a long and happy life. When this all started I couldn't deal with the thought of some other woman replacing me after I'm gone. But I'm over that. I know she won't replace me. I also know you need someone to help you pick up where we left off. The other day while you were at work Big Jim and Angel came to visit me. I adore them, and I'm so happy that Jim has found someone to share his life after your Mom died. They asked me what everybody asks me. "Is there anything we can do?" I always say no. But this time I asked them to please help Mike get on with his life. Jim wasn't sure he knew what I meant, but Angel did. So don't be surprised if they fix you up with some nice woman one of these days. And don't be mad at them. They have my blessings.

It's now time for my confession. I told you in the last letter that I had a secret I've been keeping from you. It's about Frankie. Two years ago he came to me in desperate trouble. You can guess the details. He needed money. $20,000. I had it from the money my mother left me, and I gave it to him. No strings attached. I told him he didn't have to pay me back, but he could never ask me again. Jim found out (how the hell does he know everything?) and he was a little pissed at me and a lot pissed at your brother. The reason I'm telling you is to apologize. I know *it wasn't the best thing to do for Frankie, but I love him, and he was so pathetic when he asked that I had to.*

Please forgive me and forgive him. He's going to need a lot of help to get over his addiction, and he's running out of people who give a shit. Please, please, please don't be one of those people. Don't stop loving him. Don't stop trying to get him better.

Long before I got sick Jim told me something he heard on his favorite television show. When somebody close to you dies, you lose a friend here on earth, but you have an angel in heaven. I'll do what I can for Frankie from heaven, but he still needs help down here. Don't give up on him. Be his angel here on earth.

I'm too exhausted to keep writing. This is only the seventh monthly letter, and I hoped to write at least twelve. Not sure I'm going to make it. Just in case this is the last one, I want you to know that I've said everything that's been on my mind. If I die in my sleep tonight, I'm ready. I'll wait for you in heaven. Take your time.

I love you for eternity.

Joanie

I lowered the letter to my lap and looked up at God. I opened my mouth. But I couldn't think of anything to say.

CHAPTER 48

PENINA BENJAMIN HELD hands with her six-year-old son Dov as they walked along the tree-lined street toward the synagogue. Ari, her ten-year-old, had long ago given up public handholding.

"Eemah, can I go ahead?" Ari asked his mother.

"Yes," she said. "Don't run."

Ari ran. Dov pulled away from his mother's hand and chased after his big brother. The two boys bounded up the steps of the synagogue, raced through the open double doors, and entered the building.

"I win," Ari said.

"You cheated," Dov said.

The brothers stood in the open doorway and looked around the lobby. It was a typical, modern-day Southern California synagogue. Five-thousand-year-old traditions expressed in a contemporary chrome-and-glass statement that the architect convinced the Building Committee would have the look of their Jewish heritage without feeling so old-fashioned.

Several ushers, men with white carnations in their lapels, stood at the doors to the sanctuary on the opposite side of the lobby and smiled at the boys. One beckoned with his hand, but the two brothers didn't move.

Penina entered. She was 6 feet tall with the beautifully proportioned body of an athlete, shoulder-length black hair that picked up the luster of her crimson silk blouse, and dark eyes that were filled with concern for her young sons. She was a magnet, and all eyes immediately shifted from the boys.

"Eemah," Dov said, looking upset. "There's no soldiers, no security."

Penina squeezed his hand. "It's alright. Things are different here. It's safe."

Three ushers made a beeline to the door to greet the beautiful woman.

"I got it fellas," said the man who had first waved to the children. He clarified his statement by elbowing them out of the way and reaching his hand out while he was still ten feet away from Penina. "*Shabbat Shalom*," he said. "I'm Jerry Goldstein."

Penina extended her hand. "*Shabbat Shalom*. Penina Benjamin. These are my sons Ari and Dov."

Goldstein was about sixty, a short compact man, with a full head of hair, most of which was still the original reddish-brown. But the Wilford Brimley mustache that accented his toothy smile was heavily peppered with gray. "Welcome to the best Jewish Congregation in all of Costa Luna, California," he said. "Also the only one."

"There's no security," Ari said. "No metal detectors. No soldiers."

"You're visiting from Israel, am I right?" Goldstein said.

The boy nodded his head.

"We don't have that kind of security," he said. "But the ushers know all the members, and when strangers come, we size them up."

"How do you know we don't have weapons?" Dov asked.

"Oy, the little one too is worried?" Goldstein shook his head at Penina. "Wait, I'll be right back."

He walked to a small table, opened a drawer, and returned with a hand-held scanner. "Okay boys. Arms out." He ran the wand slowly over each child, stopping to look concerned when their belt buckles or buttons set off the beeper. Finally, he said, "Now Mom. Would you open your bag please?"

Penina opened her purse and Goldstein took a perfunctory look inside. "Looks fine to me. Services start in five minutes. I'll take you in."

He escorted them inside the sanctuary doors and down the center aisle. "Are you a Sabra?" he asked.

Penina smiled. "No, I was born in New York, but I've lived in Haifa since I was Dov's age, so I feel like a Sabra."

"Are you visiting family here?"

"Not family. Familyland. The boys have been hocking me for years to come here, and the airlines finally had such a good price, I couldn't say no anymore. So here we are."

"And here *we* are," Goldstein said, as he stopped at the fifth pew from the front. "This is my wife, Roberta. Sweetheart, these are the Benjamins. Penina, Ari, and Dov. They're visiting from Haifa."

Roberta Goldstein was tan, trim, and tastefully dressed. Her hair was cut and colored expensively, with the blonde highlights that Penina was beginning to think were mandatory in the state of California.

Her soft brown eyes brightened as soon as she spotted the boys. "*Shabbat Shalom*," she said, giving them a warm grandmotherly smile. She extended a hand to Penina. "You have family in Costa Luna?"

"I already asked," Goldstein said, and quickly filled his wife in on the pertinent details.

"Just you and your sons are on vacation?" Roberta said, fishing for more information.

"My husband, he should rest in peace, was killed four years ago. A suicide bomber."

"My condolences," Goldstein said. "Now I understand why your son was so concerned with security. But this is America, Ari. It's not like *Eretz Yisroel*. Yes, we look for terrorists. But in a little synagogue in the middle of nowhere, we don't look so hard."

"Are you staying for the Kiddush or are you running off to Familyland?" Roberta asked.

"It's Shabbat. We're not going to the amusement park today," Penina said, looking at her sons. Dov rolled his eyes just enough to show that his vote hadn't counted as much as hers.

"I'm impressed," Goldstein said. "Very few tourists even come to temple on a Saturday morning. They're always running to go on the rides. This isn't as much fun as Familyland, but at least the lines to get in are shorter, right, boys?"

Dov shrugged. Ari smiled.

"Plus you're closer to God," Goldstein added.

"I don't think so," Ari said. "Yesterday when I was riding the Space Plunge, I prayed a lot harder than I do in synagogue."

The three adults laughed.

"How long are you staying in Costa Luna?" Roberta asked.

"Tomorrow we're going back to the park," Penina said. "Then Monday we fly home, with a short stop in New York to visit my late husband's parents."

"So today you can join us at our home for Shabbat lunch," Roberta said.

"Oh no, we'll have lunch at the hotel," Penina said.

"You would pass up my wife's brisket and kasha varnishkes for hotel food?" Goldstein said.

"Really, we hate to impose."

"It's not an imposition. She cooks for twenty people, and we only have seven. Our Stacey and her husband are coming with our two grandsons. They leave toys and video games at our house, so Ari and Dov wouldn't be bored."

"Also our son Alex is coming. He's a successful accountant, very handsome," Roberta said. "He's divorced, no children."

"Roberta, this is a lunch, not a matchmaking service. You'll scare her away," Goldstein said. He shrugged and smiled at

Penina and the boys. "Please, it would be a *mitzvah* for us to entertain people from the Holy Land."

Mother and sons communicated in silence for a few seconds. Then Penina said, "That would be lovely. We accept."

"Settled," Goldstein said, just as the Rabbi and the Cantor entered from a side door next to the ark.

Penina looked around the sanctuary. She got the sense that several of the hundred or more people in the congregation were looking at her. But she was an attractive woman and used to being stared at. She was also a stranger in their midst, so it was to be expected. But, she thought, Ari is right. There's no security here. A madman could walk in and kill us all.

"*Shabbat Shalom*," the Rabbi said, and Penina put the thought out of her mind.

CHAPTER 49

STATISTICALLY SPEAKING, SATURDAY, April 23, was business as usual for the LAPD. The first stabbing occurred at 12:08 a.m. in a bar on 137th Street in Compton. The first shooting was twelve minutes later and twenty miles west on the more fashionable Admiralty Way in Marina Del Rey. Both victims survived.

The first homicide occurred at 3:15 a.m. It was a classic recipe for disaster. Take two bikers and one biker chick, add generous amounts of drugs and alcohol, bring to a rapid boil, pepper the chick with an AK-47 until dead. Serve twenty to life.

Throughout the day, cars were stolen, homes were burglarized, drugs were dealt. Yet with all that crime to distract them, no one of consequence in the LAPD, the Mayor's office, or the Governor's office seemed to care about anything accept the Lamaar murders. Terry summed it up eloquently. "Everyone who is anyone in the state of California is on our fucking case."

"Aren't you the same Terry Biggs that just a few weeks ago was moaning about the fact that we haven't been catching any high-visibility homicides?"

"Right now I'd settle for a low-profile crime," Terry said. "Like picking your nose at a red light and flicking it out the window."

I asked Muller to do a background check on Ike Rose. He came back an hour later with the top line. "Graduated from

Northwestern, did comedy development at NBC, had a string of blockbuster films at Universal before he got to Lamaar. Like most studio bosses he has his detractors," Muller said. "A couple of vocal stockholders, a radio shock jock, the usual assortment of petty little feuds, none of which seem like motives for murder."

"How about his sex life?" Terry said.

"He's a powerful Hollywood exec, so there's no shortage of gorgeous women. He whored around a lot, but that stopped ten years ago when he married his wife Carolyn. Since then no rumors, no scandal. He's got three more years left on his contract with Lamaar. Stands to make around two hundred million if he stays on track. Is he a suspect?"

"No," I said. "It just bothers me that two people at Lamaar got killed, and he's trying to distance the company as far away as he can."

"That could just be the corporate culture," Muller said. "Lamaar always had a history of covering up anything that could hurt their image. Then they got taken over by Nakamachi. The old stereotype about the Japanese wanting to save face may be a cliché, but it's true. Rose flies to Tokyo every three months to report in to the Japanese brass. I'm sure he doesn't want them to add 'What's the current body count?' to their agenda."

I thanked Muller and told him to put Rose on the back burner and go back to what he was doing.

The high point of our day came at noon. Terry's wife Marilyn brought chicken sandwiches, potato salad, and lemonade. "I didn't plan to feed you boys," she said, "but I was at the supermarket and saw this." She handed us a newspaper. The headline was in red ink. *Gay Lover Beats Ronnie Lucas to Death.*

The story, typical tabloid bullshit, said Lucas was killed by his homosexual lover because he wouldn't divorce his wife.

"It's the work of a twisted genius," Terry said. "This was planted to make Lucas's death look like your classic Hollywood sex scandal."

"Who would do that?" Marilyn asked.

"A public relations person whose job is to distract people from the truth. And it looks like she's pretty damn good at her job."

Lunch was excellent. My day went downhill from there. Thirty cops each putting in an eight-hour shift equaled 240 hours of dead ends and brick walls.

And for my evening's entertainment, I was going to talk to my dumb-ass brother and see if I could help him not get himself murdered.

So far it had been a hell of a Saturday.

CHAPTER 50

BIG JIM HAD mobilized the dogs. Normally, Skunkie has the run of the house, while the other three are relegated to the kennel out back. But now Dog Security had been upgraded to DEFCON 1.

Jett, the black Lab, was posted in the front yard. I could hear her barking a quarter of a mile before I got to the driveway. I parked and quieted her down by rubbing her belly, which is not a trick I would recommend to strangers.

Houdini was on duty inside the house. He's a black-as-coal German Shepherd. Depending on the situation, he can nuzzle a baby or rip the throat out of a man with a gun. Obviously, Jim felt that little Skunkie needed backup. The rear flank was being protected by a pitbull named Shotgun. "The Lomax K-9 Division is looking good," I said to Jim, who met me at the front door.

"We sleep well, but the FedEx guy is afraid to deliver."

Frankie, Jim, and I sat down in the living room. Jim lit up a cigar. "I want to lay out a few ground rules," he said. "Frankie, no bullshit and no gaping holes in your story. Don't make Mike pump the details out of you. As for you, Detective, don't act like a cop. They're too judgmental. Listen like a brother."

"Fine. As long as we're doing preambles," I said, "I want to say something to Frankie. I know Joanie gave you $20,000. Dad knows too. I say that not in a judgmental cop way, but in the interest of full brotherly disclosure. If you want my help, don't dance around any of the old secrets. Otherwise, you're on your own. Understood?"

Frankie smiled. He was a handsome son of a bitch. Five days ago he looked like a bum. Today he looked like he'd spent a month at a spa. He had always been in great physical shape, and his T-shirt did justice to his well-toned arms and chest. His gray face had returned to its original Southern California surfer dude color. His eyes, which had been all the colors of the American flag, were minus the red, and the ratty clump of brown hair that had been matted to his head was now casually tossed.

"I swear I'll tell the truth," he said. "Sorry about hitting Joanie up for the money. I was desperate, and I couldn't ask you or anyone else. I didn't tell Pop, but I know he found out, because he threatened my life if I ever do it again."

"And who's threatening your life currently?" I said.

"Vicki Pardini. Don't bother doing one of those police searches on her. She's never been arrested, but I seem to have inspired her to turn to crime. She put a contract out on me. No bullshit. She hired someone to kill me."

"Who and why?" I asked.

"I don't know, and it's a long story. A year ago I started managing the health club. Vicki was a member. Thirty-five, fantastic body, married, no kids. She came on to me right away. Your basic bored Beverly Hills housewife. I've been there and didn't want to go back. Especially since her husband's got an Italian name and he's in the construction business. So I was friendly, but I kept my distance. I even made up a fake fiancée and talked about her a lot."

"Is her old man in the mob?"

"No. She told me he wasn't, but she said he's a real asshole. Tries to intimidate people, makes lots of jokes about his cement mixers, acts likes he's Don fucking Corleone."

"So far, you haven't done anything wrong," I said.

Big Jim blew a cloud of stogie smoke into the air. "It gets better," he said.

Frankie ran his fingers through his hair. "You know me, Mike. I gamble. I'm trying to reform. I go to G.A. meetings and stay away from the old haunts and the old gambling buddies. But I'm not entirely recovered. I play the stock market. Some of the TVs in the club are tuned to the financial channels, and when I catch a look at the ticker, I react. One day, Vicki asks why I'm so excited. I tell her about this one software stock I bought at sixteen. It's up to twenty-three, and I think it can go to forty. She asks me to buy some for her. She has some money that her husband doesn't know about. If I buy the stock for her, she'll pay me a commission."

"Did you mention that health club managers are not licensed to do that?"

"I told her it's against the law for me to act as a broker. She says, Screw the law. Buy her two thousand shares, pay the broker's commission, then take a cut for myself. This way her old man will never find out. So I say, What the hell, and she says she'll wire fifty grand to my account. I tell her she's overpaying me for my services, and she says she's sure I can find a way to make it up to her."

"Subtle," I said.

"She is what she is. The next morning, I call my bank to see if the fifty G's are there, and they say they have a computer glitch; they'll call me back. Ten minutes later the phone rings, but it's not the bank, it's Miggie Spinks."

"If it's not too judgmental, let me remind you that Miggie is a total scumbag. He's hosed you over ten times since high school."

"Now it's eleven. Miggie's a broker and he's raving on about this stock Medibon, a small drug company in France. He says they're about to announce a cure for rheumatoid arthritis and all the big drug companies will get into a bidding war for the patent. He says I should jump in now at a buck a share and the stock will go to twenty in a week. I multiplied fifty thousand times twenty and it's a nice, round million bucks, so I bought fifty thousand shares."

"You bought $50,000 worth of snake oil for Vicki."

"No. I bought it for me. With her money."

I looked at Big Jim, who remained curiously silent. "OPM," I said. I turned back to Frankie. "What did you tell Vicki?"

"I lied. I told her I bought two thousand shares of the software stock at twenty-three. By the end of the day, it had jumped a point and half, so she was already up three thousand. She says how smart I am, and I'm thinking I'm gonna make a fortune off her money, and she'll never know she staked me."

"Just a wild guess," I said. "The Medibon stock tanked."

"The next day the frogs announced that the drug works, but a bunch of the patients developed liver failure and a few died. Back to the drawing board. By the time I could sell off my shares the stock dropped to nineteen cents. I got about nine grand back from Vicki's fifty."

"So you're now forty-one thousand in the hole," I said.

"Fifty-one thousand," he said. "Because by now, the software stock I was supposed to buy her was up to thirty."

"But you originally bought some for yourself, so you're making money."

"Mike, I'm a nickel-and-dimer. I only had a hundred shares. I was up like fourteen hundred bucks."

"I'm getting bogged down in the math," I said. "Get back to the story."

"Okay, I know I'm in deep shit, but I'm not totally freaked, because she's not ready to sell. I'm thinking I still have some time to undo the damage."

"What did you do next?"

"I started sleeping with her."

I laughed. "Sorry," I said. "You caught me by surprise with

that one."

"Yeah, well, I told her that I dumped my fiancée because I was crazy for her. It seemed like a good idea at the time, but of my many dumb moves, this turned out to be the dumbest."

"Don't be judgmental," I said.

"We went at it hot and heavy for a month. We got so involved that I'm thinking, the sex is good; she's not gonna ask me for the money. Then one day, she tells me she wants to sell the stock. It's at thirty-five, so she thinks she's got seventy grand and she wants to buy a painting. I tell her it's a bad idea, that the stock was going to take another upturn. A week later it does and now I owe her eighty-two thousand. So I took the nine grand I had left, plus I sold whatever stocks I owned, and I pulled together seventeen grand."

Once again, I knew what was coming, but I clamped my jaw tight.

"I took the seventeen to Vegas," Frankie said. "I've been cold before, but this was like ice. The dealers were pulling twenty-one out of their asses. Whatever I did, I couldn't win. I blew the whole wad in an hour. I knew I was in deep shit."

"Just curious, what casino did you go to?" I said.

"Camelot. It's my lucky casino. At least it was."

Small world. "So you lost all your money and you came to us," I said.

"No. First I went to Vicki. I knew I had to face the music sooner or later, so I told her the whole ugly story."

I smacked my hand down hard on the arm of my chair. The dogs perked up. "Bullshit," I said. "You would never do that. You doctored the story so she wouldn't figure out that you were planning to make a million with her dough. Don't skate around the truth. One more lie, and I'm out of here."

"I'm not skating. I just didn't think all those details were important."

"I'm a cop. As far as I'm concerned, I'm investigating a

homicide. Yours. The first thing I go for is motive. Don't spare me any of the details of what went on between you and the woman you stole $50,000 from. Now, you told her you blew the money, what was her reaction?"

"She unzipped my fly and started sucking my dick. I swear it was like the money didn't mean shit to her. We banged our brains out. She was like an animal, and I gave her whatever she asked for. You want the details on that?"

"Get to the part where she hires somebody to kill you."

"Right after the sex she goes into the shower. Two minutes later she comes storming out dripping wet, screaming bloody murder. She figured out the timing. She realized that I didn't start screwing her till after I lost the money. She starts beating on me, kicking, throwing anything that wasn't nailed down. She goes, 'You steal my money, and then you start fucking me to make it right? You could've fucked me first, and I would've given you the $50,000, you dumb shit.'

"She tells me to get the hell out, so I start putting on my clothes. Then she says, 'You cost me a *hundred* grand, but you'll pay.' And I say, it's not that much. And she says, 'It will be by the time I finish paying someone to kill you dead. You better start running now.' So I ran."

"Hell hath no fury like a woman scorned," I said.

"Yeah," he said. "I heard that. Some famous guy said that once, right?"

"Every guy has said that. At least once."

Jim put out his cigar. "So," he said, "what do we do?"

"We need to get him out of the limelight." I said. "This has to be the first place they'll look. Why don't we send him off to rehab for twenty-eight days?"

"Hey, I'm not a drug addict."

"You could've passed for one Monday night," I said. "And by the way, how come you showed up looking like some hit man had already hit you?"

"After I left Vicki I wanted to come here, but I couldn't face Dad. I spent five days in a men's shelter. Drank a lot of coffee. Didn't sleep much. I can't go to a rehab, bro. You know people in the FBI. How about the Witness Protection Program?"

"How about the *Witless* Protection Program, bro?" I snapped back at him. "Sorry. Cheap shot."

"It's okay," he said. But I knew it wasn't. The last thing he needed was a Big Brother lecture.

"Tell me what you know about Vicki's husband," I said.

"His name is Jack Pardini. If you go by the size of his house in Beverly Hills, his construction business is doing damn good. And if he found out I was doing his wife *and* lost her money, he'd kill us both."

"Let's cut to the chase," Jim said. "Where do we net out on all this?"

"I don't know, Dad. I gotta let this percolate. I'll be in touch." I stood up. Frankie didn't. I headed for my car.

Jim and the dogs followed. "Question," he said, as the dogs roamed off to pee. "How'd you find out Joanie gave him the twenty thousand bucks?"

"It was in next month's letter. I opened it in a moment of weakness."

"Did she say how I know?"

"She said she had no idea."

"The truth is, she told me."

"You're kidding. Why wouldn't she tell me that she told you?" I said. "No, no, forget that. Better question. Why would she tell you and not me?"

He rubbed his chin. Correction, chins. "She was a teacher. She had this philosophy. You never work with a student in a vacuum. You're part of a chain. Whatever you learn that will help other teachers help that kid, you pass on. That's why they have report cards and teacher evaluations that follow you from year to year. She didn't tell you because you're not Frankie's teacher. I am.

She was quite a woman, Joanie. The world lost a real gem. We all did."

I grabbed a pad and pencil from the car and jotted down Vicki's name and a few other pertinent details that I didn't want to forget.

"What are you writing?" Jim asked.

"My 'Things To Do' list. Buy dog food, catch serial killer, save brother's life."

"Not in that order," he said. "Thanks." He gave me a hug, then he whistled for the dogs and lumbered back to the house to stand guard over his wayward son.

CHAPTER 51

JERRY GOLDSTEIN HAD been right. Roberta's brisket and kasha varnishkes were excellent.

Roberta, on the other hand, had exaggerated. Her very handsome son had big ears, small hands, bad breath, and was four inches shorter than Penina.

Do Jewish mothers ever tell the truth about their sons when they're trying to fix them up, Penina wondered. Then she laughed quietly to herself. *I will, but that's only because my sons are perfect.*

The afternoon went by quickly, and, while the boys had fun playing with the Goldstein's grandsons, Dylan and Sammy, Penina had no doubt that Ari and Dov were counting the hours until they could go back to Familyland.

The next morning it was still dark when Penina felt Dov crawl into her bed. She snuggled up to him and said, "Go back to sleep. The park isn't open yet."

By the time the sun came up Dov was dressed. When Penina woke up at 7:30, he stood next to her bed and said, "I'm ready."

"That I can see," she said. "But I'm not, Ari's not, and the people at Familyland are not ready for you."

"Eemah," the boy whined, "get out of bed. We could be the first ones there when the gate opens."

"Shush, you'll wake your brother."

Ari mumbled something unintelligible from the other bed.

"He's up," Dov said. "Can we go now?"

"Can I go to the bathroom first?" she said, swinging her legs out of bed, grabbing him with two hands and kissing his forehead.

She sat on the toilet and changed her Tampax. She knew this would be the heaviest day of her flow. Perfect timing for riding the roller coaster, she thought. By the time she showered and dressed, Ari was awake. The TV was tuned to a black minister who was praising Jesus. "Church programs?" she said.

"This is the channel that always has the best cartoons," Dov said.

"Americans don't watch cartoons on Sunday morning," she said. "They show the church programs."

"Why?" said Dov. "It's boring."

"So they don't have to go," Ari said. "They turn on the TV, and they say they were at church, but all they did was watch TV. It's cheating."

"Don't judge others," Penina said.

"*Slichah*, Eemah," Dov said, apologizing.

The trip from their fifth-floor room to the rooftop restaurant took less than five minutes, but the boys had to turn it into an adventure. The hotel had slipped envelopes under the doors of every guest who was expected to check out that morning. "They're printouts of people's bills," Penina explained. "So they can look over all the charges before they check out."

"No," Ari said. "They're notices from Rambo that you're banished from Familyland and you have to go home." He ran down the corridor looking for rooms that had an envelope peeking out from the doorsill. "Room 547," he said, raising his hands and pointing all ten fingers at the door, "you're banished." He moved along and found the next envelope. "Room 539, you are also banished."

Little Dov ran ahead of his big brother. "Room 526," he said, mimicking Ari by raising both hands and pointing at the door, "you have offended the Gods and now you are banished from Familyland forever."

Just as he made his pronouncement, the door to Room 526 opened wide and a plump woman in pink shorts and a black McGreedy Moose T-shirt stepped out. "What do you mean I'm banished?" she said.

Dov shrieked and raced down the hall. Ari threw himself on the floor and rolled in mock laughter. "It's not that funny," Penina said, as she walked past him. "Behave yourself." She smiled at the woman and said, "Boys will be boys."

They rode the glass elevator to the rooftop. Happily for Penina there were no other passengers, so she let the boys hop, jump, and boomerang around the glass cage and then bow to the totally oblivious audience in the lobby below.

"I'm not hungry," Dov said as soon as they entered the restaurant.

"You're sitting at this table for thirty minutes, whether you eat or not," Penina said. "So don't think we'll leave any earlier if you starve yourself."

"In that case I'll have pancakes," Dov said.

Penina watched her two sons color the cartoon characters on their place mats with crayons while they waited for breakfast. "I think I'd like to go back to the Space Shuttle Restaurant for lunch," she said. "The food was good, and it's much faster than the fancy restaurants. Would you like that?"

Dov perked up. "Yes, fast restaurants are the best. I want an Astroburger and two bags of Spaceman Ice Cream Pellets. Chocolate and strawberry."

"How can you eat those?" Penina said. "It's all chemicals."

"I like chemicals," Dov said. "They're delicious. Especially the chocolate."

Penina laughed. "Fine. It's your stomach. I like their Caesar salad with grilled chicken," she said. And I like the small bathroom I found there, she thought. Much cleaner than the

241

big ones with a million toilets and all those women and little girls chattering like magpies. And much more private, she said to herself, as she looked in her purse to check on her supply of tampons.

They arrived at the gate by 9:04 and headed for the rides that the guidebook told them had the shortest lines early in the morning. Penina had delegated that responsibility to Ari, and he had planned it well. "I'm very proud of how you organized our morning," she told the ten-year-old. "Very efficient."

"Like my *Abba*," he said.

"Yes," she smiled, "very much like your father."

Ari's master plan included a beat-the-crowd lunch at exactly noon. The Space Shuttle Restaurant was only a few minutes from their last ride of the morning, and they arrived at 12:07. There were plenty of tables, the lines were short, and the streamlined fast-food operation moved people along quickly.

Penina found a table near the rear, convenient to the small ladies room she had discovered several days ago. As they ate, she looked around the restaurant and thought once again about her sons' observation in the synagogue. Security here was non-existent. So unlike Israel.

The salad was as good as she remembered. "You're finished," Dov said, when she finally put down her fork. "Let's go."

"You didn't eat all your ice cream," Penina said.

"It's freeze dried. I can just close the bag and put it in my pocket. It lasts forever."

"Well, my diet Coke is wet," she said. "I need time to drink it."

"Carry it with you," Dov said.

"I would also like to go to the ladies room," she added.

"Again?" Ari said. "You're going to mess up my whole schedule. We're supposed to get on line for The Freedom Train. This is the best time to go."

"Where is it from here?" Penina said.

"Close," Ari said. He took a dog-eared map from his pocket.

"Can Dov and I go first and get on line? You could catch up. We won't get lost. Please."

"You'll hold his hand?"

Both boys jumped up sensing victory. "Yes, yes, yes," they chanted.

"Alright, I'll catch up. But be careful. Don't talk to strangers. And don't get on the ride without me."

They bolted from the table before she could change her mind. She watched them walk out. Each in his own way was so much like his father.

She had met Yaakov in the army when they were both twenty. He was strong. He was handsome. He was brave. But he also had a sensitive side. He was a poet. A dreamer. His passion was his writing. Over the course of their ten-year marriage, he wrote seven books of poetry, none of which were published. But he always said, "If I could just sell that first one, people will want to read the others."

He supported his family doing what he had to do. Driving a delivery van, night janitor in a hospital, and of course, waiting on tables. As many hours a day as he could spare, he wrote. They lived in a one-bedroom apartment. The boys took the bedroom; Penina and Yaakov slept in the living room. They had no money for life's little luxuries like dinners at fancy restaurants, family vacations, or sadly, life insurance. So when Yaakov was killed in the bus explosion four years ago, Penina didn't even have the money to bury him.

The government paid for the funeral. And as the widow of a terror victim they gave her a monthly income. It was enough to get by, but never get ahead. She and the boys lived hand to mouth. And then, Chaim Schlott changed all that. Chaim owned five restaurants, including the one where Penina worked as a hostess. He was fifteen years older than Penina, a large, beefy man, with thick bushy eyebrows and hairy knuckles. He was coarse, he was dull, and he was physically unappealing. Chaim

Schlott was not a poet, but he was rich.

He ogled her body with all the subtlety of a pauper drooling outside a bakery shop window. I know I have beautiful legs, she thought, but that won't feed my children. So she spread her legs and undid her bra, and she let Chaim inside the bakery. In return he bought her jewelry. Expensive pieces which she sold and replaced with fakes. She pawned a pair of diamond stud earrings for $4,000 and replaced them with cubic zirconium. She sold a pearl necklace for $6,000 and substituted it for an imitation that cost only a few hundred.

He was very generous, and now he wanted to marry her. Her stomach knotted at the thought. She took another sip of her diet Coke, then reached into her purse, removed her wallet, and flipped it open to their last family picture.

Yaakov was forever handsome, forever young. He was wearing white shorts and a faded blue polo shirt with the logo of a restaurant he had worked for long ago. He was six-foot-three and had one arm around Penina's shoulder, and in his other arm he cradled the two-year-old Dov. Ari, who was only six at the time, stood between his parents. The picture had been taken on one of the rare Sundays that Yaakov didn't have to work. They had spent the afternoon in the park, and the camera had captured green trees, blue sky, and other happy picnickers in the background. Penina wondered how many of them were still as happy as they had been that Sunday.

"Yaakov," she said, in a whisper. She looked around to see if anyone was watching her, but everyone else was busy with their own lunch, their own families, their own lives.

She turned back to the photograph. "Yaakov, the boys and I could be happy with no money if you were here with us. But without you, I can't bear to see them living in poverty. Please forgive me for the things I must do."

A family of four entered the restaurant. The wife, a roly-poly redhead in too-tight khaki pants and a lime green T-shirt, pointed at the menu on the wall to let her husband know what she wanted. The husband and kids got on line, while the woman made her way toward the ladies room in the rear.

"Judy!" the husband yelled after his wife. She stopped.

Her name is Judy, Penina thought, as she stood up from the table and headed toward the bathroom herself.

The husband tilted his hand to his mouth and tipped it back and forth. "What're ya drinkin'?"

"Sprite," Judy called back. "Large." Then she continued on her way to the ladies room.

Penina got there first. Some of the rest rooms have dozens of toilets. But this one was tucked in an out-of-the-way corner, with only three stalls, two sinks, and a baby-changing table. Penina stepped into the first stall, locked the door, opened her purse, and removed a fresh Tampax and a small plastic pouch about the size of paperback book.

She quickly changed her Tampax. Then she unfolded the contents of the pouch and slipped them on. When she heard the chubby redhead enter the bathroom, Penina pressed the Start button on her stopwatch. The woman sat down in the third john, and soon Penina could hear the loud, steady stream of urine splashing into the toilet, followed by Judy's soft sigh of relief.

Penina flushed, went to one of the sinks and turned on the tap. Judy came out of her stall and stepped up to the other sink, oblivious to Penina, who was now wearing a pale blue jumpsuit of paper-thin Mylar over her clothes. Her shoes were covered with booties made of the same impenetrable material. A hood was pulled snugly to her face covering her hair and ears. Her hands, which she pretended to be washing, were encased in double-thick latex gloves.

The woman leaned over the sink, wet her hands, pushed the soap dispenser, and began lathering. Without hesitation, Penina plunged the dagger into Judy's carotid artery. Blood spurted like juice from a ripe grapefruit. Judy slumped over the sink and slid to the floor. Penina toppled her onto her back, removed the dagger, placed a Ziploc bag over the woman's left breast, and drove the blade through her heart, pinning the plastic bag to her chest.

She checked her stopwatch. It had taken seventy-two seconds from the time Judy had entered until Penina had ended her life. The next ninety seconds were critical. Penina cracked open the bathroom door and hung a yellow-and-black *Closed For Cleaning* sign on the outer knob. Then she wedged the door shut with a rubber doorstop.

She stepped over the pool of blood and returned to the stalls. Quickly, carefully, she removed her blood-spattered jump-suit. She took a pair of scissors from her bag and began cutting the suit along the lines she had marked earlier. She took the first three pieces, dropped one in each toilet and flushed. By the time the toilets had swallowed the evidence and recycled, she had finished cutting the rest of the jumpsuit. She pitched the bloody pieces into two of the toilets and flushed. The gloves and booties went in the last toilet. Six flushes, and every bloodstained fiber of her disposable assassin's outfit was flowing through Lamaar's state-of-the-art, high-power waste removal system.

Penina knelt close to the body. "Forgive me, Judy," she whispered. "I don't know who you are, only that you are some poor soul who was at the wrong place at the wrong time. You gave your life for my children. I promise to say the *mourner's kaddish* for you every day for a year."

The final toilet recycled at two minutes, forty seconds into the crime. Five seconds faster than when she had rehearsed it with a second jumpsuit on Friday.

Penina tiptoed back to the door, avoiding the growing red puddle. She removed the wedge, opened the door, removed the *Closed* sign from the outside knob, and jammed the sign and the doorstop into her purse.

She walked casually past her table, where a busboy was wiping it down. She did not look at the line where Judy's husband and children were now placing their order. Three minutes and fourteen seconds after it all began, Penina was outside heading toward the meeting with her two children.

CHAPTER 52

A FEW MINUTES LATER Penina found Ari and Dov waiting on line for The Freedom Train. As Ari's guidebook had predicted, the line was relatively short.

"Where were you?" Ari asked. "The train gets here in a few minutes. We were afraid you were going to miss it."

"Well, I didn't," she said. Then she took a tissue from her purse, wet it with her tongue and began wiping Dov's mouth. "It may be freeze-dried, but it's still chocolate." The boy squeezed his eyes shut, but held still for the cleaning.

The Freedom Train was the longest ride in the park. It circled the perimeter of most of the property, stopping at five stations along the way. Passengers could get on or off at will. Most people only took it two or three stops, to get from one end of Familyland to the other. That was Ari's plan. They were headed for The Spirit of '76 on the opposite end of the park.

Penina heard the train whistle and looked at her stopwatch, which was still marking time. Just under ten minutes. The locomotive was a beautiful replica of trains Penina had seen in the American movies of the Old West. The passenger cars were open, so people could get on and off quickly, as well as get an unobstructed view of the scenery.

About fifty people exited the train, and the line to board started moving. Ari and Dov ran to the front and sat in the first car directly behind the engineer, a robust, middle-aged black man, whose name tag said Samuel. Nice Jewish name, Penina thought, as she caught up with her sons and stepped aboard.

And then came the sound she had been waiting for. Three musical chimes rang out from every speaker in the park. They were the signal that an announcement was about to be made on the Public Address system.

"Buddy Longo, please report to Area 47," the voice said. "Buddy Longo, Area 47. Thank you."

Penina looked at her stopwatch. Thirteen minutes and twenty-seven seconds. She stopped the timer and reset it.

None of the park visitors paid attention to the announcement. But the employees all stopped when they heard the words 'Buddy Longo.' She could see in their faces they knew something was wrong. They just didn't know what.

A dark-skinned woman in a conductor's uniform was in the cab behind Samuel. Her name tag said Valencia. "Buddy Longo," she said to the engineer.

"Haven't had one of those in about two months," Samuel said.

"Where's Area 47?" Valencia asked.

Dov had set his bag of ice cream pellets on the seat next to him. Penina picked it up and pretended to read the label, so she wouldn't be noticed tuning in to the conversation between the engineer and the conductor.

Samuel pulled a spiral-bound book of maps from his pocket and flipped through the pages. "Forty-Seven. The Space Shuttle Restaurant."

"Kitchen fire, I bet," Valencia said.

"No way, kid. Buddy Longo is for the big stuff. Heart attack, probably."

"You ever have a Buddy Longo on the train?" Valencia asked.

"Nope," he said. "Seven years. Plenty of vomiting, a bunch of first-aid stuff, but no Buddy Longos."

A man in a RedKap uniform held up the line of passengers.

"Freedom Train's all full up, folks," he said. "Next one's in eight minutes."

Samuel turned around so he could see Dov and Ari in the front car. "Which one of you young gentlemen wants to help me blow this train whistle?"

The brothers jumped up, each yelling, "Me! Me! Me!"

"Take turns," Samuel said, handing Dov a long metal chain. The boy pulled it and the train whistle tooted loudly. He passed the chain to Ari who yanked it hard. The whistle blew for a solid five seconds before Samuel gently removed it from his hand. The engine chugged and they started to move.

"All aboard! All aboard the Freedom Train," Valencia bellowed. "Please remain seated and keep your hands and legs inside the train at all times."

Penina sat back in her seat and tried to come to grips with what she was feeling. She had killed before. When she was younger, she and Yaakov were operatives in the army. They had killed to survive. In Israel, even poets learned to kill. This, she reasoned, was no different. This too was about survival.

Yes, thought Penina, I have just earned more money in one brief span of time than Yaakov earned in his entire life. Now my sons will have what they need, and never again will I have to see, smell, or touch Chaim Schlott.

She closed her eyes and felt the cool breeze on her brow. She breathed in deeply, anticipating the sweet smell of the poppies and wildflowers that bloomed along the tracks. Instead her nostrils filled with diesel fumes spewing from the locomotive. She smiled. This, she decided, was a message from Yaakov.

"*My darling*," he said to her. "*You and the boys have suffered long enough. Your own personal journey aboard The Freedom Train has finally begun.*"

CHAPTER 53

WHEN YOU'RE TRYING to solve the highest profile homicide in the Department, you don't get days off. It was Sunday. I was working. So were Terry and the rest of the Lamaar Task Force. Everyone showed up, except Matt Diamond, who called in to let us know that his wife Rae was in labor.

"How many centimeters dilated is she?" Terry asked.

"Three," Diamond said.

"Can you come in and work till she's up to nine?" Biggs said, in his best official, by-the-book, police detective voice.

Diamond, who is new to our squad, panicked. He started to stumble through an explanation of why he couldn't possibly leave his wife alone, when Biggs let him off the hook. "Just busting your balls, Diamond. Twisted cop-working-on-a-Sunday joke. Have a nice baby."

Terry hung up and threw his hands in the air. "First Falco and now Diamond. This maternity crap is dragging us down. Goddamn horny cops can't keep their dicks in their pants."

"I wondered why we couldn't solve this case," I said.

The Chief of the Los Angeles Police was working Sunday too. He showed up looking very natty in his Protestant golfwear, and gave me and Terry twenty minutes to debrief him. He was teeing off with the Mayor and wanted to be able to answer any and all questions. The Mayor, in turn, would be attending a black-tie dinner with the Governor that evening and also needed to be kept in the loop. All those powerful people working on our behalf, and so far we had squat.

Ziff the Sniff, my friend in Narcotics, was also working Sunday, and he called to say they had arrested a suspect in the Trachtenberg murder. Tino Santiago, a low-level drug runner who settled an old score with Dr. Trachtenberg by sticking an ice pick through his heart.

"Well, at least there's some good news today," I said.

"I don't think it's gonna wind up being such good news for the widow," Ziff said. "Santiago lawyered up, and he's willing to drop a dime on a couple of big rats in the drug sewer if we lower the homicide charge to something lighter."

"Like what?"

"He'd like it to be self-defense, but the D.A. will go for voluntary manslaughter."

"That sucks," I said.

"Tell it to the D.A.," Ziff said. "I already did. I told him hang Santiago; I'll figure out how to get the drug lords. I don't want to give up this homicide."

"I guess a homicide collar looks good on your record," I said.

"Screw my record," he said. "I'm the best Narc they got. I could walk into the Chief's office, piss on his desk, tell him it's part of a new urine-testing technique I'm developing, and he'd say, Keep up the good work. I don't want to give up the homicide collar because I personally believe that people who kill other people should be shot or fried or at least locked up for life."

"I'm sorry for the crack about your record," I said. "I didn't know you were so passionate."

"This is why I can't work Homicide, Lomax. I hate the trade-offs that the dickhead D.A.s are willing to make. Trachtenberg was a partially law-abiding citizen, whose biggest crime was he wanted to cop some dope. Santiago is thirty-seven years old and has been infecting the system since he was seventeen. I hate that he gets to skip, just because he happens to know some shit about an even worse bunch of scumbags. I told the D.A. don't make the deal. It's like telling Lassie not to lick his balls."

I decided this would not be a good time to remind Sergeant Ziffer that Lassie is a girl and has no balls. I thanked him and asked if he'd please follow up with the victim's family.

"Not my favorite thing to do," he said. "But I know you got your plate full with this Lucas homicide."

"Yeah," I said. Even someone as wired into the Department as Ziff still had no idea that we were chasing a serial killer.

It was about 12:45, and I was getting hungry. I went to the coffee room, poured myself some of the lukewarm brown beverage that was in the pot and grabbed a few cookies from a box that some thoughtful wife had sent in for her husband's buddies who had to work on Sunday.

The only one not working today was the voice inside my head. He wasn't saying a word, but, as usual, he wrote me a list of reminders on my mental chalkboard. *Stop Vicki Pardini from killing your brother. Take Diana out two more times so you can get to the date when you can sleep with her. Find a cure for cancer, so Hugo Cordner won't die. Get your fat ass to the gym, and stop eating cookies.* I was about to grab one more cookie, just to show him who's boss, when Terry bolted into the room. "Code Blue. Pack your bags."

'Code Blue' is not real cop-speak. It may be hospital-speak. In fact it may only be TV show hospital-speak. But Terry likes to use it instead of any of the official LAPD language that would indicate Emergency. Sometimes, when he's feeling real creative, he cups one of his hands and broadcasts into it, "Calling all cars, calling all cars." I think it's something he picked up from Dick Tracy.

I chucked the cookies and coffee and ran back to my desk for my jacket and a radio. Terry filled me in. "Another homicide at Familyland. White female. Stabbed in the ladies room. She's a civilian. A tourist."

"Number three in a series?" I said.

"Don't know yet," he said. "At this point, anybody farts in that jurisdiction, you and me are on the guest list. There's a chopper meeting us at the helipad. They don't want us to deal with Sunday traffic."

I grabbed my stuff, and we headed for the door. I took one last look at the chalkboard in my head. The cure for cancer would have to wait another day.

CHAPTER 54

THE TRIP TO Familyland was swift and angry.

A black and white was waiting for us in front of the station house, lights flashing, rear doors open.

Two uniforms were in the front seat, Brown and Pagnozzi. Brown is black and Pagnozzi is green. White actually, but he's only had about six months on the job. Brown, on the other hand, is months away from his twenty years, but the smart money says he's going to re-up. Young cop, old cop; white cop, black cop; silent cop, chatty cop; it was a marriage made in Headquarters.

"Good afternoon, Detectives," Brown said. "*My* partner and I were trying to figure out whether we wanted to finish eating our lunch or taxi you boys to the Federal Building. Thank you for helping us make the wise choice."

Biggs and Brown were old friends, and ball busting was the cornerstone of their relationship. "Hell, Brownie," Terry said, "My partner and I are so critical to this homicide investigation that we have to be there no matter whose two-hour lunch gets cut short. The Governor himself is counting on you to get us to a kiddy park so we can look at a dead body in record time." He exhaled. "Or he just needs a couple of scapegoats, and it's our turn in the barrel."

"Somebody's got a major bug up his ass," Brown said.

"I got every politician in the state up my ass," Terry said. "So hurry it up. They can't hang anybody out to dry until we get there."

Terry's flare-up was out of character. "Chill out," I said. "Witch hunts happen, but it's too soon to crucify us yet. This thing has gone from one murder to three in a week. How long did it take them to nail the Unibomber or Son of Sam? We have to get a few more at bats before there's a public flogging."

"Sorry," he said. "I don't usually give a shit about LAPD politics. I'm not sure why this one got to me."

"So we should keep going to the helipad?" Brown said. "I was about to tell Pags to make a U-turn and head for the nearest psych ward."

I knew Pagnozzi was a cowboy when he peeled out before our asses even hit the back seat. He drove like he must have dreamed about when he was a kid wanting to be a cop. The car careened to a screeching stop at the Fed Building in less than six minutes. He jumped out and opened my door. Brown turned to Terry and said, "Sorry, pal, I don't do doors or windows. Have a nice day."

I thanked Pagnozzi and followed Terry into the building through a revolving door, where we hit our first security checkpoint. We ID'd ourselves to the corporal at the desk and were escorted to an elevator by another Marine who had the steely eyes and square jaw you see in the recruiting posters.

Private Square Jaw rode with us to the top of the Fed and turned us over to yet another Marine who escorted us to a chopper. For the remainder of the eighteen-minute trip to Familyland, Terry didn't say much and I said even less. For one thing, we didn't have much to say. But mostly because you can't be heard on a helicopter unless you talk into headsets, and that's about as private as Open Mic Night at the Comedy Club.

We landed in an empty parking lot, were whisked to a black Suburban, then transferred to a turbo-charged golf cart that barreled us along the Lamaar Underground Highway. We came to a stop at a sign that said *Area 47, Space Shuttle Restaurant.*

Parking lot to restaurant, four minutes.

"We should use this travel agent more often," Terry said, as we followed our guide through a passageway that would take us to the World Above.

Terry is funny, but he doesn't know when to draw the line. Not everyone is in the mood to yuck it up at a homicide investigation. "Could that please be the last funny thing you say until we're alone again?" I said politely.

"It could," he said. "And bless you for thinking that was actually funny. We artists need positive feedback to keep us going."

The Space Shuttle looked like a Burger King on steroids. Jessica hadn't set up shop yet, so it hadn't yet taken on the familiar trappings of a crime scene. But the kitchen was closed, the cash registers were silent, and the people who stayed had been herded to one corner of the room. Crime scene in the making.

"Detectives!" It was Curry. He looked happy to see us, which I suspected was as happy as he was going to be all day.

"This is our worst nightmare," he said. "They killed a woman. A guest. She was here on vacation with her husband and two kids. We've got the family in a booth in the corner. A doc is taking care of the daughter who is hysterical."

"Where's the victim?" Terry said.

Curry tipped his head, and we followed him toward the rear of the place. "Where's your shadow?" I asked.

"Amy? She's with the family. The lawyers are circling the next of kin like birds of prey. She's actually making sure they don't jump the gun."

"Glad she has something to do besides hang with us."

"I can't muzzle her, but I told her not to dick around with you guys. She's all balls, but this has got her pretty shook up. This will probably make her easier to work with."

Terry couldn't resist. "Or harder."

CHAPTER 55

THE VICTIM WAS Judy Kaiser. White, forty-four, a soccer Mom with a minivan. She worked as a fundraiser at the local PBS station in Minneapolis. Her husband, Russell, was a minister and a Civil War buff. The kids, Luther, eleven, and Becky, fourteen, were 4-H and drug-free. The Kaisers were as close to apple pie as you could get in MTV America. The only things missing were Wally and The Beaver.

Judy's number must really have been up. Not only had she picked the wrong bathroom at the wrong time, but the Kaisers had been scheduled to visit Familyland during Spring Break a month ago. Unfortunately for Judy, she came down with the flu. So she and Russell decided to take the kids out of school for a few days to make it up to them.

She had gone to the bathroom as soon as the family entered the restaurant. Ten minutes later, she hadn't returned, so young Becky went to see if her mother was okay; an experience that will haunt her for the rest of her life. She opened the bathroom door and screamed bloody murder, which it literally had been. The father and Lori Lum, the restaurant manager, another longtime Lamaar employee, ran back to the bathroom.

Reverend Kaiser is a volunteer ambulance driver, so he knows dead when he sees it. Judy was definitely dead. He knew enough not to touch the knife in her chest, but he knelt at her side, which contaminated some of the scene. He calmed his daughter, while Ms. Lum paged Buddy Longo, setting off a chain of events similar to NORAD going on Red Alert.

The first two security people arrived within thirty seconds. They made some major dumb decisions, not because they were dumb, but because they were trained to protect the company's image, instead of the crime scene.

The Lamaar people were like terriers about their image. Even the yellow crime-scene tape ended up stretched from one inside wall to another, far from the eyes of the happy park patrons on the other side of the metal gates.

Terry and I peeked in at the body. Mrs. Kaiser was fish-belly white in a pool of her own blood. A dagger was sticking out of her chest. I got close enough to see that the knife had been driven through a plastic bag which contained an envelope. There was writing on the front, but the blood on the baggie made it impossible to read. I could, however, make out something else inside the plastic. A flipbook.

I called over my shoulder to Brian. "Did you see the murder weapon?"

"It's a letter opener with one of our characters on the handle," he said. "I'm pretty sure it's something we sell. I sent some of our people to the gift shops to check it out."

"Did you touch anything?"

"Not me. But the daughter, the husband, the restaurant manager, and one of our security people have blood on their shoes. Kaiser remembers touching his wife's face and feeling for a pulse, but he swears he didn't touch the weapon."

"Lock this bathroom up till the lab rats get here," I said. "Any witnesses? And don't hold shit back, or this is just going to be number three in a never-ending series of theme park homicides."

We sat at a table in the center of the room, and Brian signaled to a young couple to join us. The man was in his early thirties, athletic looking, buzz cut, dressed in a T-shirt and jeans like your typical tourist. Undercover Security. The woman had an innocent girlish face, and, with the right wig and makeup, could pass for fifteen. Right now, she looked like the guy's age-appropriate wife.

"These are two of our best security people," Brian said. "We've beefed up the detail in the past few days, but these guys have been with us for a while. This is Karen Gill." The woman nodded. Great smile; nice decoy.

Before Brian could go on, the man stuck his hand out. "Hi. Kenneth Dahl. D-A-H-L. Terrible thing, what happened today. Terrible."

"Detectives Lomax and Biggs," I said. "Nice to meet you, Ken."

"I prefer Kenneth," he said.

"Okay, Kenneth," I said. I didn't look at Terry, because if he were smirking, I didn't want to catch it. "Tell us what happened."

"We were walking past the Arctic Expedition, when we heard the Buddy Longo," he said. He hesitated, not sure we understood.

"Go ahead, we know what it is," I said.

"We're not supposed to blow our cover, so we didn't run. We walked real fast like we were a couple of hungry tourists. Karen and Lori, the manager, went into the ladies room. I went over to the dad and the screaming kid."

"No question that the woman was dead," Karen said. "I told Lori to shut down the kitchen and lower the electric gates."

"To keep people in?"

"Out. You can't lock guests in. Not if they want to get out."

"What are you talking about?" Terry said. "Of course you can lock *guests* in. It's a crime scene."

Brian jumped in. "Guys, we train our people to *contain*, but not *detain*."

"Meaning?"

"Get control of a bad situation, but don't detain the innocent bystanders."

Terry raised his voice. "How the hell do you know who's innocent?"

"I think in this case our people made a decision that there was an adverse situation, but that whoever did it wouldn't stick around to finish their lunch."

"Yeah, I'd say a woman with a knife in her chest is an *adverse* situation," Terry said. "Good call, Kenneth, but not so smart on letting people go."

"It wasn't just our call," I-Prefer-Kenneth said. "Even before we shut down, a dozen security guys showed up. One of the suits tells the crowd we have a medical emergency. 'Sorry to mess up your lunch, but you all have to leave, and we're gonna give you each a fifty-dollar gift certificate you can use at any of our gifts shops or other restaurants.'"

The door that connects to the underground passageway opened and Jessica Keating and her merry band of criminalists trooped in. "Afternoon, gentlemen," she said. "We've got to stop meeting like this."

Terry was livid. "Hello, Jessica. We've got one dead body and about a hundred possible eyewitnesses who might be able to ID the killer. Oh, no, wait. The crack security team sent them away and gave them spending money."

Brian stood up, which immediately gave him more presence than anyone in the room. "Whatever they saw, we've got on our surveillance cameras," he said. "And when they turn in their gift certificates, we ask for a driver's license, so we'll know who they are."

Terry stood too, until he was as eyeball to eyeball with Brian as one can be without getting kissed or hit. "Great, and we can follow them home to Kansas or Taiwan or wherever, and then ask them if they saw anything."

Brian didn't blink. "Hey, I don't expect you guys to understand Lamaar policy, but let me spell it out for you. The people who were in this restaurant are our public. They're not the same as a bunch of homeless winos who you can just wrangle up and hassle as much as you want."

"What did you think we were going to do to your precious public? Kick 'em in the nuts? Letting them go just hurts our investigation."

"Not as much as interrogating them would hurt our reputation," Brian said, his voice reaching an un-Lamaar-like decibel level. "You may think I sound like a corporate asshole, but we can't have people going back to Kansas or Taiwan or wherever telling their friends that Familyland was a real hoot, except for the part where some lady got stabbed to death in the bathroom."

A shrill whistle pierced the air. Jessica, two fingers in her mouth, had generated enough noise to hail three cabs in a snowstorm. As soon as she had our undivided attention, she cocked her head, and, in her nails-on-a-blackboard nasal Chicago voice, said, "This was supposed to be my day off. Now would one of you buckets of testosterone show me the DOA, or did I come at a bad time?"

By default, I got to play Good Cop. I took Jessica back to the ladies room and told her that whatever was inside the plastic bag was our highest priority.

"I must have sounded like a total PMS-ing shrew back there," she said.

"Don't apologize," I said. "They had it coming."

"No they didn't, but I'm glad I let them have it anyway. I wish I could be that assertive all the time." She stopped when she saw Judy Kaiser and knelt next to the body. "You poor woman," she said. Then without looking away from the victim, she added, "Lomax, leave us alone please. I've got work here."

It took the better part of two hours for Jessica and her team to take their pictures, vacuum up hairs and fibers, and dust for fingerprints, which was basically fruitless since we were dealing with a public restroom.

Amy joined us, and to Brian's credit, she was not at all

abusive, which for her was model behavior. We also learned that the letter opener was indeed another souvenir from the Lamaar gift assortment of fine murder weapons. The plastic handle was molded in the shape of J.J. Hogg, the world's richest pig.

"Sounds like a rip-off of Scrooge McDuck," Terry said.

"Not so loud," Brian said. "Disney agrees with you. They're suing us."

"Some nerve," Terry said. "Like they're the only ones who can have a billionaire farm animal?"

Brian tried to hide a smile, but the amusement twinkled in his eyes. Now that the tension between the two of them had diffused, I figured we could have some real laughs together, if it weren't for this damn triple homicide.

Finally, Jessica came out of the ladies room and announced what we were waiting to hear. "You've got mail." She held out a stainless steel medical tray. In the center was a sealed white, business-sized envelope. We all stared at it like it was the original of the Magna Carta.

"Can you open it?" I asked.

"Forensically, yes," she said. "But first let me read you the message on the envelope. Quote, *Police, deliver directly to Morris Rosenlicht or his heirs. If you open it, you'll be the cause of the next victim's death.* Unquote. Now, are you sure you want me to open it?"

"Who's Morris Rosenlicht?" Terry said.

"I think I know." It was Amy.

"Can you tell us?" I said.

"This is really very weird," she said. "Give me a minute."

She opened her cell phone and walked toward a corner.

"What about the flipbook?" I said.

Jessica held out a second stainless steel tray. The book in the tray looked like the others. "I don't want to manhandle it any more than I already have, so let me just act it out for you."

She started with a closed hand, then put her thumb and

forefinger in a circle and held the other three fingers in the air. "I think it means, 'everything's going great.' Something like that."

"It's also the 'three-ring' sign," Terry said. "Ask the man for Ballantine."

Jessica shook her head. "You lost me."

"Ballantine Beer. Gosh, Jess, I guess you're not the man you think you are."

Amy rejoined the group. "I just called Ike Rose," she said. "He's on a plane back from New York. He'll be here in a few hours."

"Ma'am, with all due respect," Terry said, as politely as I'd seen him in recent days, "we've either got to deliver this envelope, or ignore the warning and open it. We don't have time to wait for the head of the company."

"The letter is addressed to the head of the company," she said. "Mr. Rose was born Isaac Rosenlicht. He changed his name in business school. His father was Morris Rosenlicht. He's dead. This letter *is* meant for Ike Rose."

"This gets sicker and sicker by the minute," Terry said.

Brian circled his fingers in the three-ring sign. "Detective Biggs," he said. "For the first time today, you and I are in violent agreement."

CHAPTER 56

IT WAS AFTER five o'clock when Ike Rose arrived. He wanted to personally express his condolences to the dead woman's family, but we had interviewed them and sent them to a hotel over an hour ago.

He wanted to see the latest victim. We tried to discourage him, but he wouldn't take no for an answer.

"This is madness," he said, when he came back from the blood-spattered ladies room. "She was a guest. An innocent woman. A wife, a mother."

"Can you talk," I said, "or do you need some time?"

He shook his head. "I'm fine. I mean, I'm not fine. Nobody here is fine, but I can talk." He sat down at a table, lit a cigarette, and sucked in the poison.

Jessica set the envelope on the table. She had already photographed it, dusted it for prints, checked out the paper and the ink, and done a field-level analysis. If there were any clues like DNA, she'd find out in the lab.

Rose stared at it. *"Deliver directly to Morris Rosenlicht or his heirs.* That's my father," he said. "He died last year. Oh, Jesus, it says if you open it, you'll be the cause of the next victim's death. The guy's a madman."

"We don't usually take orders from madmen," Terry said. "But in this case we decided to wait till you got here."

"This is Jessica Keating," I said. "Forensics. I'd like her to open it."

"We all know what it's going to say," Rose said. "'*Dear Ike, you're next.*' I've gotten death threats before, but never from someone who has successfully demonstrated his capabilities beyond any shadow of a doubt."

"Is there a reason somebody would want to kill you?" I asked.

"Same reason someone wants to kill every politician, every corporate leader, or their gym teacher. Somewhere along the line I did something to piss him off. Only most people don't act out their resentment the way this guy has. Go ahead, Miss Keating. Open it."

Jessica sliced the side of the envelope open with an X-acto knife, then used long tweezers to pull out a single sheet of paper. She unfolded it gingerly and began reading. "*Hello, Isaac. By now we hope we have proven we can kill your employees, your customers, or anyone else who associates with Lamaar. We are capable of killing many, many more. If you'd like the killing to stop, it will cost you two hundred sixty-six point four million dollars.*"

Rose sprang up like he was zapped by a cattle prod. "What the fuck! They want money? This is Danny Eeg. He's been trying to get money out of us for years. Who else knows my father's name? You've got to arrest this guy."

"There's more," Jessica said. "*The amount is not negotiable. Once you agree to pay the money, place a notice in the Classified Section of the LA Times stating that the family of the late Buddy Longo thanks his friends and co-workers for their love and support during our time of grief. When that notice runs, you'll get further instructions. Until it runs, the killings will continue.*"

"The killings will continue," Rose said. "This is insane."

Jessica went on. "*If you don't respond within five days, I will notify the media of everything you have tried to keep secret. Mainly, that being associated with Lamaar can be extremely hazardous to your health. After that, we won't have to kill your people or your customers or your suppliers. They'll desert you in droves, and that will definitely have a negative impact on your bottom line."*

Jessica set the letter down. "There's no signature. Nothing else," she said.

Not a single person in the room had any difficulty processing the clear-cut instructions. Yet, for a good ten seconds, no one said a word. Not even Amy.

Finally, Rose spoke. "He's right. Thousands of our employees would quit if they thought that working for us would put their lives at risk. That would cripple our operations, but I think we could weather that. And if the public finds out that a woman was murdered in Familyland just because she decided to spend her vacation here, we will lose hundreds of millions of dollars in revenue. It would rock this company to its foundations, but I think that long-term we could weather that as well." His voice was calm. His thought process was no longer driven by emotions. Once again he was a CEO analyzing a business problem. He took another drag on his cigarette. "What we won't be able to deal with is Wall Street. What investor in his right mind would want to put money into a company whose customers and employees are abandoning it in fear for their lives? Lamaar stock would be in the toilet. Now, wouldn't that make Danny Eeg happy? Speaking of which, I think this would be a good time to give me an update on where you are with Mr. Eeg."

I filled him in on Falco's interview with Eeg. "I'll be honest," I said. "Even with his vendetta, Eeg never fit the profile of a serial killer. But this case is no longer just about multiple homicides. Now what we've got is an extortion plot."

"Pay $266.4 million or we'll cripple your company? I'd say that's one hell of an extortion plot, Detective."

"Mr. Rose, we've got a lot of new evidence here. LAPD will bring in the FBI and we will do whatever it takes to catch the person or persons behind this," I said. "And we would strongly urge you not to pay the ransom."

"I don't intend to," he said.

I was a little surprised he had made that decision. Amy was a lot surprised. She let out a little gasp. Rose looked at her, then turned back to me. "I've always admired the people who stood up to terrorists and refused to meet their demands. I just never thought I'd be forced to make that decision myself."

"Sir, excuse me." Amy was finally talking. "Do you plan to consult with the Board of Directors?"

"I'll tell the Board what I've decided, but I'm not going to put the burden on them," Rose said. "According to my contract, this is my call, and I repeat, I am not paying the ransom."

We were seeing a different side of Amy. The Corporate Kiss-Ass obviously disagreed with her boss's decision and she was letting him know it. "But, sir, the ransom note says that if you don't pay, they'll keep killing people connected with Lamaar."

"Yes, I know," Rose said. Then he turned to me and Terry. "That puts the pressure on you, gentlemen. Find out who's behind this. And find out fast."

He dropped his cigarette on the floor, stepped on it, and walked out of the room.

PART TWO

BOILING THE BUNNY

CHAPTER 57

WE WERE BACK in the office by 8 p.m. The chopper deposited us on the roof of the Federal Building and another pair of uniforms picked us up in a black and white. This was a male-female team. It was the first time I'd ever met them, but I'd bet anything they were teaming up after their shift was over.

Terry agreed. "Hell, yeah. Did you see his body language? He practically announced that he's banging her."

"And I thought it was my keen detective skills that had led me to deduce that," I said. "But then if I were a real detective they wouldn't be calling in the Feds to solve my case."

"Help solve," he said. Terry, who had been pissy on the way down to Familyland, had mellowed now that we were back on our home turf.

I, on the other hand, was tired, hungry, and cranky. "Sending for the Feebies," I said, loud enough for half the squad room to look up, "is like making a public announcement that the crime we're supposed to be solving has now escalated beyond our Level of Competence."

"It's not beyond our level of anything," Terry said. "You and I could've found D.B. Cooper if we'd have caught that case. But you gotta admit this one has escalated. It's a serial killer, plus big bucks extortion. And now that they're threatening to kill anybody associated with Lamaar, you got your terrorism factor.

Three mints in one. Sounds like a Federal case to me. That still doesn't mean that a couple of schmucks from LAPD can't solve it."

"Okay, schmuck, how do we solve it?"

"Divide and conquer. We both have the same learning curve, and there's too much work to do for the two of us to be doing it together."

"Flip a coin," I said. "Winner flies to New York on the corporate jet and interviews Eeg. Loser gets to stay in L.A. and tell half-truths to the FBI."

"Hey, if you think flying back and forth across the country in one day is first prize, you take New York," Terry said. "I'd rather suffer the FBI and still get home in time to have dinner with my girls."

"Deal," I said. "Let me call my travel agent." I called Brian Curry who had been waiting to hear which one of us was going and how soon we could leave.

"I'll have a car pick you up at 5:30 tomorrow morning," he said. "You'll be wheels up out of Burbank at six."

"Don't I have to check in an hour and a half before flight time?"

"No, and if you're late, they'll wait. Is there anything special you want to order for breakfast, lunch, or dinner?"

"You mean like a kosher meal?

"I mean like anything."

"No, I'll take pot luck. Just don't forget that reading material you promised me." Now that we were positive we were dealing with a crime against Lamaar, I had asked Brian to pull together as much backgrounder information on the company as he could find.

"It's already on the airplane." I could practically hear him grinning.

I called F.X. Falco in upstate New York. I had spoken to him earlier, filled him in on the latest murder, and told him to make sure Eeg didn't skip town before someone from LAPD got there.

Now I gave him my flight details.

"A friend of mine is an ATC at Stewart. I'll be watching you land from the tower," he said. "See you tomorrow."

The next call was to Kemp Loekle. When Joanie and I first rented the house, our landlord sent Kemp over to repair the washing machine. Then Joanie hired him to build shelves in the laundry room, then in the closets, and in no time flat she adopted him. Kemp is forty-five and single, and a good part of his life revolves around women, beer, and motorcycles. Most important he loves dogs. He's particularly nuts about Andre, and he dog-sits whenever I'm in a bind.

His machine picked up. Sunday night. Kemp probably had his beefy mitts wrapped around a babe, a bottle of Beck's, or the handlebars of his 1980 Yamaha 1100 XS. "It's almost an antique," he always tells me.

"So are you," I always answer back.

I left Kemp a message outlining his tour of duty as Andre's caretaker. Then I dialed Big Jim. "I'm calling from the phone in the Squad Room," I said, which was my way of letting him know we'd have to talk in code. "So, how is that mangy dog who came crawling home the other night?"

"I got him on a short leash," Jim said.

"Glad to hear that. I'll be out of town on a case, but if the dog tries to run away or do anything stupid, call me."

"Hey, if the dog tries to run away," Jim said, chuckling, "I may just put him out of his misery myself."

CHAPTER 58

WHEN I STEPPED out of the house at 5:30, the car was already waiting. Actually it was a car and a half; a stretch Lincoln with a back seat big enough to have its own zip code.

The driver held the rear door open and said a polite good morning. I picked up a slight European accent. I sat back, and he glided the car silently up and over a dark, dewy Laurel Canyon toward Burbank Airport.

Captain Ted Sheppard was waiting for me on the tarmac. He was fortyish, tall, and had the classic square-cut jaw that always gives me added confidence in any pilot's flying ability. His face was copper colored and smooth shaven, except for the sole patch of blond hair under his lower lip. "I'll give you the fifty-cent tour," he said as he escorted me up the steps of the twin-engine Gulfstream IVSP. I know enough about planes from hanging out with Big Jim to calculate that we were fifty-cent touring an aircraft that cost upwards of thirty mill.

"Seats fifteen," he said. "You could've invited fourteen friends."

In the forward cabin were two single seats upholstered in tan and gray leather, and a matching three-cushion divan. The mid cabin had a grouping of four more leather chairs, two on the left, two on the right, each pair with a polished burl cherry wood table between them.

"Captain, you're spoiling me for coach," I said.

"Hell, I'll spoil you for first class. And there's no need to call me Captain," he said, removing his navy blue uniform jacket. Underneath was a crisp, white short-sleeved shirt with blue-and-gold epaulets on the shoulder. On his left breast pocket the words 'Air Rambo' were embroidered. Below that was a colorful logo—Rambunctious Rabbit flying upside down in a biplane. "As you can see, we're a lot more informal than the other airlines. Call me Shep."

He opened the door to the aft cabin. "This is your conference room." The chairs in the conference grouping were green leather, which picked up the color of the dark green squares on the plush maroon carpeting.

"Food, liquid refreshment, and rest room facilities are back here," Shep said, as we made our way aft into a compact galley. I caught the early-morning smell of fresh coffee and cinnamon buns, plus an extremely provocative scent, which turned out to belong to an equally provocative woman.

"This is Sig," Shep said, pointing in the direction of the coffee, the buns, and the perfume. "She can feed you, hook you up to the Internet, darn your socks; you name it, she'll do it. And if she can't figure it out, we'll land and pick up somebody who can."

Sig was the flight attendant grown men dream about. Her thick, red hair had that lustrous shine you see in shampoo commercials, but never in real women standing less than an arm's length away. She wore a starched white blouse and a navy skirt that were just tight enough and short enough to show off enough of her kickass body to make me want to see more.

"My socks are fine," I said, "but I could use some of that coffee."

Sig poured some into a paper cup that had the Rambo logo on it. "I can't use the good china till after we're airborne," she said.

"Which will be in less than five minutes," Shep said. "Why don't you grab a seat? Actually, you're our only passenger today, so feel free to grab them all."

He headed for the cockpit, and I settled into one of the leather chairs in the front cabin. Take-off was effortless. I've been on corporate jets before, so unless I get invited to fly on Air Force One, I'm not that easy to impress, but I did get a kick out of the fact that the announcements from the flight deck were aimed directly at me.

"Good morning again, Mike," Shep said ten minutes into the flight. "We'll be cruising at 37,000 feet, smooth air all the way. Estimated time of arrival is 2:44 p.m. If there's anything you need, just holler. Enjoy your breakfast, and thank you for choosing Air Rambo."

Sig brought me coffee, a basket of pastries, six different jams, and three kinds of butter. She was walk-right-past-any-club-bouncer gorgeous, one-step-ahead-of-you efficient, and she left behind a light trail of perfume that wafted up into my brain and immediately started working its way south. I wondered how many times I could push the Call button before she realized all I really wanted was to get her within sniffing distance. Whatever I might still be going through over the death of my wife, my hormones were officially out of mourning.

The breakfast menu had no fewer than twenty items on it. I ordered the egg white omelet with spinach and mushrooms. Sig went back to the galley and I pulled out my notes on the man I was flying across country to interrogate. I had read the case file on Eeg a dozen times, but I had to read it again. I was like the hungry man who keeps going back to the same empty refrigerator thinking that some tasty delight will suddenly appear.

CHAPTER 59

DANIEL SVEN EEG was born in L.A. in 1947. A sister, Inge, was born the year before. His father, Lars, had been in the Army with Dean Lamaar and wound up in the inner circle at Lamaar Studios. Danny was a Hollywood kid who went into the biz after college. He made good money writing for TV, mostly cop shows. Got married at thirty and divorced four years later. A few years after that, he knocked up a twenty-two-year-old actress wannabe, Barbara Schneiderman, a.k.a. Bonita Storm, and they had a son, Colby.

Eeg was fourteen when his father got squeezed out of Lamaar. They paid Lars some blood money, and he tried to make a go of it as a serious artist. He flopped and a few years later started working at a small studio doing TV cartoons. Steady work, but a big comedown from his heyday at Lamaar. Then he developed Parkinson's. It escalated to the point where he couldn't draw.

One night in '85 he comes home, pulls his car into the garage, and leaves the motor running. Not only does it kill Lars, but the fumes leak through to the kitchen, catch a spark from the stove, and boom, the house gets leveled. Lars's wife survived the blast and moved to Albany, New York, to live with her daughter. Two weeks after Lars blew himself to Kingdom Come, Danny's girlfriend ran off. She and Eeg's son haven't been heard from since.

At this point Eeg was pushing forty and going through his own mid-life career meltdown, so he follows Mom to Albany. He got a job teaching high school English and found a law firm to sue Lamaar Studios on contingency, but the Lamaar lawyers have successfully tied up the lawsuit in the justice system since the get-go. When Eeg's mother died in 1991 he decided to leave the hectic city life of Albany and move to the relative peace and quiet of Woodstock.

He got involved in the local Democratic party, was elected to Town Council and got re-elected three times. His bank accounts showed no unusual deposits or withdrawals that would indicate he was paying off a string of hired assassins to settle his legal battles with Lamaar. The deposit of $50,000 made nine months ago turned out to be an advance on a book he is writing.

I folded my notes and set them down on the seat next to me. Seconds later Sig came down the aisle with a brown leather briefcase. "Mr. Curry said you'd be reading this," she said, "but we also have today's newspapers, the latest magazines, and a selection of DVDs, CDs, and video game cartridges."

"I'd better pass on the entertainment and do my homework," I said. "Just curious. Sig—is that short for Sigourney?"

"Signilda. It's Swedish," she said flashing me a friendly skies smile that would make John Madden abandon his cross-country tour bus and become a Frequent Flyer. "I'll be back in a few minutes with your breakfast."

The briefcase weighed about ten pounds. I'm a slow reader, but I've learned the fine art of skimming. By the time I skimmed through the first few pounds I realized it had a pro-Lamaar slant. There was a history of the company; another on Familyland; and several travel books on Lamaar's vacation spots. Each one painted a rosier picture than the last. Even the three-inch thick binder on the ongoing court battle with Eeg about royalty rights featured newspaper articles and letters that made Lamaar look like an innocent victim.

I read, ate breakfast, flirted with Sig, took a nap, had a snack and read some more. By the time Shep announced that we were on our approach I had waded through the bulk of it, and I didn't feel any better briefed than your average tourist who's planning a trip to Familyland.

Lamaar was a multi-billion-dollar player in the cutthroat world of show business, yet based on the material Brian gave me, nobody had ever written an unkind word about them. Everyone except Eeg adored them, and there was no reason anybody would want to hurt them, their employees, or their fans.

I called Terry and got his voicemail. I could have tracked him down, but I just left a message that the flight was lovely and that I had wasted the better part of six hours sifting through corporate propaganda. "As far as I can tell," I said, "this is the one of the world's finest organizations, and you and I should do everything in our power to see that no further harm befalls them."

I looked out the window at the longest runway I'd ever seen. It was clear and dry, but the patches of ground around it were covered with a light dusting of snow. All I had to keep me warm was a summer-weight blazer. I had forgotten that springtime wasn't the same in upstate New York as it is in Southern California.

Shep was right on the money. We touched down at Stewart Airport in Newburgh at exactly 11:44 L.A. time. I didn't bother setting my watch ahead.

CHAPTER 60

F.X. FALCO was your basic tall, strapping, handsome Italian law enforcement officer. He had a commanding presence, a manly handshake, and the foresight to bring me some cold-weather gear.

"You're dressed for the tropics," he said, handing me a navy blue parka. "It's thirty-five degrees, and it's even colder up the mountain where Eeg lives."

A white cruiser with a big black and gold *Sheriff* across the doors was parked in the loading zone. When we got within shouting range of the two airport cops who were directing traffic Falco yelled out, "Thanks for not towing my car, officers!"

One cop laughed; the other flipped him the bird.

"Poker buddies," Falco said, as we got in the car. "Guess which one is on a losing streak."

We headed north on the New York State Thruway. The trees were still bare, some of them with a crust of snow clinging to their branches.

Falco was in his early forties and closing in on his twenty years, which is when most cops bail out and look for a healthier means of employment. But I got the feeling he could be a lifer. He loved being a cop, and he bombarded me with questions about what it's like to work Homicide in L.A.

"We don't get the high-profile cases like your Robert Blake or your O.J. murders," he said. "We get a lot of body dumps with the hands chopped off so there's no prints. Sometimes it's the mob, sometimes the drug trade, although these days that's one and the same. I think the big difference between you and me is that you spend most of your time trying to figure out who the murderer is, and I spend most of my time trying to find out who the dead guy is."

"Well, it's a lot easier for me to ID a body," I said. "Everybody in L.A. is famous, so we recognize them even without their prints."

"Question about Eeg," he said. "I realize he's got a beef with Lamaar, but from what I know about him, he doesn't seem like the killer type."

"O.J. won the Heisman Trophy. Not all killers have a killer profile."

"O.J. was innocent," he said.

"Oh yeah, I keep forgetting. I reread Eeg's backgrounder on the plane. He doesn't look bad on paper. Life fucked him over a few times, but he has no criminal record, and according to you, since he moved to Woodstock he's become a model citizen, a Town Father, and a prince among men."

"I don't know about the prince part," Falco said, "but people like him. They voted for him four times."

"He got a girlfriend?"

"He goes out with a couple of local women, one more regular than the rest, Loretta Clarke. She's forty-five, widow, makes jewelry, sells it locally. She and Eeg play tennis, go to movies, the usual. They don't live together, but they've been dating a couple of years, and while this is probably not relevant to the case, Eeg gives her the best orgasms she ever had."

"Excellent detective work, Sheriff. Would you mind sharing with a fellow law enforcement officer how you managed to dig up that last little item?"

He flashed a shit-eating grin. "I deputized the local hairdressers."

We exited the Thruway at Kingston, which, according to the road sign, was the first capital of New York. We headed west on Route 28, and Falco asked if I knew the people in Hollywood who did the re-enactments for *America's Most Wanted*. He thought he'd make a great TV cop.

Five minutes later we turned onto Route 375, a two-lane country highway that felt like it deserved a homespun name, instead of a three-digit number. Most of the houses along the road were set back and separated from the traffic by trees. The driveways were spaced far enough apart to let me know that at least some people in Ulster County had elbowroom. "Who lives here?" I asked.

"It used to be middle class," F.X. said. "But we're only two hours away from New York, and, after 9/11, a lot of city people started gobbling up anything they could get their hands on. Drove the price of real estate to the moon. Lisa and I are lucky. We bought a fixer-upper before the boom."

We stopped at the edge of town where the Chamber of Commerce had posted a sign that said *Welcome to Woodstock, Colony of the Arts*. It also reminded folks that there was a Halloween party on October 31 and a Christmas Tree lighting ceremony on The Village Green on December 24. Today was April 25.

"I heard this town was in a time warp, but I thought that meant they were stuck in the sixties," I said. "They don't seem to know what month it is either."

"Oh, they know," he said. "No sense paying the sign painter to change it till there's something happening. Probably the Memorial Day parade."

We turned left onto the main drag and drove past a bank, a convenience store, a walk-in doctor's office, a pizza joint, a tattoo parlor, and a strip of uninspired storefronts. "Somehow I expected a town that's famous for peace, love, and rock and roll to have a little more sex appeal," I said.

"Sorry to disappoint you. Usually Richie Havens is in front of the hardware store singing "Freedom," but I guess it's his day off. Hey, if you're hungry, Vince makes a fantastic meat loaf sandwich," he said, slowing down and pointing at a sign that said *Woodstock Meats*.

"No thanks. They fed me on the plane."

We turned right onto Rock City Road. "How's that for sex appeal?" Falco said, pointing at the windshield where a mountain loomed directly in front of us.

We drove past a cemetery and a rec field and then Rock City turned into Meads Mountain Road. Half a mile later we made another right. "This is California Quarry Road," Falco said. "Funny that Eeg should live here. I mean you being from California and him being your quarry and all."

We drove about a mile up the mountain and pulled alongside a dark blue Ford that was parked on the shoulder. The driver, a baby-faced blond kid who barely looked old enough to be sitting behind the wheel of a car, rolled down his window. "Eeg drove into town this morning," he said. "Got gas, bought the paper, stopped at the post office. Been back in the house ever since."

F.X. thanked him and turned to me. "What's your gut?" he asked.

I had told Falco all about the ransom note on the phone the night before. "You sure you want to tell him everything?" Biggs had said. "It's a small town. You never know how close Eeg and Falco could be." By now I was confident that Falco was a straight shooter and I was glad I hadn't held back.

"My gut? Deep down inside I don't think Eeg is behind all this. But he knows something. He knew there was more than one homicide."

"You want me to keep quiet and let you do the talking, or can I jump in?" Falco said. "No offense either way."

"Jump in. Otherwise he'll think you're my driver."

Falco turned into the driveway. "You mean I'm not?"

CHAPTER 61

EEG'S HOUSE WAS set back about five hundred feet and couldn't even be seen from the road. It was large, two stories, white clapboard. Simple, but ample. The grounds around it were still recovering from winter, but I could see a few sprigs of yellow and purple popping up from a bed of brown earth.

We stepped out of the car. The front door opened, and a Yorkshire terrier raced down the walk and began snarling at my shoes. A man appeared in the doorway. "I see you're back, Sheriff," he said. "Am I going to need a lawyer?"

"Only if your dog bites us," Falco said.

"At least you'd get to arrest me for something. Come, Tinker," he said to the yippy little hairball. The Yorkie squeaked out two more ferocious barks, then turned and ran back to let her master know that she had it under control.

"Daniel Eeg," F.X. said, "this is Detective Mike Lomax from the LAPD."

"Come on in Detective. I was expecting you. I spotted one of the Sheriff's boys tailing me this morning. Having written my share of cop shows, I figured he was keeping an eye on me so I didn't skip town before you showed up and put the screws to me. Wipe your feet on the mat."

We followed Eeg into a large living room that was dominated on one end by a bluestone fireplace. A few cold, charred logs sat in the grate. The dog's basket was on the hearth and she had already curled up inside.

Eeg was trim and tanning-salon bronze. I knew from my cheat sheet that he was in his late fifties, but his weather-lined face and the pure white silky hair that hung down to the middle of his back added ten years. His family was Scandinavian by way of Minnesota, but he looked like a Native American Chief. I could picture him sitting around the campfire of tribal elders pitching ideas for cop shows. *How come there no cop show with Indian? Me have idea for cop who is Head of Security at Indian casino. Call it Chief Snake Eyes.*

Eeg gestured for us to take a seat on the rust-colored sofa. He sat in a matching armchair. "I hear you have a grudge against Lamaar Studios," I said.

"I have a lawsuit against them, Detective. That makes me litigious, not homicidal. As pissed off as I am, I had nothing to do with those murders."

I wondered if I would have to trick him into saying "murders," or if I would just call him on the fact that he'd said it to Falco last week. He had saved me a lot of time. "Who told you there was more than one murder?"

He smirked. "I see. And because I know there's more than one dead body that makes me the guy who killed them."

"Or had them killed," Falco said.

"You got me, Sheriff," he said. "Before you haul me away, you want me to get you the cancelled checks made out to Murderers-R-Us?"

"It would save a lot of time," I said, "but we'll settle for an explanation."

"I'm suing a giant corporation. I keep tabs on them. I have friends on the inside who keep me posted. I knew about Elkins the day after it happened."

"You're one of the few who did," I said.

"I can't blame Ike Rose for keeping the whole thing quiet," he said. "It's not good for business when your celebrity rabbits get whacked."

"How about when your customers get whacked?" I asked.

He gave me a blank stare. It could have been a bogus reaction, but he didn't strike me as that crafty an actor. The look on his face seemed genuinely guiltless. "There was a third homicide," I said. "A guest at the theme park."

Eeg shook his head. "I used to dream about killing Dean Lamaar, but I can't imagine getting even by killing his employees or his customers."

"It gets worse. There was a ransom note. Pay the price or the killings continue." I had just disclosed some highly confidential case information. But I knew what I was doing. At least I hoped I did.

Eeg didn't say anything. I could see him turning the information over in his head. Finally, he said, "That's balls. How much did they ask for?"

"I can't say. In fact, the ransom demand is also confidential."

"Ah, yes. You fed it to me to watch my reaction. How'd I do?"

I shrugged. When you've gone head to head with thousands of suspects, you develop a shit sorter. I can usually tell who's playing it straight and who's lying, but it wasn't easy with Eeg. He sounded like a badly written cop show.

"Pay up, or I'll kill off your people," he said. "Why didn't I think of that?"

"For a script," Falco asked, "or a way to settle your debts with Lamaar?"

Eeg laughed. "Do you think this is just a holdup, or do you think someone actually has a bigger grudge against the company than I do?"

"Let's just focus on your grudge," I said. "Tell us about it."

"As if you haven't heard all about it from Ike Rose and his team of dickless lawyers."

"I've only heard it from them. I came for your side of the

story."

That softened him. He clucked to the dog, who hopped out of her basket and up onto his lap. She curled up and began licking his hand.

"Alright," he said. "I've told it many times, but I've never had anyone listen to my beef with Lamaar so they could turn it into a motive for murder."

CHAPTER 62

"MY FATHER WANTED to be an artist. A real artist. Not a cartoonist," Eeg added, in case I didn't know the difference. "He was studying fine art when he got sidetracked by the war. You might think it was a blessing that he wound up in The Cartoon Corps with Dean Lamaar, because it was a lot safer making animated training films than dodging mortar shells on a beach in France. But it was a curse. Lamaar used my father. Cheated him. Did the nice folks at Lamaar mention that in their version of the story, Detective?"

He knew better than to expect an answer. He went on. "Dean Lamaar was an entrepreneur, but he couldn't draw shit with a brown crayon. It was Lars Eeg who breathed life into that rabbit and all those lucrative little characters. Lamaar paid him chump change, sucked him dry, then spit him out."

"Who spit him out?" I said. "Lamaar the man, or Lamaar Studios?"

Eeg shook his head. "Both. Back then, Dean Lamaar was the studio, and if you didn't agree with him, you got canned. He's the one who fucked over my father. But Ike Rose and Lamaar Studios continue to perpetuate the injustice. They're the ones who have to pay. Do you know what my father's share should be worth today? A billion dollars. That's billion, with a B. You know how much money he had in the bank when he killed himself? Eighty-nine hundred. That's hundred, with an H. My old man not only died broke, he died broken."

It was a line I'm sure he had used before. "That's my grudge, Detective. Do you think I had anything to do with those homicides?"

Anything? I knew he was in upstate New York when someone plunged a letter opener into Judy Kaiser's neck, but I wasn't ready to rule him out entirely. "No, I don't," I said, because that's what he needed to hear.

"Well, you're right," he said. "I'm sorry you had to fly all the way across the country just to rule out one suspect."

"That's not the only reason I came," I said. "Quite frankly, I never really bought that you were behind this, but I thought you might be able to help."

"Why the hell should I help Lamaar?"

"Not Lamaar, me. Innocent people got killed just because they happen to be connected to the company. I'm trying to prevent any more people from getting murdered."

"Y'know, Danny," Falco said, leaning forward on the sofa. "*You're* connected to the company. The life you save may be your own."

Eeg gave Falco the finger.

"Look," I said, "you know this company inside out. Give me something."

He was a smart man with a big ego, an excellent combination for a cop who is trying to pump information from someone. He rubbed his chin with one hand. "Do you think you could solve a murder in China?" he said.

"I'd need a translator, but, sure, a homicide's a homicide."

"Is it? Did you know that in China, thousands of parents kill their newborn daughters, because the law only allows them to have one child, and most parents want sons. If a lot of infant girls died mysteriously in L.A., you'd think there's a lunatic running around the maternity wards. But if you lived in Beijing, you'd know the parents did it. Because you would know the culture."

He repeated the words. "*You would know the culture. Lamaar is like a small country. They have the political clout to influence zoning, taxes, funding for roads, you name it. Yet the only things you know about them are what they show you in the movies and whatever they put in their press releases. You want me to *give you something*, Detective Lomax? I suggest that you dig a little deeper into their corporate psyche."

"Any particular area?" I asked.

"The fish always stinks from the head down," he said.

"Are you talking about Ike Rose?" I said.

"The skeletons won't be in Rose's closet. They'll be in Dean Lamaar's."

"He's dead," Falco said.

"So is JFK," Eeg said, "but they dig up new dirt on him every day."

"Do you have dirt on Dean Lamaar that might shed light on this case?"

"Nothing I could prove. And even if I could, I'm not sure how it would help solve these murders. But I can tell you one thing. Uncle Deanie — the all-American guy who created Familyland — he had a real dark side, and my father got to see it up close and personal."

I took out my pad and pen. "I'm listening," I said.

"For one thing, he was a racist," Eeg said. "Hated blacks, Jews, Asians. Some people say he secretly gave money to the Ku Klux Klan."

"Most of the film industry was racist back then," I said. "But the man who runs the company now is Jewish. The head of security at Familyland is African-American. Even if Lamaar was a racist personally, the company itself has come a long way."

"He was sexually repressed," Eeg said.

I yawned. "I'm a cop, not a shrink. Give me something I can use."

"Okay, Dean Lamaar murdered his father. Put that in your pipe and smoke it for a few minutes. I got fresh coffee. You want some?"

Falco and I passed. Eeg lifted the dog from his lap, put her on the floor, and headed off to the kitchen.

Falco looked at me. "What are we… what are you supposed to do with that information? Even if it's true, which I don't believe a word of it, how is that going to help solve this case?"

"Beats the shit out of me, Sheriff, but it sure will make for interesting reading in my report." I wrote *Dean Lamaar killed his father???* in my pad.

Eeg returned with a mug of black coffee in one hand and two books in the other. He sat down, set the books on the floor, and popped the dog back on his lap. "Dean Lamaar was born poor," he said. "His father was a fire-and-brimstone minister in the Midwest. Deanie was an only child, and his mother doted on him. But Reverend Lamaar was a miserable bastard, probably because he left one of his legs on a battlefield somewhere in Belgium. He was a boozer, too. A real hypocrite, he'd preach to the flock about Demon Rum, then go home and drink himself cockeyed."

Eeg took a slow, noisy sip of the steaming coffee. "Now Dean is a creative kid. He likes to draw cartoons. But the father forbids it. That's the way those Fundamentalists think — you'll be rewarded in the next life for abstinence in this one. Anyway, Deanie starts doing cartoons on the sly. One day, when he's twelve, the father finds his pictures. He calls him on the carpet, and he burns all the drawings and the art supplies in the fireplace. And get this, he must've really been loaded, because then he sticks the kid's hands into the fire."

And this is the kid who went on to create Familyland, I thought.

"The mother pulls the boy's hands out of the fire, but the father throws him down in the coal cellar to spend the night. It's crawling with mice and bugs. Most kids would curl up and cry themselves to sleep. But Deanie, he's not going to let the old bastard win. He picks up a hunk of coal and he draws this cartoon character on the wall. It's a rabbit. A big fucking rambunctious rabbit that can stand up to anybody. Years later, my father would turn that rabbit into a money machine, but that night Dean Lamaar created it with a piece of coal on a cellar wall, and I think it gave him just what he needed. Balls."

Eeg took another noisy sip of coffee for dramatic effect. "A few weeks later, the preacher climbs a ladder up to the roof to fix some shingles that blew off. Now, remember, he's a drunk and a gimp. Bam, he loses his balance, falls off the roof and lands on an iron rake. Bleeds to death in a couple of minutes."

"Where's the murder part?" I asked.

"Who do you think loosened the shingles from the roof? Who do you think toppled the ladder? Who do you think positioned the rake on the ground? Who do you think watched the old man bleed to death?" Eeg said, raising his voice with every question. "Dean Fucking Lamaar!"

"And how do you know about this murder that allegedly happened some seventy years ago?" I asked.

"Klaus Lebrecht was Lamaar's camera genius and his best friend. Deanie told him one night when they were both shit-faced and swapping stories about their scumbag fathers. Lebrecht swore he'd never repeat it, but how long does anyone in Hollywood keep a secret? Klaus told my father. My father kept it to himself, even after Lamaar dumped him. He finally told me the day before he committed suicide."

"So it's like hearsay four times over," Falco said.

"Good show business gossip always is."

"Even if this is true," I said, "it's irrelevant. It's not going to help me solve the three murders I'm working on."

"Maybe not," Eeg said. "But maybe you'll stop looking at the Lamaar Company like it's an innocent victim. They hide behind all those happy horseshit cartoons, but they've been a ruthless, heartless, merciless bunch of cutthroats since Day One."

He reached down and picked up the two books he had set there. "Read these. They're biographies of the late, great Dean Lamaar. This is the authorized version, available at finer bookstores everywhere." He handed me a book.

The title was *Deanie, Prince of Joy and Laughter*. The jacket had a black-and-white photo of Dean Lamaar that must have been taken back in the fifties. He was in his prime, handsome, well-groomed. And just in case you missed the word Prince in the title, an artist had inked a cartoon crown on his head.

"This was written by one of Lamaar's sycophants," Eeg said. "Deanie himself came up with the title and the artwork. It's the image he wanted to portray to the world. Hollywood's very own Prince Charming. The benevolent storyteller who made the world a better place."

"And the other book?" I asked.

"Unauthorized. Difficult to find. It will give you a different perspective on the man and the company that might be helpful in your investigation."

He handed it to me. The title was *The Rabbit Factory*. The jacket had the same photo of Dean Lamaar, but now there was a red tint over the black-and-white image of his face, and instead of a crown, the artist had drawn devil's horns. It was a very effective transformation. He looked menacing and evil.

I looked at the author's name. D. Tinker. "Where would I find this Mr. Tinker?" I said. "I might want to ask him a few questions."

"Funny thing about that. The book was written in 1991, but nobody's ever met this Tinker person before or since. It might not even be a man."

"True. Funny coincidence that your dog is named Tinker."

He stroked the Yorkie. "Actually, she's named after the main drag here in town, Tinker Street. She's smart, but I can assure you, she didn't write it."

"Whoever did must have helped you in your case against Lamaar."

"Not as much as one would hope."

"Thanks for all your help," I said, and I meant it. "One last question. Any thoughts on who's behind this?"

He leaned back in the chair so that his long, white hair fell against the rust-colored fabric. He looked intelligent, paternal, trustworthy. I could understand why people voted for him. He tented his hands under his chin. "These new developments, killing a guest at the park and making ransom demands, that puts a whole new spin on things. Remember what I said before? That it looks like someone's got an even bigger grudge against the company than I do. I think someone really hates them. And they're not just holding Lamaar up for money. It's like they're punishing them."

Punishing them. The thought had never crossed my mind. I was looking for a murderer, a blackmailer. But Eeg was right. Whoever was behind these homicides hated Lamaar to the core.

"And of course, I'm sure you're taking a good hard look at the Leone family in Vegas," he said.

I wasn't taking a hard look. Ike Rose had specifically told us not to waste our energy thinking about the Vegas connection.

"This Lamaar-Camelot venture," I said. "What's your take on it?"

"It makes sense," Eeg said. "Lamaar needs to have a serious presence in the adult market. If Ike Rose pulls off this Vegas deal, not only will Lamaar's profits start heading north, but their stock will become the flavor of the month on Wall Street. Rose's personal holdings alone will be worth half a billion."

"But you still think I should be taking a hard look at Leone."

"Yeah, because no matter how good the Camelot deal looks on paper, people connected to Lamaar have been murdered. The company is being squeezed for money. That all sounds like Cosa Nostra shit to me. And the Leone family has had Mafia blood

293

coursing through their veins for hundreds of years. As far as I'm concerned, you can't eliminate the mob factor."

"Don't worry," I said. "We haven't eliminated them."

Ike Rose may have wanted me to, but once again I was starting to think that what Ike Rose wanted wasn't always the best thing for the investigation.

CHAPTER 63

"SORRY FOR BLOWING it," Falco said, as we drove down the mountain road. "First Eeg spots one of my guys tailing him. Then I make that dumb statement about the life you save could be your own. I guess I'm just a country cop."

"You think city cops get it right every time? Last month twenty of L.A.'s finest raided a house in Compton. They lobbed flash grenades at the door and busted in because the C.I. swore there were three guys inside dealing drugs. Ex-cons who were armed to the teeth and had a pack of pitbulls guarding the place."

"Sounds like fun."

"It was, except they stormed the wrong house. There were two old ladies inside, sisters, watching a soap opera and drinking tea."

"Whoa, I bet those old broads shit their britches," Falco said.

"One did. The other one had a massive heart attack. She was dead before her sister could say, 'Does anyone know a good personal injury lawyer?' So don't apologize for fuckups until you know what a real one is."

"Thanks. For some twisted reason that makes me feel better."

"Good. Then the old girl didn't die in vain."

"I couldn't tell if Eeg was trying to help or just jerk us around," Falco said. "I finally decided it was a little of both. I'll bet he wrote that book."

"Damn straight he wrote it, and he's got such a monumental ego it was probably all he could do not to autograph it."

When we got to Route 28 my cell service kicked in. I called Terry's cell. "I'm back at Familyland," he said. "We got Victim Number Four."

I pounded my fist on the dashboard. Falco looked over at me. "Another homicide," I said. I went back to Terry. "Give me the details."

"An employee, Rose Eichmann, white, female, forty-four years old. She drove a shuttle bus between the main gate and the parking lots, picking up people when they come in, dropping them off at their cars when they leave. She was found about noon, sitting in the driver's seat of an empty bus. Her windpipe was crushed. The weapon was another Lamaar souvenir, a red necktie with a dozen happy characters on it. I'm hoping the killer had it around his own neck till he was ready to wrap it around the victim. We're checking for DNA."

"Did he leave us a flipbook?"

"Yeah. I thought it would be a hand with four fingers, but this whacko has a better imagination than you and me. It's four separate hands, and when you flip the pages each one gives you the finger."

"Where are we on the rest of the evidence?" I said. "Did the lab come up with anything on the ransom note that was pinned to Judy Kaiser's chest?"

"If you were hoping for a big thumb print right in the center, no. The paper, envelope, and the plastic bag were all generic. The letter opener was a Lamaar gift shop item just like the other weapons, but none of the searches we've done from gift shop receipts have turned up anything. Jessica pulled some DNA from the glue on the envelope. It's dog saliva. Just what we needed. A psychopath who thinks he's smarter than the cops."

"How smart is it to kill a bus driver?" I said. "Ike Rose won't cough up $266 million just because they killed off one of the little people."

"It's not only smart. It borders on brilliant. Did you catch the vic's name? Rose Eichmann. Rose Ike Man."

It was like a punch in the gut. And if I felt that way, I could only imagine how Ike must feel. "How'd Ike Rose handle it?" I asked.

"Sorry about the dead woman, but sticking with his 'We don't negotiate with terrorists' position. Amy, on the other hand, is on the warpath. She keeps reminding me that *other human beings* are going to get killed, just in case I forgot. She thinks if she's in my face twenty-four/seven, I'll solve it quicker. How did it go with Eeg?"

I gave Terry the highlight reel of my visit with Eeg, ending with the story about Dean Lamaar killing his father.

"Great. Instead of a confession he gives you another homicide. He must love pulling your chain. Bottom line, what's your take on this guy?"

"Not guilty, with an asterisk. He's got an ax to grind with the company, and he knows more shit about them than your average not-guilty party."

"We'll keep him in our thoughts. Gotta go. I've got a lot to do and I'd like to get home for dinner. Marilyn is making lasagna. Speaking of my amazing wife, I told her about that Lamaar security guy, Kenneth Dahl. You called him Ken and he says *I prefer Kenneth*? I mean who cares if somebody calls you Ken? And she says, 'He doesn't want you to call him Ken, because then he'd be Ken Dahl.'" He laughed. "You get it?"

"No," I said, as Falco swung around the traffic circle and merged into the New York State Thruway tollbooth plaza.

"Ken Doll. Like Barbie Doll's boyfriend. The Ken Doll. You get it now?"

"Yeah," I said. "It's not that funny, but leave it to Marilyn to figure out something like that. Maybe tonight she can tell you who killed Rose Eichmann."

"While I'm at it, I'll ask her if Dean Lamaar really killed his father," he said. "On second thought, I won't. You know why? Because I don't give a shit. This guy Eeg is mind-fucking us. He's pissing in our well. You and I don't care if Dean Lamaar killed his father, his mother, his scoutmaster, and his pet hamster. It's ancient history and not relevant to the case we've got on our plate. Promise me you'll get it out of your jet-lagged brain before you get back home."

"Y'know, the partner I worked with today is much nicer to me than you are, Biggs." I looked over at Falco, who smiled broadly, then tapped out "shave and a haircut" on the car horn.

"Hey, Biggsy," Falco yelled across the miles, "be nice to Lomax. He's had a tough day."

Biggs answered back. Falco couldn't hear him. But I did.

"Not as tough as Rose Eichmann," he said.

CHAPTER 64

AIR RAMBO WAS waiting with the engines idling, and we were rolling as soon as my butt hit the seat. Sig brought a drink menu. There were six wines and ten beers to choose from, most of which I wouldn't be caught dead asking for in a cop bar. I ordered a Bud.

I spent the next few hours reading the books Eeg gave me. I started with *Deanie, Prince of Joy and Laughter*. The writer was obviously paid to paint Lamaar as a rags-to-riches hero, beloved by one and all. It did everything but start with *Once upon a time* and end with *and they lived happily ever after*.

The unauthorized biography was more of a horror story than a fairy tale. The author could have called it *Deanie Dearest*, but he chose *The Rabbit Factory* because Lamaar was infamous for running a sweatshop. He was a cross between Ebenezer Scrooge and Simon Legree, demanding sixteen-hour days and seven-day weeks when a cartoon was in production. A sign on the wall of the animation studio read *If you don't show up Sunday, don't show up Monday.*

According to D. Tinker, while the public revered Dean Lamaar, the people who worked for him thought he was a real prick. And anyone who looked for a job someplace else might find himself the victim of a sadistic little trick that became known as 'rabbit baiting.'

An unhappy Lamaar employee would read about a good job in the classifieds. He'd mail his résumé to the address in the ad. The job would be bogus, and the résumé would be delivered to Dean Lamaar. The employee, of course, would be fired immediately.

When people at Lamaar finally learned to stop responding to classified ads, Deanie hired phony headhunters to call them. He was always baiting. Legend has it that over the years Dean Lamaar ambushed as many as a hundred employees, until eventually most of his workers would rather eat shit at Lamaar Studios than risk having no job at all.

While the first book glossed over Lamaar's personal life, only briefly mentioning his wife and daughter, *The Rabbit Factory* provided much juicier details. When he first started out, Lamaar hired Olivia Martin, a pretty girl of nineteen. She would type, answer the phone, and handle all of his personal needs from laundry to grocery shopping to car repair, because the business left him no time for a life. He did, however, find time to have sex with Olivia, and when she became pregnant, she continued her daily chores as Mrs. Dean Lamaar.

Their daughter, Gillian, was born with Down Syndrome and was institutionalized until she died at age twenty-seven. The founder of Familyland would never father a normal child of his own, and when Olivia died at fifty-one, Lamaar rededicated himself to bringing joy and laughter to the world and pain and misery to everyone else around him.

The most glaring difference between the two books was on the subject of the break up between Dean Lamaar and Lars Eeg. The first book didn't even mention it. The other painted a picture of Dean Lamaar as a ruthless tyrant who rode his friend's talents to success, *sucked him dry, then spit him out.* The very same words Danny Eeg had used when he told me the story.

I had no doubt that he wrote it. But I wondered why he left out the best part. Nowhere in the book was there even a hint that the untimely death of Dean Lamaar's father could have been anything but an accident.

A few hours into the flight, Sig brought me a telephone. "It's Brian Curry." I knew exactly why he was calling.

"I guess you heard we're having a bad day here," Curry said.

"Biggs told me. Has Rose changed his mind about paying the ransom?"

"Not yet, but he realizes how vulnerable we are. Seventy-two percent of our employees make minimum wage. Who's going to put his life at risk for that? As for the big stars who make millions, they'll just go to another studio. Even if these bastards don't kill any more customers, they can scare away enough employees so that we can't run the railroad."

"Last night Ike said the company could weather a mass exodus," I reminded him. "His biggest concern was the stock tanking."

"It still is. But we have sixty thousand employees around the world plus millions of customers, suppliers, and stockholders. Every one is a potential target. That's weighing heavily on him. At one point he pounded his fist on the table and said, 'They could kill some librarian in Omaha just because she rented one of our videos, and it would take days for us to find out.' That's a quote."

"Does that mean he's leaning toward paying the ransom?" I asked.

"Right now it means more pressure on LAPD to catch the perps."

"Have you figured out the significance of $266.4 million dollars? It's not a number out of thin air. It sounds like an amount your company owes this guy."

"We're still working on it," Curry said. "What did you get out of Eeg?"

"He bitched about the company, but I doubt if he's behind the killings. Brian, do me a favor will you?"

"The bodies are piling up, Mike. Anything I can do to help."

"From what my partner tells me, Amy is making his life unbearable. Can you call her off?"

"Terry spoke to me; I spoke to Ike. There's a big conference in Vancouver, and he's going to send her. She'll be out of your hair by Wednesday."

"Good, but I want to talk to her. Tell her to meet me in her Burbank office at eight sharp tomorrow. After that, you can send her to the moon."

"That's easy," he said. "I'm really calling you because I just got a message from the cockpit."

"I'm sure you did. I've been expecting your call."

"Captain Sheppard tells me you've asked him to make an unscheduled stop."

"Right. Ike said his plane was at my disposal. I'm taking him up on it. I asked the pilot to take me to Las Vegas."

I heard him exhale. "That's what he told me. I'll authorize it, but if I remember correctly Ike asked you to not to waste your time with the people in Vegas."

"I'm just following in Ike's footsteps."

"What's that supposed to mean?"

"If I remember correctly a lot of people told Ike not to waste his time with the people in Vegas. But he went there anyway. Good night, Brian. I'll talk to you to tomorrow."

CHAPTER 65

I HAD NO problem reaching Arabella Leone. As soon as I finished talking to Terry I called the Camelot. The operator connected me to Leone's office. "I've been expecting your call, Detective," she said. "Where are you?"

I told her and she agreed to meet me on the plane. "Have the pilot land at Henderson Executive Airport. It's private. We can avoid the tourist crowd."

"Understood," I said. "I'll be glad to avoid whatever you'd like to avoid."

It was 11 p.m. when she boarded the plane. I had seen photos of her, but she was even more stunning in person. Tall, dark, Mediterranean sexy. We sat in the conference area at the rear of the plane. She got right down to business.

"If you're wondering how much I know," she said, "it's everything. The perv in the rabbit costume, Ronnie Lucas, the woman at Familyland, and the bus driver this afternoon. I also know about the note asking for $266 million."

"Do you know who's behind it all?"

"I know it's not me, which I'm sure crossed your mind. Ike's company and mine have been joined at the hip for the past four years and anything nasty that happens to them affects us. If I were going to try to extort money out of Lamaar I wouldn't have invested so heavily in the partnership."

"What about your competition?"

"Good thought. In my world, if your business is going well, the other guy tries to put you out of business. So we looked into it, and we looked deep. None of the other casinos are behind it. Not in Vegas, not Atlantic City, not even Asia. I offered a big fat informant's fee. I guarantee you if another casino were behind this, some low-level gavoon would have picked up on it and ratted out the big guys in a heartbeat."

"What about Lamaar's competition?" I said. "If business is going well in Ike's world, do you think any of the other studios would try to hurt Lamaar? Did any of them lose out to Lamaar when you were looking for a partner?"

"A few, but they're so big, what they lost out on is chump change. The business may be full of scumbags, but that's not how they operate. I think we have a better shot at solving this if we focus on individuals, not companies."

"I didn't realize *we* were trying to solve this, Ms. Leone."

"I'll give it to you straight, Detective. Ike and a lot of smart people at Lamaar have been helping us create a vacation resort that will make every other hotel in Vegas look like a ho-hum honky-tonk. We're supposed to open the first phase of the new Camelot next month. There are billions of dollars of investor money on the line, not to mention my personal reputation. I can't wait for the Los Angeles Police Department and the FBI to get their collective thumbs out of their asses and figure out who's threatening my business partner. I'll help you if I think it's in my best interest, but don't spend a lot of your valuable time trying to hold me back. You'll wind up getting dragged."

"Ike Rose didn't want me to meet you," I said. "Is it because he thought I couldn't handle the abuse?"

She smiled. Beautiful white teeth framed by soft red lips and warm olive skin. "What's the matter? You don't like strong women?"

"Not if they get in the way of me doing my job."

"I won't get in your way," she said. "If anything, I'll help."

"You want to help? What do you know about Ike Rose that I don't?"

"Plenty." She went on to tell me about Ike's business successes and failures, his family, his friends, his enemies, the women he slept with, the women he didn't sleep with, you name it.

I wasn't sure if it would lead me anywhere, but it was incredibly thorough. "You seem to know a hell of a lot about Ike Rose," I said.

"I know a hell of a lot about anyone I get involved with. It's something I picked up from my grandfather. During his career he had more than five hundred informants on his payroll."

"How many do you have?"

"Not nearly that many. Mostly I rely on LexisNexis, D&B, Bloomberg, and Google. I even managed to find out a few things about you."

"Like what?"

"For one thing, my grandfather wouldn't have liked you."

"Because I'm a cop?"

"No, Detective. Because you're an honest cop."

We talked for another twenty minutes. We were both trying to solve the same problem, but there was no question that we were on two different sides. We agreed to keep the channels of communication open.

"After *you* solve this case," she said, carefully choosing the right pronoun, "come back for a weekend, and I'll comp you across the board. Private plane, deluxe suite, gourmet meals, the best shows, the complete high-roller package."

"Thanks," I said. "And if *you* solve it, I'll pick you up in my Acura, drive you to L.A., and take you on all the rides at Familyland."

CHAPTER 66

TEAM RAMBO, AS the executives at Lamaar are known, have their offices in a ten-story glass-and-chrome building in Burbank. It's right up the street from NBC and a short twenty minutes from my house.

I had asked Amy to meet me there at 8:00 sharp. I got to her office at 8:52, and I was far from sharp. I braced myself for a verbal drubbing as only Amy can drub.

Instead I got a cheery welcome. "Good morning, Detective. You must be exhausted from criss-crossing the country in one day. Where's your partner?"

As far away from you as he can get. "We decided to divide and conquer," I said. "He's busy conquering the FBI. You'll have to settle for just me."

"My pleasure, but I did want to apologize to Detective Biggs. I was pretty crazy yesterday. I practically ordered him to solve this case on the spot."

"He might have mentioned that you were a little upset," I said.

"If he said *upset*, then he's a real gentleman. I was a total bitch. Angry, frustrated, scared. Shit, I'm still scared. I mean, I work for Lamaar, too. That makes me just as much a target as Rose Eichmann."

"I'll pass on your apologies to Terry," I said.

"I'd tell him myself, but I'm headed to Vancouver for three

days. But you probably know that already." A. Cheever was a lot of things. Dumb was not one of them. She knew she had been voted off the island. And she knew that I knew.

She had on a charcoal gray skirt and a mint green cashmere sweater. She sat on the sofa and crossed her legs. She looked smashing. I sat in a chair facing her and handed her my copy of *The Rabbit Factory*. "Eeg gave it to me."

"Wow, these are hard to come by. Dean Lamaar bought up every available copy when it came out. Then he let the big book distributors know that if they touched it they would never sell another Lamaar product again."

"So much for freedom of speech. Have you read it?"

"I read everything written about the company," she said. "Part of my job is to separate fact from fiction."

"And which is this? Fact or fiction?"

"For starters the author's name is a lie. Daniel Eeg wrote it. What I don't understand is why he gave it to you. Is it supposed to help your investigation?"

"Maybe yes, maybe no. Eeg wanted me to know that Dean Lamaar isn't the saint he's made out to be. He's suggesting that whoever is out to hurt the Lamaar organization hates the man as much as the company."

"But the man is dead," she said.

"That may not be enough for whoever is behind this. They may be out to destroy his legacy. So I repeat the question. How much of this is true?"

"You want truth? Dean Lamaar was a legend, a visionary in an arena where it's not easy to break new ground — wholesome family entertainment. His name is right up there with Walt Disney or Jim Henson or Mr. Rogers. The public adored him. All true." She clasped her hands and rested them on one knee. That was apparently all the cooperation I was going to get.

"Amy, I know your job is to hype the good stuff, but I need a little help with the shady side. Go off the record for a minute, will you?"

"You told me the other night that cops don't go off the record," she said. "Anything I say can and will be held against me." She gave me a wink. God, she was sexy, even when she was being a bitch.

"I'm sorry I ever said that. You can talk off the record."

"And you won't hold *anything* against me?" she said.

I didn't have to be a detective to read the double entendre. I had turned down her invitation for a bowl of chili and a romp on the Calvin Klein sheets, and now she was paying me back. Like I said to Frankie, hell hath no fury like a woman scorned.

"No, but I can really use your help," I said.

"Alright, I'll tell you what I know. Then maybe one day you can do something nice for me. Deal?"

"Deal." I wasn't sure whether or not I had just sold my soul, but after working in Hollywood for less than a week, I felt like I fit right in.

"I didn't know Dean Lamaar personally, but a lot of people who did thought he was a bastard. He was definitely a sexist, and probably a racist, a homophobe, and anti-Semitic. He was not the most politically correct man, but remember, he lived in an era when nobody was politically correct. The Civil Rights movement didn't happen till the sixties. Women didn't burn their bras till the seventies. In his defense, he was a product of his time. But even with that as an excuse, he was still a first-class shit. I've heard stories about how ugly it was to work here back in the old days, especially in the animation studio. Low wages, long hours, no benefits, no unions. Basically, you either worked under the terms Dean Lamaar dictated or you didn't work at Lamaar."

"That's what the book says. Is it true?"

"Probably. Hollywood's a scummy place to work *now*. I'm sure it was no better fifty years ago. Especially for women and other minorities. But I doubt if Lamaar Studios was much different from Universal, Fox, or any of the others."

"Did Lamaar write an autobiography?"

"I wish he had, but no. Every writer in Hollywood offered to ghost it for him, but he refused. Said his personal life was too boring."

"Too bad. I've read enough bios. I was looking for some kind of personal statement."

"We could take a look at *Deanie's Farewell*," she said. "A few days before he died Dean Lamaar made a tape about the history of the company. That's as personal as it gets."

"It's also a major coincidence, and detectives don't believe in coincidences. Didn't you ever think maybe it was kind of just too perfect that he made this definitive tape right before he died?"

"I love the way you think, but no. He made videotapes for all kinds of programming or events or special occasions. In this case we have an attraction at Familyland, The Homestead. It's a replica of the house Dean grew up in, kind of a mini-museum of his personal archives. He made the tape to run on a screen at The Homestead, but it's so boring we never used it. It would have just faded into oblivion, but Lamaar died a few days after he made it, so it took on a whole new significance. It became our founder's final words. *Deanie's Farewell*."

"I'd like to see it."

"It's in the archives at Familyland. I'll have them send you a copy."

"I'd like to see it now. I'll drive back down there. It would help if you came along."

"I was hoping you'd ask me out to a movie," she said. "Let's go."

CHAPTER 67

DISNEYLAND HAS MAIN Street. Familyland has Crane Street. The house at 23 Crane was a reproduction of the house where Dean Lamaar was born. As long as I had made the drive back to Costa Luna, I figured I'd check it out.

If the designers wanted to capture the look of a genuine Depression Era home, they succeeded. Young Dean's room was frozen in time, with clothes draped on the chair and shoes on the floor like he was still a carefree kid. His schoolbooks and toys were placed strategically around the room and his early drawings were proudly displayed. From what Eeg said about Lamaar's father, the art on the wall was revisionist history. If Eeg was telling the truth, Dean hid his drawings, or the old man would kick the shit out of him in a drunken rage.

There were photos of Mom and Dad with accompanying bios that made them sound like the all-American family. So who was lying? Eeg, with his horror story about the abused boy who murdered his father? Or Familyland, for portraying the Lamaar family as if they were Ward, June, and the Beaver?

We golf-carted to the Dexter Duck Building and took the elevator down, this time to B Level. I followed Amy through a labyrinth of corridors. "Brace yourself for Maxine Green," she said. "She's a real character."

"Cartoon variety or just another delightfully zany Lamaar

employee?"

"More acerbic than zany. She's got a razor-sharp tongue. She's also the first black employee Mr. Lamaar ever hired."

And he stuck her down here in the bowels of the building, I thought.

We got to a door marked *Video Archives*. Amy swiped her ID card and we entered a room that was two basketball courts deep and crammed with rack after rack of videotapes. A tiny wisp of a woman with cocoa brown skin and white hair pulled back in a bun was seated at the front desk. Amy introduced us. "Maxine Greene, this is Mr. Lomax." I noted that I had been downgraded from Detective to civilian.

"Max has been in charge of Video Archives since before they invented video," Amy said. "It used to be called Film Archives."

"And before that it was Stone Tablets," Maxine said, totally deadpan. "What can I get you this morning, honey?"

"I need a copy of *Deanie's Farewell*," Amy said.

"I have it filed right here under Boring," she said, tapping on her computer keyboard. Ignoring the glasses that were dangling on a gold chain around her neck, she leaned forward and squinted at the screen. "I've also got it with Spanish or French subtitles, so it can put you to sleep in three languages. Oh, and I've also got the source tape."

"I'll pass on the subtitles. The English version is fine," Amy said.

"Excuse me," I said. "What's the source tape?"

Maxine reached for the gold chain and put on her glasses. Apparently she could see without them, but she could speak better with them on. "It's everything they shot that day. It's what they edited from."

"Sounds interesting," I said. "Can we get that, too?"

"Mike, source tapes go on for hours," Amy said.

"Not this one," Maxine said. "Dean Lamaar hated being on camera. He'd shoot everything in one take, maybe two if he flubbed a line." She removed her glasses and squinted at the screen again. "Let's see, the final edit is twelve minutes; the source tape is eighteen minutes, forty-two seconds."

"We'll take both," I said.

"I'll get them," Maxine said, "but I'll be damned if I can figure out how these are going to help you in your investigation."

I could see the panic in Amy's eyes. "What investigation?" I said.

"Oh, please, *Mister* Lomax," Max said. "You're one of the detectives investigating the Ronnie Lucas murder."

"Do I look like a cop?"

"No, honey, with that suit and tie you look like a middle-aged rap star," she said. "But I just finished filing away all the news footage of Ronnie's murder and your face is all over it."

"You'd make a good witness," I said. "Yes ma'am. I'm investigating Ronnie Lucas's murder."

She must have been seventy years old and weighed ninety pounds. Or maybe it was the other way around. She stood up to her full four-feet-ten-inches. A good stiff breeze could have blown her to the next county. But when she put her spindly little hands on her hips, she looked like a geriatric black Wonder Woman.

"Ronnie was one of my favorites," she said with her jaw clenched. "I hope you catch the fucker who did it. I'll get your tapes."

CHAPTER 68

MAXINE SET US up in a private screening room. Amy and I watched the final edit first. The tape consisted of Dean Lamaar, the white-haired patriarch, sitting behind a desk telling folks how terrific his life had been.

Looking more like everybody's favorite uncle than a gazillionaire Hollywood mogul, Lamaar talked about how it all started with "the simple drawing of a rabbit with attitude." He didn't mention the possibility that a good chunk of that attitude may have come from the pen of Lars Eeg.

He went on to explain how "that single rabbit evolved into a company that has come to symbolize the family values that make America great." It was totally self-serving. Now I understood why they didn't use it in the exhibit. Most people would rather spend their time on long lines waiting to risk their lives on Cosmic Cat's Space Plunge.

"Maxine was kind," Amy said. "This is worse than dull."

She put the source tape into the VCR. It opened on the desk we had just seen, but Lamaar wasn't seated yet. I watched the time code tick by on the bottom of the screen.

"And you thought the first version was hard to watch," Amy said.

"Why the hell is the camera running if nothing's happening?" I said.

"Tape is cheap," she said. "With film they're very selective about what they print, because processing is so expensive. When they're shooting a busy executive like Mr. Lamaar they just keep the tape rolling."

After about a minute an off-camera voice said. "Hey Deanie, I'm all set up here. Step in." Lamaar entered the frame, sat behind the desk, and the camera moved in to the shot we had seen in the final.

"I'm just going to do an audio slate," the voice said. "Dean Lamaar, Vision Statement, May 19, 2002, Take One. In five, four, three, two."

There was a pause, then Lamaar began to speak. And now, once again, Amy and I were subjected to the avuncular Mr. Lamaar droning on about how he had shaped the values of America by giving it a cartoon rabbit.

My eyelids started to droop. About ten minutes into Lamaar's self-tribute, the picture started to shake violently. Lamaar screamed, "What the fuck was that?" which I distinctly recalled was not in the final edit.

The off-camera voice yelled, "Earthquake! Deanie, get under the desk, get under the fucking desk!" The old man took direction well. The camera captured Lamaar as he scrambled under the desk and disappeared from the picture.

According to the time code at the bottom of the screen, the earth shook for twenty-two seconds. Then it settled. The camera recorded it all. Finally, the off-camera voice said. "It's over. Deanie are you all right?"

Lamaar surfaced from under the desk. "Yeah, yeah, I'm okay," he said. "That was some fucking jolt. What do you think—5.6? 5.7? Definitely under six." He sat back down behind the desk.

After he settled back in, the off-camera voice said, "You want to take it from the top?"

"Hell, no," Lamaar said. "You got everything but the last two pages. Find a place where you can pick it up."

The off-camera guy didn't say anything for about twenty seconds. Finally, he said, "Why don't you back up a paragraph and pick it up from the phrase, 'Our history makes us strong, but our vision makes us stronger.' I'll start in close and pull back so that it won't jump cut from where we left off."

Lamaar grunted his approval. The camera pulled in tight. Then the off-camera voice gave the countdown. "In five, four, three, two," and Lamaar picked up his speech. About a minute later he finished.

"And cut," the voice said. "Excellent. Anything more you want to do?"

"I want to get the fuck out from under these lights before the aftershock shakes them loose and kills me," Lamaar said. I heard the beginning of a laugh from the man off camera and then the tape went dark. The time code on the bottom said eighteen minutes, forty-two seconds.

Amy was speechless. Finally she found just the right words. "Holy shit."

"There you have it folks," I said. "A direct quote from the Director of Lamaar's Corporate Communications."

"I've seen the edited tape before," she said, "but I never saw the source. I'm surprised they didn't erase the part with Mr. Lamaar saying 'fuck.'"

"They were in the middle of an earthquake," I said. "They probably didn't even hear themselves cursing. Who was the guy off-camera?"

"At first I thought it was just some random studio director they pulled off the lot. But nobody called him Deanie unless they knew him well. So I listened a little more carefully and I think it may be Klaus Lebrecht. He was real close to Mr. Lamaar."

"How close?"

"Did you ever hear of The Cartoon Corps?"

"Yeah, Lamaar's old cronies from his Army days."

"Klaus Lebrecht, Mitch Barber, and Kevin Kennedy were the

last of The Cartoon Corps. A few weeks after Mr. Lamaar died, all three of them retired on the same day."

"That's weird."

"It didn't seem that weird at the time," she said. "They were old, their Lord and Master died, and they didn't much like the new Lamaar."

"They didn't much like the new Lamaar?" I repeated. "I don't remember seeing their names on any of the grudge lists."

"I doubt if they had a grudge. They had a great life here. I think they just decided to cash in their chips. They worked as a team, they left as a team."

"Where are they now?"

"Probably living in Palm Springs with trophy wives and more money than they can spend. *Fortune Magazine* did an article on them when they left. The end of an era. I can get you a reprint if you want to read about them."

"Get me their addresses too. I'd also like to talk to them. And I'll need to borrow the tapes."

She handed me the videotapes. "I'll be back from Vancouver Friday night. No late fees if you drop them off at my apartment Saturday around 8:00."

I had no intention of showing up, but I had already turned her down once. "Thanks," I said. "I'll drop them off."

"Don't forget. If you don't bring them back, Maxine will kill me."

Maxine wouldn't kill her. But somebody would.

CHAPTER 69

I TOOK AMY back to Burbank, picked up two copies of the
Fortune article, and drove to my office. Terry was at his desk.
"I've got great news," he said.

"Did Forensics come up with something?"

"No, but I just saved a load of money on my car insurance by
switching to Geico. I heard you hijacked an airplane last night."

"Yeah, I'm also working with the mob. I'll do anything to fight
crime."

I tossed him a copy of the *Fortune* article and sat down to read it
myself. It was written a few months after Lamaar died. Kennedy,
Barber, and Lebrecht gave their own sugarcoated version of the
company's golden days. But according to *Fortune*, the Lamaar
balloon officially burst on October 19, 1987, the day the go-
go eighties came to a crashing halt. After that the company's
balance sheets were dripping with red ink.

To complicate matters, Dean had no heirs to pass the company
to, and because he kept the power all to himself, there were no
likely candidates who could fill his shoes.

By the early nineties Dean Lamaar started to make big
mistakes. Clinging to the tried and true, he spent a fortune on
hand-drawn animated features that were expensive to produce
and weren't right for the times. The movie division lost money
three years in a row. His TV shows did better, but the up-front

costs were high and the paybacks from syndication wouldn't happen for five years.

Lamaar stock kept dropping, and by the late nineties Wall Street had lost faith in the company, which was still being managed with an iron hand by its aging founder. In 1999, shortly after Dean's seventy-fifth birthday, Nakamachi, a Japanese electronics company, made a hostile takeover bid to buy Lamaar Enterprises.

Dean tried to block the sale, but he didn't have enough votes. Nakamachi bought the company for the bargain price of $22 billion. They promised Deanie a lifetime contract and total creative freedom. Everything would be the same, they said, except they would assume the financial burden that was draining him dry.

Ike Rose came on board as CEO. His immediate goal was to drive the stock up. With ten million options of his own, he had plenty of incentive.

Ike brought in new blood to fill the executive suites. Long-range plans were made, new business units were formed, new areas in the world of entertainment were researched and developed. It quickly became clear to Dean Lamaar that creative freedom did not translate to corporate power.

He still played a key role in the company. He was the patriarch, the icon, the symbol that America trusted. So they trotted him out at parades and let him make boring videos for an attraction that nobody wanted to visit. He was a Minister without Portfolio, and, while his remaining years were miserable, he refused to leave the company he founded. So Kennedy, Barber, and Lebrecht stuck with him. The day after his funeral the three of them resigned.

I had wondered why they all left at the same time. The last few paragraphs of the article put their decision in perspective.

There's no question that these are three talented men who made enormous contributions to the entertainment industry. But they were followers. And when their leader passed from the scene there was no place for them at the new Lamaar Company.

Klaus Lebrecht summed it all up with these words. "We could have given notice and slowly phased out of our jobs, but we all knew our time was up. We left the company the same way we came to it and the same way we worked at it for half a century. As a team. We're sure Dean Lamaar would approve."

Terry was reading the article in the men's room when Brian called me. "If I tell the FBI something, do they pass it on to you?" he said.

"No. They keep the best clues to themselves, and then all of a sudden the Special Agent in Charge calls a press conference and says Colonel Mustard did it in the Conservatory with the Candlestick, and we're all dumbfounded because we never got that clue. What did you tell them that might help us?"

"We've been working on the significance of the $266.4 four million, and I think we hit on something. We had a movie that was released five years ago. *Home for the Holidays.* It grossed $266.4 million. It doesn't feel like a random coincidence."

"My wife and I saw it," I said. "Is that the one where the family reunites for Christmas and somebody kills the father?"

"Right. And then you find out that he had sexually abused his daughter and now he was doing it to the granddaughter."

"A Christmas classic. I never realized it was a Lamaar movie."

"It was and it wasn't. Ike Rose read the script and knew it had the potential to be a hit. But it was too ugly to put the Lamaar name on it, so he created a new division, Freeze Frame Films. Now all of our R-rated movies come from Freeze Frame. It's very profitable, but some of the old-timers at Lamaar think it hurts our image. They call it Sleaze Frame."

"Was there any bad blood when you made *Home for the Holidays?*" I asked. "Actors getting fired? Writers screwed out of royalties? There's got to be a good reason why someone would ask for every penny the movie grossed."

"No, it came out on time and on budget. Things went smooth.

People got along. It was a hit at the box office and got nominated for Best Supporting Actress, Best Director, and Best Original Screenplay, but none of them won."

"What did the FBI guys say when you gave them this?"

"Nothing."

"That's exactly what they passed on to us. Nothing." I thanked him and put in a call to Garet Church, the senior FBI Agent on the Lamaar investigation. I had worked with Garet before and I liked him. He was less of a jerk than most of the Feds I had dealt with.

"Hello, Lomax," he said. "You got any information to deposit in the FBI bank or are you calling me to make a withdrawal?"

"I'm calling to give you a possible a lead. The Cartoon Corps."

"The three old men? Old news. We questioned them already."

"And you didn't share your findings with LAPD?"

"We talked to them yesterday when you were in New York chatting with Eeg. Nice of you to share those findings."

"Shit. I hate being caught not cooperating. You should have a copy of my report in the morning."

"Save the paper," he said. "We sent our own team out to see Eeg today."

"Well, then," I said, "in the spirit of interdepartmental cooperation, what did you get from Kennedy, Barber, and Lebrecht?"

"Zip. They're three old farts with prostate problems. We didn't tell them all the gory details, but we did tell them about the extortion plot. None of them can imagine anyone wanting to hurt the company except Eeg."

"And you're satisfied that their noses are all clean?"

"They're all over eighty years old and barely spry enough to organize a lawn party. Besides where's the motive?"

"I'm not sure, but it could be the same motive as Eeg. Dean Lamaar might have cheated them out of money. Like, I don't know, 266.4 million bucks."

"Actually that was the box office gross on one of Lamaar's movies."

"Gracious of you to finally share that little tidbit with LAPD."

"The difference between you and me, Lomax, is that I love being caught not cooperating. I don't have a clue if the 266 million is something Lamaar held out on with the three old geezers. But if you smell a motive, why don't you go talk to them and see what you come up with? Maybe you're right. Whoever hired these professional assassins doesn't have to be spry."

"Professional assassins? It sounds like you know something."

"Actually, we know exactly who murdered Eddie Elkins. Those Familyland surveillance DVDs from the day he got killed panned out."

"I thought LAPD was working on that."

"You were a little understaffed, so we pitched in. We have a name and lots of pictures. We also have strong leads on two of the other hits."

"Would you care to share some of the details with your local police?"

"There's a Joint Task Force Meeting tomorrow morning at nine. And you, my friend, are cordially invited. I was just about to call you."

"Thanks for keeping us in the loop. See you tomorrow."

I told Terry about the meeting.

"You know what a Joint Task Force Meeting is, don't you?" he said. "A bunch of cops getting together to see who has the biggest dick."

"Biggs, nobody likes a dick-measuring contest better than you," I said.

"But I got class. I only take out enough to win."

CHAPTER 70

TERRY AND I met for an early breakfast at the Denny's on Sunset. The plan was to go to the Joint Task Force Meeting, then see what we could learn from the three old men who had spent fifty years working with Dean Lamaar. We were just mopping up the last of our Grand Slam breakfasts when my cell rang.

"This is Ike Rose. Those bastards broke into my daughter's bedroom."

"Where are you now?" I said, throwing money on the table and heading out the door. Terry didn't wait for an explanation. He was right behind me.

"I'm at my house. We're okay. I mean we're physically okay. How fast can you get here?"

"We're on our way."

"Don't send for backup. I don't want fifty squad cars parked outside with their lights flashing." He hung up.

We took two cars. When we got to the house on Mapleton Drive, Mr. Lu was standing inside the front gates. As soon as he recognized us, the gates swung open. He jumped into my car. "What happened?" I said.

"Mr. Rose will explain," he said. "Just drive fast please."

I drove fast. Terry was right behind me. We came to a screeching cop-movie stop on the cobblestone and raced up the marble steps. Rose was standing in front of the double doors.

"Thank you for coming," he said. "Motherfuckers."

I assumed those were two separate thoughts.

"Look at this," he said, sprinting up the Y-shaped mahogany stairway. We followed him and stopped at the second room on the left. The door was closed. "This is Hannah's room. Lu was up here this morning and noticed that the door was shut, which it never is. So he opened it." With that, Rose swung open the bedroom door and we saw what had sent him over the edge.

The room was a Hollywood designer's vision of a rich girl's dream bedroom. Large and predominantly pink, it had pricey white furniture, plush pink carpeting, a mural of hundreds of Lamaar characters covering one wall, shelf after shelf of toys, dolls, and stuffed animals, and a massive canopy bed.

The bedding was saturated in what appeared to be blood. There was no body, but there was a white outline of one on the spattered red sheet. It was child-sized. In the center was a pink teddy bear that had been slit from its neck to its crotch. White stuffing spilled out, some of which had soaked up the red.

"Oh Jesus," Terry said. "Where's your little girl?"

"I sent Hannah and my wife out of town Sunday night. They're safe."

Terry sniffed the sheet. "I don't think this is real blood," he said, "but this is Hollywood, so you can probably buy prop blood at Wal-Mart. It's damp, but it's been drying for a while. They probably got in while you were asleep."

"We have a pretty decent alarm system," Rose said.

"So does Bank of America," Terry said, "but it doesn't keep everybody out. We're probably dealing with pros."

"They left a note on her night table." Rose picked up a plastic bag that looked like the one that had been jammed into Judy Kaiser's chest.

"If that's evidence," Terry said, "please don't handle it."

"Way too late. I opened it. I wanted to make sure they weren't holding her hostage. This was inside the bag."

It was a 5-by-7 photograph. Rose held it up by the edges so Terry and I could see it. It was a picture of an open hand. The killers were now up to five fingers. In the center of the hand it said, *You can't hide your family forever. Are you really sure you want to save Lamaar $266.4 million?*

"Direct and to the point," Terry said, sliding the picture back into the bag.

"Thank God I sent Hannah away. If she had been here…"

"Whoever did this knew she wasn't here," Terry said. "The fake blood, the chalk outline, even the note says they know she's in hiding. They came to give you a message. This is what *could* happen."

"Are you sure Hannah is in a safe place?" I asked him.

"I just called. My wife and daughter are both…" He held back. But only for a second. "They're both fine. Arabella Leone's people are guarding them."

"Good choice," Terry said. "The Leones have been in the protection business almost as long as LAPD."

"I know the history of the Leone family. But I've also worked with Arabella for four years. I trust her. After you were here last week I went to Vegas and I told her what was going on. She told me straight up and down that whatever might be happening to Lamaar was our own dirty laundry. She offered me her help. I said yes." He pointed a finger at me. "I understand you paid her a visit as well, Detective."

"She offered me her help, too," I said. "I said no."

"She's got resources at her disposal that LAPD doesn't have." Ike said.

"True," Terry said. "Her people have a much better view of the bottom of the barrel than we do."

Rose rubbed his hand over his chin. He hadn't shaved yet or combed his hair. His eye sockets were dark from lack of sleep. He looked more like a desk sergeant who had pulled a double shift than a millionaire CEO.

There was a picture of Hannah on her dresser. She was wearing a green-and-white gym uniform and had her right foot on a soccer ball. Rose picked it up and stared at it. "You got kids, Detective?"

"Three daughters."

"If their bedroom looked like this, what would you do?"

"I would do whatever it takes to keep my kids safe."

"So would I. I've decided to pay the ransom."

"Are you sure you want to do that?" Terry asked.

"My mission at Lamaar is to get out from under the shadow of the cartoon bunny rabbit image. Next month we cut the ribbon on Phase One of a multi-billion-dollar entertainment complex in Vegas. Whoever is behind this extortion plot is threatening to destroy that deal. I was willing to fight them. But they have a gun to my head, their finger is on the trigger, and the safety is off. I'm paying the money before my family or someone else gets hurt. I'm only sorry I waited. An innocent woman died because I was stupid enough to think I could go up against these bastards."

"It's your decision," I said.

Mr. Lu appeared in the doorway with a telephone in his hand. Ike waved him off. "Not now, Lu, I don't want to..."

"It's Brian Curry. It's bad news." He held out the phone and Rose wrenched it from his hand.

"Brian, it's Ike."

Rose listened for about twenty seconds. I watched his face and body slowly contort in anguish. "Oh, God. They didn't have to do that," he said. "I'm gonna pay. I swear I was ready to pay. Oh, Jesus."

Rose handed me the phone. "Brian, this is Mike. Terry and I are both here. There was a threat on Hannah's life, but she's alright. What's going on?"

"They took down our plane," he said. "It left Burbank early this morning on the way to Vancouver. I don't know if it was a surface-to-air missile or if they planted a bomb on board, but it doesn't matter. The plane was blown out of the sky. Everyone's dead. Amy, four of our senior executives, and a crew of three."

Amy? Dead? I could hear the sound of my own breathing. Labored little inhales followed by loud, painful exhales. "What about the crew? Was it..."

"Yes, Mike. It was the same crew you flew with on Monday."

I looked at Ike Rose. He was still holding his daughter's picture and was pressing it to his chest. The powerful head of one of the biggest entertainment enterprises on the planet looked at me with pleading eyes. I had seen that look too many times before. They were the eyes of a crime victim who can't believe that what is happening is really happening to him.

He shook his head back and forth. "I was ready to pay," he said. "They didn't have to kill anyone else. I was ready to pay. I was ready to pay."

CHAPTER 71

THIRTY MINUTES LATER our Forensics Team was in Hannah's room. Terry and I waited downstairs with Rose in a large room with a bar, a billiard table, a pinball machine, and several other expensive adult diversions. A maid brought in a cart with coffee and pastries.

Rose took a silver cigarette case out of his pocket. "I want to write an autobiography when I'm through with this corporate shit," he said, tapping a cigarette on the case. "So I keep a journal. Every time I screw up big time, I write it down, and I tell myself it's all part of the overall experience. The book won't be interesting unless you've failed along the way. But this...?"

He lit the cigarette and blew a lungful of noxious chemicals into the air. I was jealous. Seven years and I still missed the poison.

Twenty minutes later Brian showed up. "I'm driving to the crash site to meet with investigators from the FAA, NTSB, and the FBI," he said, "but I figured I'd stop by and see if there's anything I can do here."

"Thanks," Rose said. "I wish I could go with you, but I've got our financial people coming over so we can talk about how we're going to pull the ransom money together."

"They still don't know what brought the plane down," Brian said, "but it has to be sabotage. They threatened to kill our people and they did."

"What about all that post-9/11 security hype?" Terry asked.

"Security is a hell of a lot better on commercial flights since 9/11," Brian said. "But corporate and private jets are pretty lax. Ask Mike. He just flew that plane on Monday."

I looked at Terry. "The driver took me right to the tarmac," I said. "I got on without being searched. And I was carrying a gun."

Brian stayed for less than ten minutes, then left for the crash site. Terry and I decided to stick around to hear from Forensics. Rose smoked two more cigarettes while we waited. I always tell myself that one of these days something is going to happen to push me over the edge and I'm just going to pick up again and start inhaling where I left off. Joanie's death didn't do it. Maybe it was because I had time to brace myself. But the Lamaar plane going down with people I hardly knew had a much stronger effect on my addiction. I really wanted a cigarette. I settled for one of the pastries.

It didn't take Forensics long to confirm what Terry had assumed. The blood on Hannah's bed was a mix of corn syrup and red food coloring, the basic formula used in movie making. And the burglar alarm had been disabled by an expert. He even overrode the feature that signals the security company when someone tampers with the system.

By 11 a.m. Terry and I were back in the squad room. Kilcullen was waiting for us. "I spoke to Garet Church at the FBI. He rescheduled the Joint Task Force Meeting for 2 p.m."

"Nice of them to wait for us," Terry said.

"They pushed it back to give the new people time to get there."

"What new people?" Terry said.

"Now that it looks like the plane crash is connected to the other murders, we've got the FAA involved. Plus the Governor's Office wants representatives from the California Bureau of Investigation, the State Troopers, and the Office of the Attorney

General."

"What?" Terry said. "They didn't invite the good folks from the Department of Fish and Game?"

"We're lucky they invited LAPD. Why didn't you guys solve this mess last week like I asked you to?"

We filled him in on what went down at Ike Rose's house.

"I wish he wouldn't cough up the money," Kilcullen said. "Now the Feds will be in charge of the ransom phone calls and the payoff and whatever else goes down. They're the lead agency. I'm not kidding. I wouldn't be surprised if they told LAPD to go back home and write traffic tickets."

"I know Garet Church," I said, "and he isn't going to pull us off this case. Terry and I have too big of a learning curve."

"Plus we got closer to Ike Rose in a week than any of those Federal agents could get in a fiscal year," Terry said. "They'd be crazy to ask us off."

"Is that your ego talking?" Kilcullen said. "Or do you really think you can make a difference?"

"Both," Terry said. "If we get pulled off now, it will always be our failure. If we hang on, we have a chance to be in on the collar."

"And if there is no collar?"

"Then you can take us out behind the bowling alley and shoot us."

Terry's way of dealing with the darker side of our job is to joke his way through it. I on the other hand felt a deep sense of loss. Amy, Captain Sheppard, Sig, all dead for one reason. They were connected to Lamaar.

CHAPTER 72

THE 2:00 MEETING was in the FBI offices at 11000 Wilshire. At 1:50 Terry and I were on Sepulveda, squeezing from three lanes to one to get around an accident involving a Hummer and a vanload of Koreans.

Terry flashed his lights, crossed over the double yellow line, and scattered the oncoming traffic. "Sorry to take your life in my hands," he said, "but I hate being late to a dick-measuring contest."

I've been to enough meetings with the FBI to know that they have several conference rooms that can seat forty people around one big table. It helps promote the misguided feeling that all agencies are created equal. This time there was no such pretense. The meeting took place in a theatre. Garet Church stood in front, so that the rest of us who sat facing him would have no doubt who was in charge. It was a none-too-subtle mind fuck.

Being a homicide cop, I've had to break the bad news to a lot of people that someone they loved or were close to had been murdered. The most common response is *"But I just saw him yesterday, but I just kissed her goodbye this morning, but I was just on the phone with him a few hours ago."*

People think that if they *just* saw you, you couldn't possibly, suddenly, inexplicably, be dead. It's a reaction I see a lot, and now I was going through it. So I didn't feel like saying much.

I let Terry do the talking. He gave the group an update on the break-in at Rose's house and his decision to pay the ransom.

As we expected, Church assigned his people to hang twenty-four/seven with Rose, to make sure the Bureau had first crack at the bad guys when the ransom call came.

"Rose is running the ad in the Classified Section of tomorrow morning's *L.A. Times*," Church said. "We've got electronic surveillance teams set up to cover his home phone, his office, and his cell. When the call comes, we'll try to get a trace, but don't count on it. These people are smart.

"We have no idea if they're going to ask Rose to wire the money to the Caymans, pay it out in gold bars, or leave a check under the doormat. Best guess is they'll ask for good old American greenbacks. Our job is to follow the money. Are you listening to me, people? We're not playing with Monopoly money here. This is going to be 266.4 million of Uncle Sam's finest. Some packets will be rigged to send out electronic signals so we can track it with a GPS locator. And we *will* track it. Then we'll nail whoever is on the receiving end."

Church tapped a button on the podium and a large screen lowered behind him. "We've made some headway in the killings. I'll start with Elkins. There are about a thousand surveillance cameras throughout the park and down underground where the employees are. We isolated only those cameras that Elkins passed through from the time he started work in the morning.

"One man, dressed like your average tourist, consistently took the same route as Elkins. He didn't follow Elkins directly. Sometimes he'd show up in a frame a minute behind Elkins and sometimes he'd be ten seconds in front of him, because he probably did a dry run and knew Elkins's itinerary. Here's a video of him entering the front gate on the day of the murder."

The lights dimmed and the screen lit up with a surveillance tape of the Lamaar main entrance. People were streaming through the gate eager to get into the park. Garet hit a button and the video froze on one happy group.

"See this bunch?" Church said. "Six people. Five of them are Belgian tourists traveling together. Two couples and one woman who is the sister of one of the husbands. We know who they are because they stayed at a hotel on the Lamaar property and we were able to cross-check. But this short guy with the sunglasses, he doesn't belong with them. He hung close to them, because one guy alone in a place called Familyland is going to stand out to Security."

He rolled the tape to a second scene. "Same guy again. Only now he's walking alongside a different group. Each time he pops up he tries to blend in so he doesn't look like a solo act, and each time he's following the route that Rambunctious Rabbit took through the park."

A voice from one of the seats called out. "Do we know who he is?"

"His name is Angelo Innocenti. Interpol ID'd him for us yesterday. He's a professional killer; home base is Palermo, Sicily."

A third video went up. "This is Signor Innocenti going through security at LAX that night. He took Lufthansa 451 to Frankfurt, and by the time Elkins's body was discovered the next morning, he was back home eating pizza and drinking Chianti. We don't have the manpower or the jurisdiction to smoke him out of whatever cave he's hiding in, and frankly, I don't give a shit about him right now, because he's just a pair of hands for hire."

A female voice called out. "If Innocenti went back to Sicily after the Elkins murder, then someone else killed Ronnie Lucas. Correct?"

"Correct. The Lucas killer was eight inches taller than the Elkins killer. One person who was on the breakfast line that morning swears that the tall guy who talked to Lucas sounded Albanian. Now admittedly our eyewitness has been homeless for twelve years and is not as mentally stable as some of you folks…" He paused for the laugh and he got it. "But a few other people thought the suspect sounded Eastern European. Again, the doer is not who we're after."

"What about the Judy Kaiser murder?" Terry asked.

"That only happened a few days ago. But something jumped out on the surveillance tapes from the restaurant. A woman came in with two kids. They bought lunch, then sat in the back out of range of the cameras. About twenty minutes later we pick up the two kids leaving. But the Mom stayed behind. Then the Kaiser family comes in and Judy goes off camera toward the bathroom. Four minutes later we pick up the Mom leaving the restaurant. We track her to the train ride where she catches up with her kids."

"Was she in the bathroom with the vic?"

"Hard to tell," Church said, "but she was definitely in that little alcove in the rear, so she must have seen Judy. She's either an innocent bystander or a soccer Mom who brought her kids to Familyland, then murdered one of the other patrons to help pay for the trip."

He put up a shot of a striking, dark-haired, dark-eyed woman and two young boys. "Fortunately she also stayed at one of the Lamaar hotels, so there were cameras everywhere. This was taken when they checked in. Her name is Penina Benjamin and the kids are her two sons. She's an Israeli."

There was an audible "ah-ha" murmur from the room. Sort of a collective conclusion that if a beautiful young mother with two kids is from Israel, she's more likely to be a trained commando than an innocent bystander.

"Mrs. Benjamin and her kids flew to New York early Monday morning, spent the night, then flew El Al back to Israel yesterday. We want to talk to her, but with all the bureaucratic crap that goes on between the U.S. and Israel, that's not going to be very high on anybody's list. More important than picking her up for questioning is that once we get a suspect who might have hired these killers, we'll see if his passport shows that he made a shopping trip to Israel, Italy, and Eastern Europe."

My cell phone vibrated. I checked the Caller ID and bolted out of the room. I got to the corridor and answered on the fourth ring.

"Hi, it's Diana."

"I know. You think I pick up for every beautiful, blue-eyed blonde who calls me in the middle of a multiple homicide investigation?"

"Oh, gosh," she said. "I caught you at a bad time."

"It's never a bad time when you call. How are you?"

"I'm fine, but Hugo has had a few rocky days. His fever is up, his blood count is down, and he's rejecting platelets. He's stable now, but... I'm sorry, I hate to ask you this when you're so busy."

"Would it help if I came over and visited him?"

"Yes." She lowered her voice. "The sooner the better."

"I'll be there by 6:00."

"Thank you," she said, still whispering, making her sound both grateful and sexy at the same time. "You know I wouldn't ask if I didn't think it would make a big difference."

We hung up, and I went back to the meeting. I still didn't feel like saying much. But after thirty seconds on the phone with Diana, I felt a hell of a lot better than when I walked out.

CHAPTER 73

THE MEETING DRAGGED on till 5:00. It took another two hours to go back to the office, follow up on phone calls and deal with Kilcullen. I didn't get to Valley General until 7:45. Diana was waiting at the sixth-floor nurses' station.

"I did the best I could," I said, "but you can never believe a cop who says he'll meet you at a civilized hour. Sorry."

"Don't apologize. You've already gone above and beyond. I didn't tell Hugo you were coming. He's going to be thrilled to see you."

She took my arm and led me down the corridor. "I should warn you. He's lost more weight and the meds have really taken their toll."

I nodded. I had seen Joanie in her final months. I knew what to expect.

Hugo was in bed, connected to a network of tubes and wires that snaked their way out of his body to a multi-limbed IV tree. A monitor hung from one of its metal arms and beeped efficiently. Also dangling from the pole were six plastic bags filled with high-tech potions that would either cure him or kill him.

A woman, whom I recognized as Hugo's mother from the Christmas in Sundance T-shirt, was sitting in a chair near his bedside. She stood up and introduced herself. "I'm Nola Cordner. You must be Detective Lomax. Diana told me all about you.

Hugo, look who came to visit. It's your hero."

Hugo looked smaller, paler, and much sicker. He contorted his face in a grimace. At first I thought he was in pain, but then I realized it was just typical teenage embarrassment. "Mom," he said, stretching the word out into three syllables. "I never said hero. What am I, eight years old and he's Batman?"

He looked over in my direction, but my old LAPD baseball cap was pulled down low on his face, so I couldn't see his eyes. "I didn't say hero," he said.

"Well, even if you did," I said tapping on an IV bag filled with Da-Glo yellow glop, "I'd just figure it was the drugs talking."

"Tell my Mom about the revenge of the flowers," he said. "It's the best story, but if I told it, she'd probably say I was making it up."

"Well, let's see," I said, turning to Nola. "I was about your son's age, and I had no thought about going into police work."

"He was going to be a stuntman, like his mother," Hugo said. "Well, she was a stuntwoman, but you know what I mean."

And so it went. I told the story, and Hugo would jump in with the details. After a few minutes, he asked Diana to help him sit up, and by the time I got to Donny Hovsepian's arrest, Hugo had transformed from an inert gray lump to an excited, animated child.

"That was a wonderful story," his mother said, her eyes wet to the brim, but not quite spilling over. "Thank you. Thank you very much."

At 8:30 Diana called a curfew. I took Hugo's hand. It was cold and his grip was weak. "I don't want to hurt you like I did the last time," he said. "So you're getting the wimpy handshake." His eyes were drooping and he closed them as Diana lowered the head of his bed. I said good night to his mother, and he was asleep before Diana and I left the room.

We took the elevator down to the lobby. "Are you hungry?" she said.

"Starved."

"What kind of food are you in the mood for?" she said.

Whatever you have in your refrigerator, I thought. But I knew better than to say it. My wife had passed away less than seven months ago. My brother was in deep shit, and my father needed my help digging him out. And my partner, my boss, and the Governor of California needed me to solve the crime of the century. The last thing I needed at this point in my life was a serious relationship with Diana Trantanella. Then she repeated the question.

"Earth to Mike, I asked what kind of food you're in the mood for."

"Whatever you have in your refrigerator," I heard myself say out loud.

And then I felt her arms around my neck and her lips gently kissing mine. "Are you sure?" she said.

"No," I said. "Maybe if you kissed me again."

She did. It was long and deep and went directly to every pleasure center in my body. "I'm sure," I said.

Twenty minutes later we were in her bedroom furiously peeling each other's clothes off. I'd have to call Big Jim in the morning and thank him for meddling in my life.

CHAPTER 74

DIANA AND I made love, raided her refrigerator, made love again, watched Letterman up to the Top Ten List, and then, despite my advancing years and lack of sleep, managed to make love a third time. She was impressed. I was even more impressed.

"Don't get used to it," I said. "It's like a parlor trick. I never do it again for the same crowd."

"What about your dog?" she said, suddenly sitting up.

"Andre can do it six times a night," I said. "But then he doesn't call you in the morning. The French can be so rude."

She laughed. "I mean, don't you have to go home and walk him?"

"If I did, you and I would be in *my* bed right now, and Andre would be trying to wedge his way between us. My friend Kemp is dogsitting."

She turned over on one elbow and ran a pearly pink fingernail from my navel to my left nipple, which apparently was not too tired to rise to the occasion. Then she worked her way directly over my heart and slowly began stirring up a patch of chest hair. "Did you plan that in advance because you thought you might not be going home tonight?"

"I've been putting in twenty-five-hour days lately," I said. "So it's not fair to leave Andre sitting around the house with his legs crossed."

"What crime are you trying to solve?"

There was such a delightful ingenuousness to the way she asked the question. Like, *What color will you be painting the ceiling, Mr. Michelangelo?*

"I'm not supposed to give you the details. You could be a security risk."

"You can frisk me if you want," she said, sliding her soft, warm body on top of mine and slowly kissing me on the eyes, the nose, and finally the lips.

I told her everything. I figured if Terry could tell Marilyn, which I knew for a fact he did, it would be only fair for me to have someone's ear. Although her ear wasn't what I focused on as I unfolded the gruesome details of the past eleven days. Besides, what could the Department do to me if they found out I broke the rules while I was naked in bed with a beautiful blonde? If they drummed cops out of the corps for pillow talk, the city of Los Angeles would be totally without police protection.

I slept till dawn, then drove home to change. Kemp's truck was parked outside my house. He was in the living room with Andre, who bounded across the room and had his paws on my shoulders before I could close the door.

"Good morning, Detective," Kemp said. "You look like you had a rough night keeping the peace."

"I was doing some serious undercover work. Thank you for taking care of Andre. Did the *L.A. Times* get delivered? It wasn't on the front step."

"I was reading it in the bathroom. I'll get it." He returned a minute later with the dog-eared sections in a bulky pile. "Sports section is a little wet," he said, "but it's only water."

The lead story was the Lamaar plane crash, which was reported as suspicious and under investigation. There was a picture of Amy and two of the other victims on Page One. I shuffled through the rest of the sections till I found the Classifieds.

Kemp was leaning over my shoulder. "Looking for a job?" he

asked.

"No. I'm looking for a handyman who can mind his own business."

I turned the pages till I got to the Personals. Kemp grinned, but didn't say anything. I ran my finger down the columns until I found it. *The family of the late Buddy Longo thanks his friends and co-workers for their love and support during our time of grief.*

There was no turning back now. I crumpled the entire section into a ball and threw it across the room.

"I don't know what you're looking for in the Personals," Kemp said, "but I'll give you the same advice my father gave me. Even though I never paid much attention to it."

"Lay it on me. I need all the advice I can get."

Kemp bent down, began scratching Andre behind the ears, looked up at me, and said, "If it's got tits or wheels, it's gonna give you problems."

CHAPTER 75

IKE ROSE WAS a stubborn son of a bitch. Despite the fact that he had to be within arm's reach of a telephone so he could accept the ransom call, he refused to stay in one place. "I'm not rescheduling my life," he said. "My phone can follow me wherever I am. I do it every day. Call Forwarding."

He had an early breakfast meeting at The Four Seasons with a couple of investment bankers, stopped at his Burbank office for an hour, then drove down to Familyland where he was shooting a promotional video for the park.

Terry and I were part of the entourage that followed him, which also included Garet Church, his partner Henry Collins, and a four-man electronic surveillance team, who had forwarded Ike's home, office, and cell phones to a single black handset.

When we got to Familyland, Ike and the Feds went to The Rainbow's End, the location where the video was being shot. Terry and I were politely asked to wait in Brian Curry's office till it was time for Ike to head to his next gig. "No sense in everybody cluttering up the same space," Agent Church told us.

"I wonder if he wants us to just sit here and do nothing," Terry said, when we got to Brian's office, "or if we should go screw ourselves while we're waiting."

We speculated on what kind of person it took to mastermind a crime like this one. "Speaking of masterminds," Terry said, "it's been five days since Judy Kaiser was killed. Somebody smart is managing to keep it out of the papers."

"You remember Ike's assistant, Richard Villante?" Brian said, clearing his throat hard on *assistant*. "Ike was darn lucky to find an assistant who graduated top of his class at Yale Law. Richard has an uncanny ability for keeping things out of the news."

But no number of lawyers could keep the Lamaar plane crash out of the news. We flipped from CNN to MSNBC to Fox. None of them referred to it as an accident. The theories and hypotheses all focused around terrorism, although one so-called expert was convinced it was caused by a suicidal pilot.

"You jackass," Terry said to the TV. "A pilot would commit suicide by plowing the plane into downtown Burbank, not by blowing it up in midair."

"Let him talk," Brian said. "Ike needs idiots like that obscuring the truth."

Brian tried to work, but for the most part Terry and I kept distracting him. I picked up the double-sided picture frame on his desk. I pointed to the older couple. "Your Mom and Dad?"

He smiled. "Married when they were seventeen. Mom taught first grade. My Dad was a railroad cop for forty years. He's a hell of a guy. They broke the mold after they made him."

"They broke the mold with my Dad, too," I said. "Actually we're pretty sure it was cracked before they even started."

Curry laughed. "What did he do?"

"He's devoted his life to bugging the shit out of me. He's still at it."

"I hate to interrupt this fascinating repartee," Terry said, "but the three of us are as useless here as tits on a bull. Let's go out and get some lunch."

Curry shook his head. "I don't think we should leave."

"Why?" Terry said. "Because the FBI needs us? As far as they're concerned, we're the dummies that couldn't solve it. Explain it to him, Mike."

"Terry gets cranky when he's running on empty," I said. "Come on, it won't hurt to run out and grab a quick bite. We've got radios. They'll find us."

"Alright," Curry said. "Let me just check my e-mail."

"And I'll check my pee mail," Terry said. "Point me toward a urinal."

Curry didn't answer. He was preoccupied by whatever was on his computer screen. Terry and I were about to find a men's room on our own when Curry stopped us. "Don't go!" he yelled. "Get Ike and the Feds in here. I've got to shut down Ramona."

"Who's Ramona?" I said, my voice and my blood pressure kicking up a few notches.

"The Ramona Rabbit Parking Lot. I'm shutting it down. Those maniacs just e-mailed me the ransom demands."

Terry took off to get the others, and I scrambled to the other side of the desk and scanned the screen. Curry grabbed a radio from his desk and pressed the Talk button. "Security One to Ramona Parking, come in Ramona."

The radio squawked back. "This is Ramona. Go ahead Security One."

"Shut Ramona down," Curry said. "Divert everything to Dexter. Now. You copy that?"

The voice on the other end was young and female. "Yes, sir. Shutting down Ramona now. Just a minute, sir."

I could hear the young woman yelling at the other parking lot attendants. "Yo! Julie, Melissa, we're shutting Ramona down. Divert those cars to Dexter. Yo! Jason, don't let that Mazda sneak in. Thank you."

"It's a little nuts here, sir," she said, over the sound of horns honking. "The guests are not thrilled that they have to divert, but we're on the case."

"How many cars in Ramona right now?" Brian asked.

"Rough estimate, maybe only three hundred, sir. We just opened this lot about ten minutes ago."

Brian turned to me. "We're in luck. Ramona holds six thousand cars, but we operate the parking sectors on a stagger system. We don't open one until the lot in front of it is full." He went back to his radio. "How many guests are waiting for the shuttle?"

"Fifty, sixty," she said.

"Get them back in their cars and send them to Dexter. Then tell shuttle dispatch no more service in or out of Ramona until further notice from me. This is Brian Curry, Head of Security. Who am I talking to?"

"This is Caitlin Farley, sir."

"You're doing a good job, Caitlin. Over."

Ten minutes later Ike Rose and the six Feebies piled through the doorway of Brian's office. "They made contact," Brian said to Ike. "E-mail."

Rose sat on the edge of a chair. The rest of us stayed standing. "It's from b.longo@yahoo.com, sent today at 11:47 a.m.," Curry said checking his watch. "Fifteen minutes ago. Subject: *payoff time*. Message: *Curry, pass this on to Ike Rose and the Keystone Cops who are bumping into each other as they hover around him*."

Curry looked up to see if anyone wanted to comment, but nobody said a word. Not even Terry. Curry went on. "*Send two men, unarmed and shirtless to the black Ford van in row fourteen, space nine, of the Ramona Parking Lot. Take the twenty-seven duffel bags from the back and fill them up. Put exactly ten million in hundreds in each bag, 6.4 million in the last bag. Put the bags back in the van by 5 p.m.*"

"Are they crazy?" Rose said, springing up from the chair. "They want us to make the payoff in our own parking lot? That's the dumbest plan I ever heard of. That lot is filled with people going back and forth all day."

"Not any more sir," Brian said. "I just shut it down."

"What if people want to get their cars back so they can drive home?"

"There are only three hundred vehicles parked there now," Brian said. "If it were up to me, I'd get a bunch of tow trucks and flatbeds and move them all except the black van. But I'm not in charge here." He looked over at Church.

"Good call locking up that parking lot," Church said. "I agree that we should move every single vehicle, but I don't give a shit about people getting their cars back. I just want to isolate the van."

"Put the bags back in the van by 5 p.m.," Brian said, returning to the e-mail. *"A few minutes after that, we'll be picking it up."*

"And then what?" Rose said. "They just drive it off the property? Would they like us to provide them with a police escort?"

Terry could no longer resist. "I doubt if they're going to want us Keystone Cops mucking up their getaway, sir," he said.

Sometimes Terry pushes too far, but this time even the FBI guys laughed.

"Let me finish," Brian said, quieting the room down. *"There are video cameras on, in, and around the van. We're watching every move you make. Any tricks and the first ones to die are Rose's family."*

Rose's shoulders slumped. He was only five-foot-four, and now, surrounded by a room full of six-footers and beaten down by terrorists who invaded his home and threatened his family, he looked even shorter than usual.

"Get the bags," he said. "I've got the money downstairs."

CHAPTER 76

'I'VE GOT THE money downstairs' was an understatement. Six stories below the fun and the fantasy was an impenetrable steel fortress where an army of bean counters processed the millions that poured into Familyland daily.

"We call this place Little Switzerland," Brian said, as he took me and Terry on a tour of the facilities. "Every dollar, franc, and yen spent in the park is counted, re-counted, and accounted for. Every credit card receipt is authenticated, substantiated, and validated."

We stopped in an area where four workers wearing rubber aprons were dumping bags of coins into sudsy water. "And this must be where the money gets laundered," Terry said.

Brian shook his head like he'd heard that one before. "We have thirty-two fountains on the property. We encourage people to toss in a coin, make a wish, and help a child who can't be here. The money we collect goes to Ike's favorite charity, Vitamin Angels. Then he personally matches it. He's a good guy."

I nodded in agreement. He sure seemed like one.

We finally arrived at the room where the ludicrous sum of $266.4 million was being prepped for delivery.

Until the e-mail arrived, nobody knew for sure how the ransom would have to be paid out. But Church's gut instinct told him that the killers would ask for cash. So Ike had a Wells Fargo armored truck with the $266.4 million standing by. Now, the Bureau's mad scientists were in the Familyland subterranean bank deftly doctoring random packets to send out electronic tracking signals. *Our job is to follow the money*, Church had said repeatedly.

Terry and I had the honors of being the unarmed shirtless bagmen who would carry the duffel bags from the rear of the van. We had volunteered as soon as Ike left Brian's office.

"That money is pretty heavy," Church said. "I got younger, stronger guys who can do it."

"C'mon, Boss," Terry said. "This may be the only chance Mike and I get to work topless."

A slo-mo grin spread across Church's face. He didn't say anything, but I knew what he was thinking. *You waited for Ike Rose to leave the room before you volunteered. If you had asked while he was still there, you would have put me in an embarrassing position, because he's your new rabbi and he would have pushed me to give you the job. But you didn't do that. If you did, you'd be back at LAPD complaining about how the Feds cut you out of the loop.*

"Okay," he finally said, loud enough for all his agents to hear. "Lomax and Biggs will be the bagmen."

Once again Aretha was right. R-E-S-P-E-C-T.

Ramona was the smallest of seven parking lots on the Familyland property. According to Brian it *only* held six thousand cars. The north and east ends were open to allow the free flow of traffic. The southern and western perimeter was surrounded by trees, which were being carefully combed by a team of agents.

Row after row of uniform parking spaces were neatly painted and numbered. The lot was dotted with stainless steel columns that rose sixty or seventy feet in the air. Each pole ended in a cluster of floodlights. It was still broad daylight, but I got the impression that darkness never fell on Ramona.

Retrieving the duffel bags was easy. The Feds set up a command post, a thirty-foot Winnebago parked half a football field away from the van. Terry and I stripped to the waist, walked slowly to the rear of the shiny black Ford, and opened the rear door. The inside was completely empty except for the driver's seat. I saw at least three tiny video cameras. One, perched on the dash, was pointing right at us. Two more fish-eye lenses covered the parking lot. They said they were watching every move we made and I believed them.

The bags were strapped together in four separate piles. Terry and I grabbed two piles apiece, shut the door, and returned to the command center, where a second team took them to the underground bank to be filled with cash.

While the money was being counted, the car population of the Ramona Rabbit Parking Lot was diminishing rapidly. Twelve tow trucks, seven large tractors, five teams of horses, and four elephants were rounded up to drag a total of 288 vehicles to the Dexter Duck Parking Lot a mile to the east. By 3:30, the black Ford van in row fourteen, space nine, stood alone.

By 4:15, the duffels were filled, packed onto a flatbed, and ready to roll.

"Should we strip down again?" Terry said to Agent Church.

"No, they said 5:00. I'm not giving it to them any earlier," he said.

Ike Rose was standing next to the truck, his hand resting on a bag that contained $10 million. "How the hell do they think they can drive off with a Ford van full of money?" he said.

"My best guess," Church said, "is helicopter. The e-mail said put the money in the van, then *we'll be picking it up*. I think they're going to swoop down with a cargo chopper and lift up the entire van."

"Then maybe we made it easier for them by clearing the cars," Ike said.

"We also made it easy for us to see what they do," Church said. "And if they airlift it, those money wrappers will give off a signal we can track for miles. I've got our choppers standing by. We can tail them and still stay out of sight."

"And what if someone just gets into the van and drives off?" Rose said.

"We'll still follow them from the air. Sooner or later the driver's got to deliver the money to whoever planned this whole thing. They're smart, but they're not that smart," Church said. "We'll get them."

"From your lips," Ike said.

At 4:40, Church turned to me and Terry and said, "Show time, boys."

We took off our shirts. Terry got behind the wheel of the flatbed and I sat on top of one of the duffel bags. He drove at five miles an hour and pulled up behind the black Ford. I opened the rear doors.

Each bag weighed eighty pounds, so it was easier for us to both grab a handle and haul it up onto the edge of the cargo bed. "When I leave the job and go into stand-up," Terry said, as he climbed inside and dragged the first bag to the front of the van, "this little drama is going to make great material. I don't know what's funny about it yet, but I'm definitely going to work it into my act."

On the fourteenth bag, Church called out on the bullhorn. "Pick up the pace, boys. It's ten to five."

My shoulders, arms, and back were feeling the burn, but nobody else had to know that. We loaded faster. Also, as the van filled up, we didn't have to drag each bag so far. We finished at 4:56, jumped into the flatbed, drove back to the command post, and put our shirts back on.

"Now we wait," Church said.

CHAPTER 77

WE DIDN'T WAIT long. At 5:02 Church got the first radio call. "Incoming chopper, two miles due west of the drop zone. He's at nine hundred feet."

"Positions," Church yelled, and most of the agents took cover in the tree line at the west end of the lot, just in case the idiots in the helicopter decided to pick off cops while they were picking up the money. Ike, Brian, Terry, and I followed Church and two agents into the Winnebago.

Inside, a technician sat in front of three monitors. One camera was locked on the black van; the other two were scanning the sky. "Got him on Two," the techie said, but none of us turned to watch the monitors. We could see the chopper through the window. He was half a mile away and closing fast.

The sky was clear and visibility was excellent. "He doesn't care if we know who he his," Church said. "His BuNo is plain as day."

Sure enough, the BuNo, the FAA's identifying serial number for all aircraft, was clearly visible on the underbelly of the blue-and-white helicopter. "November, five, eight, two, niner, Charlie," Church said, reading it through binoculars.

The chopper was small, like one of those bubble-front traffic copters that zip up and down the freeways. "He's not big enough," I said. "That bird could never lift that van."

"You're right, he looks like a Bell Jet Ranger," Church said. "They're fast, but they can't lift more than half a ton." He grabbed a radio. "Command One to Air Support. Air One, stand by to follow the chopper. Air Two, don't move till the van is rolling. It looks like they're going to drop a driver."

But the helicopter didn't drop anybody. It buzzed right past the van and kept heading east toward Familyland.

"What the hell?" Church said, and stepped out of the Winnebago to get a better view. We all followed him and watched as the helicopter flew directly over the theme park.

Seconds later, the sky was filled with a ribbon of yellow.

"He's dropping leaflets," Church said, as tens of thousands of sheets of paper fluttered in the wind. "Command One to Air One. Go, now."

As a cop, my mind focused on the fact that if they were only dropping paper, nobody could get hurt. But as the CEO of Lamaar, Ike had a grasp on the real significance of the drop. "Those sick bastards," he said, pounding his fist on the side of the Winnebago. "They're going public on us."

Brian was on the radio. "Security One to all stations. They're dropping flyers over Sector Seven. I want to know what they say."

The sky was now littered with flapping yellow pages. Some seemed to be defying gravity as they got caught in an updraft and rose even higher, but the bulk of them were floating slowly to the ground. The helicopter was now a speck on the horizon and fading out of sight. Air One was about a mile behind.

Curry's radio snapped to life. "Security Twelve to Security One. Brian, it's me, Mel Gelade. This is really sick."

"Read it," Brian said.

"There's a Lamaar logo with a slash through it. Then it says *Death to Lamaar and all those who associate with them. We've killed twelve so far, and we will continue to kill employees, customers, and all those who support Lamaar in any way. This is your only warning.*"

"What's the crowd reaction?" Brian said.

"Not many people have read it yet, but a bunch of them who have are hauling ass to the gates. A few think it's a prank and they're happy that the lines are getting shorter. It's not a prank, is it?"

"No. Just a minute." Brian turned to Ike. "White Star," he said. Ike just nodded. Brian went back to his radio. "Security One to all stations. Operation White Star is now in effect. This is not a drill. This is the real deal. Repeat, Operation White Star is now in effect."

Brian turned to us. "We're closing the park," he said. "We should have about ninety-eight percent of the visitors and half the employees off premises in an hour. White Star is designed to get people out of the park in the least amount of time with the least amount of panic."

"When did you do your last dry run?" Church asked.

"Monday," Brian said. "The day after the ransom note came. I was thinking that maybe I was being a little paranoid, but now I'm glad I did it."

"I don't get it," Rose said. "We had a deal. They asked for the money. There it is." He pointed to the van, which didn't seem nearly as important as it was just minutes ago.

"It's a vendetta," I said. "I guess it was never about the money."

And then a voice boomed out. It was human, but it was electronically distorted. "Good afternoon, Mr. Rose." Somewhere, someone was talking into a voice changer and the sound was coming from a loudspeaker in the Ford van. It went on. "We didn't keep our end of the bargain, did we?"

Ike Rose started walking toward the van. "You bastards. What the hell did I do to you?"

"You have no soul, Mr. Rose," the voice said, echoing slightly. "No values. Your days of peddling smut are over."

Ike raised a fist in the air. "You sanctimonious hypocrite. You kill my people; you break into my home and desecrate my little girl's bedroom; and you talk to me about values?"

The only response was maniacal laughter. Then the laughter doubled and tripled into a chorus. The person operating the voice changer wanted to piss Ike off. It was working. He was livid, flushed with anger. "I paid your ludicrous price. What more did you want?" he yelled, still moving toward the van.

The van answered back, equally angry. "Do you really think we want money? Do you think money will stop us?"

And in that moment I knew what was about to go down. I'm sure the other cops would have figured it out. I just happened to be the first. "Take cover!" I yelled. "Get in the Winnebago! Now, now, now!"

Church and his men didn't need to be told twice. They started running. But Ike kept advancing toward his invisible accuser, his voice and his fist raised. I grabbed him by the arm. "They don't want the money!" I said. "Run, run!"

"Run?" Rose shrieked. "I'm not running from those bastards! They're destroying my company."

Terry was right behind me. He grabbed Rose's other arm. Together, the two of us dragged and shoved the hysterical CEO toward the Winnebago.

The voice on the loudspeaker continued. "Lamaar is doomed, Mr. Rose, and you're the person responsible for sending it to its grave."

The Feds piled into the Winnebago. Terry and I tried to push Rose in, but he smashed his shin into the metal step and started to yelp in pain.

Church's partner, Henry Collins, who has arms that look like they were fabricated in a steel mill, reached down from inside the motor home and yanked Rose up in the air and pulled him in. I made it up the step and Terry was right behind me, shoving me through the door.

"Take cover!" I yelled. "Stay away from the windows! They're going to…"

I didn't get to finish my sentence. The explosion finished it for me. The van had been wired with a bomb. I caught a quick glimpse of the fireball as the van and the twenty-seven duffel bags stuffed with money blew sky high.

As my partner tumbled through the door, the blast knocked the Winnebago on its side and we slid across the macadam.

CHAPTER 78

I'VE NEVER BEEN shot. But in my mind I've always been prepared for what it would feel like to take a bullet.

This I was not prepared for.

I threw myself down and managed to get most of my upper body under the video equipment table, and immediately decided it was the wrong choice. I tried to protect my head with my hands. My ears were covered but I could still hear metal shredding, glass breaking, and Garet Church bellowing out in agony. We skidded to a stop and the horrendous sounds gave way to frightening smells. Burning electrical cables, scorched rubber, spilled gasoline.

I kicked what glass was left in the front windshield and crawled out onto Ramona Rabbit. One by one the others crawled out after me. All except Terry. I screamed his name. No answer. I crawled back in.

The motor home was on its side and Terry was lying inside a shattered window frame. His face was covered with blood that sparkled with tiny shards of glass. His arms were clutching his chest and he was gasping for air.

Like most cops I've had some medical training. In a post-9/11 world, we've become first responders. I'm a few steps up from Eagle Scout and a few notches below an EMT. The good news is I know enough to diagnose the problem. The bad news is I know just enough to make me fear the worst.

And the worst in this case was pneumothorax. Collapsed lung.

"You get hit in the chest?" I said, trying to keep the panic out of my voice.

He grunted something that felt like yes.

Shit, shit, shit. I know what this is and I'm not equipped. I could hear my own heavy breathing. In my worst-case scenario, his lung was punctured; air was filling up his chest cavity with no place to escape. His lung would collapse and he would die in minutes. *Come on God, don't dick with me. He's got three kids. We need this man.*

I put my ear to his chest. I couldn't hear a thing. I ripped his shirt open and pressed my ear hard and flat against his skin.

"No mouth... to mouth... you homo," he said, between shallow breaths.

"If ever in your life you stopped trying to be funny, this would be a good time, asshole!" I yelled. "Breathe, damn you!"

It was hard to hear what was coming from his chest, but it felt like breathing. Labored, but it sounded like his lungs were expanding and contracting. "Sit up," I said. "This is a better position."

He sat and I looked out through the windshield at the Ramona Rabbit Parking Lot. A few agents were on their feet. Garet Church was clutching his right shoulder and his face was contorted in pain.

A column of fire and black smoke rose up from row fourteen, space nine. Ike Rose, bleeding from a gash over his left eye, stared upwards as hundred-dollar bills swirled around the flames and dissolved into orange embers. I could hear sirens as the fire trucks and emergency vehicles headed our way.

And then my cell phone rang.

There was nobody on the planet I wanted to talk to. But I had a brother who was living under a death threat. Or it could be Diana with news about Hugo. Or maybe the Governor was just wondering how things were going on the Lamaar case. I didn't care. I let it ring a second time. And a third.

"You're giving me... a headache," Terry said. "Answer... the damn... phone."

I flipped it open. "Hello."

"Detective Lomax?" It was a man's voice, but I didn't recognize it.

"Yeah, this is Lomax," I said, as the wailing fire engines pulled up to the burning van.

"Sounds like you're busy out there," he said. "This is Danny Eeg calling from Woodstock. I hope I'm not catching you at a bad time."

PART THREE

RUN, RABBIT, RUN

CHAPTER 79

THE THREE REMAINING disciples of Dean Lamaar sat quietly, absorbing the silence. As soon as Klaus Lebrecht had detonated the bomb, every microphone, camera, and electronic connection to the van was obliterated. The conversation with Ike Rose was over.

"Gentlemen," Lebrecht said giddily. "We seem to have been disconnected."

"Do you think he's dead?" Kevin Kennedy said.

"I don't know," Lebrecht answered. "I was trying to lure him closer to the van. Then, somehow, that cop figured it out and they started running. I pushed the button as fast as I could, but the relay must be slow. Even if he's not dead, I'll bet he's cut up pretty bad. There was a lot of shrapnel flying through the air."

"And a lot of money," Kennedy said. "A shitload of money."

Lebrecht poured himself some wine from a Baccarat decanter and held his glass up in a toast. "*Alea iacta est,*" he said.

The others needed no translation. They'd heard it from him before. It was the phrase Julius Caesar had uttered when he led his troops across the Rubicon River and began his successful campaign to conquer Rome.

Alea iacta est. The die is cast.

"I thought the die was cast when we whacked Elkins," Kennedy said, waving off Lebrecht's offer of wine and pouring himself more vodka. "On the other hand, if you mean we just let a quarter of a billion dollars go up in smoke and we'll never get it back, then yeah, that die is cast. I realize it made for great theatre, but don't tell my wife that I gave up a shitload of dough just to make a point, or this Mick will be cast. Castrated."

"That piece-of-ass wife of yours will outlive you by fifty years and still have a small fortune left over when she dies," Lebrecht said. "And, for the record, I have no regrets about blowing up the money. My only regret is that this is the last bottle of 1959 Gruaud Larose in my cellar."

He poured some wine into Mitch Barber's glass. "Alright, let's focus on Act Three. We've got Sophocles in New York, Yeats in Dallas, and Cervantes is still in L.A. They're waiting for their marching orders."

Barber took a sip, then swirled the Gruaud around his tongue. *How did it get this far*, he wondered. He was the writer who made movies with the great Dean Lamaar. And now, he was writing death threats and ransom notes.

Kennedy was an alcoholic. But Barber's addiction took on a much more acceptable form. Workaholic. No matter how hard or how late Dean Lamaar worked, Barber worked harder and later. In part, he was driven to succeed, but mostly it was his need to constantly impress and be near the Boss.

Deanie was God. *And if I can't be God*, Barber used to tell his analyst, *I want to at least be recognized as the second in command. The Son of God.*

"Did you hear me, Mitch?" Lebrecht said. "They're waiting for their marching orders."

Marching orders? We won't be giving them orders to march. They're waiting for their killing orders. Barber drank some more wine and spoke. "Maybe we should hold off. We've made the threat. Shouldn't we wait and see what happens?"

Lebrecht's lips pursed. "You losing your nerve, Mitch?"

"Hell, no," Barber said quickly. "I just don't want us to lose sight of what we're trying to do. The objective is to put Lamaar out of business. Not to kill off their customers and employees one by one. Don't you think a dozen dead people makes a big enough statement? Let's wait for the public reaction. Maybe killing more people is unnecessary."

"If we quit now, it'll be business as usual at Lamaar a month from now," Lebrecht said. "This is war. There are going to be casualties. I made my peace with that when we started. I want to see the company die before I die. Besides, we're only going to kill those *who support Lamaar in any way*. Your words Mitch, not mine. If nobody supports them, nobody gets killed."

Kevin Kennedy refilled his glass with vodka. "Sorry Mitch," he said. "I know where you're coming from, but it's too late for regrets or conscience or whatever it is that's got you. In for a penny, in for a pound."

Barber had worked with the two of them since World War II. Whatever he dreamed up they had made happen. Kevin was one of the best damn producers in Hollywood, and Lebrecht, aside from being a narcissistic, arrogant prick, was still the best director Barber ever worked with.

Deanie had discovered them, took them under his wing, and together they had built an empire. But the empire they created had been replaced by a new one that reeked of depravity and decadence. Lebrecht and Kennedy were right. It had to be destroyed. It was too late to turn back now.

Alea iacta est.

CHAPTER 80

THE HELICOPTER THAT had been waiting on the ground to chase the bad guys was quickly brought over to airlift the good guys to UCLA Medical Center.

The top hospital brass was out in force when we arrived. Not because we were cops, but because Ike was on their Board. Terry had stabilized in flight, and as soon as the rotors stopped spinning and he could be heard, he started talking. "Never would have guessed…they'd blow up the money. Good call, partner. You saved my life."

"Happy to do it. See if you can work it into your stand-up act."

"I'll be lucky… if I can stand up." A team of men and women in green scrubs transferred him from the chopper to a gurney and wheeled him off.

I didn't need medical attention, so they set me up in a private waiting room reserved for families of their most generous patients.

It was nothing like the Day Room where Diana had taken me to meet Hugo. The furniture was polished mahogany. The walls and carpeting were muted shades of blues and tans. Even the *No Smoking* signs were gold lettering on ebony plaques. It was the first-class lounge for those who had to be inconvenienced by being in the vicinity of people who were sick.

Ike Rose joined me an hour later. He had a bandage over his

left eyebrow. "I'm fine," he said. "Five stitches hand-sewn by the second-best plastic surgeon in all of Los Angeles. The first best is working on your partner's face."

"What about his lungs?"

"According to the docs, his chest is bruised, but his lungs are fine."

Rose could read the relief on my face. "Terry means a lot to you, doesn't he?" he said.

I nodded. "He's my best friend. How are the other guys doing?"

"Collins is in audiology. He's got some hearing damage, but it will be a while before we know if it's permanent. Garet Church is having an MRI on his shoulder. He's surrounded by the best orthopedic team in California."

"It's always nice when us civil servants get quality medical care. Thanks for making that happen."

"I'm the one who should be thanking you. You saved my life. How did you know there was a bomb?"

"I don't know how I knew. My wife died last October. I think maybe I have a guardian angel up there."

"Or maybe you're just a damn good cop. Sorry about your loss."

The hospital had sent up a beverage cart. Ike opened a bottle of water and downed half. "And I'm sorry about Terry," he said. "If I had run when you told me to, he wouldn't have gotten hurt."

"You were furious. You put up a lot of money to save your company, and those bastards pulled the rug out from under you."

"I'm not that noble. I put up the money to save my daughter. When they rejected it, I knew her life was still at risk. That's why I went ballistic. You probably think I'm a hypocrite, but you have no idea what it feels like to have your family living under a death threat."

Well, not my whole family, but there is a contract killer looking to whack my dumb-ass brother.

"Who would want to do this to a great American institution

like Lamaar?" Ike said. "When they killed Ronnie Lucas I was sure it was Daniel Eeg paying us back for what Lamaar did to his father. And by the way, he does have a legitimate beef. Lars Eeg helped to make this company what it is today, and he got screwed."

"If you believe that, why don't you settle with Eeg and be done with it?"

"Eeg is a total asshole. Not only does he want a billion dollars, which is out of the question, but he wants us to make a public statement that his father was the genius behind Lamaar's success. I can't. It would tarnish our image."

"Speaking of images, the people who blew up that van seem to think you've had a negative effect on the company's 'family value' image."

"Don't pussyfoot. They called me a smut peddler. I'm the devil, the amoral bastard who subjects your family to sex, violence, and—coming soon—the perversions of Las Vegas. They also said, do you think money will stop us? *Us*. It's probably some nut-job right-wing fundamentalist religious group."

"I doubt it," I said. "It feels too personal. Whoever they are, I think they're connected to your company."

"I've racked my brain," he said. "The only ones capable of this kind of violence are the ones connected to the Leones. But they're not the type to blow up all that cash. I can't think of anyone who would destroy that much money."

"I can," I said. "Three old men who already have more money than they'll ever need for the rest of their lives. The Cartoon Corps."

He froze. "The Cartoon Corps," he said. "Kennedy, Barber, and Lebrecht." He said their names again. I could see the wheels turning.

"You worked with them," I said. "How did they feel about the R-rated movies? What did they say about your going into business with Arabella Leone?"

He ignored the questions. "The Cartoon Corps. Deanie's little henchmen. Why didn't I think of them? Nakamachi didn't just buy this company. It was a hostile takeover. Dean tried to block the sale, but he didn't have enough votes. As a gesture of goodwill they gave him a lifetime contract, but no power. He hated it. They all hated it, but they had no choice. It was my company to run."

"Did they ever tell you they didn't like the way you ran it?"

"They couldn't. It was in their contracts that if they ever got vocal in public or in private about the way the company was run, they'd be out. It shut them up. Except for one night at a big, black-tie dinner. Deanie got drunk and told me how I was destroying his legacy."

"What set him off? Was it the movie *Home for the Holidays*?"

"No, with all the major changes I made, he finally exploded over something that was almost negligible. Something I did at Familyland."

"Familyland is where this all started," I said. "What did you do?"

"Familyland is good, old-fashioned, traditional Lamaar fun. I never wanted to change it, but I started getting complaints that we only catered to traditional families. Translation: heterosexual. There are lots of alternate-lifestyle families in California and they said we never created a *comfortable environment* for them. They started a Website accusing us of discrimination. They even said that the actors inside the character costumes were instructed to avoid gay people. At first I thought it was complete bullshit..." He paused.

"Was it true?"

He shrugged. "When Dean Lamaar first opened Familyland he was personally involved in training the characters. I'm sure his homophobic tendencies crept into the process. Then over the years, it just permeated the culture. The characters would always gravitate toward the traditional mom, dad and two kids, and steer clear of *the other kind*. It was an unwritten, unspoken rule. I wouldn't admit it, but I knew I had to fix it. We developed a new training program for the characters, and the following summer, we held a Gay and Lesbian Family Weekend at the park. It was a huge success. It's now an annual event."

"But Dean Lamaar couldn't deal with it."

"That's an understatement. He tore into me that night at the dinner. *The dirty movies* weren't bad enough, he said, now I opened the doors to *his* house to perverts and sexual deviants. I was going to burn in hell."

"So he trashed you in public. Did you fire him for violating his contract?"

"No, I felt sorry for him. I tried to calm him down. I reminded him that the company was in deep financial trouble when I took over, but now we were making money, and he was making money along with everyone else."

"How did he react?"

"He reached into his pocket, grabbed all the bills out of his wallet, and threw them in my face. He said, 'Here's your money, you kike bastard.' That was the last thing he ever said to me. About a month later he died."

Rose sat down and took a deep breath. I was sure he needed a cigarette. He picked up the *Thank You for Not Smoking* sign on the coffee table in front of him and turned it face down. "Do you think the three old men are trying to get back at me for whatever they think I did to Lamaar and his company?"

"Did they say anything to you when they retired?"

"No. They left gracefully. We threw them a nice party. Gave them gifts. Not that they needed anything. They're all multimillionaires."

"So they could easily afford to hire a whole army of assassins," I said. "Knowing what you know about them, could they be behind this?"

"Definitely. They could hate what I've built so much that they want to destroy it."

"That's called motive," I said. "And we know they've got the means."

He stood up and started pacing. "They have the imagination, too. As ghastly as this is, it's pretty ingenious. Barber is a screenwriter, one of the best plot guys in Hollywood. And Kennedy and Lebrecht could put it all together. It would be like producing and directing another movie."

"And they also know a thing or two about flipbooks," I said.

"Holy shit, the flipbooks. Cartoon animation is where they started. Lomax, it all fits. They're the ones behind this. You've got to arrest them before they kill somebody else."

"It's not that easy," I said. "A couple of days ago you were sure Daniel Eeg was behind this, and you wanted me to arrest him. Now it's Kennedy, Barber, and Lebrecht. We may have figured it out, but we still need evidence. I was planning to talk to them yesterday, but, as you know, I got sidetracked."

"Okay, but now you're back on track. How do you nail them?"

"Start by asking them a few questions about the company. Tell them they know it better than anyone, and we could use their help. If we treat them like suspects we might scare them into covering any tracks they haven't already covered. So we'll just make a couple of friendly house calls.

"Fine," he said. "And if that doesn't work out, I'll hire a couple of professionals to make some house calls and murder the bastards in their beds."

CHAPTER 81

ROSE WENT OUTSIDE for a smoke break. When he came back he started giving me as much insight as he could into the three old men. Fifteen minutes into it Garet Church showed up, his right arm in a sling.

"Thank you for saving my sorry ass, Detective Lomax," he said. "You have taken the spirit of interdepartmental cooperation to new heights."

"It was totally self-serving," I said. "I hated the thought of having to break in a new guy."

"I've been on the phone while the doc was working on my shoulder. The helicopter belongs to L.A. Sky Tours. The pilot is a twenty-two-year-old kid named Darby McQuade. He's in custody, and his story is that someone from Lamaar Studios hired them to drop the flyers as part of a promotion for a new Lamaar film."

"He's lying," Rose said. "Every pilot knows that the air space over Familyland has been a No Fly Zone since 9/11."

"He claims this guy from Lamaar gave him an FAA permit to do the drop. We went back to his office and the permit is totally bogus, but we polygraphed him and he's telling the truth."

"Wasn't he just a little suspicious when he saw the *Death To Lamaar* flyers?" Rose said.

"He never read them. They were bagged and ready to be

dropped. He's just a kid. He told us that having an FBI helicopter chase him down was the highlight of his career."

I filled Church in on our thoughts about The Cartoon Corps.

"That's pretty good detective work, Detective," he said. "What do you have that looks like hard evidence?"

"Nothing hard, but Danny Eeg called me right after the shit hit the fan this afternoon. He thought maybe Lamaar screwed the three old men out of money, and they might be behind the extortion. I told him the money motive went up in smoke. But listen to this. Eeg started digging into their financial records, and they've been systematically selling off their Lamaar stock. Small sales so that nothing stands out, but they've been dumping stock for the past two years. Little by little they've unloaded ninety-five percent of their original holdings."

"That's a huge sell-off," Rose said. "Those guys are all big shareholders."

"They were," I said. "But for the past two years they've been betting that the stock was going to tank, and they sold off so they don't get burned."

"Jesus," Rose said. "And the only way they could know the stock would crash is if they're behind the plot to destroy our company. Isn't that evidence?"

"Maybe for the SEC," Church said, "but I can't arrest people just for dumping their stock in a company."

The door to the waiting room opened. It was Terry. His face was peppered with little cuts. A hundred, maybe two hundred tiny red lines that ran from ear to ear, forehead to chin. There was a greasy sheen over it all, probably an antibiotic ointment. "My modeling career is ruined," he said.

He had me laughing right off the bat. "Apart from that, how you doing?"

"My chest feels like someone clubbed it with a night stick, and I just spent three hours on a table while some Beverly Hills doctor plucked little pieces of glass out of my face with a pair of eyebrow tweezers. How *you* doing?"

"I'm just happy to see you."

"You're happy to see this face? Look at me. I used to be just another unattractive man. Now I look like the world's ugliest strawberry. Apart from that, I feel fantastic. I hope you didn't solve the case while Dr. Frankenstein was rebuilding me. I'm ready to go back to work."

"Don't you want to take some time off?" Church asked.

"Hell, no. Did you see Bruce Willis in *Die Hard*? He was in much worse shape than me and he worked right through the final credits. I just caught the tail end of what you were saying. Who's been dumping stock in the company?"

"Kennedy, Barber, and Lebrecht. The same guys who helped start it."

"If they built it, why would they want to destroy it?" Terry asked.

"Why did God destroy Sodom and Gomorrah?" I said. "He was pissed at the way they were running the operation."

"As the CEO of Sodom and Gomorrah," Rose said, "I'd be real happy if you came up with a different analogy."

"Gentlemen, it's late," Church said. "I'm tired, my shoulder is killing me, and I'd like to go home. There's a vodka bottle with my name on it that's going to help me wash these painkillers down, so let me lay out a game plan.

"I'd like you guys to interview the three old men. We might suspect them for being the brains and the money behind this, but proving it is another story. First thing tomorrow, I'll ask for phone taps. My best bet is to find a federal judge to sign the warrants. No local judges who might know them. We'll also check out their travel history. We'd especially like to know if they've been to the places where we think some of the paid killers came from. And we'll do a head-to-toe financial. Corroborate the stock transaction information Eeg gave us, and go over their bank records and credit card transactions with a microscope."

"Who gets assigned to that?" I asked.

"I don't know yet. RCFL, CART, maybe NCCS."

"Give me a break," I said. "I don't even know what FBI stands for."

"We have a Regional Computer Forensics Laboratory in San Diego. We also have an alphabet soup of computer crime squads. Some handle cyber fraud, some look for terrorists, and ever since 9/11 we keep making changes to our IT. Personally, I'm a street cop. I never remember which bunch of geeks handles what. Do you care who gets assigned?"

"No, but Terry and I work with a really good Comp Tech at LAPD. Can he be included?"

"There's always room for one more nerd," Church said. "We've got our work cut out for us. The Bureau has set up a dedicated 800-Number Tip Line on this case, and it's the lead story on the FBI website, which means we'll get lots of calls and e-mails, most of which go nowhere. But we have to follow up on everything. Two hundred agents will transfer here in the next twenty-four hours to help with the load, so brace yourself for long days and longer weeks."

"Weeks?" It was Ike Rose. "This can't take weeks. We know who's behind it."

"We *think* we know," Church said. "Remember the anthrax attacks right after 9/11? Five people died. Three different bloodhounds sniffed the anthrax letters that were sent and each one led the Bureau to the same apartment in Maryland. Everything pointed to one man. But we never proved anything. I'm sorry for the way things worked out today. When we were loading the van this afternoon I truly thought we'd nail these dirtbags. I'm trained to expect the unexpected, but I never expected them to obliterate a quarter of a billion dollars. It must be my middle-class sensibilities that I couldn't even imagine someone destroying that much money."

"If it's any consolation," Ike said. "I'm in a higher tax bracket than you and it never crossed my mind either."

"I'm sure you and your people have a lot of work to do now that the threat is public," Church said. "Have you thought about how you're going to handle it?"

"We'll keep Familyland closed. Beyond that I don't know yet. Curry and his people are working through the night to come up with a security plan. I'm meeting with them at 7 a.m. I've scheduled a press conference for noon."

"I'm going to assign a round-the-clock team to be with you."

"Thanks, but I can save the taxpayers' money and hire my own bodyguards," Rose said.

"The taxpayers respectfully decline your offer," Church said. "You're a high-profile target, but my people won't just be there to protect you. They're also there to let me know what you're up to. Whatever measures your security people are taking, I need to know about. With one exception, you're free to do what you have to do, but I need to be kept in the loop."

"What's the exception?"

"Everything you heard here tonight, especially about Kennedy, Barber, and Lebrecht, is classified. You could do a lot of damage if you told anybody what we know, what we suspect, and what we plan to do. Understood?"

"Have no fear, Agent Church," Rose said. "I've spent the last four years working with Arabella Leone. What happens in Vegas stays in Vegas."

"Alright," Church said. "Now that we're all squared away, there's one last thing I would like to get to the bottom of tonight."

"What's that?" Rose said.

"That vodka bottle with my name on it. Good night, gentlemen."

Terry and I had left our cars at Familyland when we took the helicopter. Curry had his people drive them to the hospital and leave them in the parking lot, keys in the visor.

I drove home in time to catch the eleven o'clock news. The death threat to the Lamaar organization and anyone who came near it was on every channel including the Spanish stations.

There were five messages on my machine. One from Diana saying she was going to bed and not to call after ten. One from Kemp letting me know that Andre was a great chick magnet, and he'd be glad to dogsit as long as I needed him. And three from Big Jim, who told me to call any time of the day or night. There was no immediate Frankie crisis. He just wanted to know what I knew about this Lamaar business that the TV wasn't telling him. I called him back, told him I knew plenty but I wasn't at liberty to discuss it.

I was in bed a few minutes after midnight. It was now Friday. It had been less than two weeks since Terry called me and said we had a dead guy in a rabbit suit. To say that my little homicide case had escalated to monumental proportions would be an understatement.

CHAPTER 82

THE TELEPHONE WOKE me at 6:30. It was Terry. "There's a strange man lurking at your front door," he said. "He's got hot coffee and he's here to help you with that baffling case you've been trying to solve."

I stumbled to the door and let him in. "What the hell are you doing here so early?" I said.

He had two Starbucks coffee cups. "Amazing how much time you can save in the morning if you don't have to shave." He stepped in and I got a better look at his face. I could still see the cuts, but the redness had calmed down.

"You look a hell of a lot better than last night," I said.

"I've never heard that before. It used to be some broad would wake up next to me in the morning and say 'Christ, you're even uglier in the daylight.' Marilyn fixed me up with some kind of homeopathic powder so I don't look like a full-blooded Cherokee."

"How's your chest?"

"I now know how Dolly Parton feels when she runs into a brick wall." He handed me a coffee. "They hit again. Lamaar has a kids' radio network. A bomb went off at their station in New York. They were off the air for the night, so it only destroyed the transmitter. But it scared a lot of people. Minimum casualties, maximum message. Get dressed."

I drank the coffee in the shower, dressed, and went to the kitchen. Terry was eating a bowl of Cheerios, and there was a second bowl for me. "I thought of something that might help when we talk to the three old men," he said.

"And you just couldn't wait to wake me up and share."

"Did you ever read *The True Believer* by Eric Hoffer? I read it in college."

"I was too busy getting laid in college. Can I get the Cliffs Notes?"

"The book gets inside the mind of fanatics; what makes them tick. You ever wonder how a suicide bomber can get on a bus and blow himself up just so that a few innocent civilians will die with him?"

"I pretty much figure he's out of his mind."

"He is. But he *believes* he's doing the right thing. The people who crashed those planes into the World Trade Center, they were what Hoffer calls 'True Believers.' They really thought this is what God wanted them to do. I think maybe that's what's driving these three old men."

"God is telling them to destroy the Lamaar Company?"

"Not God. Dean Lamaar. Don't laugh, but to them, he's God."

I didn't laugh. "Interesting," I said. "The first time I talked to Big Jim about Lamaar he said something like 'If your name's on that front gate, you are God Almighty.' But Lamaar is dead. Did he leave instructions telling them to destroy the company, or do they just think this is what he would want them to do?"

"Jesus is dead," Terry said. "He left instructions, and lots of people follow them. You and I can't make sense out of how a fanatic thinks. But Hoffer's book not only tells you how their minds work, it explains how your basic Joe Average can wind up crazy as a shithouse rat."

"These guys worked for a movie studio," I said. "At what point along the way did they start believing they're on a mission from God?"

"Marilyn thinks that…"

"Wait a minute," I said. "Your wife came up with this?"

"No. I did. And at four in the morning, I wanted to talk to somebody about it, and I had two choices. Wake you or wake her."

"Good call. What did she say?"

"In the beginning, Dean Lamaar created the company. She said it biblical like that to make the point. Lamaar is God. He's the Father. But for the next fifty years Kennedy, Barber, and Lebrecht shaped the company. They nurtured it. It became their purpose in life. Then along come the Japanese and Ike Rose, and the company doesn't need them any more, doesn't want them any more, and starts changing everything they built. Bingo, they have no purpose."

"That happens to lots of guys," I reminded him. "Sometimes you see a cop who retired from the force, and he's like a zombie."

"These guys didn't retire. You told me last night. They got shanghaied by the Japanese. Hostile takeover. And then Ike Rose shows up with the sexy movies and the casino in Vegas and all the smut they bitched about yesterday before they blew up the van. To them Rose is the Devil. And the company is his evil empire. So now they found a new purpose in life. If the company can't be the way the great God Dean Lamaar intended, they're going to destroy it."

"Marilyn came up with this idea?"

"I told you, I landed on it. She just helped talk me through it. You seem to be having real trouble accepting the fact that I am funny *and* smart."

"You're right. Maybe it's because your face looks like somebody used it as a dartboard. But it's a good theory. Should we call Church and tell him?"

"I'd rather talk to Kennedy, Barber, and Lebrecht first. We can't arrest them without evidence, so let's get inside their heads. The more we understand how they think, the better chance we have of getting something out of them."

I finished my Cheerios, cleared the table, and washed the dishes. It gave me time to let it all percolate. "It fits," I finally said. "These guys have spent most of their lives treating Dean Lamaar like he's God. Not just because he created the Lamaar Company, but because he created *them*."

"I like that," Terry said. "Marilyn will like that. Dean Lamaar created them."

"Last night Ike Rose gave me some more background on the three of them," I said. "After the war Kevin Kennedy went back to Boston and got a job driving a bus. If Dean Lamaar hadn't sent for him he would have wound up being just another bus driver who could draw."

"How about the other two?"

"Different details, same story. Lamaar helped all of them to live lives that were beyond their wildest dreams. I think you hit it right on the head, partner. These guys believe they owe it to his memory to destroy the new company."

"Yeah," Terry said. "The hard part is going to be catching them before they actually do."

CHAPTER 83

TERRY AND I drove to Mitchell Barber's house in Bel Air. Nobody was home. Kevin Kennedy lived half a mile away. "He's gone for the day," his maid told us. "You should have called first. I could have saved you a trip."

"There's a helpful hint for homicide detectives," Terry said, when we got back in the car. "Call ahead to let the murder suspect know you're on the way."

"Actually the fact that the first two weren't home bodes well," I said. "I'll bet the three of them are hiding under the same rock. If they're all together in Ojai, you want to run the business card play?"

"It's worth a shot. Who's our weakest link?"

"From what I read, and from talking to Ike, Mitchell Barber."

"You know what he looks like?" Terry said.

"Yeah, the *Fortune* article had pictures of all of them." I tapped my pocket. "And I got all the business cards I need right here."

We stopped in Ventura for gas, then merged onto Route 33. Counting the pit stop, it took us an hour and fifteen minutes to get to Ojai. I spent twenty of those minutes on the phone with Muller. I gave him the broad strokes, then I told him the FBI was already searching the ether for anything that would connect Kennedy, Barber, and Lebrecht to Innocenti in Sicily, Benjamin in Israel, or the tall guy from Eastern Europe. "But I thought you might have fun playing the game."

"This is a mercy assignment, isn't it?" he said. "You knew how bummed I was when Lucas got murdered and my pedophile research got thrown out, so you're just throwing me a bone. Right?"

"Right," I said. "It's strictly out of pity."

"Yeah, well all I can say is this is the best bone I've been thrown in a long time. Thanks, Lomax. I won't let you down, man."

I hung up. "Good news," I said to Terry. "There's joy in Geekville."

Compared to the Kennedy and Barber estates, Lebrecht's house was modest. Assuming you consider the five-million-dollar range modest. There were four cars in the driveway. In most places that would be a sure sign that the three people we were looking for were all there. In Southern California it's just as likely to mean that nobody is home, and the guy who owns the house is tooling around in Car Number Five.

A man in his early fifties answered the door. He was blue-eyed, thick-lipped, with a bald dome that was polished to a high gloss. He had on black pants, a starched white shirt, a pearl-gray tie, and one of those striped vests you see butlers wear in old movies. We flashed our badges and politely answered, No, we did not have an appointment. "Just a moment," he said in the same tone of voice that most people save for "fuck you." He closed the door in our faces.

"Seems like a pleasant fellow. A bit authoritative, but then, who isn't?" Terry said, clicking his heels and snapping to attention.

A minute later the door re-opened. "Mr. Lebrecht will see you in the Media Room," the butler informed us. "Follow me."

We followed. Terry, of course, had to take a few goosesteps, because what's a mass murder investigation without a few yucks.

The furniture and the art on the wall were minimalist, very Bauhaus, which made sense, considering Lebrecht's heritage.

The Media Room had three television sets, all of which were tuned to different news channels. It also contained the three old men. Before any of them could get up I walked over to Mitch Barber and shook his hand. "Mr. Barber, how are you today?"

I turned to Lebrecht. He stood up. He was tall and lanky, Lincolnesque, but without the beard. He extended his hand. I put my business card in it. "Detective Mike Lomax, LAPD, and this is my partner Detective Terry Biggs."

He looked at the card and put it in his pocket. "How do you do, Detective. I'm Klaus Lebrecht."

As soon as he spoke I recognized the voice. Amy had been right. It was the same voice I had heard in Dean Lamaar's farewell video. I turned to Kennedy and gave him a card. "And you, sir?"

"Kevin Kennedy." He put the card in his pocket without looking at it.

Barber stood up. "I'm Mitchell Barber. I don't believe we've met."

He was short and squat with a comb-over that had to take at least ten minutes to blow-dry into place. I gave him a puzzled look. *Of course we haven't met, but I want to convince your buddies that we have.* "Oh, right," I said. "My mistake. Good to meet you." *But no business card for you, Mitch.*

Terry jumped in. "This is sure a coincidence. We've been hoping to talk to you gentlemen, and here you all are. Together."

"We come here often," Barber said. "It's a short enough drive and it's the only way we get to spend time with Klaus. He hates to leave the compound."

"This will sure save us a lot of time," I said, winking in Barber's direction. "I see you're watching the news about Lamaar. We've been sent to ask you a few questions. Believe me, it won't take long. Why don't we start with you, Mr. Lebrecht? Is there a place where we can be alone?"

Lebrecht gave me an amused look. "Detective Lomax, these

men and I have been partners for more than half a century. Whatever you have to say to one of us, you can say to all of us."

"Fine by me," I said. "It's not exactly by the book, but like I said to the lieutenant, you don't need to be Sherlock Holmes to figure out why somebody would want to put the Lamaar Company out of business."

"We were just wondering that ourselves," Lebrecht said. He turned off the three TV sets and gestured for everyone to sit down. "Why *would* somebody want to put Lamaar out of business?"

"Sir, look at the garbage they're turning out," I said. "I realize that's no reason to be killing people, but it happens all the time. I mean if someone murders an abortion doctor or blows up one of his clinics, how smart do I have to be to figure out the motive? Believe me, I don't condone it. It's against the law, and if I find the guy, I'll arrest him. But I know where he's coming from."

"I agree that my old studio is putting out some offensive films these days," Lebrecht said, "but isn't that what the young audiences want?"

"I don't care what the young audiences want," Terry said. "I've got three little girls. What about what I want? You think I want them seeing movies about incest? And don't think that just because it's rated R, they can't sneak in."

"Have you seen the video games?" I said. "I won't let my boy Hugo play them anymore. If he keeps watching all that random violence, don't you think he's going to be trying to find where I keep my gun? But, hey, I apologize. We're wasting your time. The question is, what do you think is going on? Do you have any ideas who might be behind this and why?"

"We worked with a man named Lars Eeg," Lebrecht said. "His son is suing because he says Deanie cheated his father, but that's patently untrue. He might be angry enough to try to bring the company to its knees."

If I had any doubts that Lebrecht was the off-camera voice from the tape, I didn't now. As soon as he said *Deanie*, I was positive. "We're aware of him, sir, but so far that's going nowhere. How about you, Mr. Kennedy? You have any ideas on who may be behind this and why?"

Kennedy had been cleaning his eyeglasses to give himself something to do. He looked up. "Beats the piss out of me, officer."

I completely ignored Barber and turned to Terry. "I told the boss this was a waste of time."

"Not for yours truly," he said. "It's not every day I get to meet the people behind some of the best movies and most popular characters of all time. I'm a big fan. Hey, tell me Mr. Lebrecht, what was Dean Lamaar like in person?"

"Deanie was a prince," Lebrecht said. "So talented, so loving, so caring. It was a joy to work for him and an honor to be his friend. There was still so much more he could have given the world. He passed on far too soon."

"No disrespect, sir," I said, "but maybe it's for the best. Don't you think he'd be pretty miserable to see what they've done to his company?"

I could see Barber's flabby chest rising and falling. He turned to Lebrecht, waiting for him to field the question. "I'm sure Deanie would be less than thrilled, but he did sell the company to a Japanese conglomerate," Lebrecht said. "He knew that the new corporation would no longer reflect his personal sensibilities or his commitment to the traditional values of the American family."

"American family values!" Terry said. "That's what the Lamaar Company was always about. I understand a company has to make money. And me, I'm as open-minded as the next guy..."

"Ha!" I said, turning to the old men. "He's not. He's a real throwback. Come on, Terry, we've bothered these gentlemen enough." I stood up. "Nice to meet you all. If you think of anything, give me a call."

Lebrecht stood as well. "I can assure you we will. Thank you for driving all the way up here. Freddy will show you out."

Apparently, the humorless, bald, Nazi manservant was named Freddy. He showed us out.

CHAPTER 84

A WHITE VAN was blocking our car. Irwin's Market was making a delivery. "Move the van, asshole," Freddy dictated, in a very un-butlery manner.

The driver, who obviously knew better than to argue with the Gestapo, shrugged his shoulders, put the carton of groceries down, and backed the van out of our way, as the hulking Freddy glared at him.

"What's your take on Larry, Curly, and Moe?" Terry asked, as we pulled out of the driveway.

"They're all guilty of something, which is probably why they were glued to the tube catching the latest Lamaar disaster news. And don't tell me it's big news, and the whole world is glued to the tube. These guys had three tubes."

"You really nailed Barber," he said. "First you give him the big nice-to-see-you-again hand pump, then you pretend you don't know him, then you totally ignore him, so now the others are sure you've been talking to him."

"Ike Rose told me Barber was a great plot writer. At first I thought he might say, Cut the crap, I wrote that cop scam into a movie back in the fifties."

"He didn't say anything, because he's scared," Terry said. "Did you feel how clammy his hand was? Guilt sweat."

"Sweaty palms don't hold up in court. We need smoking guns.

Do you think they bought the whole 'Lamaar-has-turned-to-shit' routine?"

"You were fantastic," he said. "That business about the abortion clinic. And then the bit about your son Hugo. That was great."

"You didn't answer the question," I said. "Do you think *they* bought it?"

"It's always a crapshoot when you try to gain some scumbag's confidence by telling him you believe in the same things he believes in. I hate it when I've got a rapist in the box, and I'm trashing the victim, saying, 'I know her type. I bet she was asking for it.' I got three daughters. It makes me feel dirty."

"You still didn't answer the question. This whole True Believer theory was your idea. You said the only way we're going to pry anything out of these guys is to *enter their world. Make them think we believe what they believe in.* So we tried it. At the risk of repeating myself, do you think they bought it?"

"Lebrecht is the leader. He's a real True Believer. Did you hear his little tribute to Lamaar? I think he felt comfortable saying those things in front of us. We made more of a connection than if we tried to strong-arm him."

It sounded like the answer to my question was a definite maybe. I figured that was as much as he'd commit. "What about the other two guys?" I said.

"I think Kennedy does whatever Lebrecht tells him. And Barber, he got tangled up in all of this and wishes he hadn't."

"In that case, he and I have a genuine connection. I feel the same way. This case sucks."

"It's been sucking for a while now," Terry said. "Turn on KFWB. They probably know more than we do."

They did. They reported on a fire in a movie theatre in New York, where a Lamaar film was playing. "Several people were taken to St. Luke's Roosevelt Hospital where they were treated for smoke inhalation," the reporter said. "Fortunately, there were very few patrons inside the theatre." Then he dropped his voice for dramatic effect. "But twenty-four hours later and it would have been packed with kids for a Saturday matinee.

"In related news a bomb went off earlier this morning at a New York City radio station owned by Lamaar. And in a third incident, also in the New York area, a woman in Macy's department store found a dead rabbit in a pile of Lamaar character sweatshirts. Having seen the Lamaar threats on TV, she immediately made the connection and reported it to the police. The store has been evacuated while bomb-sniffing dogs do a thorough search."

Terry turned off the radio. "Dead rabbits," he said. "What's next?"

CHAPTER 85

DECLAN BRADY KILLED his first person when he was fifteen years old. He put a rusty ice pick against Bobby Bodine's temple and whacked it in with the palm of his hand. That motherless wanker never woke up from his drunken stupor.

Declan didn't even know the man he murdered. All he knew was that Bobby was Megan Bodine's uncle, and the bastard had been raping her since she was eleven. Megan didn't have any money to pay Declan, but he assured her that the most beautiful redheaded girl in all of Ireland could find other ways to reward him for his services.

Five years later he killed again. This time it was for money. Two thousand pounds. After that the jobs started to come in pretty regular, and his price worked its way up. The pay was good and the hours were even better. It gave Declan the time he wanted to practice his guitar, box at the gym, and hang with the guys. He was pushing thirty now. He had thick, dark hair and a sharp, lean face like Sean Penn, only without the scowl.

He had met the three old men over a year ago. That slimy little ferret-faced cab driver Liam Flaherty had brought them to the back booth of The Pig and Whistle and introduced them as businessmen from America. No names were exchanged. The three of them squeezed into the booth, and Liam brought a chair over for himself.

"If this works out," Declan said to Liam before he could even sit down, "you'll get your cut. If you put your scurvy Mick arse in that chair, your widow will get it."

"The boy's got a wicked sense of humor," Liam said to the old men. "I'll be waiting in the taxi."

Declan sipped from his pint as Liam backed out the door. He sized up the three men in front of him. "You sound like a Yank," he said to Kennedy, "but you got *Erin Go Bragh* all over yer mug. Where you from?"

Kennedy looked at him with a straight face. "Lithuania."

"The Pope's plums, you are," Declan said, laughing. "If you won't tell me, then it's probably out of shame. I'm guessing Cork. It's pretty, but there's bloody goats everywhere. Goats and bad pubs. Last beer I had in Cork, I swear to Christ the barman pissed in the jar and gave it to me."

"And you being from Belfast, I'll bet you drank it," Kennedy said. "My mother came from Tralee. County Kerry. Much nicer than Cork."

"It's still in the bloody South. And where you from?" he said to Barber.

"Texas."

"You vote for that crazy Texan George W. Bush?"

"Every smart American voted for Bush," Barber said.

"And you, sir?" Declan said to Lebrecht.

"I'm one of those dumb Americans who voted for John Kerry," Lebrecht said. "But I'm originally from Chicago, so I voted for him six times."

They drank, talked, and danced the dance. The three men followed Declan's lead. His rule was that he had to get to know someone before he went into business with them. About forty minutes into the harmless banter, Declan popped the question. "And what business are you three gents in?"

Chicago did the talking. "We're looking for someone who will do anything for money."

"Define money," Declan said.

"One million dollars, American."

Declan felt the blood rush to his head. He hoped it didn't show on his face. "Look no further," he said.

The man smiled. "Would you like me to define what I mean by *anything?*"

"Not necessary," Declan said. "I'll do it." *Shit, for a million American he'd kill his mother and fuck her dead body up the arse.*

Declan didn't hear from the old men again till two months ago. And now he was in Dallas ready to earn the biggest payday of his bloody young career.

He'd been to America twice before. Both times to visit family in Brooklyn. This was his first time in Texas. He'd been here six days, staying in a different motel every night.

It seemed like an easy enough job. Except he didn't relish killing innocent people. He'd rather kill scumbags like Bobby Bodine, but the payoff was too big to let this one slip through his fingers.

He was driving south on I-45 when he saw the Burger King ahead. He signaled, slowed down, and pulled the silver Ford Taurus into the parking lot. He'd been here three times before. Easy in, easy out, right on the highway.

It was 11 a.m. The breakfast crowd was long gone and the lunch business hadn't picked up yet. There were about a dozen vehicles in the lot, half of them pickups. He passed up the spaces in front and parked behind the building. He got out of the Taurus, left the doors unlocked and strapped on the backpack. He pulled the peak of his Texas Rangers baseball cap down over his sunglasses.

He walked over to the side window and looked in. Mostly men. No kids. That's why he had decided to do it now. The kids would all be in school.

He stepped around to the front. There was a large color poster on the window. *Win a Free Trip to Familyland.*

He opened the glass door and went inside. There were two guys in cowboy hats, a couple of Mexicans in paint-spattered overalls, a fat man in a cheap suit arguing with someone on his cell phone, two women in their sixties wearing tennis whites, and a smattering of others who were either looking up at the menus on the wall or looking down at their food.

Declan went directly into the men's room and locked the door. The sanitary inspection sign on the wall was initialed in the 11 a.m. spot. Nobody would be back to clean up or empty the trash until noon. He removed the backpack and deposited it in the wastebasket. Then he covered it with paper towels. He took a leak, washed up, went to the counter, and ordered a Whopper with cheese, large fries, and a chocolate shake. To go.

He was back in the parking lot when the minivan pulled in.

Damn! The driver was a pretty, ivory-skinned lass with long red hair. She could have passed for Megan Bodine's sister. She pulled into a space and Declan heard the clamor of kids ready to swoop into the Burger King for a meal that he knew they would never get to finish. He looked at his watch. *Four minutes.*

He walked calmly over to the van, just as the beautiful young mother stepped out. She had two gorgeous daughters in the back seat. One was about seven. The other was about nine months younger. Irish twins.

"Excuse me, Miss," he said. "An old fellow in there just had a seizure. Fell down and split his head open. They already called 9-1-1, but there's blood and vomit all over the floor. Not very pleasant for the little ones."

She opened the back door. "Stay in the car, girls." She closed the door and turned back to Declan. "Thank you. We'll go to McDonald's. We actually like it better, but the kids insisted on coming here. They're trying to win a free trip to Familyland. I'll just go in, ask for some game cards, and leave."

Declan reached into his bag and pulled out a red, blue, and

silver scratch-off card. "Here. Give them mine."

"Thanks, but two kids, one card? I'll never hear the end of it. I better run in and try to get another one."

"Don't go," Declan said, forcefully enough to make her back up a step. He softened his tone. "It's not a pretty sight in there for them or for you. Hold this." He handed her his bag of food and ran back into the restaurant. *What in Jesus's name am I doing? Am I out of my bloody mind? Three minutes.*

There was no line at the counter. "Give me another one of those contest tickets," he said. He didn't know the rules about how many tickets you could get, but Declan had a face people didn't argue with.

He ran back to the parking lot. The rear window of the van was open and the two girls were anxiously waiting for their game cards. He handed the second one to the mother. Her eyes were green and her smile was radiant. And the girls were the spitting image of their Ma. Declan was glad he went back.

"I'm Bonnie Dolan," she said. "This is Colleen and this is Kelly. Normally, they'd be in school, but we had parent-teacher conferences today." She handed each girl a card. "What do you say, girls?"

"Thank you," the older one said. She began scratching the card.

"I'm Kelly Dolan," the younger one said. "What's your name?"

"I'm Liam Flaherty," Declan said. "I hope you win the contest."

Kelly sat back down and began working on her card. *Two minutes.*

"Well, it was lovely to meet you, Mrs. Dolan," Declan said, opening her driver's side door. "We better skedaddle before the ambulance gets here."

She didn't budge. "You sound like you're from the old sod," she said. "My family is from Ireland. Whereabouts do you live?"

Jesus, this effin' chinwag can't shut up. "Brooklyn, New York. Moved there twenty years ago, but I just can't seem to get rid of the brogue."

"Well, don't ever lose it. It's charming. I told the girls that the kitchen is closed, but believe me, they only care about winning that free trip. I know they can't win. But even if they did, this is one family that's not going to Familyland. Have you heard what's going on? People were murdered, and terrorists have threatened to kill anybody who has anything to do with Lamaar."

Then why enter their bloody contest, ya nimrod? Declan never asked or cared why the target had to be a Burger King, but last night, when the news about Lamaar broke, he had figured it out. "Terrible what this world is coming to," he said. "I hear a siren, so let's clear a path for the ambulance." *Sixty seconds.*

"I hope your lunch didn't get cold," she said, handing him his bag back. She climbed into the van and Declan shut the door. "You're a genuine Irish gentleman, Mr. Flaherty. Thank you."

"My pleasure." He smiled and waved at the girls until she pulled out. Then he raced for the Taurus. *Thirty seconds.*

As he started the car he saw the Mexican painters get into their truck. *This is your lucky day, amigos.* Declan felt good that they got out in time. He felt even better that the guy yelling into the cell phone was still in there. He laughed as he pulled out of the driveway onto I-45. *I'd have killed that fat minger for free.*

CHAPTER 86

THE FLYERS THAT were dropped over Familyland said *We've killed twelve so far*. But the killers wanted to make sure the world knew who, when, where, and how. So they released the specifics to the media. Now the newscasters seemed to revel in repeating all the gory details.

"This is like reliving all the shit we've been through in the past two weeks," Terry said, as we listened to the radio on the drive back to L.A.

I didn't need KFWB to tell me that people were scared, but they told me anyhow. The threat itself was terrifying, but the radio station bombing, the theatre fire, and the dead rabbit at Macy's had spooked people even more.

Reporters interviewed moms and dads on the street, and the response was universal: *I'm not taking any chances. My kid isn't going near anything that has anything to do with the Lamaar Company*. This was the anthrax scare and the D.C. sniper to the tenth power.

Ike Rose's press conference was scheduled for noon. We got to The Beverly Wilshire Hotel at 11:45, found Garet Church, and did a quick debriefing.

"A judge authorized the taps," Church said. "I'm also going to put tails on the three of them. It'll burn up eighteen agents a day, but it's worth the manpower. I like how you set up Barber. When should we bring him in?"

"Let's see how the other two react first," Terry said. "I once pulled this bit on a bunch of drug pushers. Gave three of them my card and said 'Catch you later, Armando' to the fourth. They shot Armando before I got back to the office. Instead of a drug bust we put the rest of them away on a murder rap. You gotta love happy endings."

"We heard about the incidents in New York," I said. "Any leads?"

"A few sketchy descriptions. Our guys in New York are looking at the security tapes from Macy's. But we may have something worse than a dead rabbit. I got a report from NYPD that a teenage girl was pushed in front of a subway and killed. She was wearing a leather jacket with Lamaar characters painted on the back. Nothing positive that tells us it's connected, but if it is, she's the first to die since they went public with the threat."

"*Death to Lamaar and all those who associate with them,*" Terry said. "You bet your ass it's connected."

Garet looked at his watch. "It's 11:55, gentlemen. Time for Meet The Press."

CHAPTER 87

THE GRAND BALLROOM of The Beverly Wilshire Hotel was crammed with photographers with cameras pressed to their faces, reporters with laptops perched on their laps, and security people with guns strapped to their hips.

Church, Terry, and I found a spot in a corner at the front of the room, where we could watch the speaker and the audience at the same time.

The microphones had all been lowered to Ike Rose's limited height, and, at precisely noon, the head of the most beleaguered company on the planet stepped up to the podium, looking poised, self-possessed, and downright unflappable.

"I have a brief statement, and then I'll take questions," he said. "Lamaar Studios, Familyland, Rambunctious Rabbit, and all the other Lamaar characters are American institutions that symbolize our values and way of life. Someone is determined to destroy those values by attacking our employees, our customers, and our business partners. I don't know why this animosity is directed toward us, but I have spoken with the Director of the FBI, the Secretary of Homeland Security, and the President, and they have assured me that protecting and defending this great American institution is a national priority. Questions."

Dozens of reporters jumped out of their seats, all yelling at once. "Debbie," Ike said, pointing at a lady in the third row.

Thank you, Mr. Rose. Debra Alonzo, L.A. Times. *What precautions are being taken to protect those who are at risk?*

"We are in the process of shutting down all our public facilities. As you can imagine this is a major undertaking. We have hotels filled to capacity, cruise ships at sea, and other venues that can't be evacuated as quickly as Familyland. We're also increasing security at all facilities that are vital to our day-to-day operations. In an effort to further safeguard the public, I called the heads of the major theatre chains. All Lamaar and Freeze Frame films will be pulled from distribution immediately. We will issue security updates on a regular basis. Next question."

Trish Conrad, Fox News. *Ronnie Lucas was killed on April 20, which is ten days ago. Did Lamaar know then that there was a plot to kill its employees?*

If the question made Ike uncomfortable he didn't show it. "When Ronnie was killed, LAPD suspected there could be a connection between his murder and the death of Eddie Elkins, which took place three days earlier, but at that time there was no concrete evidence that any other Lamaar employees were at risk."

Byron Barclay, CNN. *When Elkins was killed he was wearing a Rambunctious Rabbit costume. Why was a high-profile murder like that kept from the press?*

"Mr. Elkins was an ordinary citizen, not a high-profile celebrity. His murder was thought to be personally motivated and not related to the costume he wore. We didn't keep it from the press. At the time it was just another tragic L.A. homicide that didn't make the headlines."

It was a smooth answer. Amy Cheever would have been proud.

Follow-up question. Judy Kaiser, a visitor to Familyland, was killed on Sunday, April 24 inside the park. Surely by then you knew that your employees and the general public were at risk. Why didn't you issue a warning then? Why did you wait for nine more of your employees to be killed, and even then it was the people behind the killings who went public with the information.

"Lamaar has over sixty thousand employees worldwide. Hundreds of millions of people watch our movies, buy our products, and use our services. I made a decision that to go public would create panic. I hoped that the FBI could catch the murderers before any more damage was done. That didn't happen."

Ron Frank, Wall Street Journal. *Were you afraid that going public with the information would hurt your stock?*

"No. Our stock value didn't play a factor in the decision that was made."

Terry leaned over and whispered in my ear. "And I did not have sexual relations with that woman." We both knew Rose was full of shit. My guess is that the guy who asked the question knew it too.

Follow-up question. When The New York Stock Exchange opened this morning, they immediately halted trading on Lamaar stock for two hours. When trading resumed your stock opened at $95, down from yesterday's closing of $127.50. It's now at $72 and declining. Will you try to convince the Exchange to halt trading indefinitely while your company is under siege?

"I wish I could, Ron, but as you well know, that's not the way the market works. Whenever there is a significant imbalance between buyers and sellers on a stock, trading is halted long enough to allow the exchange specialists to set a new price range. They did, and our stock went into play again. It's frustrating because the price is being driven down, not because of poor performance on our part, but as a direct result of crimes against the company."

"Sir!" It was Brian Curry. He stepped up to the podium, whispered in Rose's ear, and handed him a single sheet of paper. The room went silent as Rose read it carefully. The only sounds were the clacking of keyboards, the snapping of shutters, and the whirring of camera motors.

Rose finally stepped back up to the microphones. "I have some bad news," he said. I could hear the tremor in his voice and see pain on his face. "A bomb was set off at a Burger King in Dallas, Texas. Four people are dead and about ten customers and employees have been injured."

A chorus of voices wanted to know what this had to do with Lamaar.

"I was getting to that. We are in the middle of a fifty-million-dollar promotion with Burger King. The top one hundred winners were to be flown to Familyland and ride on floats down Fantasy Boulevard with the Lamaar characters during our big Fourth of July parade."

There was a raucous flurry of questions. "Please, let me finish!" They quieted down. "Our hearts and prayers go out to the dead, the injured, and their families. I will call the senior management at Burger King immediately and cancel the promotion, and I will ask my people to contact every company we partner with to shut down all Lamaar merchandising and tie-ins."

He paused and the reporters began firing away again. "Please," he said, "I have a message for the American people. I don't know why these crimes have been directed toward Lamaar, but I do know that innocent people should not have to suffer by association. In light of this tragedy, I am asking every man, woman, and child in America to disassociate from our company, our products, and our services. I apologize if you have been put at risk. I thank you for your understanding and ask only for your prayers. No more questions."

Rose stepped down. Shutters clicked like a swarm of locusts. There was only one easy exit, a side door. Church, his arm in a sling, got behind Rose and shoved him toward it. Curry, Terry, and I were right behind them.

We went through two sets of double doors before the sound of reporters calling Ike Rose's name finally faded. We were standing inside the Grand Ballroom's huge industrial kitchen. It was empty. No chefs, no waiters, no food. Just stainless steel as far as the eye could see.

Brian Curry pounded the heel of his hand on the counter. "Shit! We had started to pull the plug on all promotions, but we have hundreds of them going on. We need more time."

"They don't want us to have time. They want us dead," Rose said. He nodded to me and Terry. "I thought you'd be out talking to Kennedy, Barber, and Lebrecht."

"We did," I said. "They're still high on our short list."

"Why don't you just arrest them?" Rose said.

"They aren't doing the killing. There's a network of paid assassins in New York, Dallas, Los Angeles, and God knows where else. Locking up the old men won't necessarily stop the wheels that are in motion."

"I agree," Church said. "We'll keep them under surveillance until we have something we can arrest them for. Right now we don't have any grounds."

"No grounds," Rose said. "So four people died this morning. And more will die tomorrow. And more the day after that. What about those people?"

"Nothing is more frustrating to a cop than to watch innocent people die because we can't get our job done fast enough," Church said. "It sucks. But it happens. The military has come up with a real ugly term for it."

"I was in the Army," Rose said. "I know the term."

We all knew it. *Collateral damage.*

CHAPTER 88

ROSE THOUGHT IT would be a good idea for Terry and me to meet with Curry's team to get an up-close look at what they were doing and to fill them in on our morning visit to Ojai. Church agreed.

The three of us decided to take one car so we could talk on the way to Burbank. "Why didn't your team just take some space in the hotel?" Terry said.

"The team is more like a battalion. More than three hundred people." Curry laughed. "We can't afford the room rates at The Beverly Wilshire. I was only in the hotel this afternoon because Ike wanted me at the press conference. I got the call about the bombing just after he started. It took me a few minutes to decide whether or not to break the news to him while he was up there, but I'm glad I did. His response was perfect. He got the message out for people to disassociate from Lamaar. That's going to make our work easier."

"What exactly is our work?" I asked.

"They said they'd kill anyone connected to us. Our job is to disconnect Lamaar from the world, then be ready to bounce back as soon as this is over."

"How do you do that?" Terry asked.

"I have no idea. I have a lot of people helping, but none of them have any experience making a multi-billion-dollar corporation disappear into thin air. We're making it all up as we go along."

"What have you made up so far?" I said.

"We've divided people into three groups. The first is the Input Team. It's made up of department heads, production people, traffic managers, database management, and a few old pros who know the company inside out. Their job is to help us find all our fingerprints."

"What does that mean?" Terry said.

"It sounds ludicrous, but this company is so spread out, there's no one person who could ever know all the things we're into. Sure, we make movies and TV and have a theme park, but that's just the tip of the iceberg. We're also in sports marketing, travel, education, food service, theatrical production, cable, Web development, and a dozen other businesses. Each business has permeated the public culture in its own way. Our Merchandising Division alone has over twenty thousand active licensing agreements. The Input Team is compiling lists of all things Lamaar.

"That data gets fed to the Implementation Team. They're handling the logistics of shutting everything down. TV and movie productions have to wrap, hotels have to close, cruise ships have to dock, and arrangements have to be made to fly the passengers home. Then there's the nightmare of dealing with retailers who have to remove billions of Lamaar logo items from their shelves."

"Why do you even have to call them?"

"After what happened at Macy's, every major retailer is working overtime to strip the shelves bare. That's the good news. The bad news is they're all calling us. Wal-Mart wants to know who's going to pay for all the manpower that takes. Target asks who's going to cart all that contaminated shit away. Let's say the answer is us. How do we do that? And if *we* do, then what do we do with it? And to top it all off, our lawyers have told us that if we help a billion-dollar customer like Wal-Mart, we also have to help Patti's Pet Emporium in Poughkeepsie get rid of their Slaphappy Puppy dog collars."

"It sounds like we can get it all done by 5:00," Terry said. "Which is good, because I promised my daughter I'd show up at her volleyball game."

"We did computer projections," Curry said. "It will take a minimum of ten days to dismantle a company this global and hide ninety percent of it from view. That means they're going to keep attacking us. So we have a third team. The Think Tank. They come up with 'what-if' scenarios to show us where we could be the most vulnerable. That's who you'll be working with."

We got to Burbank by 2:00. The office space was a forty-eight-thousand-square-foot sound stage. Hundreds of desks and conference tables had been arranged in small clusters and surrounded by temporary partitions that served both as dividers and makeshift bulletin boards. Most of the workers were dressed in jeans, shorts, or sweats, although a few men wore shirts and ties. Everyone wore a headset. People were talking on the phone, typing on laptops, and tacking color-coded cards onto the temporary walls.

It was chaotic, yet it felt organized. "I'm impressed," I said. "You put this together in less than twenty-four hours?"

"We started setting up Sunday night right after the ransom demands. Ike wanted a command center. It was a contingency. We didn't know if or why we would need it. Last night we opened for business. Everything is wireless, so it's not nearly as difficult as having to hook up hundreds of phones and computers. There's also a smaller stage next door. That's where the Think Tank is."

The second stage was divided in three. A dining facility, a dormitory area, plus a walled-off square about a hundred feet on a side that had a lot of the comforts of home. Overstuffed furniture, private workspaces, and large communal areas.

A large man with orange-gold hair saw us enter and came over to say hello. "Detectives Lomax and Biggs! It's good to see you boys again."

It was Ben Don Marvin. "I told you I wasn't behind this," he said. "I guess you believed me, because I got a call to fly in and help out."

"Excuse me," Terry said to Curry. "Would you mind explaining how someone gets promoted from the suspect list to the A-Team?"

"Sorry," Curry said. "I should've told you. He's here because he's done this before. Right after 9/11 he and a bunch of writers worked out hundreds of scenarios on how terrorists could hurt us."

"He told us. That's how he got the idea for the eBay scam."

"That's the other reason I was invited," Marvin said. "I think like a criminal."

There were twenty people in the Think Tank. Ben Don was the only felon. "Remember what Ike told you the first night you met him?" Curry said. "That he had resources no police department ever dreamed of. A Rolodex with presidents, prime ministers, and princes he could call on for help. He wasn't kidding. Let me introduce you to the rest of the group."

There were no princes, but we had four psychologists, two counter-terrorism experts, an Oscar-winning screenwriter, two best-selling mystery authors, a retired member of the Joint Chiefs of Staff, several people who just gave their names without saying what they did, and one guy who introduced himself as Bond... James Bond. Curry told us that he was a former member of the Israeli Mossad and that he was the most expensive person in the group.

"They're not doing this out of the goodness of their hearts?" I said.

"They're consultants," he said. "They dropped what they were doing as a favor to Ike, but they still get paid."

"*Cuanto?*" Terry said.

"On average, ten grand a day. Some a little less, some a little more. One a lot more. But ultimately it won't cost us a penny. Ike is taping it. After this is over, he's going to edit it and market it to big corporations that have similar security fears."

Terry poked me in the shoulder. "And you said Ike was dumb."

There was a twenty-foot-long black wall labeled *HPHVT*. Hundreds of neatly lettered white cards were velcroed to it. Each card was also marked with a red star, a green triangle, a yellow circle, or some other color-coded symbol. "Those are the High-Profile, Highly Vulnerable Targets," Curry explained. "There are millions of potential targets. We can't protect them all. So we're just trying to come up with our version of the World Trade Center and the Pentagon. Then we have to figure out how to prevent those targets from being attacked.

"The colors indicate levels of vulnerability and potential damage. This sound stage, for instance. The people in here are violating the directive. We're working for, associating with, and supporting Lamaar. But it's unlikely that they'll ever know we're here. We've also got armed men around the perimeter and air support, so we're basically safe. Yellow circle."

He pointed to the only card on the wall that had three red stars. It said *families*. "See this one? Hundreds of our top people have agreed to stick with us. We can protect them, but what about their wives and kids? You saw how they went after Ike's daughter. Right now protecting the families of people who are willing to stay is our highest priority, but I guarantee you we'll resolve it fast."

"How about the one that says *Camelot Hotel, Las Vegas*," Terry said. "It doesn't have any Lucky Charms on it."

"We contacted them. They know they're a target, but they said they'll handle their own security. Not our problem."

We sat down with the group and filled them in on what we knew about the Cartoon Corps. Then we stayed for eight hours of brainstorming and head banging. It was totally exhilarating.

They didn't think like cops. They had something most cops either don't have or don't use. Imagination.

I've always believed that if the federal government didn't have its head up its ass, they could have prevented 9/11 by doing exactly what Ben Don Marvin had done and what we were doing now. Put a bunch of creative people in a room, and instead of saying here's how we've always dealt with the enemy in the past, ask them to think outside the box.

We were back in Terry's car by 11 p.m. and he was driving me home. "This is the most fascinating day I've ever spent as a cop," I said. "I've never seen so many smart people in one room."

"I guess you've never been invited to a Biggs family reunion."

"You may think you're smart, Detective Biggs, but you and I were the dumbest ones in the room."

"Bullshit. I thought we held our own. What's the difference between us and them?"

"Ten thousand dollars a day." For once, he let me have the last laugh.

CHAPTER 89

ANOTHER SIXTEEN-HOUR day. I was glad to be home. I reached into my pocket for my key and stopped dead. There was something hanging on my front doorknob. I backed off.

I was connected to Lamaar. Two of the three old men had my business card. All of them knew my name. I was a target. There was a bomb hanging on my front door.

"Are you out of your mind? Mass murderers don't come to cops' houses and hang bombs on their doorknobs." It was the little voice inside my head. It had a point.

My car was right there in the driveway. I went to the trunk, got a flashlight, and shone the beam on the front door from ten feet away. There was a bubble-pack envelope, about the size that you'd use to mail a videotape, taped to the knob. *Mike Lomax* was neatly printed on the front in black marker.

"If that's a bomb, it's a pretty small one. The worst it could do is blow off a few fingers. Use your left hand." I thanked the voice for his help and told him I could take over from here.

I removed the envelope from the knob with my left hand, unlocked the door with my right and went inside. Andre wasn't there. I called his name. He didn't come. He was still with Kemp. I didn't need the little voice to tell me I was jumpy. I *was* jumpy. I went from room to room checking the house. Nothing out of place. I felt like an idiot.

I put the envelope on the table, got a knife from the drawer, and sliced open the top. There was a box of candy inside. A large box. The kind you buy at the movies when you're willing to pay four bucks for twenty cents' worth of sugar. It was one of my favorite candies from when I was a kid. Red, yellow, orange, and green jelly beans. Mike and Ike.

I opened the box. No candy. No problem, I wouldn't have eaten it anyway. I dumped the box onto the table. A cell phone fell out.

I reached inside the box and pulled out a handwritten note.

I can help. Dial 77#. Then hit Send.

I have a bunch of informants. Some of them have strange ways of contacting me, but none of them would ever leave his number programmed into a cell phone, put it in a Mike and Ike box, and hang it on my front door. That's pure show business.

I'd bet a week's pay that if I dialed that number, the great Hollywood screenwriter himself, Mitch Barber, would be on the other end.

CHAPTER 90

IT HAD NOT been a good day for Klaus Lebrecht. It started with an encrypted e-mail from Sophocles in New York. He was supposed to set off a bomb in a toy store that hadn't yet removed the Lamaar displays. But the bastard backed out. "Too many kids. I can't do kids."

Lebrecht offered him more money, but the answer was still no. Sophocles agreed to wait for further instructions. "But no kids," he said. "If you want to kill kids you should have hired a Turk."

Then those two cops showed up. Lebrecht knew they'd come asking questions eventually, but these two acted like they knew Mitch.

After the cops left, the three old men had watched Ike Rose's press conference together. "I told you my boy Declan was good," Kennedy said when Rose announced the Burger King bombing. "I liked him from the get-go."

"You said he was an arrogant sod," Barber said.

"Maybe that's what I liked about him," Kennedy said. "It doesn't matter. Whatever I thought about Declan at first, he's been worth every nickel."

"Yeats," Barber told him. "We agreed to use code names."

"Yeats, it is. Our fine Irish poet, William Butler Yeats is doing a *bang-up* job in Dallas." Kennedy laughed, then turned to see if Lebrecht was enjoying the joke as much as he was.

"You find this funny?" Barber said. "You seem to have made the transition from jovial, drunken Irish producer to jovial, drunken Irish mass murderer without any problems."

"Up yours, Mitch," Kennedy said, every ounce of joviality gone. "You feel bad about the people who died? I don't. I just hope some of them were the same bleeding bastards who voted to let the Japs and the Jews take over Lamaar Studios. You thinking about backing out? Well, think about this. You've been riding one man's coattails for your whole life. You don't jump off the ride because you don't like what's coming up at the next turn."

Kennedy reached into his pocket and pulled out Lomax's card. He threw it at Barber. "Here. I'm not gonna need this. And that cop didn't seem to think you needed one either."

Barber stood up. "That's an old trick. Cops do that shit to drive us apart."

"Well, it's working!" Kennedy yelled.

"Stop it," Lebrecht said. "You think we're shooting some movie where you can argue over a line item in the budget or a scene that got cut? Our balls are on the chopping block here. What happened to honesty, loyalty, unity?"

The three magic words. Deanie's words. They were the glue that held the team together, he used to say. Now they were Lebrecht's mantra. "We can't afford dissension, we can't afford a rift," he said. "Mitch, if you're having second thoughts about..."

Barber jumped in. "I'm not having second thoughts."

"But you're not happy with the way this is escalating," Lebrecht said.

"Do I think it's necessary to keep killing more innocent people? No. But did I go to the cops? I shouldn't have to answer that. After all these years you either trust me or you don't."

"I'm sorry," Kennedy said. "I trust you."

"I trust you, too," Lebrecht said. But he wasn't sure he did.

Freddy brought in lunch, and they watched the news while they ate. The Lamaar story filled the airwaves. The cameras captured store shelves being stripped, movie titles being removed from theatre marquees, and the grounds of Familyland being patrolled by armed guards and bomb-sniffing dogs.

People who were interviewed were almost unanimous in their willingness to do exactly what the flyers had demanded. "I'd have a hard time giving up beer," one young man said. "But cartoons, no problem."

Still, reporters managed to find their share of people who refused to follow the crowd. One truck driver plastered Lamaar posters all over his eighteen-wheeler and dared the terrorists to come and get him. Three teenage girls wore Rambo sweatshirts, but had drawn a circle and a slash around his picture. "That way we can still wear the shirts, but the terrorists will think we support them." The reporter informed the audience that a few minutes after the girls were taped, they changed their minds, "because the terrorists might not get the joke."

Lebrecht turned off the TV. "We're not terrorists," he said to the others.

"It doesn't matter what they call us," Barber said. "We are what we are. I've got to get going. I promised my wife I'd be home for dinner."

Mitch left. Kennedy poured himself a drink. "I believe him," he said.

"I don't know what to believe," Lebrecht said. "When I was a kid—six, maybe seven years old—my father took me to Cedar Point in Sandusky. I couldn't wait to go on the big Ferris wheel. I had never been before. He says, You sure you want to go? Yes, yes, yes. Well, we get on, and as soon as that wheel got to the top and stopped, I started crying. This wasn't what I thought it would be. I wanted off. You know what my father did?"

Kennedy shrugged.

"He picked me up, held me out over the safety bar, and dangled me three hundred feet over the midway. He said you want off, Klaus? If you want to get off in the middle, this is the only way."

"You had one nasty ass father," Kennedy said.

"Maybe. But I learned a lesson. You make a commitment, you stick with it."

"Mitch didn't go to the cops," Kennedy said. "He's scared, but he's not stupid."

"Well, if he didn't, then those cops were setting us up. And that means they didn't just come to talk. They suspect us."

"Of course, they suspect us," Kennedy said. "They suspect everybody who was ever connected to Lamaar. But they don't have shit. They're fishing."

"And what if they're not fishing? What if Mitch talked to them?"

"Klaus, I've known Mitch all my life. He would never rat us out."

"Answer the question, Kevin! What do we do if we find out that Mitch talked to the cops?"

Kennedy shook his head. Klaus was a master of manipulation. "I guess if we're going live by your father's rules, we throw him off the Ferris wheel."

CHAPTER 91

THERE WAS NO sense calling Terry to tell him that Barber had taken the bait. He was halfway home and would only insist on driving back. I turned on the cell phone, dialed 77#, and hit Send.

"Hello, Detective Lomax." The voice on the other end was strong, confident, and female. It wasn't Barber. It was Arabella Leone.

Every now and then I get caught flat-footed. This was one of those times. "Ms. Leone," I said, "you could have just called me at the office."

"Sorry for the intrigue, but your friends at the FBI have a bad habit of listening to my private phone calls. I wanted this to be extra private."

"Whatever you give me on the case I'm going to share with them," I said.

"This is not about the case," she said. "You have a brother Franklin."

"Frankie, yeah. What do you know about Frankie?"

"He's a crook," she said. "He stole money, and the injured party wants him to die for his sins."

"How the hell do you know this?"

"I told you, Detective. I do a thorough background check on everyone I come in contact with. You came up clean. But we have a Franklin Lomax in our database who's been here a number of times; the last one was a few weeks ago. He played recklessly, lost everything he came with. I have it on videotape."

"Spare me the pictures. I heard all about it firsthand."

"When someone is that desperate, we keep an eye on him," she said. "Just in case he thinks the best way to get the money back is to take it at gunpoint."

"That's not his style."

"We didn't know that at the time. So I had Rhonda, one of my bartenders, buy him a few drinks and get him to pour his heart out. Apparently he set up a woman in L.A., Vicki Pardini, and ran a stock scam on her."

"I don't think he set her up to scam her," I said. "It just got out of hand."

"He didn't *mean* to steal her money? Is that still a valid defense in your line of work?"

"You're right," I said. "He committed a crime. But the punishment is way harsh."

"I agree. And now that I find out that he's your brother, I'd like to help."

I had now been caught flat-footed twice. "I appreciate your concern," I said, stammering just a little, "but I couldn't possibly accept any help from…"

"From me? That's what any self-respecting, live-by-the-book cop should say. But if you're too principled to even listen to my offer, the only decent gesture I can make now is to send flowers to the funeral home."

"I'm not used to decent gestures. I'm a cop. Mostly we get bribes."

"This is not a bribe. It's a favor to you and to Ike."

"Does he know about this?"

"No, and he never will. I don't want payback, not from him or from you. If I need a traffic ticket fixed, I have plenty of friends in the Vegas Police Department."

"Alright, I'm listening. How can you help?"

"I have a business associate in L.A.," she said. "Joseph Cappadonna."

Joey the Cap. Mid-level mob guy in the protection racket.

"As luck would have it, Mrs. Pardini's husband is in the construction business, and Mr. Cappadonna's firm does security work on all Mr. Pardini's job sites. As a favor to me, Mr. Cappadonna is willing to talk to Mrs. Pardini and try to convince her to accept the money your brother owes her and cancel any vindictive reprisals she may have planned."

"And how would I repay Mr. Cappadonna for his kindnesses?" I asked.

"Don't worry. I told him you're a straight shooter," she said. "It's strictly business. He brokers a meeting between you and this woman; he helps both parties negotiate an amicable settlement; and you pay him a fee. It's all handled aboveboard with no damage to your integrity or your reputation."

"Or my brother."

"Exactly," she said. "Are you interested?"

"How much time do I have to think about it?"

"None."

"Let me repeat this so we're clear. I pay Cappadonna the money my brother owes, plus a fee for his services, and he makes Vicki Pardini an offer she can't refuse. He doesn't expect any Get Out Of Jail Free cards or other favors."

She had a sexy laugh. "That's not the way my attorneys would put it, but just between you and me, that's it."

"I accept," I said. "How do I get in touch with Cappadonna?"

"He'll call you. Just hang onto that cell phone. Don't use it to call me again. I'm out of the loop. Good luck with Cappadonna, and good luck catching the bastards who are trying to put me and Ike Rose out of business."

She hung up before I could thank her.

CHAPTER 92

I WAS SOUND asleep when the cell phone rang. I fumbled for it, slid it off the night table, and flipped it open. "Hello."

"Mike?" A man's voice.

"Yes. This is Mike."

"This is Dr. Joseph's office. You have a private consultation scheduled with the doctor. Be at the corner of Highland and Beverly in half an hour and wait for further instructions. And Mike, the doctor has very sensitive diagnostic equipment. So no metallic objects."

"Highland and Beverly. Half hour," I said, and the phone went dead.

I checked the digital clock. 3:45. I got dressed and left my gun and badge in my dresser so they didn't set off Dr. Joseph's sensitive diagnostic equipment.

I drove to Highland, which is a nice wide street. Traffic was non-existent, and I got to Beverly five minutes ahead of schedule. I parked at the hydrant on the corner. Twenty seconds later the cell phone rang. "Follow the Suburban." It was the same man's voice.

A black Chevy SUV with tinted windows pulled alongside my car. It turned right onto Beverly, and I followed. I looked in the rearview mirror. There was a pair of headlights right behind me.

Our little caravan followed Beverly east through Hancock Park, then headed south on Western. When we got to the edge of

Koreatown we went west on San Marino, then turned onto Saint Andrews, a quiet little street. Definitely not mob territory. The SUV parked in front of a small brick church. I pulled in behind him and was immediately sandwiched in by the car in the rear.

There was enough light coming from a street lamp that I could make out the two drivers as they got out of their cars and walked toward mine. I know a little about the faces connected with organized crime in L.A., but I had never seen these guys before.

The SUV driver was clean-cut with dark hair and distinctly Italian features. He had on cream-colored pants and a royal blue shirt and was good-looking enough to make the grade as a struggling actor/waiter in Hollywood.

The guy who drove the second car had pale, non-Mediterranean skin and a blond buzz cut. He was wearing the official uniform of all twenty-something Los Angelinos. Black pants and black V-neck over a black T-shirt. He opened my door and said, "Dr. Joseph's office is this way."

They didn't look like mobsters. I guess they were Thugs-In-Training. They escorted me to the side of the church. A well-lit sign said *Rectory Entrance, Private. For Office Business Please Use the St. Andrews Street door.*

We must not have had office business, because we entered the rectory. We walked down a corridor, which had white stucco walls, dark wood trim, and wrought iron sconces. We stopped at a wooden door that had a ten-inch-high stained-glass cross embedded in the center.

Mr. Cream Pants frisked me, and was not remotely shy about probing and squeezing every possible area where I might have a concealed weapon. *A guy like you could make a pretty penny doing that in West Hollywood*, I thought. But I knew that this was not the time for cheap jokes that could get me killed.

He removed the two cell phones from my pockets, looked them over carefully and handed mine back. "This one's yours," he said.

Black V-Neck opened the door, and as soon as I went through he closed it behind me. The room was lit by two, maybe three, dim bulbs. It looked like a sitting room of sorts, with two small sofas, two stuffed chairs, and a small wooden writing desk. A woman was sitting in one of the chairs. Joey Cappadonna was in the other one. He stood up to welcome me.

"I apologize for the early morning hours," he said. "I'd have rather met you for lunch at The Ivy, but I didn't think either of us wanted to be seen together in public. Thank you for coming." He extended his hand.

"Thank you for meeting me," I said, and shook the hand that had in its time done God-only-knows what.

Cappadonna looked more like Andy Garcia than Tony Soprano. Trim and tan, fit and forty. He had on gray slacks and a pale blue Sea Island shirt, which even in the dim light set off thick, dark, wavy hair that was a little long in the back and a little gray at the sides.

"This is Mrs. Pardini," he said, gesturing to the woman. Frankie had described Vicki Pardini as thirty-five, fantastic body, your basic bored Beverly Hills housewife. He hadn't exaggerated the body, but this housewife was far from bored. Sitting only a foot away from Joey the Cap, my guess would be she looked to be somewhere between petrified and shitting in her pants.

"We're all adults here," Cappadonna said, "so let me get to the point. Your brother Frankie took $50,000 from Mrs. Pardini with the understanding that he would buy her a particular stock. Instead he bought something else, thinking he'd make a mint for himself with her money, but it turned out to be crap and he lost it all. Am I right so far?"

"Yes," she said. "He took my fifty thousand."

"The questions are for Mr. Lomax, sweetheart," Cappadonna said. "You just sit tight. Have I given a fair account so far, Mr. Lomax?"

"Yes," I said.

"So now, the stock he should have bought has gone up and up and up. But since your brother doesn't have the money, he decides to seduce Mrs. P. in the hope that *amore* would triumph over good business practice. Correct?"

"That's the way I understand it," I said.

"Good. Now, your brother has taken advantage of this lovely woman's trusting nature and her virtue, and in an emotional moment she recruited someone to teach him a permanent lesson. However, a mutual friend of yours and mine, who does not want to see your brother dead, contacts me, and I contact Mrs. Pardini, because I think I can help her regain her money and her dignity. It's the ebb and flow of business. One hand washing the other. The only barrier to success here is, does your brother currently have the money?"

"How much does he owe?"

"The new bottom line is $115,000. The stock he should have bought is now worth ninety thousand. Then there's a $10,000 fee from your brother to me for brokering this transaction. Then there's another $10,000 brokerage fee from Mrs. Pardini to me, which as a gesture of contrition your brother will pay on her behalf. If you're good with numbers, you probably added it up, and it's only a hundred and ten. The other $5,000 we'll put in the poor box, because the church was kind enough to let us use their space for a private function. Payment is due at noon tomorrow. And we don't accept American Express."

"That's a lot of cash," I said. "Most banks are closed on the weekend."

"I hear that's an excellent time to make a large withdrawal." He handed me an aluminum attaché case. "It should fit nicely in here."

"And where do I deliver?"

"Tomorrow, you go to the Century City mall. Park on the lower level and go upstairs to the 12-Plex. Buy a ticket for the noon movie in Theatre Six. You got that?"

"Theatre Six. Noon."

"My two associates will be sitting in the next-to-last row with one empty seat between them. You sit in the last row directly behind the empty seat, put the case on the floor and slide it under the seat in front of you. The lights will go down, they will leave with the money, and you will sit tight for fifteen minutes."

"What if I want to stay and watch the rest of the movie?"

He laughed. "It's good to see you haven't lost your sense of humor. You can stay there till Christmas. What you can't do is move for fifteen minutes. By then, we'll have double-checked the contents of the package. If it's all there, your brother is free to go about his business without fear of reprisal, and Mrs. P. is free to go about hers without fear that her husband, who is a business associate of mine, will ever have to be troubled by knowledge of her error in judgment. Your basic win, win, win."

I took another look at Mrs. P. She didn't look like she was on the winning team. "And the brokerage fee that my brother pays," I said, "that would be the extent of our family's obligation to you for your services?"

"Well I would hope that you would remember me fondly if I ever get a summons for jaywalking," he said, patting my shoulder like we were old friends.

Jaywalking. This coming from a man who has been quoted as saying the only way for two men to keep a secret is if one of them is dead. He turned to Vicki. "Say goodbye to Mr. Lomax. You won't be seeing him again."

She barely moved. "Goodbye," she said.

"I apologize for my brother," I said. "I'm sure he didn't mean to hurt you. He has an addiction. He gambles."

"I have an addiction myself," she said. "I keep getting involved with assholes."

Cappadonna shook my hand. "You're a lot classier than your brother," he said, as he walked me to the door. The two thuglings escorted me to my car and watched me drive out of sight.

CHAPTER 93

I DROVE HOME, made coffee, showered, shaved, and thumbed through the *L.A. Times*. According to unconfirmed reports, four thousand Lamaar employees had resigned. It seemed like a small number considering the magnitude of the threat. But the paper pointed out that most low-level workers wouldn't bother resigning. They would just stop showing up. And there were thousands of mid-level employees who wanted to quit, but they couldn't find any bosses to quit to.

At 6:00 I called Big Jim. "Good news," I said. "They agreed to call the dogs off Frankie. It'll cost money, but he'll live to self-destruct another day."

"*Thank God*," he said. Not, *How much. Thank God.* That's Big Jim.

"The price tag is a hundred and fifteen thousand," I said.

"Ouch," he said. "There goes my plan for retiring before I die."

"It's expensive raising kids. And we need it in cash by noon tomorrow."

"No problem," he said. "I got it right here in the safe."

"Of course you do. Who doesn't have a hundred and fifteen thou just lying around the house?"

"It was Angel's idea. She said sooner or later we're going to need it, so I cashed my CDs. When they say 'substantial penalty for premature withdrawal' they ain't kidding. The guy at the bank told me I was making a mistake, and I told him I made the mistake when I decided to get your mother pregnant for the second time. What kind of crooks are you dealing with that won't take a check?"

"Technically, they're not doing anything crooked," I said. "They just happen to have the juice to help us out. The only crook here is Frankie."

"I'm sorry you had to get your hands dirty," he said. "I'm amazed you found time. I've been watching the news. I figured you'd be up to your nuts with the Lamaar fiasco."

"I got three hundred FBI agents and the Secretary of Homeland Security helping me on Lamaar. I decided they wouldn't miss me for a few hours if I worked the Frankie Lomax fiasco."

"Thanks," he said. "How do we make the payoff?"

"There is no *we*. You deliver the money to me tomorrow morning at 10:00. I'll deliver it to them."

"Why can't I go with you?"

"Because you'll annoy the shit out of them, and they'll want more money. Dad, this is my operation. We are doing it my way."

"You're so incredibly stubborn. You take after your mother," he said. "Alright, fine, I'll bring you the money. Diana's apartment at ten."

"What makes you think I'll be at Diana's apartment?"

"Because, Detective Numbnuts, you don't *just* take after your mother."

CHAPTER 94

I HATE WORKING weekends. Especially when I'm one of two hundred cops looking for a terrorist in a haystack. It reminds me of voting. You know your vote doesn't count, but you go through the motions, because it's been drummed into your head that you might be the one person who makes a difference.

I got to the FBI offices at 8:45. I'd been awake five hours and felt like I'd already put in an exhausting day. My partner, on the other hand, was raring to go. "The tip lines are lit up like Figueroa Street on Cinco de Mayo," he said.

Tips on major crimes come in from psychics and psychotics, publicity hounds, and cat ladies who want nothing more than a detective to come over to the house and chat over a cup of tea. It's frustrating, time-consuming, and usually unrewarding work. But occasionally, someone with a legitimate lead gets through, which is why we're willing to open the floodgates.

"We got a break," Terry said. "A woman in Dallas saw the guy who bombed the Burger King yesterday. This just came in from the Bureau Chief down there. Garet said we should stroll by his office when we finish looking it over. I read it. You may want to move faster than a stroll."

He handed me a thin stack of paper that had been stapled together. I grabbed it and started reading like a kid at summer camp who finally gets his first letter from home.

Bonnie Dolan, a thirty-five-year-old freelance fabric designer, called the local FBI office two hours after the explosion. She had been tentative at first and asked the agent if an old man at Burger King had had a seizure and busted his head open before the bomb went off.

After some prodding, the agent determined that Mrs. Dolan and her two daughters had gone to Burger King just minutes before the blast, but a man in the parking lot had convinced them to leave so they wouldn't have to see the seizure victim. When the news broke, Dolan began to wonder if the man kept her out of the restaurant to keep her kids from getting hurt in the explosion.

"He had a thick Irish brogue," Mrs. Dolan had said, "and Lord knows those people know a thing or two about bombs. He said his name was Liam Flaherty and he lived in Brooklyn, but I wouldn't be surprised if that was as big a lie as the old man supposedly bleeding on the floor."

That day's surveillance tapes had been destroyed in the blast, but there was an Arby's across the road that picked up Mrs. Dolan's minivan as it pulled out of the Burger King. It also picked up a late model Taurus that pulled out directly behind her, but the plates were unreadable.

Working under the theory that the bomber scouted the place in advance, the agent got Burger King's surveillance tapes from the past seven days. The same Taurus had been there three different times before Friday, but the driver wore sunglasses and a baseball cap that hid most of his face. The car was identified as having been rented from Hertz six days prior at DFW Airport.

Hertz had recorded the entire transaction, with sound, on high-quality tape. This time the man was in plain view. Mrs. Dolan positively identified him as "the gentleman who kept her family from getting blown up."

He had used a New York driver's license, but both the name and number turned out to be bogus. Based on the time stamp on the rental contract, the agents — there were now twelve of them working the lead—pinpointed an American Airlines flight as the one that had brought him to DFW.

His passport said Declan Brady. Interpol verified that the man on the Hertz video was indeed Declan Brady, a mercenary from Belfast who was suspected of five professional hits, but never arrested. In the grand scheme of things Brady was considered a low-level nuisance because his victims were usually other lowlifes whom Interpol was happy to see eliminated.

The report noted that while Mrs. Dolan had made a positive ID, she had mixed emotions about being Brady's accuser. "He must have some good in his heart," she told the agent. "Look at what he did for me and my girls."

The Taurus had been returned to a Hertz office in downtown Dallas thirty minutes after the bomb blast. The car had been cleaned and re-rented long before the agents had even gotten the first phone call from Mrs. Dolan.

Airport security tapes were scanned, but there was no indication that Brady had left Dallas on a flight out of DFW.

His picture was distributed to every cop in Dallas, all rent-a-car offices in the area, and all checkpoints along the Texas-Mexican border.

The heat was on.

We didn't stroll to Church's office. We flew.

CHAPTER 95

CHURCH WAS SITTING at his desk. The sling was gone.

"How's the shoulder?" I said.

"Hurts like hell, but I hate walking around looking like a casualty."

"Did you want to talk about this field report from Dallas?" I said.

"First things first," Church said. "I just spoke to Ike. I wanted to let you know before the press picks it up. He's gone underground. Snuck out of town in the middle of the night."

I was surprised, and a little disappointed. "That's too bad," I said. "I thought he was the kind of leader who would tough it out with his people."

"He is," Church said. "They're just not going to tough it out in L.A. He went to higher ground, and he took fifteen hundred of his people with him."

Terry let out a low whistle. "That's almost as big a posse as the one that travels with Britney Spears."

"Ike's biggest concern has been the well-being of the people who are sticking with the company. He feels like they're on the front line, so he moved them out of harm's way. And they took all their family members with them. It was a mass exodus, and they pulled it off without a hitch."

"Do you know where they are?" I asked.

"Yes. And some of my men are with them. I'd rather not tell

you guys until you have a need to know."

"I don't want to know," Terry said.

"I don't want him to know either," I said. "He tells his wife everything."

"Now let's talk about the field report from Dallas," Church said. "What did you guys think?"

"It's great," I said. "If Dallas can nail this Brady guy, he'll give up the people who paid him. This could be the break we've been looking for."

"Yeah," Terry said. "This is the best news we've had since we found out that the dead guy in the Rambo suit was actually a dead pedophile."

"It's good to see you so upbeat," Church said. "Most guys who work a hundred-hour week get cranky by Saturday."

"Speaking of working around the clock, I need some personal time tomorrow morning." *I'll be forking over my father's life savings at the 12-Plex to save my kid brother's ungrateful ass.* "How about if I come in around 2:00?"

"How about if you and Terry both take tomorrow off. You've been working double shifts for two weeks straight. Get your batteries recharged."

I was seeing Diana tonight. The thought of extending it into the weekend, with just one small interruption to pay for Frankie's sins, was tempting.

I knew where Terry's head was. He'd be thrilled to have a day with his wife and kids. He looked at me and shrugged. "Your call, Mike."

"It sounds good, but don't you think Kilcullen would be happier if we came in?"

"Tell Lieutenant Kilcullen that I pulled rank on him," Church said. "Shut up and take the day off."

"Thanks," I said. "We accept."

Terry dragged me out of the office before I could change my mind.

CHAPTER 96

IT WAS 2:15, and I was regretting the Jalapeno roll-ups I had for lunch, when Muller called. He's the Master of Understatement, so when he said, 'I think maybe I got something,' I knew he didn't mean maybe, and it would be a lot more than something.

"I've been working with the Federalés," Muller said. "Nice folks. This one guy went to MIT and he contributes open source code for Mozilla…"

"Muller, I'm glad you made friends," I said. "But can we jump to the part where you got something. What is it you got?"

"Credit card records. Your three boys went on a spending spree. Sicily, Israel, Ireland, and a few other places where one might shop for saboteurs and other freelance hooligans."

"And it was right there on their credit cards for anyone to see?"

"Not anyone. The Feds didn't catch it. Even the Alpha Geek was impressed when I figured it out."

"How fast can you get over here and brief us?"

"I thought you might say that. I'm in the lobby."

Five minutes later Terry and I, Church and Collins, and half a dozen other agents were seated at a conference table, pens poised, waiting for the details.

Muller stood at the front of the room. He looked like a high school kid who still hadn't started shaving yet, and a few of Church's guys smirked. But as soon as he started talking, the grins disappeared.

"We started out looking for unusual credit card activity," Muller said. "Big bumps that would indicate they took a trip to hire these killers. Nothing. Then it dawned on me. Maybe we should be looking for unusual *inactivity*."

Terry winked at me. LAPD Pride.

Muller went on. "These guys use their credit cards a lot. Expensive restaurants, travel, clothes, jewelry—Kennedy shops regularly in one jewelry store on Rodeo Drive—and Barber can easily spend twenty, thirty grand a month on rare books. Two years ago, for twenty-four days straight—middle of August till early September—none of those guys used a single credit card."

Church raised his hand, but didn't wait to be called on. "So they all had a zero balance bill?"

"It wasn't that obvious, sir," Muller said. "They all have automatic credit card charges, like club dues, that show up on their bill every month. Also the twenty-four days were spread across two billing cycles, so their August and September bills had charges. But the totals for those two months were a lot less than usual. I'd let that slide with one guy, but not all three of them. So I analyzed their day-to-day spending. Turns out none of them used a single credit card for twenty-four days."

"What does that prove?" Church said.

"Nothing yet. So I went to the credit card companies and asked them to look for three *different cards*, all Southern California based, that ran up a hefty bill during those twenty-four days, but charged nothing before and nothing since."

"I'm liking this," Church said.

"The Small Business Division of American Express opened a new account for a company called Drum Roll Productions. It's not uncommon in the movie business for a production manager to set up a separate charge account for each project. That way he can track which expenses get charged to which film. It's also not uncommon for a producer to run up huge bills during a short period of time, wrap the production, and never use that card again.

"Three cards were issued to officers of the new company, Curvin O'Connor, Maxwell Harper, and Kurt Schmidt. The billing address for all three is the same: a Mail Express in Ojai, California."

"Kid," Church said, "you have a future in police work. What got charged on the cards?"

"Airfare, hotels, restaurants, car rentals, just your basic travel expenses."

"Are you sure they didn't do anything a little more incriminating?" Terry said. "Like walk into Murder For Hire and order half a dozen assassins to go. Because then we could wrap this up in no time."

"It's not *what* they charged," Muller said. "It's where they charged it. Haifa, Belfast, Athens, Palermo—place for place their itinerary matches up with what we know about the actual killers."

"Why do you think they left a paper trail?" Church said. "Wouldn't it have been easier to pay cash?"

Muller's eyes twinkled. Like he was waiting for that question. "I don't know, sir," he said. "If you were interviewing people who commit cold-blooded murder for money, how much cash would you carry?"

Everyone laughed, including Church. "Excellent, Mr. Muller. Since you're way ahead of me, have you thought about how we can prove that the men who made those charges are actually Kennedy, Barber, and Lebrecht?"

"Yes sir. Once they had the credit cards, they kept building their new identities. Eventually they took their phony credentials to the passport office, and a week later they've got genuine U.S. passports, all with fake names. The only problem is, they can't fake their faces. The pictures have to look like them.

"So now all we have to do is call the State Department, give them the bogus names and ask for copies of their passport photos. If O'Connor, Harper, and Schmidt look like Kennedy, Barber, and Lebrecht, you won't have any trouble getting a federal prosecutor to sign a warrant."

"Day off or no day off," I said, "if we're making an arrest, Terry and I want to be there."

"Relax," Church said. "I won't let you guys miss out on any of the fun. First we have to contact State."

"I already did, sir," Muller said. "I figured we should get the process moving. You know how slow the federal government can be."

Church cracked a smile. "Yeah, thanks, kid. I heard."

CHAPTER 97

I HAVE A fifties CD and I played Paul Anka singing Diana six times on my way home from the office. I took a twenty-minute power nap, showered, touched up my morning shave, and spent more than the usual thirty seconds brushing my hair.

I tried not to overthink my wardrobe, but I went through three different combinations before I settled on my most comfortable pair of gray slacks from Nordstrom, my Ralph Lauren blue-and-white tattersall shirt, and my predictable navy blazer. I was only running ten minutes late when I left the house.

I stopped at the Sav-on drugstore on Rodeo Drive and bought a dozen condoms for me and a gift for Diana. I got to her apartment building on Wilshire and the doorman announced me. I took the elevator to the fourteenth floor and she was standing in the doorway of her apartment waiting for me.

I had only seen her in pinks and pastels, and tonight she was wearing black. She looked stunning. The dress was open at the neckline and tied at the waist. "You should wear black more often," I said. "You look incredible."

She kissed me hello, but it wasn't enough for either of us. She pulled me inside the apartment, and we threw our arms around one another and kissed passionately. Slowly it settled into one of those tender, enduring, movie kisses, two lovers reunited after four long years of war.

431

"This is only our third date," she said, when we finally came up for air. "At the risk of scaring you away I have something to tell you. I missed you."

"It would only scare me if you said you didn't. I brought you a present." I held out the little white plastic bag with the drug store logo on it.

"Condoms?" she said.

"Actually I bought some of those for myself," I said, and tapped the box in my jacket pocket. "But I'd be delighted to share them with you. This is a real gift. And don't be fooled by appearances. This isn't from just any Sav-on. It's from the one on Rodeo Drive."

She reached into the bag. "A Snoopy wrist watch," she said. "What's the occasion? Have I been late for things?"

"No."

"Let me try it on," she said, unstrapping the Rambunctious Rabbit watch from her left hand.

And then she let out a little gasp. She understood.

"I may be overprotective," I said, "but in my head the fact that you're wearing a Lamaar character watch makes you a target. Nobody seems to have it in for Snoopy, so I'd feel a lot better if you wore him."

She sat down on the sofa. Her eyes welled up and several tears spilled over and ran down her cheeks. "I'm sorry if I upset you," I said.

"I am not upset," she said, sniffling. "It's just been a long time since anybody cared about me like this. Thank you."

A long-haired white cat hopped up on her lap. She stroked it behind the ears.

"This is Blanche," she said. "You didn't meet her last time because I locked the bedroom door." Diana lifted the cat off her lap and plopped it down on the floor. Wispy white strands of cat hair clung to the dress. "She's the reason I hardly ever wear black."

432

We drove to a Japanese restaurant on West Third that wasn't trendy enough to attract the noisy Saturday night date crowd. By mutual agreement we talked about anything and everything but the Lamaar case.

Two hours later Blanche was locked out of the bedroom again.

I don't know how many women I've slept with in my life. Enough so that I have a basis of comparison. Not counting Joanie, sex with Diana was as emotional an experience as any I've ever had.

She let her dress fall to the floor, then stood there waiting for me to remove the black bra and panties, looking like the fantasy of every man who ever lusted over a *Victoria's Secret* catalogue.

When I was nineteen and trying to hump everything in sight, I remember thinking, *Why do they call it making love? It's fucking*.

With Diana I made love, as slowly and tenderly as I possibly could, considering that my hormones were popping like bottle rockets.

We woke up in a spoon position, her back to my front. I cupped a breast in one hand and began nuzzling the back of her neck. Within seconds we were both breathing heavily and in rhythm. "Come in me," she said. I started to roll over to the night table to get a condom and she said, "No. I don't have a disease and I won't get pregnant and I want to feel you inside of me. Please."

She didn't have to say please. I slipped easily into her and my brain exploded. I know that condoms make sense. I know they prevent disease, help avoid pregnancy, and, if more people used them, the planet would be a healthier, safer place. But there is no feeling in the world like the first time you enter a woman you're falling in love with and you're skin to skin the way God intended.

I came in less than a minute, and Diana was only seconds behind me. Her body continued to heave and shake and I realized that her orgasm had subsided but she was sobbing. I rolled over and kissed her lips and gently licked her tears. I didn't want to say, "What's the matter," because I know it's a Dumb Man Question. So I just tilted my head a little like a curious puppy who wonders what's going on.

She understood the question. "I never thought I could be this happy again," she said, still teary.

I let the annoying little voice inside my head go through all of its mental gymnastics. "Should I respond? Should I say what I feel? If I do will she believe me? Is it too soon? Does it sound like a commitment? Am I sure?"

Finally, the questions stopped and the voice said, "There will never be another moment quite like this."

I pressed my lips gently against Diana's ear. "Me either," I whispered.

CHAPTER 98

I WAS IN the middle of a blissful steaming shower when Diana tapped on the frosted glass door. "The doorman just rang up. Your father is downstairs in the lobby."

"He's delivering a package to me, but he's an hour early."

"That's okay, he can have breakfast with us. I'll tell him to come up."

"Wait," I said. "Have the doorman show him where my car is. There's a silver attaché case in the trunk. Tell Jim to bring it up here."

I stood under the pounding hot water for another ten minutes. By the time I got dressed Jim was sitting in the living room, the aluminum attaché at his feet, Frankie's ratty black duffel on his lap.

"Good morning," he said. "I'm Secret Agent Lomax." He patted the bag. "The hot cross buns are in the oven."

"Transfer your buns to the other oven, while I explain to Diana that this is not something I do with my crazy father every Sunday morning."

He opened the duffel and dumped the money on the floor. "I already explained. She looked trustworthy."

Diana smiled. "He gave me top secret clearance."

"They had a videotape of Ike Rose on the news this morning," Jim said, as he neatly stacked a chunk of his life savings into

Joey the Cap's briefcase. "He took off for parts unknown with hundreds of Lamaar execs and their families. Trying to keep them safe."

"I knew that was happening," I said. "But what did he say on the videotape?"

"Sort of a big 'fuck you' to whoever's behind this. *You can't intimidate us; this shit just makes us stronger; we'll run the company from a secret location until the cops bring you to justice; no matter what you do, we'll rebuild.* Even if the terrorists weren't watching, it's a good message to put out to the public. Maybe convince investors not to dump their Lamaar stock."

Jim put the last of the bills in the case and snapped it shut. He still had something in his lap and he held it up. "Speaking of videotapes, where did you get these tapes of *Deanie's Farewell?*"

"Do you have *any concept* of personal boundaries?" I said. "I was looking at them for the Lamaar investigation. The woman who gave them to me was *killed* before I could return them, and they've been sitting in the trunk of my car until you decided it was perfectly okay for you to help yourself."

"It was in the middle of a pile of crap along with old sneakers, jumper cables, and a broken umbrella. How the hell am I supposed to know it's *Important Police Evidence?*"

"It's not evidence. It was just another blind alley. The point is…"

"So then what's the big deal?" he said. "I used to be Dean Lamaar's driver. I just wanted to look at the videotapes. And by the way, for a hundred and fifteen thousand bucks I should get some popcorn with my movie."

I threw my hands up in the air and turned to Diana for some help.

"Can I look at them, too?" she said. "I already have top secret clearance."

"And you wonder why I like her so much," Jim said. He handed her one of the tapes. "Here, honey, pop this in the VCR."

"That's the source tape," I said. "It's longer than the final edit, but it's got something real cool in the middle. Do me a favor, Dad. Pay attention to the voice off-camera."

Diana put the tape in the VCR, and we watched it from the opening frame until Lamaar said, "I want to get the fuck out from under these lights before the aftershock shakes them loose and kills me," and the tape went dark.

I turned to Jim. "For starters, did you recognize the guy off-camera?"

"Klaus Lebrecht. And it's not just his voice. Lebrecht was one of the few guys who called the old man Deanie to his face. They were best friends." He winked not too subtly. "Some people say maybe more than friends."

"They were gay?" I said.

"Lebrecht is gay," Jim said. "He thinks he's in the closet, but in this town people know. Most of us suspected that he was in love with Lamaar. But Lamaar was homophobic. It was never gonna happen."

"If we're finished with the payoff money and the police work," Diana said, "can we think about Sunday breakfast? Waffles or omelets?"

"Both sound good to me," Jim said. "I'm starved. I mean, if I'm not butting in, I'd love to stay."

He stayed.

CHAPTER 99

"WHAT ARE YOU two kids doing today?" Jim said, as he worked on his second omelet. "I mean after you get rid of my hundred and fifteen thou."

"I rented a plane at Van Nuys," Diana said. "I thought we could cruise up the ocean to Malibu and look at how the rich people live."

"Today is May first," Jim said. "May Day."

"I know," she said. "May is my favorite month."

"Question," I said. "If May Day is one of the most gorgeous days of the year, how come pilots say 'Mayday' when a plane is in trouble?"

"Your father is a pilot," she said. "Ask him."

"I did when I was ten years old. He said, 'Beats the shit out of me, kid.'"

"Still does," Jim said between bites.

"Mayday for pilots has nothing to do with the month. It comes from the French word, *m'aidez*, which means 'help me'," she said, coming behind my chair and kissing me on the cheek. "Anything else I can teach you that you couldn't learn from your father?"

I turned around so I could return the kiss. "I'm sure there is," I said. "Isn't it time for you to get on the road, Dad?"

"It's Sunday morning. Angel's in church. Frankie's asleep, and two of my drivers are in the kitchen, just to be on the safe side. Do you mind if I hang out here a few more minutes?"

I minded like hell. Diana, on the other hand, started brewing another pot of coffee.

We made small talk until 11:15, at which point I picked up the briefcase. "Time to take care of business," I said.

"I'm right behind you," Jim said. "I got your back."

I was furious. "You think I can't figure out why you've been stalling? You are positively not going, damn it. That was the deal, and if you don't go home right now, I'll go there and shoot Frankie myself."

Jim looked at Diana. "Mayday," he said. She shook her head and covered her mouth with both hands. She was definitely staying out of this one.

He walked up to me and wrapped his arms around me. "Okay, but be careful, Mikey. Don't do anything stupid. Call me when it's over."

"Thanks for your concern. Now get out of here."

He left and as soon as the door closed Diana started laughing into her hands. "Oh, my God," she said, "my father's a rabbi, and I thought *he* was a Master of Jewish Guilt. Yours is even better at it than mine."

"I knew we had a bond between us," I said. "We're the adult children of pushy men of different faiths. Grab your bag and your pilot stuff. We gotta go."

"*We*? I thought it was dangerous."

"Only if my father goes. Otherwise, it's like going into a loan office and paying off a debt. It doesn't make sense to leave you here alone. We've already lost enough of our private time. You can just sit in the car or walk through the mall while I take care of business. The whole deal will only take fifteen minutes. I'll be done at twelve fifteen and we can go flying."

"Cool. But if he ever finds out that you took me to the mall for the Big Payoff, he'll go ballistic."

I let out a long sigh. "I know. It will be the highlight of my week."

CHAPTER 100

I PUT THE briefcase and the videos back in my trunk, and Diana and I headed for Century City.

"Can I ask you a dumb question?" Diana said, as I pulled onto Wilshire.

"If it's 'Who was that fat man and why do you put up with his constant bullshit?' don't bother asking. I don't have an intelligent answer. Anything else, fire away."

"It's about the Lamaar video. Was that earthquake staged?"

I tried not to laugh, but a small chuckle slipped out. "Why would you ask that?"

"See? I warned you it was dumb."

"Sorry. I only laughed because I'm intrigued. Why would you *think* they staged the earthquake?"

"When the tape started you told Jim to listen to the man off-camera. You meant the voice, but I didn't know that, so I focused on the words. When he says Take One, he also says the date, May 19, 2002."

"Right. That's the day they shot it."

"But there was no earthquake in Los Angeles on that day. So I thought maybe they faked it. But that's crazy. Why would they do that? So then I thought maybe they just didn't shoot it in L.A."

"No, they shot it here. I remember Amy talking about Dean

441

shooting it on the Lamaar lot."

"Well, then your guy Lebrecht got the date wrong," Diana said, "because there was no earthquake in L.A. on that day."

We were on Beverly Glen. I slowed down so I could catch a red light. I turned to look at her. "How can you remember a specific day when there was *no* earthquake?"

"Because my husband and I moved here from New York in April 2002, and I was very nervous about the quakes. He said once you've gone through your first one, you'll see that it's not so bad. My first earthquake in L.A. happened on May 23, 2002."

"And you're sure of the date," I said.

She smiled. "Remember I told you May was my favorite month? I was hoping you'd ask me why. May 23 is my birthday."

The guy behind me tapped on his horn and I pulled out. My mind was trying to put the pieces of the puzzle together. "Tell me about the quake," I said. "Do you remember where you were and what time of day it happened?"

"You don't forget the details of your first earthquake. I was asleep. I woke up and the bed was shaking. I freaked. I was screaming, Why the hell did we move here. My husband tried to calm me down by saying, It's your birthday present. I wanted to surprise you. I just screamed till it stopped. He said it gets easier the next time, but he was wrong. They still scare me."

I wished Terry were in the car. We have a rhythm, a patter. I'd have to talk it through without him. "Let's go over it again," I said. "On the tape Lebrecht says it's May 19, which is two days before Dean Lamaar died. But you say the earthquake happened on May 23, two days *after* Dean Lamaar died."

"Maybe that wasn't the real Dean Lamaar on the tape."

"No, it's him." *They might be able to fool me with Hollywood makeup, but they couldn't fool Maxine Green.* "But if Lebrecht lied about the date, then the tape was shot on May 23, which would mean Dean Lamaar didn't die on the 21st like they said he did."

It was impossible to believe. Yet, as my mind raced through the events, facts, rumors, and unanswered questions of the past two weeks, it was just as impossible not to.

"And if Dean Lamaar didn't die when they said he did," I said, as I slowly worked my way to the next logical conclusion, "then I'm willing to bet that he didn't die at all."

CHAPTER 101

I WANTED TO spin the Acura around and head for the Federal Building, but I wasn't driving to the mall to catch a movie. I still had a brother in deep shit.

I turned onto Little Santa Monica and into the parking garage. There were spaces everywhere. I pulled into a spot near the multiplex, killed the engine, and turned to Diana. "Are you *sure* about the date?"

"I know I'm blonde, so some of the things I say are highly suspect, but I felt my first earthquake on May 23, 2002, my birthday. At least I think it's my birthday. Would you like to see my driver's license, officer?"

"Only if I can frisk you." I kissed her lightly. "Is it possible that there *was* an earthquake on the 19th and what you felt on the 23rd was just an aftershock?"

"You mean being an inexperienced, seismically deprived New Yorker I might not have been aware of the first series of gut-wrenching shocks. But four days later, I had developed the sensitivity it requires to feel my bed doing the cha-cha around the room."

She returned the kiss and whispered in my ear. "Interesting theory, Detective, but I seriously doubt it will hold up in court. Now go get your bag of cash, give it to the Mafia guys, and make your Daddy proud. I'll wait in the car."

"I like a woman who does what she's told." I popped the trunk, grabbed the metal case, and took the escalator steps two at a time. As soon as I got to street level I pulled out my cell and dialed Muller at home.

"Write this down," I said. "We have a videotape that supposedly was shot in L.A. on May 19, 2002. Now we think it could have been shot May 23. There was a small earthquake during the shoot and the camera picked it up."

"Gotcha," Muller said. "So the earthquake time-stamps it. And if I tell you when the quake happened you'll know when the tape was made. Easy."

"I also need the magnitude and the duration of the shock. The one on the video is twenty-two seconds long, and it was a duck-under-the-desk, shelf rattler."

"You just made it even easier. Unless you're trying to protect the ignorant, tell me why we care if this video was shot on the 19th or the 23rd."

"Because the star of the tape is Dean Lamaar," I said. "And if you believe everything you read in the papers, he died on May 21. I'll call you back."

I got to the box office, bought a ticket, and went into Theatre Six. The lights were still on. Cappadonna's boys were in the next-to-last row. I sat behind them and leaned forward in my seat. "Sorry, boys, change in plans," I said.

They both stiffened. V-Neck leaned forward in his own seat. "Stay away from the ankle holster," I said. "I have the money. What I don't have is fifteen minutes to sit around while you count it. So here are the new rules. I leave. You stay. If your boss has a problem with that, tell him to call our friend in Vegas, because what I have to do is important to her and she wouldn't want me wasting time staring at the back of your thick necks and inhaling your cheap cologne."

The house lights dimmed. I shoved the case with my foot and they could hear it scrape the floor beneath them. "Are you cool with that little change?"

Cream Pants reached down and put the case on his lap. "Flexibility is our middle name."

"Good. Now sit back, relax, and enjoy the show."

CHAPTER 102

"YOU'RE FAST," **DIANA** said, when I got back in the car. "Usually it takes me at least an hour to spend that much money in the mall."

We pulled out of the garage and I called Muller. "What have you got?"

"May 19, 2002, there were six earthquakes that registered over 3.5. Uzbekistan, Guatemala, Greece, The South Sandwich Islands, Taiwan, and the Molucca Sea. Nothing in the U.S. Repeat, nothing."

And Lamaar didn't fly to Uzbekistan to shoot a video. "How about May 23?"

"Five quakes. India, Chile, Siberia, the Molucca Sea again — and bingo, Southern California. It registered a 5.2, and lasted twenty-two seconds. The epicenter was Inglewood, but it rattled cages from Long Beach to Thousand Oaks."

"Would they have felt it at Lamaar Studios?"

"The night watchman would if he was awake. The first jolt came at 4:49 a.m. Middle of the night, so most people would have slept right through it."

Perfect time for a dead man to shoot a video without attracting any attention.

"Thanks. I owe you." I turned to Diana. "You were right. The earthquake was on May 23. Do you realize what this means?"

"Yes, now that you know my birthday, you have no excuse for not buying me a gift." Then she tapped her forehead, "Oh, and I helped you solve the crime of the century. Where are we going, partner?"

"You're going home. I'm going to work. This is big."

"Lights and sirens big? As long as you're dumping me, you could show me a good time on the way home."

"You can have lights." I grabbed my Kojak light, slapped it on the roof, and it started strobing. "But no sirens. I have to call my other partner."

"First call your father and tell him both his sons are okay."

Exactly the way Joanie would have put it. Not a nag; just the right thing to say. I called. "Dad, it went fine. Tell Frankie he's officially an unmarked man."

"If I were smart I wouldn't say a word," Jim said. "Then he'd stay locked up in the house and keep his ass out of trouble."

"C'mon, Dad, where's your sense of adventure? If Frankie doesn't get in any more trouble, our lives would become meaningless and boring."

I hung up, called Terry, and told him the news. "Leave it to you to figure out a way to ruin my day off," he said. "Let me put on some pants."

"Excuse me, Romeo," I said. "Sorry if I interrupted you and Marilyn."

"Marilyn's not home. It's just me and my parish priest."

I laughed; he thanked me for laughing; then I called Church. "Did the Bureau know about this Dean Lamaar tape?" he asked.

"I don't know. It's been gathering dust in a vault at the Lamaar Studios," I said. "Talking to Eeg kind of helped lead me to it."

"We interviewed Eeg, too, but you got more out of him than we did. Do you think Eeg knows Lamaar is alive?"

"No. I think Eeg believes Lamaar is an evil man who murdered his own father and then drove Eeg's father to suicide."

"If Lamaar is alive and behind this, *evil man* doesn't even begin

448

to put a label on it," Church said. "And if he is alive, where has he been hiding?"

"The most logical place is Lebrecht's house in Ojai."

"State is still working on those passport photos, but we're arresting these crazy old coots now. I don't want anyone else murdered on my watch."

CHAPTER 103

YOU NEVER KNOW what's going to make the difference in solving a crime. When David Berkowitz, the Son of Sam, went off to kill his sixth victim, he couldn't find a place to park. So he left his car next to a fire hydrant, and a seemingly insignificant parking ticket led to his arrest.

I had a seemingly insignificant videotape, a brother who needed to be bailed out of trouble, a nosy father who just had to see what was on the tape, and a girlfriend who could remember the date of an earthquake. An incredible confluence of events. And I'd get credit for being a smart cop.

I dropped Diana at her apartment, ran the rest of the lights on Wilshire, and made it to the FBI office in three minutes. Terry showed up from the Valley only five minutes behind me.

We screened the source tape with Church, Collins, and a dozen other agents. "I'm sure your boy Muller is right," Church said, "but I'm going to ask Hogle to give us a second opinion."

Don Hogle was the guy Muller called the Alpha Geek. He wasn't the tall, square-jawed, blond, buzz cut, stereotypical agent you see in the Hollywood version of the FBI. He was short, compact, bookish, with salt-and-pepper hair and a pair of love handles, which I suspect were handled mostly by lovers of the same sex. "How much time do I have?" he said.

"It's 1:00. Take all the time you need," Church said. "As long as you're back here by 2:00."

He was back at 1:45. "I cross checked six ways to Sunday," Hogle said. "The earthquake on the tape had to have happened on May 23, 2002. There are no other possibilities. I also did a voice analysis on Dean Lamaar. That's him on the tape. Reports of his death on May 21 were greatly exaggerated."

At 2:20 Agent Kinya Chandler came back from the Hillcrest Country Club, where she had gone to track down a federal judge. "Any problems?" Church said.

Chandler was an attractive young African-American woman, who obviously had a comfortable relationship with her boss. "Thanks for sending me to an all-white country club, Garet," she said. "I had to take drink orders for three people before I could find Judge Aronson. But when I told her what we had on these guys, not only did she sign the search and arrest warrants, she said if I came back with a warrant to cut their balls off, she'd sign that, too."

"Good job," Church said. "But if you made any tips taking those drink orders, you're going to have to turn them into Accounting."

It had been a relatively quiet Sunday at the Bureau, but now a steady stream of agents came in from their day off, and Church dispatched two teams of ten to back up the units already watching Kennedy and Barber.

"Twenty more Quantico-trained, razor-sharp, anti-terrorist operatives to stake out two old farts," Terry whispered to me. "And you wonder why the federal deficit is a hundred zillion dollars."

The teams tailing the old farts reported in every fifteen minutes. Kennedy and his wife were shopping. Barber was visiting his grandchildren in Culver City. Lebrecht was at home with Freddy the houseman.

"I want to get Freddy alone and ask him a few questions before we move in," Church said. "If he has any information worth buying, I'll cut him a deal."

"I know how to pry him out of the house," Terry said.

"Lay it on me," Church said.

Terry grinned. "First, we'll need that delivery van from Irwin's Market."

At 2:45 a caravan of no fewer than thirty of us headed toward Ojai. An hour and fifteen minutes later Church and I rang Irwin Pearlman's doorbell. Irwin was in his late sixties and more high-energy than a box full of puppies.

When we informed him that a grateful nation needed his help and his delivery van, he practically hugged us. "I can wear a wire," he said. "I was in Vietnam. I'm a marksman. Just tell me what you need. I'm your man."

Church explained that we wanted to question Freddy Schlecht about an FBI matter, and if Irwin could come up with a reason why his van might make an unscheduled stop at the Lebrecht residence, we would take it from there.

"That's easy. Every few weeks my wife bakes up a bunch of chocolate babkas that are to die for. It's Mr. Lebrecht's favorite. I have a standing order to let Freddy know whenever she makes a fresh batch. I could just call and ask him if he wants me to send any over."

"You think you can pull it off?" Church said.

"Are you kidding? I'm in a local theatre group. I just did *Streetcar*."

Irwin turned out to be a convincing actor, and at 4:20, Agent Hector Nava, a Hispanic agent, drove the delivery van up to Lebrecht's house and rang the bell at the service entrance.

Freddy opened the door. "*Buenos dias, Señor*," Nava said. "Delivery."

"Well, bring it in," Freddy said.

Nava put his head down. "Sorry, *Señor*, but I can't read so good. Just please tell me which is your box, and I carry."

"Where is the regular driver?" Freddy said.

"Is Sunday. He's drunk, maybe," Nava said. "I'm just fillin' in. They say there's good tippers in this neighborhood."

"Don't hold your breath, you little illiterate wetback," Freddy said, storming down the back stairs and toward the van. "If I have to come out and show you which box is which, then you get shit."

He opened the rear door of the van and the long arm of the law grabbed him. Actually it was eight long arms, four of which belonged to Terry and me.

Nava kicked Freddy in the ass as he got yanked into the van. "Illiterate wetback?" Nava said. "I was *magna cum laude* from Georgetown, you fat Nazi scumbag." He slammed the back door, jumped in the cab, and we drove off.

CHAPTER 104

FREDDY CRUMBLED LIKE a sack of tacos in a food fight.

He started whining as soon as he hit the floor of the van. "I'm only Lebrecht's butler. If that old coot is up to no good, I got nothing to do with it."

We drove to a high school parking lot about a mile away. It was empty except for two joggers and a young couple playing Frisbee with a dog. At the far end of the lot were a Winnebago and six SUVs. Nava opened the back door of the van, dragged Freddy out, and shoved him into the motor home. Church, his partner Henry Collins, Terry, and I all followed and closed the door behind us.

Freddy was sitting on a folding chair. Church smiled at him. "I'm Special Agent in Charge Garet Church," he said. Then he turned to Collins. "Iron Man, why don't you see if you can get some straight answers from Mr. Schlecht."

With that, he stepped aside and made way for this blond block of granite. Collins's nickname came from the fact that, just for the heck of it, he competed in two or three triathlons a year. He had a boyish smile that had transformed into a menacing snarl as soon as he crossed the threshold of the Winnebago.

Collins loosened his tie and removed his suit jacket. He was wearing a short-sleeved white shirt that hugged his body. Even I was intimidated by the massive chest, thick neck, and chiseled arms. He looked down at Freddy. "How many people are in the house, shitbag?"

"Three," Freddy said, sweat beading up on his bald dome. "Mr. Lebrecht is there and Dean Lamaar. He's alive. I know you're looking for him."

"That's two. Who else is in there?"

"Jesus is with Mr. Lamaar," Freddy said.

Collins grabbed him by the shirt, digging his nails deep enough to rip at skin and chest hair. Freddy let out a shriek that was more fear than physical pain. Collins screamed back. "Jesus? Don't screw with me, you fat piece of shit."

"No, his name is Jesus. He's Mexican. He pronounces it *Hay-soose*," Freddy said, "but Mr. Lamaar makes us call him Jesus. He's Lamaar's nurse."

"What does Lamaar need a nurse for?"

"He's got bad kidneys. They have a whole dialysis setup in the house. Lamaar gets five hours of dialysis every other day," Freddy said.

"Is Jesus armed?" Collins asked.

"No, no way. He's just a nurse. I think he's gay."

"Are these guys behind the terrorist activity that's targeting the Lamaar Company?" Collins asked.

"I don't know," Freddy said. "I just work for..."

Iron Man lunged at Freddy and shoved him backwards. The chair went down and Freddy hit the floor hard. His right ankle got caught under the metal rung of the folding chair and Collins stepped down on it. "Quiet everyone!" Collins yelled. "The next sound you hear will either be that of Mr. Schlecht telling the truth or the first of many bones snapping."

"Alright, alright, don't break my ankle. I'll tell you everything."

"Do it," Collins said. "We already know most of the details, so if you try to con us or if you leave out a single word, it will cost you an arm and a leg."

Freddy sat back in the chair. "Mr. Lebrecht interviewed me

about six years ago. It was a good job, big money just for taking care of one rich old guy. He told me he knew about the trouble I had in Austria, but he'd overlook it."

"You had a record?" Collins said.

"I was working in a hotel in Salzburg. I was young, I had a passkey, you know how it happens. I pulled three and a half for robbery. It was way before I came to the U.S. I don't know how the hell he knew, but he did. He said he trusted me. All he wanted in return was loyalty."

"All he wanted was a loyal ex-con," Collins said. "No strings attached."

"It was a real cushy job. Health benefits, bonuses, paid vacations. In the beginning it was all on the up and up. Then one day he tells me Mr. Lamaar was going to go into hiding. He would live in our house. All I had to do was swear secrecy and not ask any questions."

"And you agreed."

"Hey man, I didn't give a shit. I didn't do anything illegal. I thought maybe it was an insurance scam, but these guys were too rich to fake being dead for money. So I figured they're just a bunch of crazy old codgers, the two of them and their buddies, Barber and Kennedy. After a while, it was totally natural. I'm serving breakfast to a guy everyone thinks is dead."

"Who *did* die?" Church said. "They cremated someone."

"No they didn't," he said. "Lebrecht bought off the crematorium, he paid for the phony death certificate. Money talks. That part was easy."

"Why did Lamaar make that video two days after his so-called death?" Collins said.

Freddy looked confused. "What video? I don't know what you're talking about. If this is a trick so you can break my leg, I swear to God..."

"Shut up, you whining little pussy," Collins said. He banged his fist on a tabletop and Freddy squeezed his eyes shut.

Church leaned over and whispered something to Collins. Collins touched his two palms together then threw back his arms like a rodeo cowboy who just roped and tied a calf. Then he stepped back. Church stepped in and put his good hand on Freddy's shoulder. The man shuddered, then opened his eyes.

"My friend is angry because innocent people have died, like those folks at the Burger King in Texas, and because he himself was injured in an explosion that your employer sponsored. Now, I can keep him calm, but you're going to have to tell us what you know about those murders and what they have planned next. Now, I believe you when you say you had nothing to do with it, but you're the butler. Butlers hear things. Tell us what you heard, and I'll help you when the time comes to sort out the 'guilty' from the 'only-guilty-by-association'."

"You can get me off?"

"I said I can help," Church said. "The more I get, the more I can help."

Freddy nodded. "They've been planning a long time. At first I thought it was a movie. They were talking about the script and pre-production and casting the right people. Then one day, it dawns on me that it's a caper."

"It just *dawned* on you, Freddy?"

"Hey, I got curious," Freddy said. "The three of them, Lebrecht, Kennedy, and Barber, took a bunch of trips a few years ago. I stayed home and babysat Mr. Lamaar. One day he says something like, 'I miss the guys. I can't wait for them to come back from their casting trip.' So after they get back, I thought I'd poke around Mr. Lebrecht's room to see what's going on."

"And lucky you, you don't even need a passkey to break into his room," Collins said.

Freddy flared for a split second. His mouth started to form the F sound, but he caught himself. He wasn't about to drop an F-bomb on Iron Man. "I'm in his room, and I'm looking at a diary that's just sitting on the dresser. He's got notes on different people. Names, where they live, prices, and specialties."

"Give us a for instance of a specialty," Church said.

"Explosives, garrote, karate, marksman. Then I check out his passport, but it's..." Freddy thought about holding back, but as soon as he hesitated Collins started moving toward him. "His passport... it's phony. It has his picture, but a fake name, Schmidt, Kurt Schmidt. And he's been to Cyprus, Israel, Russia, all dicey places. So I figure he's not casting a movie; he's looking for guys who do wet work."

"And so, good citizen that you are, you called the cops," Church said.

"No. Mr. Lebrecht has always taken care of me. I'm loyal."

"Plus now you got some good shit on him that maybe you can use to blackmail him some day," Church said.

Freddy looked offended. "I would never do that to Mr. Lebrecht."

Church put his face up against Freddy's. "It's so hard to get good help nowadays, Freddy. You're a real find," he said, exhaling hard so that Freddy could feel, smell, and taste the same disgust he had already seen and heard.

Church and Collins took turns questioning him for another twenty minutes, but Freddy didn't know much. He wasn't even a small fish in the pond. He was a bottom feeder who would give up whatever he had if it could save his own scaly skin.

"Alright Freddy," Church said. "We need to talk to Mr. Lamaar. I'm sure he's not sitting in his rocker on the front porch. Where in the house is he?"

"The bookcase in the Media Room opens up like one of those Hollywood sets you see in the movies," Freddy said. "That's where Mr. Lamaar hides out. It's Sunday afternoon, so he'll be in the sterile room getting dialysis from the nurse. Don't forget. You promised to give me a break if I helped you."

"You have been very helpful, Freddy," Church said. "And how could I forget? It's not every day that someone leads me to Jesus and tells me how to bring Dean Lamaar back from the dead."

CHAPTER 105

IT HAD BEEN less than two weeks since Terry and I rode through the Rabbit Hole on a golf cart to look at the body of the late Eddie Elkins.

It was now 6 p.m. on a sunny Sunday in May, and we were in the lead vehicle as a sextet of Government-Issue Chevy Suburbans returned to join the agents who were watching Lebrecht's house.

Church, Collins, Terry, and I waited while the rest of the team surrounded the house and covered every possible escape route, including the roof.

"It's been over an hour since we grabbed Freddy," Church said, "so they know he's missing. But they haven't tried to escape."

"It might be hard for Lamaar to get around unnoticed dragging a dialysis machine behind him," Terry said.

The four of us went to the front door. "Why don't you do the honors, Mike," Church said. "You cracked the code."

Actually Diana cracked the code, but I decided not to mention it and just rang the doorbell on her behalf. "FBI and LAPD," I yelled. "Open up!"

Lebrecht opened the door. He was wearing blue jeans and a gray sweatshirt that was devoid of logos, pictures, or sports team affiliation. "Hello, Detective Lomax," he said. "I suppose you and these other gentlemen are the reason I have to fix my own dinner. Where did you take Freddy?"

"Freddy is in good hands," I said. "And I have excellent news. You won't have to fix your own dinner ever again. The United States government will be happy to fix it for you. We have a warrant for your arrest."

I read him his rights, while Collins signaled eight agents to move into the house. "We have a search warrant," I said. "Let's start in the Media Room."

The agents fanned out through the house and the four of us walked into the empty Media Room. The control button was recessed into a decorative wall panel and was practically invisible. We would have found it eventually, but Freddy bought himself some get-out-of-jail-sooner points by telling us exactly where it was. I pressed it, and a five-foot section of bookcase swung open.

The room behind it was small, about twelve by fifteen feet. In the center was a brown leather recliner. Facing me, his body adjusted to a forty-five-degree angle, was the childhood icon of generations of children, my own included. Dean Lamaar.

A series of tubes ran from his left arm to a large column that was a foot square and five feet high. The tubes, filled with blood, snaked their way through a rotating pump and back into his arm. There was a video display at eye level that monitored his progress. A small, dark-skinned man of about fifty, wearing white pants, white shoes, and a white T-shirt, was seated at his side.

I scanned the room and a feeling of déjà vu crept over me. "Jesus," I said.

The man dressed in white stood up. "*Si, Señor*," he said.

I turned to Church. "I wasn't talking to him," I said, laughing at the comic ludicrousness of it all. "I meant Jesus, would you look at this room. It's an exact replica of the room Dean Lamaar grew up in. There's another one just like it at Familyland."

"With or without the dialysis machine?" Terry said.

Except for the medical miracle that was detoxifying Lamaar's blood, the room looked exactly like the Homestead exhibit Amy had taken me to. The furniture, the books and toys on the shelves, the drawings on the wall, everything. Dean Lamaar had returned to his boyhood home.

He was wearing navy slacks and a blue-and-green checked shirt. A pale yellow shawl was draped across his lap. He was no longer the same vibrant, healthy Dean Lamaar I had watched in the video. The head full of white hair had thinned, and the rosy Reagan glow had turned gray and waxy. But his eyes were still fiercely alert, and his voice still commanded attention.

"Gentlemen," he said, welcoming us and despising us in a single word.

"You're under arrest for the murder of Ronnie Lucas and numerous others," Church said. "You have the right to remain silent..."

Lamaar snapped back at him. "What if I don't wish to remain silent?"

"Anything you say can and will be held against you in a court of law."

"Fine, I understand my rights. I want to talk, but I'll be plugged into this contraption for..." Lamaar leaned over to read the monitor. "...another hour and fifty-two minutes."

"Then I guess we'll wait," Church said.

"No," Lamaar said. "We'll talk now. You can question me here."

"Do you want an attorney present?" Church said.

Lamaar sneered at the suggestion. "All I need is Jesus," he said.

"Okay," Church said. "I'm going to want to tape it."

"Klaus has got video equipment," Lamaar said. "What do you need?"

"Thank you, sir," Church said, "but we brought our own."

"Make sure it's working," Lamaar said. "I don't do more than one take." *The Prince of Joy and Laughter* laughed, but there

461

was no joy. The laughter sounded like dementia. The Prince had become King Lear.

CHAPTER 106

ONE TECHNICIAN SET up the video equipment, while a second clipped a lavalier mic to Lamaar's shirt. "This dialysis machine's a bit noisy," the sound man said. "I'll lay on an extra mic just to make sure we pick everything up."

He was lying. The second microphone fed into a voice analyzer. It's not as reliable as a polygraph, but it can detect stress in a person's voice and measure ten different levels of truthfulness ranging from Boy Scout honesty to avoidance to out-and-out bullshit.

Church walked up to the recliner. "I'm Special Agent in Charge Garet Church," he said politely. Then he pointed to the shawl on Lamaar's lap. "Sir, may I take a look under the blanket?"

"If I had a gun under there, I'd have shot you when you came through the door," Lamaar said, handing him the shawl.

Church checked the recliner, then set the shawl back on Lamaar's lap. "And what's that button in your left hand, sir?"

"Sodium release. I press it if my blood pressure drops."

Church thanked him, stepped back, slated the tape with the date, time, and location, and read the Miranda. "You understand your rights, sir?"

He did. "I'm ready to confess all my sins," Lamaar said. "Can I just tell it my way? I was never any good at questions and answers."

"I have one burning question first," Church said. "There are still hired guns out there murdering innocent people. The first order of business is for us to find them and tell them the war is over. We need names and places."

"I had nothing to do with casting," Lamaar said, as casually as if he were talking about a movie and not a massacre. "I left that to the other three. You'll have to talk to them. Klaus Lebrecht is more likely to open up than Barber. Mitch is a zealot. Dedicated to the cause."

"What about Kennedy?" Church said.

"Kevin had prostate cancer a few years ago. It kicked in again and has started to metastasize. Kevin will be dead before he tells you anything."

"Excuse us a second," Church said. I followed him outside.

The technician who set up the voice analyzer joined us. "The part about the cancer is true," he said. "But he lied about the first two guys. I'd say Barber's our weakest link."

"I'll have the surveillance units bring in Barber and Kennedy," Church said. "Get Barber in the box with Patch. He'll put some heat on him."

A few minutes later, we were back in the room with Lamaar. Church gave him an icy nod. "Go ahead, sir. Tell it your way."

Lamaar cleared his throat. "I was eight years old when I drew my first cartoon character. I was twelve when my father beat me savagely for it."

For the next ninety minutes Lamaar talked. Some of it I'd heard from Big Jim or Eeg, but that had been Hollywood hearsay. This was direct from the source. I remember Amy saying that Lamaar wouldn't let anyone ghostwrite his autobiography because his personal life was too boring. I only wished she were here to witness this. When Lamaar finally spilled his guts it was mesmerizing.

"As a boy, I instinctively knew to keep my pictures private," he said. "I wanted to share them with Mother, but I knew she would be consumed with fear of how Father might react. He had forbidden me to even read comic strips. But I had a destiny and nothing was going to stand in my way. Nothing.

"So I sinned. I would sit in my room by the light of a tallow candle and my colored pencils would sweep and swoosh and shade. Father had his leg blown off in the Great War and some nights I would hear him hop, hop, hopping to the toilet without strapping his wooden leg on. I would quickly douse the light and hide my pads and pencils in the hollow wall behind my closet.

"It was the perfect hiding place. Until the coon died. She must have been sick and burrowed her way into that space. When the stench of dead coon became powerful enough, Father went in search of the carcass.

"It was on the day of my twelfth birthday, and I came home from school, excited about what treat Mother might have for me. Along with Christmas, it was the only other day of the year that Father permitted her to give me a gift.

"He was sitting there, a whiskey glass in his hand and hatred in his eyes. The sanctimonious hypocrite. Oh, he would preach about the dangers of alcohol, then go home and drink himself mean and ugly. He had my pencils and pads on the table next to him, and he demanded to know how I got them. My bowels went loose and I prayed to the Good Lord not to let me crap in my pants.

"I told him I bought them at Goldberg's Emporium with money I earned cleaning Mr. MacDaniels's barn. He started to scream. *You should have given that money to your Lord Jesus Christ, not to that thieving Jew merchant, Goldstealer.* And then he held up my drawing pad. *What are these evil pictures?* I explained that they were cartoons, but he didn't see cartoons. He saw animals dressed like people. Cows and dogs and pigs, dancing and smoking. Female animals with bosoms. And then he saw Miss Kitty. Little flecks of foam bubbled from his lips and he went into a rage. *A cat, dressed like a whore, and what name do you give her? Kitty? The name of my sainted dead mother? God will strike you dead for this, Deanie.*

"God didn't strike me. Father did. I had suffered his belt before, but this time twenty lashes weren't enough. This sin called for greater pain. He dragged me to the fireplace and made me throw my drawings and pencils into the fire. I was crying and bleeding and begging. *And now, sinner*, he said and he forced my hands into the flames screaming, *this is what it will feel like in Hades.*

"Mother had been cowering behind the kitchen door, but she couldn't watch any longer, and she ran into the room and pulled my hands out of the fire. She begged him not to hurt me, especially on my birthday, and that set him off even more. He pushed me to the cellar door and threw me down the stairs, yelling, *For your birthday dinner you can eat water bugs and mouse droppings!*

"It was dark with just a little daylight coming through the window. A water bug as big as my fist darted across the floor. I tried to step on it, but I missed. I was petrified, because I thought that the bug was angry, and he'd bring back his friends. Now I was afraid to sit on the floor. I had never seen a water bug in the coal pile, so I climbed to the top, careful not to collapse it. The window was dirty, but there was enough light to see for another hour. I picked up a lump of coal and began to draw on the cellar wall.

"There was a character that had been inside my head for years. A rabbit. Defiant, confident, dauntless, daring—everything I wished I could be. That night in that dungeon, he came to life, and he comforted me and sustained me through my loneliness and fear. In the morning, I gave him a name. Rambunctious. I knew he was part of my destiny and no one would ever stand in our way. I decided right then to murder my father."

Lamaar paused, and the only sound in the room was the whir of the dialysis machine. "It took me a few weeks," he said. "Not to get up the courage, but to come up with a plot. I was only

466

twelve, but I was very creative. One night, after Father had passed out from liquor, I climbed a tree, crawled out on the roof, pried loose some shingles, and let them slide to the ground. The next morning he saw them and told me to hold the ladder while he repaired them.

"He hobbled up fifteen rungs, and just as he lifted his good leg to step onto the roof, I shoved the ladder backwards. He came crashing down and landed in a pile of garden tools that I had placed on the ground. I ran to him, ready to bash his skull with a shovel, but he fell on an iron rake and cut an artery. I will never forget the look in his eyes, first pleading for me to get help, then horror as I whispered, *I'll see you in hell.* I stood over him until he bled to death.

"Everyone accepted it as just a tragic accident. But at the cemetery, as they lowered him into the grave, Mother hugged me tight, put her lips to my ear and whispered, *Thank you, thank you, thank you.* We never spoke of him again."

A tray was attached to the right side of Lamaar's recliner. There was a box of tissues in it, a large syringe with no needle, and a can of Pepsi with a straw sticking out of the top. He reached over with his right hand, took a sip, then gestured his head toward me. "I've been trying to place your face," he said, as if we were casual acquaintances at a studio party. "I saw you on TV after the Ronnie Lucas murder. And we watched you on the Web cam. You and your partner put the ransom money in the van, but you were the one who realized we were going to blow it up."

"Yes, sir," I said. "You almost killed us."

"Don't take it personally. You're Lomax, right?"

"Detective Mike Lomax, sir. LAPD."

"Lomax," he said. "Years back, I had a driver named Lomax. Big Jim we called him. Good man."

"He's my father, sir."

"I'll be damned," he said. "I guess Disney was right. It's a small world after all. You and your Dad get along okay?"

"Very much so, sir."

"That's a real blessing," he said. He took another sip of the soda. "I had two overwhelming feelings after Father passed. The first was the sheer sense of relief. But the other came as a complete surprise. I loved the feeling of power. Taking someone's life is the ultimate God-like act, and for me, power was a rush. I like being in control. That's been my strength and my Achilles heel.

"In 1937 Disney released *Snow White* and followed it up with *Pinocchio*. Two Hollywood blockbusters. I was living in Manhattan at the time." He laughed. "Manhattan, Kansas. I made a very, very low-budget animated short about a farmer who couldn't start his tractor. *The Intractable Tractor*, I called it. Boy, was it bad. I had a lot to learn and nobody to teach me. But then I got lucky. The Japs bombed Pearl Harbor. I joined the Army, and instead of shipping me overseas, they sent me to Fort Belvoir, Virginia, and assigned me to a unit that produced military training films. A lot of it was animation, because everything had to be simple enough for the average GI Joe to understand. That's where I met the men who would become my lifelong friends."

"The Cartoon Corps," I said.

He smiled. "You've done your homework. Uncle Sam bought us lots of sophisticated equipment, but we were in over our heads, so they flew in some of the best animators in the business to teach us the tricks of the trade. One week a guy would help us make a film on how to avoid venereal disease, and the next week he'd be back home working on *Fantasia*.

"We learned a lot and after the war, Lars Eeg and I went to Hollywood. Lars was a better animator than I was, but I became the successful one. I think it's because he always had pretensions of becoming a fine artist. My goal was to create cartoons that would capture the essence of the twentieth-century American family. Did you ever wonder why Familyland isn't called Lamaar Land? Because I wanted the name Lamaar to be synonymous with family.

"I love children. Did you know that in 1970, *Scholastic Magazine* did a nationwide survey of kids under ten. If they could spend one day with any person, living or dead, real or fictional, who would it be? Their first choice, ahead of Babe Ruth, Superman, Santa Claus, and Elvis Presley, was me. It's ironic, isn't it Mike?"

"What's that, sir?"

"I murdered my own father in cold blood, and somehow I became a father figure to millions."

CHAPTER 107

LAMAAR TOOK US on a guided tour of the rise of his empire, including his split with Eeg. "He was never a team player," Lamaar said. "His family still thinks they're entitled to more money than I gave him, but they're wrong. Lars only perfected my idea. He wasn't down there in that vermin-infested cellar when I created it.

"Sooner or later all good things come to an end. By the late nineties the company was losing money. We had been down before, but this time was different. We were old men. Our stockholders had no faith in us and the Japanese had money. They stole the company out from under me.

"They promised me total creative freedom and a contract for life, but they began destroying my baby before the ink was even dry. They hired Ike Rose. The Great Jewish Hope, all five-feet-nothing of him. I remember my first meeting with him. He kissed my ass like everyone who ever drove through our front gates. Mr. Lamaar, you're a genius, Mr. Lamaar, you're a legend, Mr. Lamaar, let me kneel at your feet and bask in your brilliance. I knew right then he'd be trouble.

"Three weeks later he issued his famous *Memo From the Beach*. After living, breathing, and soaking up every aspect of the Lamaar Company for less than one calendar month, he spent a weekend at his beach house in Malibu and wrote a fifty-seven-page document on how to fix it. He never said fix. He used 're' words. Reshape, revitalize, resuscitate, reinvigorate, rejuvenate, re-energize, and my favorite—reanimate.

"*The world has changed*, he said. And for that they paid him millions. *A new millennium is upon us. We have to give the people what they want.* And for that they heaped stock options on him. And what in Mr. Ike Rose's Talmudic opinion did the people want?"

Lamaar struggled to lift his head from the pillow and screamed at the camera. "Violence, profanity, infidelity, nudity, fathers defiling daughters and granddaughters. Incest. Innnnncesssst."

His head fell back on the pillow. He put one hand over his eyes and took short, shallow breaths. A minute passed before he removed his hand from his eyes and spoke again. This time, his voice was calm, softer, a little raspy from the beating he had just given his ancient vocal cords. "Do you know the word heterodoxy, Mr. Lomax?" he said.

"No, sir."

"It's like heresy or blasphemy. A sin against God. My father used to use it in his sermons. Ike Rose committed heterodoxy. His first foray into reanimating my vision was a movie called *Home for the Holidays.*

"I told him it was a huge mistake. I said it would ruin the Lamaar image. He opened a new division called Freeze Frame to release it. He said this way the Lamaar name won't be associated with an R movie. But that's bullshit. The Fundamentalists know it's a Lamaar film, the Christian Right knows it, The Moral Majority knows it. Who does that kike bastard think he's kidding?

"I wanted to stop him, but I was powerless. They turned me into another Colonel Sanders. He created Kentucky Fried Chicken then sold it to a conglomerate. They put his face on every bucket of chicken, but he had no say in running the company. I too was stripped of my power. To make matters worse, the movie was a blockbuster. It cost $30 million to make and pulled in $266.4

million. Wall Street loved him.

"I knew what that meant. Little by little, the balance would shift until debauchery and depravity replaced morality and virtue. Familyland would become Paganland. My partners told me to stay calm. Today's audiences aren't looking for 1950s family fun, they told me. Lebrecht said R-rated movies are a sign of the times. But then I found out Ike Rose wasn't stopping there. He's been negotiating to build a multi-billion-dollar complex in Las Vegas. The Lamaar name right in the middle of America's cultural hellhole—gambling, prostitution, drugs, all run by organized crime. That's not the legacy I wanted when I died."

He was breathing heavily, but while the voice analyzer clearly registered stress, the technician bent his thumb upwards to signal that it was also registering honesty.

"I hated Rose and everything he was doing. I couldn't sleep. And then one night, I realized that Father had been right. My simple drawings had turned into a company that was a purveyor of filth. My only salvation was to destroy the Sodom and Gomorrah I had built. I was indeed its Creator, and I had the right—no, the obligation—to wipe it from the face of the Earth.

"I met with Kevin, Mitch, and Klaus. They were wealthy beyond imagination and they all knew I was responsible for the lives they had been blessed with. They were loyal. I didn't have to prod them.

"We decided I should fake my own death. Everyone knew I hated the way the company was being run. If I were still alive, I would be a suspect. But if I were dead, I would have the power to orchestrate its demise. We put together a master plan the same way we used to produce a feature film. It didn't happen overnight. It was fine-tuned, perfected. Nothing was left to chance. I have a question, Detective. How did you figure out I was still alive?"

"You made a videotape two days after you supposedly died," I said. "We watched the source tape and there was a minor earthquake in the middle of filming. That time-stamped it for us."

Lamaar shook his head. "Damn," he said. "The earthquake…
the goddamn earthquake." He let out a pitiful sigh.

"I have a question," I said. "Why did you make the tape after
you faked your death? Why didn't you make it before?"

"I did, I did," he said. "We shot it on May 19, two days before
I died. It was supposed to be shown at my funeral. But the day
after I faked my death and moved in here, Klaus came racing in
and told me that the tape had been destroyed. It was sent out to
be duped, but somehow it wound up in a box of tapes that were
scheduled to be erased for re-use.

"I was devastated. I had wanted that tape to be my legacy, a
testimonial to what I had created. Klaus said we could reshoot
it. I remember ranting and raving that we couldn't reshoot
because I was dead. But he had a plan. Before dawn on May
23 we sneaked back into the studio, shot a second version, and
backdated it. No one saw us. I remember that earthquake. I
thought it was my father rumbling down in hell, pissed off that I
really wasn't dead."

Henry Collins entered the room and held up a clear plastic bag.
Inside the bag was a pink-and-white fuzzy hunk of fabric and wire
mesh with a jagged cut along the bottom. It was Rambo's ear.

"LAPD has a rabbit head that's missing one of those," I said.

"This is just one of a dozen things we've found that connects
them," Collins said. "Including Lebrecht's phony passport. They
didn't go out of their way to hide anything."

Church looked at the time remaining on the dialysis machine.
"Another eight minutes and we'll be done irrigating Lamaar's
kidneys. Let's transport him back to L.A. I'll need a Med-Evac.
Set it down at the high school."

"I'm on it," Collins said and left.

"Mr. Lamaar," Church said. "We have no more questions for
now. As soon as you get unhooked from that machine we're
going to take you back to Los Angeles."

"I don't want to go back," Lamaar said.

473

"Sir, with all due respect," Church said, "you don't have a choice. We're in charge now."

"No," Lamaar said. "You're not." He picked up the empty syringe from the tray at his side.

"Sir?" Church said, and started to move toward him.

"Stop right there," Lamaar said.

"What's in the syringe, Mr. Lamaar?" Church asked.

"Nothing." He smiled. "Just air. Thirty ccs of God's good air." He snapped the syringe into a piece of blue plastic that was on one of his blood lines.

"*Dios mio*." It was Jesus.

"Jesus, what the hell is going on here?" Church yelled.

Jesus moved toward the recliner. "*Señor, por favor.*"

"Don't come any closer," Lamaar said, and Jesus stopped a few feet from the chair. "The man asked you a question. He wants to know what's going on."

"There's a luer lock on the return tube," Jesus said. "It's there if I have to inject antibiotics into the lines. But he just connected an empty syringe. The air bubble is like instant death. It will kill him in seconds."

"Mr. Lamaar," Church said. "We can negotiate here. You don't even have to go to jail. A good lawyer can…"

"A good lawyer can what? Get me a nice corner suite at a home for the criminally insane? Save it, Mr. Church. I'm in charge of this production. Detective Lomax, I didn't hear anyone yell 'cut.' Is that videotape still running?"

"Yes, sir," I said.

"Good. Because you're only gonna get one take."

His right forearm tightened as he pressed his thumb down hard on the plunger. He gasped sharply. His body seized up and convulsed for a few seconds, then his hand fell to his lap and his head dropped. A red light started to strobe and the monitor let out a series of shrill beeps alerting us to what we already knew.

The Prince of Joy and Laughter was finally dead.

CHAPTER 108

"MOTHERFUCKER!" CHURCH SCREAMED. "Cocksucking, son of a…"

"Tape's still rolling," the technician said.

Church stormed over to the recliner and shoved two fingers into Lamaar's carotid artery. "Jesus, turn that thing off." The nurse killed the beeping monitor.

Church pulled his fingers from Lamaar's neck. "I think he's done with the dialysis, too." Jesus turned off the pump and began to recite the *Hail Mary* in Spanish.

"Quiet!" Church yelled. He checked his watch and turned to the camera in total disgust. "8:11 p.m. The suspect, Dean Lamaar, using an empty syringe, apparently pumped air into his dialysis line and killed himself. The coroner will determine actual cause of death. Stop the videotape."

"Tape stopped," the tech said.

Church scowled at Lamaar's lifeless body. "You worthless scumbag. You slimy bastard." Jesus stared at the floor, his lips moving rapidly, either in silent prayer, or he was cursing out Church for hurling insults at his late patient.

"Come on, Garet," I said. "Let's step to the other side of the looking glass." I put my arm on his shoulder and walked him through the magic bookcase into Lebrecht's media room.

"When I was a rookie, I used to work with this old-timer,

475

Sergeant Paulivici," I said. "We had this running gag between us. Every time something really weird would happen on a case, I'd say, Paulie, now I've seen everything, and he'd say, Kid, you ain't seen nothing yet. He was always right."

"I think maybe this time you're right," Church said. "Now you have seen everything."

Church assembled his agents and filled them in on the most recent demise of Dean Lamaar. "But don't worry if you missed it," he said. "The fucker killed himself on videotape, so the whole world can see how vigilant we are when we question a suspect. Henry, you still got a chopper coming to pick up Lamaar?"

"It'll be here in fifteen," Collins said.

"Get him a hearse," Church said. "Lomax, Biggs, and I are taking the chopper back to L.A. You stay and finish searching the house. What's the story on Lebrecht and Freddy?"

"They're on the way back with Chandler and her team. Are we charging the nurse with anything?'

"I doubt if he's involved with the operation, but I don't want him wandering the streets just yet," Church said. "Bring him in. Tell him he's a material witness to a crime."

Collins shrugged. "What crime?"

"Suicide."

CHAPTER 109

WHEN WE GOT back to L.A., Terry called Kilcullen, and I asked Church how to reach Ike Rose. "I think we should give him the good news."

He frowned. "Bad idea." Then he shook his head. "What the hell? The guy's been through enough. Call him, but if it leaks that we nailed the people behind it, the rest of the network will scatter like roaches when the lights go on."

He gave me a number with a 573 area code. Curry answered. "We got them," I said. "You can't come out of your spider hole yet, but we got them."

"Hallelujah," he said. "Who are they?"

"Kennedy, Barber, Lebrecht, and believe it or not, Dean Lamaar."

"Elvis isn't in on it, too, is he?"

"I know it sounds like movie magic, but I just spent two hours talking to Dean Lamaar."

"*He's alive?*"

"Not exactly." I took Brian through the events of the past two days, ending with Lamaar's on-camera suicide. His only response was a loud exhale.

"Can you tell me where you are?" I asked.

"I guess I can now. We're guests of the President of the United States at the Fort Leonard Wood army base in Missouri."

"How'd you swing that?"

"Ike called the President and said he needed to get his people the hell out of Dodge. Ten minutes later The Secretary of the Army called back and gave us a choice of four military bases. This one came with the continental breakfast, a Jacuzzi, and a strict no-tipping policy. Plus it's in the middle of goddamn nowhere, which helps us sleep better at night. When can we come back to L.A.?"

"Lamaar still has some wet workers in the field," I said. "Give us some time to sweep them clean."

"The stock market opens in the morning," Brian said. "The sooner Ike can announce that these guys have been caught..."

"Brian, Garet was nervous that I could be jumping the gun by telling Ike. The people who are out there doing the killing are still out there. If Ike goes public, Garet Church will do a lot more than cut off his rabbit ears."

"Understood. I'll keep him in check," he said. "Congratulations, bro. You just solved the biggest case of your career."

"I didn't solve it on my own. There were hundreds of people involved, including my girlfriend, who figured out that there was something fishy about the *Deanie's Farewell* tape."

"Mike, I got a flash for you. The TV news shows don't want to interview hundreds of people who were *involved*. They want heroes. And you're the guy who cracked the code. When this story breaks, it's going to be front page from here to Oshkosh. And you, Detective Lomax, are about to become a media star."

Brian was close. I didn't exactly become a media star, but I definitely got my fifteen minutes.

CHAPTER 110

MITCH BARBER SAT in The Box, one ankle shackled to the leg of a gray metal table. It was a sterile room with gray industrial flooring and four white walls, one of which had a four-by-six-foot mirror built in. Barber stared at the mirror. Church, Terry, and I sat on the other side of it, staring back.

The door behind Barber opened and Agent Mal Strang, known to one and all as Patch, entered the room. He was tall and lanky, with parchment skin and wispy red hair. He was pushing retirement, the oldest agent I'd seen so far. He wore a black eye patch over his left eye.

"What happened to his eye?" I asked.

"Nothing," Church said. "He only wears it to put people off."

"Good evening, Mr. Barber," Patch said.

"I want a lawyer," Barber answered. "They read me my rights. I told them I want a lawyer."

"If I had murdered as many people as you, I'd want one, too," Patch said. "How old are you?"

"Eighty-one."

"Enlighten me, sir," Patch said. "At your advanced age, does the death penalty scare you?"

"Of course it scares me."

"It's not that bad, sir," Patch said. "They strap you to a gurney, put the needle in your arm, turn the spigot. It's not a bad way to die. In fact, in your case, it would be a fantastic way to die."

Barber looked at him like he was nuts.

"And, sir, if you tell me what I want to know, I can personally guarantee you that you will die by lethal injection."

"Are you insane? That's your guarantee?" Barber said. "What happens if I *don't* tell you what you want to know?"

"That would be ugly, sir," Patch said. "You'd still get the death sentence, but we'd lock you up with a prison population of lifers, murderers, and sickos. No solitary. No isolation. No protection. It's amazing how many convicted killers have a warped sense of justice. They see this rich old white guy and they think, *Hey man, somebody's gotta pay for them poor souls who got murdered at Burger King.* But they don't kill you right away. You'll wish they did, but they never do. Now *that's* a terrible way to die. Would you like to avoid that?"

Barber started to whimper. He nodded his head.

"That's where I come in, sir," Patch said. "You and your partners have a bunch of hired assassins out there. I will give you thirty seconds to tell me who and where they are. When the thirty seconds are up, I'll leave the room, and make the same offer to one of your partners. The first one of you to accept will live to see the needle. The other two get fucked." He laughed. "Often and hard. Your thirty seconds starts now."

Barber panicked. "It's a good offer," he said. "I'll talk it over with my lawyer when he gets here."

"I hope he doesn't get stuck in traffic, sir," Patch said, looking at his watch. "This offer will be retracted in sixteen seconds. Fifteen, fourteen, thirteen."

"I have a good defense," Barber said. "I was brainwashed by the others. They said they'd kill me if I backed out."

"Ah, the famous Third Reich defense," Strang said. "'I was only following orders.' Six, five, four."

"This isn't fair. This is blackmail," Barber said.

"See what I mean by a warped sense of justice?" Patch said.

"Here you are, a mass murderer, and you're angry at me, a humble blackmailer. Your time is up, Mr. Barber. I guess I pegged you wrong, but I have the feeling that Mr. Kennedy is more the kind of man who will tell us anything to avoid being gang raped. Goodbye."

He turned and headed for the door.

Barber screamed. "Stop, please, stop!"

Patch kept walking. He opened the door, stepped out, let the door close most of the way, then stuck his head back in the room. "Yes, sir?" he said.

"I accept," Barber whimpered. "I'll talk."

CHAPTER 111

HE TALKED. NAMES, specialties, how they were recruited, how they were paid. "We had a cast of ten," he said. A cast. Three of them were still active.

Church took over for Patch. "What are they planning to do next?"

"Lebrecht told them to sit tight and wait for instructions."

"And they're willing to do that?" Church asked.

"They get paid by the day whether they work or not."

"Well, let's put them to work," Church said. "That's the only way we're going to flush them out. How do you contact them?"

"Klaus contacts them by e-mail."

An hour later Lebrecht's PC was in the FBI computer lab. He had trashed his e-mail program, but it took the techies about a nanosecond to restore it.

We already knew the man behind the Burger King bombing. Declan Brady, code name Yeats. The guy in L.A. was a Basque, code name Cervantes. And the one in New York was Greek, code name Sophocles. "I hope you catch that weasel," Barber said. "He was more trouble than he was worth."

Barber created scenarios for their next targets. It was almost midnight when we e-mailed each one and told him to catch an early morning flight. We sent Yeats to Chicago, Sophocles to San Francisco, and Cervantes to Miami. Then we faxed Brady's photo and sketches of the other two to every office in the net.

"Now we wait till morning," Church said.

"It's my day off," Terry said. "I think I'll go home."

I didn't want to go home. I went to Diana's apartment. "Sorry to wake you," I said, when she let me in.

"Shut up," she said, and kissed me.

She led me to the bedroom. I peeled off my clothes and crawled into bed with her. Human contact never felt so good.

"I have good news," she said. "Hugo's counts are up. The docs tell me this is the sign of remission we've been waiting for."

"I thought you weren't going to the hospital today," I said.

"I didn't, but I still called in."

"That's fantastic," I said. "Tell Hugo as soon as he's ready, he's invited for the grand tour of our squad room."

She kissed me. "Have I told you lately that you're a very nice man?"

"I don't believe you have," I said. "Ever."

"Oversight. So, how'd it go at the office for you today?"

"Excellent, but I'd rather give you the details in the morning."

"Well, I'm wide awake now," she said. "I hope you're not going to just roll over and go to sleep."

I held her close. "Have no fear."

CHAPTER 112

SOPHOCLES WAS THE first to be caught. He pulled up in a taxi at the American Airlines terminal in JFK at 7 a.m. At least a dozen agents were waiting for him, posing as skycaps, gate agents, and fellow travelers. He entered the terminal and was looking up at the departure screen when two of the agents grabbed his arms and a third one cuffed him.

Cervantes met the same fate at LAX. Henry Collins headed up the team who made the capture. Both arrests were clean and simple, almost routine. There was a lot more drama in Dallas.

The FBI agents at DFW had staked out every airline that had direct or connecting flights to Chicago. But Yeats took a cab to the international terminal, then hopped on the monorail that circles the airport. He arrived unnoticed at his departure terminal and actually got as far as the gate, when the FBI agent behind the counter recognized him.

She was nervous and must have given herself away, because Yeats knew he'd been spotted and he bolted. Three agents chased him down the corridor.

There's a lot of pent-up energy in airports since 9/11. People eye their fellow travelers suspiciously. Who's carrying a bomb? Who smuggled a deadly pair of tweezers past airport security and plans to storm the cockpit? So when the three agents ran down the corridor, one of them yelled out something that caused all that pent-up energy to explode. *"Stop that man, he's a terrorist!"*

Weary travelers heard the call and rose to the occasion. At least half a dozen men lunged at the fleeing criminal, but the one who nailed him was, appropriately enough, a 330-pound football tackle from North Dallas High School, a seventeen-year-old kid named Darryl Jenks.

The photo on Page One of almost every newspaper the next day showed young Darryl with his knee dug into the back of an Irish citizen named Declan Brady. The headline in The *L.A. Times* said *Teen Tackles Burger King Bomber*.

As soon as the last assassin was accounted for, Ike Rose was ready to hold a press conference. He and Brian had flown in the night before, leaving his senior management in Missouri to figure out how they could downplay the involvement of their much-beloved founder.

Ike's first proposal was that we sweep Deanie under the rug. "Just say you captured a gang of terrorists and skip the details."

"Yeah, that should fly in twenty-first-century America," Church said. "Especially with this Freedom of Information Act we've got going for us."

Ike didn't press the point. "I knew you wouldn't buy it," he said, "but I had to take a shot." I hoped that Amy Cheever was looking down from on high and laughing at the sheer audacity of it all.

We agreed to a more believable and almost accurate story. We would let the world know that Dean Lamaar had faked his death and embarked on a mission to destroy the company he had birthed. But we would also emphasize that he was suffering from severe mental illness and that at this time, the extent of his involvement was not clear.

"I think that'll hold the press for now," Ike said. "I've got four of our best screenwriters working on a story that will make Dean Lamaar sound more like a confused victim than an evil perpetrator. It won't be the Whole Truth and Nothing But the

Truth, but we have to preserve our image. If we give the public full disclosure, it could wind up destroying the company, and Dean and his partners in crime will have succeeded."

"I appreciate the need for a corporate cover-up," Church said, "but you're going to have to talk to someone higher up the food chain than me."

"I understand," Ike said. So he called the highest person up the chain he knew—the President of the United States. He in turn called the Director of the FBI, who agreed that it was in the country's best interest not to go public with details of the crime, lest it hurt one of America's premier corporations and damage the nation's economy. It took less than an hour for the Director to pass down the official FBI position to Garet Church.

"Pretty impressive," Terry said to me, "especially when you consider that it took me five months to clear up a two-hundred-dollar overcharge on my Visa bill."

The press conference was at 2 p.m., which guaranteed it would be the lead on the six o'clock news in the East. By order of the Los Angeles Chief of Police, Terry and I were both on the platform with Garet Church and Ike Rose.

Church read an opening statement. When he got to the part about Dean Lamaar being alive, the reporters went nuts. When he followed up by saying that Dean had been part of the conspiracy, they went ballistic. Forget that he was in the middle of a prepared script; they started screaming like a bunch of adolescent groupies at a Justin Timberlake sighting. Church didn't give the details of how the case was solved, but he did give me a lot of the credit.

Ike read a statement that promised the American people that Lamaar Enterprises would return bigger and better than ever. He thanked the law enforcement agencies for their tireless efforts in bringing an end to the crime spree, the public for their support and understanding, and the President for making this an issue of national concern. He went on and on and on. At one point Terry leaned over and whispered in my ear, "If this were the Academy

Awards, they would have cut to a commercial five minutes ago."

Ike announced that the company would reopen for business in the morning and that all employees who had quit were welcome to return. Those who took a leave of absence would be paid. Familyland would reopen on Saturday. Admission for the first one hundred thousand people would be free.

"One more thing," Ike said. "Our company stock has gone down significantly, because investors weren't sure how badly these crimes would affect us. Now that the ordeal is over, I can promise you that the future looks brighter than ever for Lamaar.

"With that in mind, tomorrow morning when the market opens, I will be buying $10 million worth of Lamaar stock. Every senior executive who was with me throughout these difficult days has agreed to also buy at least $200,000 worth of stock. We are going to make Lamaar Enterprises great again, and we're all putting our money where our mouths are. Thank you."

I don't think the media usually applaud during press conferences, but this group did.

CHAPTER 113

LIEUTENANT KILCULLEN WAS waiting for me and Terry after the press conference. He was with a woman I didn't recognize. Five-foot-two, early thirties, minimal makeup, no-nonsense pants suit.

"Good job, boys," he said. "This is Shannon Treusch. The Chief will ram a hot poker up my ass if LAPD doesn't shine as bright as the FBI when the kudos are given out for solving the crime. Shannon is your publicist. She'll set up all your interviews and coach you along the way."

I shook her hand. "Do we really need a publicist?" I said.

"Maybe *you* don't," Shannon said. "But the Department does. We get enough bad press. Hero cops are what I live for." She walked up close to Terry and looked at his face. "I heard you got all cut up in the explosion."

"We can cover it with makeup," he said.

She laughed. "The hell we will. I don't want it to heal. A wounded hero cop is as good as it gets."

"In that case," Terry said, "tomorrow I'll shave with a Swiss army knife."

Shannon spent the next hour briefing us. It was a real education.

She picked us up at 4:00 the next morning and took us to a TV studio, so the East Coast audience could see us chat live on *The Today Show* with Katie Couric. At 4:45 we were having a similar

488

chat with Diane Sawyer on *Good Morning America*. Terry ate it up.

After that it was a barrage of newspapers and radio. Then on Friday night, we made the big time. We were on *The Tonight Show*.

The producers let us know that Jay Leno would interview us with all the respect and dignity a case of multiple homicides deserves. "But Jay is a comic, so he's going to look for a place to get laughs."

Leno was good. And at one point he said, "Now that you guys have solved the Super Bowl of homicides, I guess you're going to Disney World." It got a laugh.

But Terry got the biggest laugh of the night. Leno asked him what happened after the explosion cut up his face. "They took me to UCLA Medical," Terry said. "The doc walks in and he says, 'Don't worry, I'm one of the top plastic surgeons in L.A. I work on all the big stars.' I say, Like who? And he says, 'Joan Rivers.' So I shot him."

The taping was over at 6:00 and Diana and I drove out to have dinner and watch the show with Big Jim, Angel, and Frankie.

After dinner Frankie asked if he could talk to me alone. We went to Jim's office at the far end of the house. The walls are cheap pine paneling that gives it a 1950s Dad's Den look. The floors are covered with mismatched carpet remnants, because according to Jim, "My boots are always dirty, so why would I want to spend good money on fancy carpeting?"

In one corner of the room is the desk that Jim made from an old barn door and a couple of double-drawer steel file cabinets that someone at Universal threw out thirty years ago.

Four bookcases, all painted dark green to create the illusion that they actually matched, were placed against various walls, not based on how they looked, but whether or not they fit. They were filled with car and truck manuals, parts catalogues, ledger books, files that hadn't yet made it to the file cabinets, and a hodge-podge of crap that was my father's life as a Transportation Captain.

The room was musty and dusty and absolutely off limits to any interloper with a vacuum cleaner or a bottle of Windex. "I know where everything is," Jim always said. "A cleaning lady would totally screw up my system."

My Mom had a different point of view. "A rampaging bull running through it every hour on the hour couldn't screw it up any worse than it is."

Frankie and I love Jim's office. It's where we used to come as kids to hear our nightly bedtime stories. It's where we shared our first father-son beers.

"This place brings back memories," I said.

"It does," Frankie said. "Hey, I like your girlfriend."

"And I thoroughly enjoyed meeting yours."

"You would've liked her better a couple of months ago," he said. "She was a really nice person till I walked off with her fifty thou."

"Well, try not to let it happen again," I said.

"That's why I wanted to talk to you," he said. "Did you ever hear of Claymore House?"

"It's in Montana. They have a twenty-eight-day inpatient program. No alcohol or drug addiction. Just gambling," I said. "Don't look so surprised. I've researched every rehab from here to Tokyo."

"I should have known," he said. "I'm dealing with a detective."

"No," I said, "you're dealing with a firstborn. Taking care of our baby brothers and sisters is the cross we all have to bear. What about Claymore?"

"I want to go," he said. "I'm ready for it. There's just one small snag."

"Let me guess. You need money."

He laughed. Then I laughed. "Ironic isn't it?" he said.

"Pack your bags," I said. "I'll pay for it."

"I'll pay you back. I promise." He caught himself. "Shit, I guess I'm addicted to promising, too."

"Frankie, there's only one way you can pay any of us back," I said. "And that's to get your addiction under control before it ruins your life."

"Again," he said. "Before it ruins my life again. I was holed up here with Dad and Angel for two weeks. I can't tell you how many times I prayed to God for one more chance. I'm not going to blow this one Mike. I prom…"

I punched him on the shoulder before he could make another promise. Then I followed up with a serious hug. "Now let's get back and watch me on TV. I'll bet a month's pay that halfway through the show Dad says, This is boring, let's watch Letterman."

Frankie looked at me and lifted both hands in the air. "Nice try, bro," he said. "But I'm not betting."

CHAPTER 114

THE NEXT DAY was Saturday and we were guests at the grand reopening of Familyland. Terry brought Marilyn and the girls. I brought Diana, Hugo, his parents, and two sisters. Hugo only stayed for two hours, but you can see a lot in a short time when you have a golf cart and you get back-doored to every ride.

Saturday night Terry and I turned down at least ten dinner invitations. Everyone from the Mayor of Los Angeles to some film studio executive I had never even heard of had us on their A-List. The only invitation we accepted was to come on over to Brian Curry's house for his own personal secret recipe barbecued chicken.

It was a nice low-key way to end a heady week. Brian's wife Giselle was an entertainment lawyer. She also made a mean coconut custard pie. After dinner, we were sitting on the deck and Giselle asked if anyone had called us about turning the Lamaar case into a movie.

Marilyn Biggs let out a little shriek. "Oh God, no, please," she said. "Terry's been impossible to live with ever since he talked to Katie Couric. And after Leno, forget it. A movie would ruin our marriage."

"But just suppose it happened," Brian said. "Terry, who would you want to play you in the movie?"

"It's a toss-up between Tom Cruise and Brad Pitt. Unless

there's a nude scene with Michelle Pfeiffer, in which case I'd have to play myself."

He got a big laugh from the group and a punch in the arm from Marilyn.

"How about you, Mike?" Brian said. "Who should play you?"

"I don't know, Brian. I'm thinking maybe Denzel Washington."

"The hell you say. If Denzel's in this movie, he's definitely playing me."

We carried on like that till midnight. Three couples, friends who had been through hell together, eating, drinking, laughing, and sitting under the stars on a warm spring night. I had forgotten what it felt like to be normal. It was almost like living someone else's life.

Diana and I went back to her apartment and made love. It started out soft and tender, but there was a passion that had been building in both of us and what began as gentle lovemaking ended in a heaving, sweaty heap of pure animal sex. I didn't just come, I exploded. The orgasm reached that intense peak when I normally would have collapsed, totally spent, but instead it kept cresting and I rode through it to a state of sexual bliss I had never experienced before. In the middle of it all, I buried my face in Diana's neck and said, "I love you, I love you, I love you," over and over and over.

When the sex ended I stayed inside of her and held her. After a few minutes we caught our breath, and I lifted my head so I could look in her eyes. Maybe the first time I told Diana I loved her had to come from a screaming libido in order for me to get it out. But this time I let it come from the heart.

"I love you," I said.

Her eyes turned liquid. "I love you too," she said.

Sunday we stayed home, watched the Dodger game on TV, played Scrabble, cooked dinner together, and just generally basked in each other's glow.

On Monday morning I went back to my office. Terry and I

had no doubt that we would be razzed relentlessly about our TV appearances, and sure enough when I walked into the squad room, everybody was wearing sunglasses. Throughout the day ball-busting cops yelled Hollywood inanities at each other.

"Get my agent on the phone."

"Dah-ling, you look deeee-vine. Let's do lunch."

"I can't believe the Cannes Film Festival is next week and I have nothing to wear."

Terry and I bitched and moaned that Lieutenant Kilcullen forced us to become media whores, which only made the other guys stick it to us harder. We loved every minute of it.

By the end of the day, we also got handshakes and back pats from every cop in the room.

Things settled down, and by mid-week we had wrapped up all the paperwork on the case and caught a couple of new ones: a shooting in a beauty salon and a stabbing at a car wash. It was great to be back to normal.

On Friday night Diana and I went to Big Jim's house for Frankie's going-away dinner. He had to be at Claymore House Monday morning, and Jim and Angel were driving him to Montana.

"Are you following Lamaar stock?" Frankie said, when we all sat down.

"No," I said. "I'm trying to detach myself from all things Lamaar."

"It was down eighty-five points by Monday night," Frankie said. "Dad and I bought a thousand shares first thing Tuesday morning. It's up thirty-two points already. That's a $32,000 profit in three days."

"And you're going to rehab for what?" I asked him.

"Don't yell at him," Jim said. "It was my idea, my money. I just asked Frankie if he thought it was a good investment."

"And what was Frankie's advice?" I said.

"He told me it was a sure thing. I even had him call a bunch of my friends and turn them onto the stock."

I pounded my fist on the table. "Damn it, Dad! What the hell are you thinking?" And then the two of them started to laugh like a couple of underage drunks at a fraternity party.

"Gotcha," Jim said.

"Gotcha real good," Frankie said. "Welcome home, Mikey. We missed having you around."

"Why just last week this time he was sitting on Jay Leno's couch," Big Jim said. "And now look at him. Humble once more."

By now Angel and Diana were laughing, and I had to admit it was pretty damn funny, so I laughed along with them.

The following Tuesday was May 17 and Lebrecht and company went before a federal judge. They pleaded Not Guilty. Trial was set for the following March. That was it. No hoopla. No TV cameras. Just three old men, standing up one at a time, uttering two words apiece to let the judge know that they really didn't do anything bad.

Freddy was turned loose. In the grand scheme of things he really was a small fish. And as Terry explains it, "We don't have any proof that he aided, abetted, or participated. He just butlered. He did it badly, but that's not a crime in this country."

Three of the hired guns were locked up, and the FBI was working with the Mossad, Interpol, and the police bureaucracies in several countries in the hopes of being able to extradite the rest of the people that Kennedy, Barber, and Lebrecht had hired. It wouldn't be easy. But it wasn't my job.

That night Diana switched shifts with a friend, so I was on my own. I called Kemp and told him it was time for me to reunite with my dog yet again. I got home at 6:00 and Andre showed up just in time for dinner. Some dogs can be pissy when their owners finally come back after leaving them for a long time. But when Andre came through the front door he jumped on me, licked my face, barked his happy-to-see-you bark, rolled on the floor, and in general let me know that he wasn't the kind of dog to hold a grudge.

I apologized to him for being away and explained that it was partly business, but mostly love. I gave him as much of an update on Diana and her cat as I thought he wanted to hear. Then I rubbed his belly and told him that she and I were talking about living together, and wouldn't it be cool if we were all one big happy family.

At 7 p.m. my cell phone rang. No Caller ID. I answered.

"Hello, Detective Lomax, this is Danny Eeg in Woodstock."

"Hello. I'm surprised to hear from you."

"I won't take much of your time," he said. "I just wanted to thank you for whatever it was you said to Ike Rose."

"In regard to what?"

"In regard to my lawsuit against the company."

"I didn't say anything."

"Well, something happened to influence him," Eeg said. "They made me an offer. It's significantly less than what I asked for, but of course that was grossly overinflated anyway. What's important is that they agreed that I have money coming to me because of the contributions my father made to Lamaar."

"I wish I could take credit, Danny, but I had nothing to do with it."

"Don't sell yourself short," Eeg said. "The Lamaar lawyer we've been talking with said that Ike Rose respects you. You must have said something that changed his mind about me."

"I told him that you tried to help," I said. "Ultimately, I think that little talk we had in Woodstock led me in the right direction to solve the case. I think I might have mentioned that to Ike."

"I think maybe you did," Eeg said. "Thanks."

It was a warm night, so I took Andre out for a light jog. When we got back I waded through a stack of bills that had been piling up. I did my laundry, cleaned out the fridge, and got into bed by 11:30. I was about to go to sleep when I remembered what day it was. I turned on the TV and watched the first half hour of Leno.

At midnight I turned off the television, got out of bed, and opened the wooden box that was still sitting on top of Joanie's dressing table. I ran my finger over the plaque *Mike and Joan... till death us do part.*

It was officially the 18th of the month. Today I was supposed to be reading letter Number Seven, but I had cheated and opened it weeks ago. I couldn't wait till June to read the next one or July to read the one after that. I pulled out letters Number Eight and Nine.

CHAPTER 115

THE ENVELOPE HAD a big number eight on the front. Joanie had filled in the top circle of the eight with a happy face. The bottom circle had a sad face. Conflict.

The letter was dated four days before she died. It was written in black ballpoint on yellow legal pad paper. Apparently neatness didn't count. The handwriting was shaky, and when she made a mistake or changed her mind, she just scratched out the words she didn't want and kept on writing.

Dear Mike,

I'm out of time. Today is October 14 and I don't think I'm going to be around for Halloween, unless maybe I come back and visit you as a ghost.

So this is the last letter I'll write. I know, I know, you already have letter Number Nine, so how can this be my last letter? Well, Detective, that's because I wrote Number Nine a few weeks ago, before the OxyContin took its toll on my brain. It's filled with my memories of the times we shared together. Sweet memories, happy ones, sad ones, stupid ones. Just memories. And then I found myself writing about the future. Things I wish we could do together if I didn't have to die. And finally, I started writing about a different future. Yours. Without me.

And now that I poured out all my hopes and dreams for your life, I'm writing to tell you that I don't want you to open it. Not next month, not next year, maybe not ever. But I don't want you to throw it away either. I just want you to keep it close.

When I was in high school I read this really cool short story by O. Henry. It takes place in New York City in the 1890s. Two young women artists, Sue and Johnsy, are living in the Village and Johnsy gets pneumonia. The doctor says she doesn't have much of a chance, because she's made up her mind that she's going to die.

It's late autumn and Johnsy just stares out the window at the brick wall on the next house. An old vine is growing against the wall, and as the leaves drop off the branches, she counts backwards how many are left. Twelve, eleven, ten, nine, the leaves continue to fall. Johnsy refuses to eat. She tells Sue that when the last leaf falls, she too will wither and die. Sue pulls down the shade and puts her to sleep.

In the apartment downstairs there's this old artist. He's always saying he's going to paint a masterpiece but he's a failure. To make some money he agrees to model for Sue. She tells the old guy how the vine is killing Johnsy. He carries on that Johnsy is an idiot for thinking like that.

That night there's a freezing rain. In the morning Johnsy tells Sue to pull up the shade. One leaf is still on the vine. It's dark green and yellow, and it's hanging from a branch high off the ground. Johnsy says it will fall today, but the next morning, after another cold night of wind and rain, the leaf hangs on.

Johnsy decides if the leaf can cling to life, so can she. She asks for a bowl of soup and vows to get better. The next day the doctor tells Sue that Johnsy is out of the woods, but that the old artist died this morning. Two days ago they found him in his apartment. His clothes were cold and wet all the way through. Then they found a ladder in the yard, and a lamp, and some brushes, and some green and yellow paint.

Sue tells Johnsy to look out the window and says, Do you know why that leaf is still there? It's the old artist's masterpiece. He painted it on the brick wall the night the last leaf fell.

Do you get the metaphor? I'm not the dying girl. You are. I'm the crazy artist and letter Number Nine is my masterpiece. My last leaf. But if you read all the things that were in my heart, then you'll know everything I think, everything I feel, everything I am, everything I could have been. And then you'll have nothing more of me to look forward to.

But if you don't open the letter then there will be one piece of me, still unknown to you, that you can wonder about, daydream about, get mad at me about because I haven't yet shared it with you. And that, to my drug-addled brain, becomes the part of me that will never die.

I'm dying much faster now. You know it, I know it, the doctors know it, so this is the last letter I will be able to write. Let it be the last one you read. Keep the other one sealed till you're about 80 or 100. Just keep it. Cling to it.

My life is slipping away, and I can do nothing to stop it. But I don't want my love to slip away. Hold me in your heart forever.

I love you. I love you. I love you.

J.

I folded up the pages and put the letter back in its envelope. I picked up the last unopened letter. It had nine number nines on the envelope. I squeezed it between my thumb and forefinger. It was thicker than any of the others. I'm sure it was filled with feelings, secrets, instructions, confessions, and all the wit, wisdom, and wonder that were Joanie.

I went back to her dressing table and picked up the double-sided silver picture frame. "I don't buy your logic," I said to her picture. "You're not the old artist keeping me alive. You're just helping me keep you alive. Thanks."

I put both letters back in the wooden box, closed the top, and went back to bed.

ACKNOWLEDGEMENTS

If you have dreams of writing your first novel, it doesn't hurt if you know James Patterson. Jim and I worked together in the advertising business. A few years after he became a literary legend, we had lunch and I pitched him the bare bones concept of this book. "Good idea," he said, "but what if..."

I sat there dumbfounded as The Master Storyteller suggested ways to make it better. He has continued to give me encouragement, advice and support. Recently he paid me the ultimate compliment. He said, "I don't know why I still talk to you. You're the competition now." Well, Jim, since that lunch you've published 24 new books and I managed one. Some competition. I am in awe of your talent and grateful for your generosity.

I would also like to thank Marty Delaney of the Bergen County New Jersey Prosecutor's Office, Dr. Paul Pagnozzi and the staff of the Kingston Hospital Dialysis Center, Alan Wagner, Matthew Diamond, Steve Darien, Hal Eisenberg, Larry Dresdale, and a true Word War II hero, Irv "Uncle Icky" Ziffer.

Thanks many times over to Detective Frank Faluotico of the Ulster County Sheriff's Office for helping me give my criminals and my cops the ring of truth.

Special thanks to Sandi Gelles-Cole who helped take the fear and the mystery out of how to fill 600 blank pages. And to Jonathan Pecarsky, who pushed me to do "just one more rewrite" at least three times.

My gratitude to David Poindexter and his team at MacAdam/Cage; Scott Allen, Melanie Mitchell, Dorothy Carico Smith, Julie Burton, Melissa Little and especially to my editor/consigliere/point man, Jason Wood.

And last but not least, thank you Craig Alan. You're a real life saver.

Thank you for reading *The Rabbit Factory*. It was my first book, and I didn't exactly know what I was doing, which is why it has so many pages and, for some of you, far too many

F-Bombs.

For those of you who prefer zero profanity, my apologies. My books are about murder and mayhem, cops and killers. I did try to write a scene without any swearing, and here's how it came out:

The knife came from nowhere, slicing through the air into the back of his hand, and pinning it to the table.

"Oh, fudge," he screamed. "That's an ouchy."

My editor sent it back with a few F-Bombs of his own.

The follow-up book, *Bloodthirsty*, has fewer pages and much less cursing.

I have to confess that the fictional characters I murder in *Bloodthirsty* are based on real people I worked with in Hollywood. Killing them on the page is totally legal and extremely cathartic. However, the research was gruesome.

I spent an entire morning at the LA County Morgue. Forget the wall of sliding steel drawers, the neatly zippered body bags, and the crisp, clean autopsy rooms you see on TV cop shows. The real deal is more like something out of Edgar Allen Poe. More than a hundred bodies on gurneys parked helter-skelter, the air ripe with the smell of disinfectant, formaldehyde, and decomposing humanity.

I also took a crash course in exsanguination, the fine art of draining someone's blood and slowly sucking the life out of him. Talk about your Hollywood metaphors.

Anyway, if you liked hanging with Mike Lomax and Terry Biggs in *The Rabbit Factory*, here's a sample of what they're up against in *Bloodthirsty*.

— Marshall Karp

ABOUT THE AUTHOR

MARSHALL KARP co-created and co-authored the first six books in the #1 bestselling *NYPD Red* series with James Patterson. Starting with *NYPD Red 7,* Marshall will become the sole author of the series, which features Detectives Kylie MacDonald and Zach Jordan as members of an elite task force dedicated to solving crimes committed against — and sometimes by — New York City's rich and famous.

He is also the author of the critically acclaimed *Lomax and Biggs Mysteries* featuring LAPD Detectives Mike Lomax and Terry Biggs, who work homicide out of the Hollywood Division.

After a successful career in advertising, Marshall's first mid-life crisis transported him from New York to LA, where he wrote and produced numerous TV sitcoms and a feature film, *Just Looking,* a coming-of-age comedy loosely based on his own embarrassing teenage years. It was during his time in Hollywood that Marshall met many of the people he kills off in his novels — a cathartic yet perfectly legal way for a writer to exorcise his demons.

Marshall lives and writes in the Mid-Hudson Valley of New York State. Since 2001, he has worked closely with Vitamin Angels, a non-profit organization that brings lifesaving supplements to millions of women and children in the US and around the world.

For more information, visit www.karpkills.com.

Ready for more Lomax and Biggs?

Read on for a sneak peek at

BLOODTHIRSTY

It's a bloodthirsty town, Hollywood is.
No matter how popular you are, there's always
someone who'd be happier if you were dead.
And in some cases, you can be so despised,
that **everyone** *would be happier if you were dead.*

CHAPTER 1

ROGER AND AGGIE held hands as they watched the kid bleed out. He was on his back, head flopped to the left. The gurgling in his windpipe had stopped, and now there was just a silent stream, as if Roger had left the tap open.

"Practice makes perfect," Aggie said.

Roger accepted the compliment by giving her hand a gentle squeeze. He was definitely not the type to slit somebody's throat without doing some serious prep work. So he had practiced. On pigs. He tracked down a copy of *Comparative Anatomy and Physiology of the Pig* at the Texas A&M library. After that it was just a matter of working on his technique.

"Did you know that swine have the same basic characteristics as people?" he had said to Aggie. "That's why they use 'em in biomedical research. You could live for years with a pig heart in you."

"I think Ermaline Hofsteader's already got one in her," Aggie said. "You see how that girl eats?"

Roger slaughtered four hogs in all. By the third one he got the hang of it, but he did one more for insurance.

"You sure you can't switch over to cows or chickens?" Aggie said one night at dinner. "I'm getting pretty damn sick of pork."

Four pigs, one Mexican, Roger thought, looking down at the kid. The only difference was that the kid's blood wasn't bright red like the pigs'. In the murky light under the freeway it looked more like Hershey's syrup.

The pool of chocolate soup got wider, caught a crack in the concrete, and one satellite stream oozed its way toward Roger's left foot.

"Careful it don't get on your boots," Aggie said.

Roger backed up a few steps. "The boots are fine," he said. "More'n I can say for my..." His lips started to form the F-word, but he caught himself. He had given up profanity for Lent. The results had been spotty at best, so on Easter Sunday he made a silent vow to try and hold off cursing another fifty days till Pentecost. "More'n I can say for my dang shirt."

He looked down at his right sleeve, sopping with the kid's juices. "Darn kid spurted. Got blood all over my good Roper."

"Told you ten times not to wear that shirt," she said.

"I must not have heard you," he said. "And it was more like a hundred and ten times."

"Don't worry. I can get it out. I'll take it to a laundromat tonight."

"Good idea," he said. "And make sure you buy a big box of that new Tide with DNA Remover."

"I can get out the blood."

"Blood's not DNA. Trust me, this muchacho's genetic code is in this shirt till I burn it. Besides, a lot of these laundromats in Los Angeles have security cameras, and I don't want to star in no movie about you and me washing blood out of no shirt."

"It wouldn't be you and me in the movie," she said, "because when in the past twenty-seven years did you ever help one time with the washing?"

"Same amount of times you ever split one stick of firewood."

Aggie looked down at the body. Eighty feet over her head she could hear the hum of tires rolling along concrete. She inhaled a noseful of freeway fumes and caught a whiff of garlic. The kid's last meal, probably.

Roger knelt down beside the body and tightened his grip on the knife. It was a seven-inch Ka-bar, the same Marine Corps fighting knife he had carried with him since Nam. "Let me get this over with," he said.

"Don't," Aggie said, grabbing his arm. The shirt was wet and sticky, but she didn't let go. "Leave him be."

"Ag," he said, "we decided."

It had made sense when they were planning it. Make the murder look like a rival gang did it. Mutilate the kid's face beyond cosmetic repair, so that even his own mother couldn't look at him. Street revenge.

"It ain't necessary," she said. "The cops won't investigate a dead gangbanger. How old is he? Fourteen? Fifteen? You gave some poor woman a dead son. At least give her one she can bury in an open coffin."

"I don't know why I bother planning, if you're gonna change everything last minute." Roger felt the F-word welling up in his throat. "Fine," it came out.

She released the grip on his arm and rubbed her hands together to dry off the blood. "Thank you. You saying he got his DNA in your shirt?"

Roger stood up and slipped the Ka-bar back into its leather sheath. "Yep. Never get it out."

"Then fair is fair. We should leave him a little DNA of our own."

She puckered her lips and sucked them in and out, gathering up a generous gob. She let it fly. The frothy mix of saliva and bile hit the kid's vacant left eye and trickled down his brown cheek toward an ear.

A few minutes later, they were in the Chevy pickup creeping along the freeway with the rest of the rush-hour traffic. He could feel her eyes on him. Reading him. "You upset?" she finally said.

"About what?"

"About the high cost of chintz in China. You just cut a boy's

5

throat. You upset about killing someone?"

Roger forced a little laugh. "No big deal. I've killed people before."

"But that was always in the line of duty."

Roger wiped one watery eye with a wrinkled blue bandana. "Yeah. Well, that's what this was, Aggie. Killing this little fucker was the line of duty."

CHAPTER 2

IF YOU'RE LOOKING to get rich, being a cop is not the way to go. Especially the honest variety.

Last year I made ninety-three grand working homicide for LAPD. My partner, Terry Biggs, who is one pay grade lower, managed to make eighty-eight with overtime. Not bad money. Except that my plumber cleared one-fifty. And he didn't get shot at. Of course, I don't have to snake toilets. Life is full of trade-offs.

Then one day the phone rings and some guy offers me and Terry fifty thousand dollars to option our last big homicide case for a movie. I hang up. It's a con job. Ever since we cracked the Familyland murders and got our minute and a half of fame, every cop we know has been busting our balls.

The guy calls back. He swears he's Halsey Bates, the director. "Sure, you are," I say, as I Google him. "Where'd you go to college?"

"Penn," he says.

"Wrong," I say and hang up.

Next day Halsey Bates shows up at the station house, in the flesh. "You might have solved a big murder case, Detective Lomax," he says, "but you don't have a clue where I went to school." He holds up his college diploma. "*Universitas Pennsylvaniensis*. Penn."

"Hollywood Online says Penn State," I tell him.

"They also say Clay Aiken's dating a supermodel. Let's talk."

Two weeks later, Halsey hands us each a check for twenty-five big ones. "And that's just your first taste," he says. "This movie catches fire, and you boys will be building yourselves swimming pools."

"I already have a swimming pool," Terry told him.

"This one would be for your money."

"What if I just drained the pool I have?" Terry said. "How long would it take you to refill it with cash?"

"Depends on how long it takes me to find someone with sixty million bucks to bankroll us."

"I got three daughters. The twins are starting college in September."

"It took ten years to find the money to make *Forrest Gump*," Halsey said. "How were you planning on paying for college if I didn't option your story?"

"Mike and I were going to stick up the Wal-Mart over on Crenshaw. My other choice was to sell a kidney, but Mike refuses to part with one."

"Well, if you're in a hurry, we could sell our souls to the devil," Halsey said. "I have his home number."

The devil, in this case, was Barry Gerber, a legendary industry prick. Over the years he made dozens of films, zillions of dollars, and zero friends.

"I hear he's a real Hollywood asshole," Terry said.

"That's redundant," Halsey said. He gave us both a big toothy smile and ran his hand through his thick, straight, dirty-blond hair. The hair is the only thing straight about him.

I've met a lot of schmucks in the movie business. Halsey Bates isn't one of them. He's a decent guy, with an ugly past.

Seven years ago he was directing a movie and met Kirk Jacoby, a struggling young actor who had the three basic ingredients guaranteed to make him a star. He was talented, great looking, and bisexual. Kirk would sleep with anyone if he thought it could help him get ahead in the business.

They spent the day shooting at an LA country club, first on the tennis court, then the locker room, and finally the showers. Halsey was so hot for Kirk he wrapped early, and they drove to Halsey's house, which was well stocked with booze, dope, and condoms.

Jacoby had one agenda. He wanted a bigger part. Halsey offered him a few more scenes, but Kirk wasn't stupid. He knew they'd wind up on the cutting room floor, so he said goodnight and staggered toward his car. He was not only too drunk to drive; he was too drunk to walk. He cut across the lawn and fell into the koi pond. Halsey offered to put him up for the night, but Jacoby insisted on leaving. *Absolut* logic prevailed, and they decided that Halsey should be the designated driver. Jacoby flopped into the director's Saab convertible and immediately fell asleep in the passenger seat.

He never woke up. They weren't the only drunks on the road that night. Heading east on Beverly Boulevard they were T-boned by a young couple in a pickup running a light at Highland. Jacoby, unbelted, was thrown 120 feet and killed instantly. The driver of the pickup had his chest crushed and his girlfriend's head was severed when she went through the windshield.

Even with the best lawyers money could buy, Halsey spent the next four and a half years in prison. But it was time well spent. From his jail cell he used his clout, his talent, and his ingenuity to raise enough money to open a drug and alcohol rehabilitation center in downtown LA.

By the time he got out he had added a rescue mission and a battered-women's shelter, and his charity, One Brick At A Time, had become as popular among the rich and famous as Japanese hybrids. Hollywood is nothing if not forgiving.

The day he got out was a media gangbang of O.J. proportions. TV crews from around the world were camped outside the gates.

The first one to welcome him back was Barry Gerber. He announced that he was hiring Halsey to direct his first post-prison film. He then whipped out a contract and a pen, offered up his back, and the cameras rolled while Halsey signed on the dotted line. It was a great stunt, and the media gobbled it up.

"What's the movie about?" half the reporters yelled at once.

Gerber just smiled. "I can't say."

It was an old Hollywood ruse. Tell them what you're trying to pimp, and you're lucky if they print a word of it. Don't tell them, and they'll invoke the First Amendment.

"Come on, Barry," a woman from *People* demanded. "Give us something."

Gerber held his hands up and shook his head. The man was a master at getting millions of dollars' worth of publicity without spending a dime.

The press refused to take no for an answer.

Finally, Gerber acquiesced. "Alright, just a taste. It's about a good-looking, charming, successful man who makes a terrible mistake," he said, putting his arm around the good-looking, charming, successful man, who had spent four and half years paying for his own terrible mistake.

"What kind of mistake?" came the inevitable response.

Gerber grinned. "He kills his boyfriend."

CHAPTER 3

IT TOOK THE better part of a month for Halsey to set up a meeting between us and Barry Gerber. Living legends have busy schedules, so I figured we'd be lucky to get five minutes with him in his office. But that wasn't Barry's style.

"He wants you at the premiere of our new movie," Halsey said. "Sunday night. The Pantages Theatre. Red carpet, black tie."

"Do you really think we should pitch him the Familyland idea when he's surrounded by a theater full of people?" Terry said. "Why doesn't he just meet us in St. Peter's Square and bless us from the balcony?"

"It's the perfect time," Halsey said. "He loves making deals when he's feeling triumphant and expansive. I once saw him green-light a feature at a Lakers game. They had just won in double overtime."

"Can I bring my wife?" Terry said. "She hates when I go to these Hollywood premieres on my own."

"Bring your entire posse," Halsey said. "We'll make a night of it."

Our posse consisted of Terry's wife Marilyn, my girlfriend Diana, my father Big Jim Lomax, and his wife Angel. Jim has a fleet of cars, trucks, and production vehicles that he rents out to film crews. He decided that the best way for us to show up at the premiere was in a thirty-foot stretch Hummer.

Jim is about the size of a Hummer himself, loud as a Harley, and prone to bear hugs. He was sitting across from me in the limo, Angel's tiny brown hand resting on his picnic ham of a thigh. She's twenty years younger, two hundred pounds lighter, and at least three times as stubborn. When my mother died six years ago, Angel did what anti-depressants, shrinks, and weekly visits from our parish priest couldn't. She made him smile. I grinned at the happy couple and gave Jim the official Lomax Wink of Approval.

He caught it, directed his gaze toward the lovely Diana Trantanella sitting at my side, creased one eyelid, and tossed back a paternal wink of his own.

"So, what's this movie about?" Marilyn asked Halsey. Marilyn is Terry's fourth and, I'll bet every nickel of my movie-option money, final wife. She's one of those plus-sized women, so it's ironic that she wound up changing her last name to Biggs. But she's Biggs and Beautiful, with delicate pale skin, fiery red hair, and a quick wit that lets her go wisecrack for wisecrack with her wannabe-comedian husband.

"It's called *I.C.U.*," Halsey said. "It's a thriller, so all I'm going to tell you is that Damian Hedge plays a neurosurgeon who murders someone he's having an affair with."

"I love Damian Hedge," Marilyn said. "Do you think you can direct him to have an affair with me?"

"Marilyn, my pet, you are far too good for Damian Hedge."

"I'm far too good for Terry, but I still sleep with him."

"Excuse me, folks." It was Dennis, our driver. "I don't think Damian will be at the premiere. We have the contract with his studio, and I've been driving him around for the past three or four weeks, but he canceled the limo."

"Maybe he heard Marilyn was stalking him," Terry said.

"It's more likely that he hates Barry Gerber's guts, and he's standing him up just to screw him over," Halsey said.

"Oh God, Halsey," Marilyn said. "Do you know why Gerber

fired him? I would kill to find out."

The Barry Gerber–Damian Hedge feud had been one of the hotter topics in La-La Land. It started out as gossip, but the threats of lawsuits and countersuits got it kicked up to the business pages. Frankly, I didn't give a damn.

Halsey had filled six glasses with champagne, and his own with Perrier. "I have no desire to discuss why the most obnoxious man in this town isn't talking to the rudest one," he said, passing out the glasses. "But I do have a toast to a much more promising business relationship."

Big Jim tapped on the divider. "Dennis, slow down. You got designated drinkers back here, and I don't want them spilling this stuff on the upholstery."

The stretch eased to a smooth glide, and Halsey raised his glass. "To Mike and Terry, my new partners in crime. If the gods are smiling tonight, you'll meet the man who will put up the money to make the movie that will make you rich."

Terry raised his glass. "Halsey," he said, "if you're right, and this movie sells, you will have single-handedly destroyed the very principle on which I have based my entire adult life."

Halsey turned on the Big Toothy Grin. "And what would that be, Detective Biggs?"

"I've been working under the ridiculous assumption that crime doesn't pay."

CHAPTER 4

WE WERE IN a caravan of limos on Hollywood Boulevard inching our way to the Pantages Theatre.

"Explain something to me," Terry said. "They can orchestrate a twelve-minute car chase through the streets of LA, but they can't figure out how to drop people off at a movie theater without creating a major traffic jam."

"It's all part of the game," Halsey said. "People drag their asses getting out of their limos so they get more camera time. They know everybody else is behind them, and they're thinking, let those losers wait."

"But you're the director," Angel said. "You shouldn't have to wait."

"Everybody sits in traffic," Halsey said. "Streisand, Scorsese, everybody. Just play the game. They won't start without us."

It took us ten minutes to go three blocks. When we got to the front of the line, two hunks of beef in tuxedos opened the doors and helped unload the precious cargo onto the red carpet. A third gave Dennis instructions on where to park and how to pick up his passengers at the end of the night.

Big Jim exited the Hummer first, then helped Angel out.

The mob behind the velvet rope sized them up. One woman actually said, "Who are they?" Half a dozen fans quickly fielded the totally uncool question. "Nobody. They're nobody."

14

Of course, celebrity stalkers know that Nobodies never arrive alone, so the crowd strained to see which Somebody would finally emerge from the limo. Terry, Marilyn, Diana, and I followed, and I could see that the crowd was getting impatient. I stepped away from the car door, so Halsey could have his moment.

But Big Jim stepped in front of it, threw his arms up in the air, and yelled, "You are the greatest fans in the world."

The man is a six-foot-four, 300-pound people magnet. People started cheering. A few of us Nobodies waved, and the cameras started snapping.

"Ladies and gentlemen," the Trucker Ringmaster bellowed, "the man you've all been waiting for, the director of *I.C.U.*, Mr. Halsey Bates."

Halsey stepped out and the crowd let out a roar. *So you got drunk and killed someone. You make great movies. All is forgiven.*

I could see Terry lapping it all up. I slammed the car door, and Dennis started to drive off when we heard the siren. One of the beefy parkers slapped the side of the Hummer and yelled, "Hold it up; let him pass." He pulled out a walkie-talkie and said, "I thought LAPD was redirecting all traffic to Sunset."

I couldn't hear the comeback, because the siren got louder and the flashing lights of an ambulance came into view. Then a reporter on the red carpet started yelling at her cameraman, "Freddie, shoot it, shoot it."

She shoved me and Diana out of the way so Freddie could get a better shot of the ambulance as it passed.

But it didn't pass.

It came to a screeching stop right in front of the Pantages. The front doors opened and two big-titted blondes in skimpy nurses' outfits jumped out, ran around to the back, and flung open the rear doors.

Out stepped Damian Hedge. The fans started yowling, reporters started shoving, and the LA cops who thought they could coast through the evening began shoving back.

Damian was wearing a white tux and had a stethoscope around his neck. One of the blonde nurses bent forward so he could listen to her colossal chest. Apparently the stethoscope didn't work. He tapped it, hit it against his palm, and finally shrugged and tossed it into the crowd. Then he buried his ear into her cleavage and pronounced her extremely healthy. The crowd ate it up.

Halsey shook his head. "Big stupid douchebag ham."

"And he didn't have to wait in traffic," Terry added.

By now the crowd was chanting, "Day-mi-an, Day-mi-an," and the big stupid douchebag ham walked past us into a sea of cameras and microphones.

"Let's not wait for sloppy seconds," Halsey said. We headed inside.

CHAPTER 5

THE PANTAGES THEATRE is a piece of Hollywood history. Even without a movie, it's worth the price of admission. It's art deco heaven, with ornate ceilings, massive chandeliers, and thousands of thick, plush, red velvet seats.

The ushers were all wearing green hospital scrubs with a red *I.C.U.* logo on the back. One escorted Big Jim and the women to the mezzanine level. Halsey, Terry and I were walked down the aisle to a section marked Reserved.

We barely sat down when a man with a Bluetooth headset in his ear appeared and knelt down beside Halsey's aisle seat. He was about thirty-five, but it was a weary thirty-five, and the lines around his eyes told me he had either spent too much time in the sun or in the line of fire.

I could make out the Waspy good looks that must have served him well at Yale or Dartmouth, but his cheeks were doughy, his jaw was sagging, and his sweat glands were working overtime. The theater was cool, but his face was glistening and his tuxedo shirt had wilted. He looked like a *GQ* cover boy gone to seed.

"Hey, Tyler," Halsey said. "Fellas, this is Tyler Baker-Broome, the man who runs Barry's life. T.B., I'd like you to meet—"

T.B. didn't want to meet anybody. "We have a problem," he said.

"I know. I saw Damian make his grand entrance. I'll bet Barry

17

is livid. Where is he? I want him to meet Mike and Terry."

"He's not here," Baker-Broome said. "That's the problem."

"Where is he?"

"I don't know where he is," Baker-Broome said, lowering his voice into a nasty whisper. "I only know where he isn't."

"Did he walk out because of Damian?"

"He didn't walk out because of anything. He never showed up. I spoke to him this morning. He was fine. I called him again at noon. No answer, so I left a message. I called him again at one. Since then I've been calling every ten minutes. I tried the office, the house, his cell, everything. He was supposed to be in the theater an hour ago. He's never missed an opening in his life."

"Did you call the cops?"

"Are you out of your mind? You know Barry. He's probably got his nose in some blow, and his dick in some underage coke whore. You want me to call the cops?"

"Excuse me," Terry said. "None of my business, but he hasn't been missing long enough for the cops to get involved."

Baker-Broome had ignored us so far. Now he gave Terry a condescending sneer. "You're right. It's none of your business, Mister..."

"Biggs," Terry said, getting up from his seat. "Detective Terry Biggs. Los Angeles Police Department."

Terry Biggs is not a pretty man. In fact, he'd be the first to agree that he's ugly as a mud fence. His face is pitted and has an unfortunate bone structure that makes him look like a cross between Mick Jagger and a weasel. At six-foot-three, he doesn't have to work hard to look menacing. He loomed over Baker-Broome, who was still squatting, all of two-foot-nothing.

Baker-Broome clenched his face like he had just missed the final Jeopardy question. He stood up and nodded toward me. "You a cop too?"

"Detective Mike Lomax," I said. "You have the right to remain silent."

"A little late for that," he said, holding out his hands to be cuffed.

"Relax, Tyler," Halsey said. "They're cool. I'm sure they don't give a shit that Barry is out somewhere getting his brains fried or his knob polished."

"Actually, we do," Terry said. "I only rented this tuxedo so I could meet him and pitch him a movie."

"I make most of Barry's appointments and all of his apologies," Baker-Broome said. "Sorry he stood you up. As soon as I talk to him, I'll get you on his calendar." He handed each of us a business card.

"Tyler's been with Barry for years," Halsey said.

"Sixteen and a half," Tyler said.

"His job description says he's supposed to be making deals or movies, but he spends most of his time cleaning up after Barry. We call him Tyler Baker-Broome-and-Shovel."

"So this is not the first time he's gone missing," I said.

Tyler laughed. "Hardly. He's pulled his disappearing act before. He's got a few perverse habits that get in the way of his judgment. But he never did anything like this. I can't believe he hasn't showed up for your opening, Halsey. Once again, I apologize. And speaking of deals and movies, I hope we're still on for lunch Thursday."

"Chiseled in stone," Halsey said.

The audience burst into applause. The four of us turned and looked up to see what triggered it. It wasn't Barry. It was Damian Hedge.

"Elvis has entered the building," Halsey said.

"Let's give Barry five more minutes," Baker-Broome said. "If he doesn't show, could you get up there and welcome people?"

Halsey agreed and T.B. went off to make more frantic phone calls.

"Sorry you had to hear all the deviant details about the man I picked to fund our movie," Halsey said. "I hope it won't keep you from taking his sixty mil."

"You said we'd be doing business with the devil," I said.

"Underage coke whore?" Terry said. "One would think Barry Gerber's taste would run to high-class hookers and movie starlets."

"He's done them too," Halsey said, "but his first choice is always street trash. Usually young, so that even when they consent, it's statutory rape. Barry's biggest problem is that he hates himself."

Halsey waited ten minutes, then stepped to the front of the theater and took the microphone. "I just got a call from Barry," he lied. "He's running late."

"You know Barry," a voice yelled out. It was Damian Hedge. "He's always getting *a little behind.*"

The crowd laughed. Apparently Barry's love of young ass was legend.

"Now, Damian," Halsey said. "Everyone is late from time to time. When we were working on this film, there were a number of mornings that you missed your call time. Rumor has it you were *all tied up.*"

Advantage, Halsey. One of the tabloids had just done a cover story on Damian's penchant for an erotic form of Japanese rope bondage called Shibari. This time the crowd responded with hoots and yells.

Halsey held the mic close to his face so his voice filled the hall, drowning out any possibility of a retort from Hedge. "Ladies and gentlemen, forgive me for being prejudiced, but I think *I.C.U.* is a terrific film. I know you're going to embrace it, and I'm sure Barry will join us at the party later this evening."

With that, the house lights went down. Halsey Bates got the last laugh. And he was right about the movie. It was damn good.

But he was wrong about Barry. The bastard never showed up. There's no people like show people.

CHAPTER 6

WHEN MY WIFE Joanie died a year and a half ago, I never thought I'd feel joy or love or anything but pain again. And then I met Diana Trantanella.

"Met" is a poor choice of terms. I was sandbagged by my meddling father. Big Jim invited me to dinner one night and there she was. I was totally pissed. What kind of an overbearing, interfering, fat jerk of a father blindsides his forty-two-year-old widowed son with a surprise dinner date? And only six months after Joanie died.

I was as uncooperative, unfriendly, and unsocial as I could be. Actually, I acted like a complete asshole. Jim wanted to kill me. Diana was more forgiving. At the end of the evening I walked her to her car and apologized. She smiled and gave me a gentle peck on the cheek. Apology accepted. Pain understood. Diana's husband had died two years before. She knew we had both just been manipulated by a Machiavellian teamster, and she forgave my bad behavior.

You don't let a woman like that go. Especially when she looks like Diana.

Ever since my hormones were old enough to form opinions of their own, when I hear the Beach Boys sing "California Girls," I picture a sun-streaked blonde with blue eyes, golden skin, and a knockout smile, running in slo-mo through the surf. Diana is the early-forties version of my fantasy girl, and if they ever met her, I bet Brian Wilson and Mike Love would update their lyrics in a heartbeat.

Diana and I are now living together. Sort of.

I still rent the little house in West Hollywood where I lived with Joanie. A month after Diana and I started dating, she moved some of her things in. But not all of her things. She keeps the rest in an apartment on Wilshire, where she had lived with her late husband.

When I realized she wasn't going to move in with me full time, I brought some of my stuff over to her apartment. So for the better part of a year it's been your place or mine. There is no ours.

Big Jim, who is never short on solutions, especially when they're for somebody else's problems, offered up his unwanted fatherly wisdom on our living arrangements. "Stop holding on to the past, and buy a house together."

When I informed him that we were happy the way we were, he informed me that we were not. He may be right, but I'll be damned if I let him know.

Halsey's movie ended at 9:30. Diana and I left the party at 11, blew off the limo, and took a cab to her place.

The sun came up about 6:20. Little Mike was up shortly after that. Diana loves to make love in the morning. Personally, I'm not fussy about the time. Just the woman. We were in that half-asleep, totally naked, post-coital spoon position, her belly pressed to my back, her fingers stroking my chest.

"I think we got this backwards," I said. "Roll over."

We twisted a hundred and eighty degrees, until I had arranged myself comfortably behind her and could cup a breast in each hand.

Diana has fantastic breasts. Tits that tit men fantasize about. Full, firm, and oh, so real. The kind that God provides, not the ones approved by the FDA.

We lay there in silence, breathing in perfect sync.

"What are you thinking about?" she said.

"Nothing." I shifted my body ever so slightly because Little Mike had actually started thinking about an encore.

"You're thinking about Paul McCartney, aren't you?"

"No," I said, "and if you bring it up again, you're going to give me a serious case of erectile dysfunction."

"Paul McCartney" is code for the state of our relationship. He was married almost thirty years when his wife died. Four years later he remarried and had a child. Four years after that, his second marriage ended in an ugly divorce.

The sociologists pounced all over it. Their bottom line is that men are quick to remarry, but that the new wife has a tough time measuring up to the memory of the sainted dead original.

Sir Paul's divorce made all the papers. The first mistake I made was to read about it. The second mistake was to share it with Diana.

"They call it the Rebecca syndrome," she said. "Widowers who were happily married have expectations that the replacement wives can't live up to. But we're fine. I'm not a replacement wife."

True. But I had thought about it. According to what I had read, the average widower waits two and a half years before remarrying. My brain started heading in that direction by the third date.

"So marry her" was Terry's solution. "If it works, it works. It took me three miserable marriages before I found Marilyn."

"It's not the same thing," I told him. "Marilyn didn't have a gold standard to live up to. All she had to do was not shoot you with your own gun, and you'd have called it a roaring success."

"You know what your problem is? You overthink everything."

He's right. Thinking is bad for me. Getting laid is good. I stopped thinking, kissed Diana's shoulder and pulled my body as tight to hers as I could. Penis trumps Brain every time. Both Mikes were ready for Round Two when my cell phone rang.

"Somebody needs a cop," Diana said.

"It's Terry. Let it ring."

"Whatever happened to Protect and Serve?" she said, unspooning. She reached over to the night table and handed me the phone.

I flipped it open. "Have I told you lately that your timing sucks?"

"And good morning to you too, Detective Lomax. I'm sorry to interruptus your coitus, but there's a body in a trash can up in the Hollywood Hills, and you're invited to the opening. If you tell us where you are, we'll send a limo."

"I'm at Diana's and I don't have my car, so yeah, come and get me."

"My pleasure. But first, ask me what this guy died of."

With Terry anytime is comedy time. "I give up, Terry. What killed the poor fellow?"

"He got a Viagra stuck in his throat. Died of a stiff neck."

"I'm hitting the shower. Pick me up in twenty minutes."

Diana grabbed the phone. "Make it thirty minutes. I'm hitting the shower with him."

CHAPTER 7

DIANA'S APARTMENT BUILDING has a semi-circular driveway, and Terry's five-year-old silver Lexus ES 250 was already parked at the far end when I got downstairs.

"Morning," I said, getting in. "How late did you party last night?"

"Some time around midnight Marilyn realized she wasn't going to live out her fantasies with Damian Hedge, so she decided to settle for me."

"At least you got laid," I said.

"One would think." He turned left out of the driveway onto Wilshire. "But on the ride home she brought up a sore subject."

"Your lackluster past performance in the sack?"

"My dick is fine. It's my bank account that's all shriveled up. Rebecca and Sarah will be in college any minute now, and Emily is only two years behind them. I think Marilyn was expecting Barry Gerber to show up last night and start writing tuition checks. So after four glasses of champagne, Marilyn decides to rehash the shortcomings of the Biggs family budget."

"Definitely not conducive to romance."

"Thank you, Dr. Ruth. You want to solve the world's overpopulation problem? Mandatory husband and wife financial discussions. It's the ultimate form of sex prevention."

"Fortunately, Diana and I file separate returns, so we had fantastic sex."

"Swell. I'll make a note of it on the official Lomax and Biggs scorecard."

"Oh, well, if you're keeping score, as of 7 a.m., it's Lomax 2, Biggs, nothing."

Terry looked at his watch. "And as of 7:35, we're both getting fucked. Do you believe this crapola?"

"I'm not sure which particular crapola you're complaining about this morning."

"A body in a trash can? That's the case we catch? And before that, we get a junkie in an alley, a Jane Doe under a pier, a night clerk at a flophouse, a pimp. Do you see a pattern here?"

"Dead people."

"Boring dead people. Ever since we signed the movie deal with Halsey, Division is sending us out on the lowest of the low profile cases."

"Obviously, somebody is determined to teach you some humility," I said. "And as your partner, I'm forced to suffer the consequences. But look on the bright side. We work out of Hollywood. We're bound to catch a superstar sooner or later."

The good news is, it was sooner. The bad news is, it was the guy who was supposed to write Terry's tuition checks. The body in the trash can turned out to be Barry Gerber.

Don't stop now.

The best is yet to come.

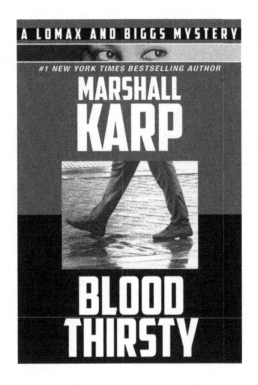

Available in paperback or e-book on Amazon

Thank you for supporting my life of crime.

— Marshall Karp

Made in the USA
Coppell, TX
27 November 2022

87195713R00312